MAKING N!

C000198985

How can the news business be re-envisioned ___
Can market incentives and technological imperatives provide a way forward.
How important have been the institutional arrangements that protected the
production and distribution of news in the past?

Making News charts the institutional arrangements that news providers
in Britain and America have relied on since the late seventeenth century to
facilitate the production and distribution of news. It is organized around eight
original essays: each written by a distinguished specialist, and each explicitly
comparative. Seven chapters survey the shifting institutional arrangements
that facilitated the production and distribution of news in Britain and America
in the period between 1688 and 1995. An eighth chapter surveys the news
business following the commercialization of the Internet, while the epilogue
links past, present, and future.

Its theme is the indispensability in both Great Britain and the United States
of nonmarket institutional arrangements in the provisioning of news. Only
rarely has advertising revenue and direct sales covered costs. Almost never has
the demand for news generated the revenue necessary for its supply.

The presumption that the news business can flourish in a marketplace of
ideas has long been a civic ideal. In practice, however, the emergence of a
genuinely competitive marketplace for the production and distribution of
news has limited the resources for high-quality news reporting. For the
production of high-quality journalism is a byproduct less of the market,
than of its supersession. And, in particular, it has long depended on the
acquiescence of lawmakers in market-limiting business strategies that have
transformed journalism in the past, and that will in all likelihood transform
it once again in the future.

Richard R. John is a Professor of History and Communications at Columbia
Journalism School, Columbia University. He is a historian who specializes in
the history of business, technology, communications, and American political
development. He teaches and advises graduate students in Columbia's Ph.D.
program in communications, and is a member of the core faculty of the
Columbia history department, where he teaches courses on the history of
capitalism and the history of communications.

Jonathan Silberstein-Loeb was Senior Lecturer in History at Keble College,
Oxford. He is a Barrister of the Inner Temple and a member of the New York
State Bar.

Making News

The Political Economy of
Journalism in Britain and America from the
Glorious Revolution to the Internet

Edited by
RICHARD R. JOHN AND
JONATHAN SILBERSTEIN-LOEB

OXFORD
UNIVERSITY PRESS

OXFORD
UNIVERSITY PRESS

Great Clarendon Street, Oxford, OX2 6DP,
United Kingdom

Oxford University Press is a department of the University of Oxford.
It furthers the University's objective of excellence in research, scholarship,
and education by publishing worldwide. Oxford is a registered trade mark of
Oxford University Press in the UK and in certain other countries

© Oxford University Press 2015

First published 2015
First published in paperback 2018

Published in the United States of America by Oxford University Press
198 Madison Avenue, New York, NY 10016, United States of America

British Library Cataloguing in Publication Data
Data available

Library of Congress Cataloging in Publication Data
Data available

ISBN 978-0-19-967618-7 (Hbk.)
ISBN 978-0-19-882065-9 (Pbk.)

Acknowledgements

This book is the result of a multiyear, multinational collaboration between a group of scholars from three countries and two continents. Central to our vision from the outset was the convening of face-to-face meetings at which the contributors could present chapter drafts and refine their ideas. Two such meetings occurred. The first took the form of a public conference at Columbia University's Heyman Center in November 2012 on "Free Market, Free Press? The Political Economy of News Reporting in the Anglo-American World since 1688"; the second, a day-long workshop at the University of Oxford's Reuters Institute for the Study of Journalism in August 2013. Following these two meetings, each of the chapters was extensively revised; this book is the final result.

Projects of this kind would be impossible without generous financial assistance. We are grateful for support from the Reuters Institute for the Study of Journalism; the Poliak Fund at the Columbia School of Journalism; the Heyman Center for the Humanities at Columbia University; the Committee on Global Thought at Columbia University; the Columbia University Society of Fellows; and the Columbia University Seminars. Special thanks to Michele Alacevich for his expert guidance in organizing the Columbia conference; to Anya Schiffrin for her comradeship and collegiality, and for hosting a memorable dinner party for our authors; and to Robert G. Picard and his staff for coordinating our workshop at Oxford.

We are also grateful to the four journalism scholars who commented on the papers that were presented at the Heyman Center Conference: Martin Conboy, Brooke Kroeger, Michael Schudson, and Andie Tucher.

Among the many other people who have assisted us in various ways, we would like to extend our special thanks to Nancy R. John, Emery A. John, Larry Loeb, and Dr Linda Silberstein.

Richard R. John
Jonathan Silberstein-Loeb

Contents

List of Contributors

Joseph M. Adelman is Assistant Professor of History at Framingham State University.

James L. Baughman was Fetzer Bascom Professor of Journalism and Mass Communication at the University of Wisconsin-Madison.

James R. Brennan is Associate Professor of History at the University of Illinois at Urbana-Champaign.

Victoria E. M. Gardner is a history teacher at Wellington College, Berkshire.

Richard R. John is Professor of History and Communications at Columbia Journalism School, Columbia University.

David Paul Nord is Professor Emeritus of Journalism and Adjunct Professor Emeritus of History at Indiana University.

Robert G. Picard is North American Representative at Reuters Institute, University of Oxford, a research fellow at Green-Templeton College (Oxford), and a Fellow of the Royal Society of Arts.

Jonathan Silberstein-Loeb was Senior Lecturer in History at Keble College, Oxford. He is a Barrister of the Inner Temple and a member of the New York State Bar.

Will Slauter is an Associate Professor at Université Paris Diderot and a member of the Institut Universitaire de France.

Michael Stamm is Associate Professor in the Department of History at Michigan State University.

Heidi J. S. Tworek is Assistant Professor of International History at the University of British Columbia.

1

Making News

Richard R. John and Jonathan Silberstein-Loeb

News reporting is expensive, yet information wants to be free. This unsettling paradox has perplexed everyone who is interested in the future of high-quality journalism. How can the news business be re-envisioned in a rapidly changing world? Can market incentives and technological imperatives provide a way forward? How important were the institutional arrangements that protected the production and distribution of news in the past?

The history of the Anglo-American news business since the seventeenth century provides one approach to these questions. From the 1770s until the 2000s, the dominant news medium in Britain and America was the newspaper, by which we mean its print-and-paper incarnation and not its digital off-spring. For over two centuries, the newspaper provided the people of both countries with a steady supply of the time-specific reports on market trends and public life that are commonly called news. The news that newspapers contained has long been indispensable not only for commerce, the creation of an informed citizenry, and the monitoring of the powers-that-be, but also for the cultivation of the habits of civic engagement, the fundamental responsibility, in the view of the moral philosopher John Dewey, of journalism in a democratic society.

News, of course, can take a variety of forms and it would be a mistake to presume that the newspaper has been the only medium for its circulation. Though the newspaper was invented in the seventeenth century, it would take over one hundred years for it to triumph over its rivals—the scribal newsletter, the pamphlet, the broadside—to become the dominant news medium.[1] In fact, one of the most surprising facts about the rise of the newspaper is how halting it has been.

Rival news providers never disappeared. From the 1770s until the 2000s, newspaper publishers adapted to and, in turn, helped to shape a dazzling array of technical contrivances that included low-cost mail delivery, the electric telegraph, radio, and television. Yet the newspaper endured.

Following the Second World War, the newspaper increasingly found itself in competition with television and radio. Even so, it has remained a disproportionately important news source. Well into the twenty-first century, according to one estimate, newspapers continued to generate fully 85 percent of all the information that journalists, pundits, and media commentators would regard as news.[2] This is true, even though for several decades the single most popular news medium in both Britain and America— at least, in sheer weight of numbers—has not been not the newspaper, but television news.[3] Although the viewership of TV news has in recent years outpaced newspaper readership, and despite the healthy profits long enjoyed by television news divisions, television journalism has disproportionately relied on reporting primarily intended for newspapers. In December 1968, for example, two news agencies—the Associated Press (AP) and United Press International (UPI)—originated 70 percent of all the domestic news stories featured on NBC, then one of the nation's two largest television networks.[4]

Since the 2000s, however, a rising chorus of journalists and media scholars in many countries—including Britain and America—have derided "dead-tree media" as a doomed genre trapped in a death spiral from which it can never recover.[5] This is unsurprising: change is disruptive, and social commentators make a living by crafting dramatic narratives with gloomy denouements.

The rhetoric of newspaper decline in the Anglo-American world is so widespread that it has been little shaken by the fact that in countries as otherwise different as Germany and India, the future of the print-and-paper newspaper currently appears to be robust.[6] Sooner or later, or so commentators assume, a combination of factors—including, above all, the commercialization of the Internet—will doom the medium even in those markets in which its financial position now seems secure.[7]

Making News is not yet another lament for a world we have lost. News is distinct from and more important than newspapers, and the theme of *Making News* is not the rise and fall of the print-and-paper newspaper, but the shifting institutional arrangements that since the seventeenth century have protected the production and distribution of news. These institutional arrangements have taken many forms: advertising, sponsored content, cartels, administrative regulations, government monopoly.

Our theme can be simply put: institutions matter.[8] To understand how news was made, neither markets nor technology but institutions hold the key. By institutions we mean the relatively stable configuration of laws, administrative protocols, organizational templates, and cultural conventions that facilitate or impede the production and distribution of news. Institutional arrangements have been, on balance, more important than market incentives and technological imperatives in creating and sustaining the organizational capabilities necessary for high-quality journalism. High-quality journalism is built on independent reporting and independent reporting rests on a solid base of financial support.

The problems confronting the news business involve the interplay of four distinct elements: technological innovation, business strategy, professional norms, and public policy. *Making News* explores the interplay of these four elements in two countries over three hundred years. Interplay is the key. Journalism has always been a challenging business to understand because it is a "public good" in two distinct ways. Economists use the term "public good" to characterize a product or service that is not depleted when it is consumed. News is such a service. Once news is produced and distributed, it can be endlessly circulated. For news providers to operate a sustainable business is not easy; in fact, the very magnitude of the challenge helps explain why they have so often created institutional arrangements to insulate themselves from the market.

The term "public good" has a second meaning. For it also denotes a product or service that is clothed in the public interest, in the sense that it is vital to the civic life of a city, region, or nation. Public goods are magnets for intervention by governments, political parties, and interest groups of all kinds. It is partly for this reason that journalism is so preoccupied with ethical norms: high-quality journalism is journalism that is infused with a public purpose.

This ever-shifting array of civic ideals, ethical norms, and institutional arrangements—public, private, and in between—is what we call the political economy of journalism. The political economy of journalism in the opening decades of the twentieth century is rooted in decisions made long in the past. To understand where we are going, it is useful to know where we have been.

Making News is a collection of original essays on the institutional arrangements that news providers in Britain and America have relied on since the late seventeenth century to facilitate the production and distribution of news. Our purpose is neither elegiac nor encyclopedic. Rather, we have recruited a distinguished team of specialists to analyze key junctures in the history of the news business, with a focus on the big picture. Each essay is explicitly comparative and each considers a relatively long time-span. While the essays differ in emphasis and tone, each analyzes the institutional arrangements that long sustained the dominant position of the newspaper as a news medium. Some were legally binding, and, thus, overtly public; others were purely customary and thus typically categorized as private. Whether public, private, or something in between, these institutional arrangements established for news providers the rules of the game.

Among the questions we have asked our authors to consider are: Who paid for the news? What institutional arrangements facilitated its collection, curation, and circulation? How did these institutional arrangements interact with technological imperatives and market incentives? How did they inform the ideological commitments of journalists?

It is appropriate to focus on Britain and America for several reasons. First, each country boasts a long history of independent newspaper-based reporting, a journalistic genre that is critically dependent on the organizational capabilities that only a well-staffed newsroom has been able to sustain; and, second, the advertising revenue that newspaper publishers relied on in each of these countries to staff these newsrooms is in steep decline. Our comparative approach has the additional advantage of showing how the political economy shaped the news business. Though British and American journalism have much in common—each places a high value on independent reporting and each has been highly commercialized since the seventeenth century—the rules of the game for news providers in the two countries have often diverged.

A case in point is the contrasting institutional arrangements that British and American news providers devised to facilitate the reporting of international news. Beginning in the mid-nineteenth century, powerful news agencies—the Press Association (PA) and Reuters in the United Kingdom and the New York Associated Press (NYAP) and its successor the AP in the United States—long coordinated international news cartels that lowered the cost of news for many newspapers. In Britain, non-London newspapers obtained overseas news at rock-bottom rates, thanks to the hefty cross-subsidies paid to the PA by the London press, the colonial press, and certain colonial governments. In the United States, in contrast, AP member newspapers obtained a steady diet of time-specific news reports that the AP refused to distribute to rival non-AP newspapers. Not until 1945 would the United States Supreme Court finally ban the AP from limiting the circulation of its news reports to member newspapers, overturning over a century of market-channeling institutional arrangements that had been no less consequential for the news business in the United States than the monopoly grant held by the British Broadcasting Corporation (BBC) had been for the news business in the United Kingdom.

Two dates serve as bookends for our project: 1688 and 1995. In 1688, the English Parliament deposed James II in favor of William of Orange in an event widely regarded as a critical juncture in British history. Known as the "Glorious Revolution," this event was a largely peaceful transfer of power that ensured that the monarchy would remain Protestant and that the Crown's authority would be constrained by Parliament, which reaffirmed its prerogative as the supreme power in the land. This event is mostly remembered for shifting the balance of power towards Parliament and away from the Crown. Yet it also had major consequences for the press. By enshrining religious toleration as a civic ideal, Parliament delegitimized long-standing institutional constraints on the circulation of information. Prior to 1688, every book, pamphlet, or newspaper published in England had to be licensed by a government censor prior to its publication. The Protestant succession and Parliamentary supremacy cleared the way for the refusal by Parliament in

1695 to renew legislation requiring the pre-publication licensing of printed items, including newspapers. In so doing, Parliament helped birth a new kind of public sphere that would hasten the rise of the newspaper as the dominant medium for the circulation of news.[9]

To peg to a single year the beginnings of the rise of the newspaper over its rivals as the dominant news medium is of course an oversimplification. The newspaper would not become the dominant news medium until the 1770s. Even so, there is good reason to credit the Glorious Revolution with enduring consequences for journalism. Much the same can be said about 1995. Just as the events of 1688 facilitated the rise of the newspaper as the dominant news medium, so the events of 1995 accelerated its decline. For it was in that year that the National Science Foundation in the United States permitted businesses to commercialize the digital computer network popularly known as the Internet, hastening a remarkable proliferation of information on all manner of topics, including news. Much of this information could be obtained free of charge, undercutting the rationale for a newspaper subscription. No less importantly, the Internet created a vast and rapidly growing online classified advertising business that eroded the de facto spatial monopoly that newspapers traditionally enjoyed over the placement of classified advertisements, a major source of revenue for over two hundred years. Of course, splashy display advertisements remain in the 2010s a stable revenue source for many print-and-paper newspapers. Yet even here, it would seem likely that a sea change from print to digital is well underway.

The decline of the print-and-paper newspaper predated the Internet. In both Britain and America, per capita newspaper circulation had been dropping for decades, partly due to shifting social norms, and partly due to the rise of broadcast news. The Internet accelerated this downward trend, not only because it provided audiences with a cheaper news source, but also because it has emerged as a superior vehicle for classified advertisements.

The following seven chapters survey the shifting institutional arrangements that facilitated the production and distribution of news in Britain and America in the period between 1688 and 1995. An eighth chapter surveys the news business following the commercialization of the Internet, and the epilogue links past, present, and future.

While the chapters defy brief summary, four themes stand out. The first is the pervasiveness in the news business of cross-subsidies; the second is the divergent priorities of lawmakers in Britain and America; the third is the influence on business strategy of political economy; and the fourth is the fallacy of what English social historian E. P. Thompson called the "rationalist illusion," that is, the presumption that the elimination of constraints on the production and distribution of news, such as, for example, the abolition of newspaper taxes in nineteenth-century Britain, would more-or-less automatically create the necessary preconditions for high-quality journalism.[10]

The pervasiveness of cross-subsidies in the news business is a theme that unites almost every chapter in the volume, with the possible exception of the chapter on the immediate post-Second World War era. To borrow from the language of the economist: in the news business, oligopoly has been the rule and competition the exception, and barriers to entry have been indispensable to the consistent production of high-quality journalism. Free trade in news has always been a fiction. Collaboration and collusion ordinarily have been the norm, and the freewheeling bottom-up creativity that many associate with the Internet an aberration. High-quality news reporting is expensive and the organizational capabilities necessary to sustain high-quality journalism require a stable long-term investment that is difficult to monetize. To complicate matters still further, with the exception of certain kinds of commercial information, the demand for news has rarely generated enough revenue to cover its cost. As a consequence, news providers have typically relied on subsidies of various kinds to balance the books. On the production side, news cartels divided the market; on the distribution side, advertisers subsidized reporting.

The pervasiveness of these cross-subsidies underscores the dependence of news providers on some kind of commercial quid pro quo. Here it is important to make a basic distinction. Notwithstanding the challenges that Anglo-American news providers have confronted in matching costs and revenue, the news business has long been a commercial venture. Indeed, the presumption that the news has been only recently commercialized—a tenet of much historical writing on this topic in Britain and America, and a premise of a celebrated philosophical treatise on the press by the German philosopher Jürgen Habermas—has surprisingly little historical warrant.[11] On the contrary, news has been a business since the seventeenth century, and commercial considerations have shaped the business strategy of news providers for over three hundred years.[12] These commercial considerations, it is worth emphasizing, have typically had little relationship to the oft-touted emancipatory potential for high-quality journalism of an unfettered marketplace of ideas. Indeed, the very presumption that there has existed anything like an open marketplace of ideas in the news business is hard to square with the evidence. Every kind of news—including, in particular, financial news—has been long subject to subtle and not-so-subtle manipulation by self-interested parties: sponsored content is nothing new.[13] A very different kind of manipulation shaped the distribution of news: beginning in the nineteenth century, news providers routinely colluded with news agencies—and, in the late nineteenth-century United States, network providers—to limit access to news reports.[14] In addition, and perhaps most important of all, high-quality journalism has flourished best in organizations that proved the most successful at keeping market forces at bay.

To be sure, Anglo-American journalism has only rarely sanctioned direct state control. With the notable exceptions of the BBC in the United Kingdom and National Public Radio (NPR) and the Public Broadcasting Service (PBS) in the United States, the news business in both countries has primarily devolved on for-profit commercial ventures that are largely, though not exclusively, independent of the state. Even so, the news business in Britain and America has been protected from market competition by a variety of institutional arrangements. Each had the effect, as was often its intention, of protecting incumbents from new entrants. In the news business, protection is a form of subsidy, competition between news providers is often contrived, and the cost of supplying the news has often exceeded the demand for its provision.

The financial precariousness of the news business is worth emphasizing, given the propensity of twenty-first-century media analysts to regard the half-century that followed the end of Second World War in 1945 as the baseline for future-oriented projections. Few assumptions have done more to obfuscate the challenging question of how it will remain possible to sustain high-quality independent journalism, including, in particular, investigative reporting.[15] In fact, if one takes the long view, the one period during which news providers consistently generated impressive profits—that is, the five post-Second-World-War decades—was the least typical. A more appropriate baseline for the future might be the United States in the early republic, a period in which public policy hastened the oversupply of news, an outcome that, as many contemporary chroniclers observed, limited its influence and undercut its authority.

A second theme that runs through the chapters in this volume is the divergent priorities of lawmakers in Britain and America. Media scholars interested in comparative media systems often lump together Britain and America as exemplars of a single, market-oriented liberal model.[16] This is true even for those scholars who are attuned to the sometimes subtle but by no means insignificant differences in the legal standing of journalism in British and American law.[17] The chapters in this volume, in contrast, show how the political economy of journalism in Britain and America shaped the business strategy of news providers. By considering the political economy as an agent of change, rather than merely as the aggregation of specific political decisions, the contributors demonstrate that British lawmakers have been consistently more willing to support centralized news providers than lawmakers in the United States. As a consequence, the news business in the United States has been more variegated and, especially early on, more financially precarious.

In explaining the evolution of the news business in Britain and America, our contributors have not focused exclusively on political factors. On the contrary, and in the best tradition of historical writing on economic institutions, they have probed the interrelationship of politics, technology, the economy, and ideology. Even so, in both Britain and America the structuring presence of the state has loomed large. For example, even ostensibly non-political decisions, such as the acquiescence of lawmakers in cartel agreements that contemporaries regarded as private, presupposed a raft of assumptions about the relationship of government and the press that had major implications for the provisioning of news.

A third theme that unites the chapters in this volume is the relationship between political economy and business strategy. The business strategy of news providers has been shaped not only or even primarily by the supposedly unstoppable juggernaut of market incentives and technological imperatives, but also by the structuring presence of governmental institutions and civic ideals. The political economy has shaped the business strategy of news providers by encouraging certain business practices and discouraging others. Particularly important has been the implicit political endorsement of the distinctive, yet complementary, cartel agreements that have strengthened the organizational capabilities of news agencies in the United Kingdom and the United States: the PA and Reuters in the United Kingdom; the NYAP and its successor, the AP, in the United States.

The influence of civic ideals on the business strategy of news providers has informed the journalistic output of reform-minded editors in Britain, America, and Britain's colonial possessions. For the nineteenth-century liberals C. P. Scott of the *Manchester Guardian* and Joseph Medill of the *Chicago Tribune*, urban politics fostered new forms of civic engagement. For Mahatma Gandhi, British imperialism emboldened a twentieth-century anti-colonial journalist to popularize an innovative form of nonviolent popular protest.[18]

A final theme that ties these chapters together is the fallaciousness of the common presumption that government policies designed to facilitate access to information will automatically generate useful knowledge. This presumption helped inspire the successful popular protest in Britain during the 1830s against the taxes that the government levied on newspapers; it would recur in the 1860s during the public debate that culminated in the government purchase of the electric telegraph. This presumption has re-emerged among proponents of "net neutrality," a principle that is sometimes invoked as a cure-all for almost everything critics find objectionable about the current digital media environment. Taken together, the chapters in this volume raise questions about this presumption. If newsgathering has almost always been collaborative—and, indeed, often monopolistic—then it would seem to be more constructive for lawmakers to encourage journalistic cooperation than to assume, in flat contradiction of the historical record, that a swarm of nimble digital start-ups can supersede the lumbering journalistic behemoths of the past.

The presumption that the news business can flourish in a marketplace of ideas has long been a civic ideal. In practice, however, the emergence beginning in 1995 of what can be plausibly characterized as a genuinely competitive marketplace for the production and distribution of news has limited the resources for high-quality news reporting. Much would be gained, and little lost, if we abandoned the marketplace of ideas metaphor and replaced it with an alternative, such as public utility, civic engagement, or even the creation of an informed citizenry. For the production of high-quality journalism is a byproduct less of the market than of the acquiescence of lawmakers in the market-channeling business strategies that have transformed journalism in the past, and will in all likelihood transform it once again in the future.

The rise of the newspaper in the period between 1688 and the start of the American War of Independence in 1775 is the topic of Will Slauter's chapter on the early modern news business. Like so many innovations in the history of Anglo-American journalism, this development received a major impetus from institutional arrangements that had little to do with market demand. Printers benefited from tax loopholes, the awarding of special privileges by government officials, and the lapse of pre-publication censorship in 1695. Even after 1695, printers who circulated information on sensitive topics remained vulnerable to arrest and imprisonment, but they could no longer be blocked in advance from publishing information on market trends and public affairs.

For a time, it was unclear if newspapers would win out in the multimedia contest with pamphlets, magazines, broadsides, and scribal newsletters. Few barriers to entry existed—in contrast to, say, the nineteenth century, when the widespread adoption of the steam press greatly increased the capital costs of publishing a newspaper. Even so, newspapers had a critical advantage that other media lacked: they offered advertisers a tool to reach a large and varied audience quickly and cheaply. Advertisements, crowed one printer in 1769, were the "Life of a Paper." Not surprisingly, advertisers—including, for example, London theater owners, eager to fill their seats—invested heavily in newspapers, helping to ensure that they would prosper. Right from the start, printers sold not only news, but also the attention of a captive audience for advertisers, and, to an extent that is often forgotten, it was the captive audience and not the news that paid the bills.

The political economy for journalism that Slauter describes differed in several respects from the political economy of the more recent past. The most obvious contrast was the limited investment in reporting. The financial resources that printers allocated for newsgathering went not to reporters, an occupational category that had yet to exist, but to the procurement of other publications, which printers mined for suitable material. Eventually, this task would devolve on a specialist known as the "editor," an occupational title that in Britain had come into use by the 1760s. Most contributors, who were known as letter writers or "correspondents," were unpaid, and it was not at all uncommon for government insiders to pay the newspaper to insert a paragraph surreptitiously to influence public opinion on one of the public issues of the day. In the absence of the unpaid labor of the letter-writers, the extensive participation by readers in newsgathering, and the ubiquitous sharing of news items between newspapers—features of the eighteenth-century press that in some ways mimic digital media conventions—it would have been hard to envision the newspaper emerging as the dominant news medium in the Anglo-American world.

Among the proudest legacies of the eighteenth-century Enlightenment was the opening to journalists of the ongoing deliberations of the national legislature: Parliament in Britain; Congress in America. Few developments did more to facilitate the systematic, ongoing coverage of public affairs. In Britain, this innovation occurred in the 1770s, when, following a political struggle, journalists got access to Parliament; in the United States, it occurred in a six-year period between 1789 and 1795. In 1789, journalists obtained access to the House of Representatives, in keeping with what lawmakers assumed to be the protocols appropriate to a government established by a popular mandate under the federal Constitution; six years later, they also got access to the Senate. The results of this innovation were subtle, yet profound. In Britain, the opening of Parliament to journalists helped to spur a reorientation in the coverage of public affairs away from international relations and back again toward national politics. In the United States, it focused the press on the national government, a circumstance that, given the decentralized, federal structure of the American polity, was by no means preordained.

The opening of the national legislature to journalists coincided with the expansion of the newspaper during the "Age of Revolution," an epoch that began with the outbreak of the American War of Independence in 1775 and ended with the final defeat of Napoleon in 1815. In both Britain and America—as Joseph Adelman and Victoria Gardner contend in their chapter on the news business in this period—it now became not only possible, but also obligatory, for journalists to report extensively on national public affairs. To meet this demand for up-to-date information, news providers in each country invented a new vocation: the stenographic reporter. In Britain, Parliamentary reporters remained subordinate to the authors of the anonymous "paragraphs" that printers inserted into newspapers. In the United States, in contrast, a small number of journalists—led by Joseph Gales, Jr, the son of a radical printer from Sheffield, England, who had fled from Britain to the United States—became influential for transcribing and then printing the debates of Congress, a role that Gales himself performed with distinction for many years.

While the opening of the national legislature highlighted commonalities between British and American public policy, other legislative initiatives pushed journalism in different directions. In Britain, press freedom was rooted in privilege. To limit the circulation of subversive ideas, early nineteenth-century lawmakers charged a heavy tax on newsprint and newspaper advertisements, increasing production costs. Advertising remained vitally important, since subscriptions barely covered the tax-augmented production costs. Yet the impact of these taxes affected different journalists in different ways. Insurgents confronted prohibitively high barriers to entry while incumbents thrived. Among the winners was the well-established London-based *Times*, which took advantage of its privileged position to assert its political independence from the powers-that-be, encouraging the ascendancy of the editor over the printer within the journalistic craft, and buttressing the emerging conception of the newspaper press as a semi-autonomous "fourth estate."

In the United States, in contrast, the political economy of journalism hastened a flood of newspapers that was without parallel in world history. Here press freedom rested not in privilege, but in opportunity. Paradoxically, however, opportunity only rarely translated into commercial success. In America, as in Britain, advertising revenue remained important for the publishers' bottom line. Yet for many news providers, advertising and subscriptions were not enough. Political subventions, mostly in the form of government printing contracts and government advertising, provided many news providers with the additional revenue they needed to stay afloat.

The remarkable proliferation of newspapers in the United States during the early republic owed much to public policy. Most obvious was the absence of the onerous newspaper taxes that had limited the circulation of newspapers in Britain. Even more important was the Post Office Act of 1792, which lavishly subsidized the newspaper press.

The Post Office Act of 1792 is much less well known than the First Amendment to the federal Constitution, with its stirring paean to the freedom of the press. Yet for well over a century, the Post Office Act had a much more immediate and enduring influence on the news business. The First Amendment would only become important for the press when it became invoked in constitutional jurisprudence. And this took a surprisingly long time: the United States Supreme Court would not hear its first First Amendment case until the First World War, and it would not be until the 1960s that the judiciary invested the freedom of the press with the quasi-superstitious aura that has enshrouded it ever since. The Post Office Act of 1792, in contrast, exerted a pervasive influence on the press from the moment of its enactment.

Three provisions of the Post Office Act proved to be especially indispensable for news providers. First, Congress admitted every newspaper printed in the country into the mail at extremely low rates, a policy that was at this time unprecedented anywhere else in the world; second, it permitted printers to send an unlimited number of newspapers through the mail to other printers without any charge whatsoever, massively subsidizing news distribution; and, third, it instituted a mechanism to facilitate the rapid expansion of the postal network that led inexorably to the enormous proliferation of postal routes throughout the vast American hinterland.[19] Just as the Internet is rapidly emerging as an indispensable platform for commerce and public life, so the postal network became in Alexis de Tocqueville's America the operating system for the world's first mass democracy, a world in which the small-town post office supplanted the big-city coffee house as the iconic communications node of the age.[20]

The modern daily newspaper was born in the 1870s in the burgeoning industrial cities of Britain and America. This is the provocative claim of David Paul Nord's chapter on the news business in the Victorian city. Newspapers in Chicago, St. Louis, and Manchester, England, popularized a new, distinctively urban style of journalism, rooted in the civic ideals of the Enlightenment, that linked the big-city newspaper with the prosperity of the cities in which they were published. The political economy of the industrial city became the journalists' "beat." Buttressed by stable subscription lists and healthy advertising revenues, these newspapers exemplified the "new journalism" that the English cultural critic Matthew Arnold decried. At their core, these newspapers were defined not by the philistine superficiality that Arnold deplored, but by their dual role as commercial enterprises and civic boosters. Early on, the *Chicago Tribune* and its English cousin, the *Manchester Guardian*, championed the highly individualistic, anti-interventionist economic liberalism known in Britain as *laissez faire* and in America as antimonopoly. Over time, however, even some of the most ardent champions of private enterprise and economic liberalism came to embrace a much more collectivistic understanding of political economy. This new sensibility, rooted in the commercial realities of the industrial city, would prove even more consequential for the press than the two journalistic innovations (both American) to emerge in the same period: the first-person interview and the investigative exposé. Labeled by contemporaries the "New Liberalism" in Britain and "progressivism" in America, this city-centric reform agenda would shape the public debate on the government regulation of big business in the two decades preceding the First World War. To solve the problems of the day, journalists combined a faith in discussion, negotiation, and the rational arbitration of conflict with an almost irrational faith in the efficacy of facts. Of every three stories on public affairs to appear in the *St. Louis Post-Dispatch* in 1894–5, one was on municipal utilities: for the first time in history, news reporting had come to focus on infrastructural improvements in a specific locality.

The newspapers that Nord describes were both politically influential and commercially successful. Yet their newsgathering apparatus remained restricted primarily to the locality in which they were published. How, then, did journalists gather news on events that originated at a distance? This question furnishes the theme for James R. Brennan's chapter on the business of international news in the half-century before the First World War. The "Age of Empire," as this period has come to be known, witnessed the heyday of imperial expansion for the United Kingdom and the first major overseas war for the United States. The international news that found its way into the leading mass-circulation newspapers—Alfred Harmsworth's *Daily Mail* in London;

Joseph Pulitzer's *World* in New York—was often generated by a new institution—the international news agency—that took advantage of the novel facilities for high-speed communications that had been created by the electric telegraph, a new medium that by the 1890s linked the world in a single global network. In Britain and America the most important of these news agencies—the PA and Reuters in Britain; the NYAP and its twentieth-century successor, the AP, in the United States—relied on distinct yet complementary business strategies to provide newspaper readers with international news.

The quality of the news that these news agencies provided was highly uneven. Newspaper coverage of the Boer War in Britain and the Spanish–American War in the United States was notoriously bigoted and unfair. Yet in no obvious sense was it market-driven. Rather, it was the logical byproduct of the institutional arrangements that newspaper publishers devised to supersede the exigencies of the market.

Then, as now, news agencies were bedeviled by a conundrum. How would they be remunerated for gathering a commodity—news—that lost its commercial value the instant it was made public? Information of enormous value to readers could not be monetized once it had found its way into print. To make matters even more complicated, at no point did the demand for international news match the cost of its supply. In the period between 1869 and 1915, Reuters's news business generated less than 2 percent of the company's total profits. To generate the revenue necessary to cover international news, Reuters and the PA relied on government subventions, cross-subsidies from the London and colonial press and other lines of business, and cartel agreements with their principal rivals (Wolff in Germany; Havas in France). The NYAP and the AP adopted a different strategy. By limiting their dispatches to member newspapers, they created a tradable asset—exclusivity—that justified the fees they charged for access to their newsfeed.[21]

In the twentieth century, the newspaper would be challenged but not overtaken as a vehicle for news reporting by broadcasting—first radio, and eventually television. Radio news, as Michael Stamm demonstrates in his chapter on the news business in the period between the first commercial radio broadcasts in 1920 and the Second World War, augmented but did not supplant news reporting by newspapers.

The boundaries between news broadcasting and newspaper news owed much to the institutional arrangements that lawmakers devised. These institutional arrangements had certain common features: in both Britain and America, lawmakers claimed as a government monopoly the electromagnetic spectrum. In neither country was it possible for a business or individual to own a radio frequency, and every radio station had to obtain a license. The regulatory differences, however, were equally marked. In Britain, Parliament also established a monopoly over radio licences, which was coordinated by the

BBC. In the United States, in contrast, Congress opposed a government broadcasting monopoly, and, as an alternative, empowered a regulatory agency to grant broadcasting licenses to as many stations as the agency presumed to be technically feasible.

Once again, in yet another variation on a pattern that went back to the Enlightenment, British lawmaking fostered centralization and American lawmaking decentralization. The outcomes for journalism, however, were quite different. In late eighteenth-century Britain, centralization encouraged news reporting; in the 1920s, however, it did not. Fearful that the BBC would compete with their own news reporting, British newspaper publishers successfully blocked it from entering the news business. Ironically, the establishment by Parliament of a monopoly radio broadcaster had led British newspaper publishers to persuade lawmakers to strengthen their monopoly over the news business. The limitations on radio broadcasting were made evident in one notorious instance in 1926, when, to mollify British newspaper publishers, the BBC broadcast the sounds of the horses' hooves beating against the track during the Epsom Derby, but not the result of the race. For many years thereafter, newspaper publishers would successfully limit the character and scale of the news reporting that the BBC could undertake. These restraints were not lifted until the Second World War, when the vivid BBC radio broadcasts of journalists such as Richard Dimbleby convinced British lawmakers that it was politically necessary for the public to listen in real time to the sounds of the war on the radio as well as to read about the war in the newspaper and to see it at the movies, in the short features known as newsreels.

In the United States, in contrast, lawmakers refrained from imposing any limitations on the kinds of news that radio announcers could report.[22] Yet this did not mean that the news business evolved in the absence of legal constraint or the intervention of newspaper publishers. In Britain, radio broadcasting was a government-licensed monopoly. In the United States, newspaper publishers quickly came to hold licenses for a substantial percentage of radio stations. Predictably, newspaper publishers were eager to exploit the commercial potential of the new medium, and American radio stations were much more aggressive than the BBC in broadcasting news reports and covering live events. CBS reporter Edward R. Murrow was but the most accomplished of a generation of talented American on-air news journalists to emerge at this time.

The influence of public policy on the news business was far less obtrusive in the half-century between 1945 and 1995, according to James L. Baughman in his chapter on this period. Yet it was never entirely absent. In both countries, this half-century witnessed the deregulation of broadcast news, a development that would fill the coffers of news moguls while weakening the organizational capabilities of the major news networks. In Britain, the BBC lost its TV broadcasting monopoly in 1954 and its radio broadcasting monopoly in

1971; in the United States, the "Fairness Doctrine"—which, by obliging radio and television broadcasters to air multiple viewpoints, had the unintended effect of limiting the range of opinions that they felt it prudent to express—was eliminated in 1987.

The deregulation of the news business helped explain why it had become so lucrative. On both sides of the Atlantic, media mogul Rupert Murdoch became a household name while television broadcasters and newspaper publishers reaped huge profits. This was not the first epoch in which the news business had been highly lucrative. A century earlier, Pulitzer and Harmsworth had made good money running big-city newspapers. Yet the post-Second World War profits spurred by the steady upsurge in advertising revenue was unprecedented, and, in certain respects, misleading. As the number of newspapers in a particular city dwindled, the advertising revenue increased substantially for those that remained, leading to a temporary burst of innovative news reporting. Only after the commercialization of the Internet in 1995 did the financial prospects of the surviving newspapers significantly decline, leading to further cuts in newsroom staffs and overseas reporting. In this context, it is worth recalling just how recent all this is: the peak year for newspaper advertising revenue in the United States was 2005.[23]

The legal strategies news providers deployed to protect the commercial value of news reporting is the theme of the final two chapters, by Heidi J. S. Tworek and Robert G. Picard. Each focuses on a different period: Tworek on the post-electric telegraph, pre-1995 past; Picard on the post-Internet present. Among the themes that they explore is the relative merit of licensing versus copyright as legal strategies and the peculiar challenges that news providers confront in their determination to protect their news stories from unauthorized use. In the pre-1995 period, news providers relied on the exclusivity of their newsfeeds to protect their organizational capabilities, a business strategy that received a major impetus following the rise of the modern metropolitan newspaper in the 1870s. As print runs became larger and the news business more capital-intensive—a shift that had been spurred in part by the widespread adoption of technical contrivances such as mechanical typesetting and the high-speed steam-powered printing press—news agencies in Britain and America devised exclusionary business strategies that enabled news publishers to block their rivals from gaining access to time-specific information. Since 1995, in contrast, the commercialization of the Internet has made it more difficult to perpetuate the exclusionary business strategies that served news providers so well in the past.

News providers have always looked to legal institutions to protect themselves from competition, Tworek observes. Yet certain strategies have been more successful than others. In the interwar period, for example, the British news agency Reuters and its American rival the AP each lobbied international standard-setting organizations to transform news reports into a form of property that governmental institutions would protect. In the end, however, this legal strategy came to naught. Far more successful was the adoption by news providers of a cartel-based business strategy that was closely aligned with the political economy of the countries in which they were based.

The limitations of copyright as a panacea for the problems facing twenty-first-century news providers is emphasized by Picard in his chapter on the news business since 1995. News providers intent on protecting their intellectual assets would be well advised, in his view, to scale back on their efforts to make copyright a trump, and focus attention instead on the establishment of licensing agreements similar to those that had worked so well for news providers in the past.

A second theme that Picard explores is the decline of the print-and-paper newspaper. Recent events, including, but by no means confined to, the commercialization of the Internet, are bringing to a close an epoch in the history of news that goes back to the Enlightenment. There are simply too many news providers and too few barriers to entry for incumbent news providers to retain their privileged position. As a consequence, the badly frayed lifeline between the production of news and the publication of newspapers has finally snapped.

The future remains open. It is hard to know how lawmakers will respond, should digital aggregators carve out for themselves a dominant position in the news distribution business and Internet service providers occupy the same functional niche in the political economy once filled by telecommunications giants such as the Bell System. Even so, it seems safe to predict that the audience for print-and-paper newspapers will continue to decline, and that digital media, including mobile devices, will become increasingly ubiquitous. It also seems likely that in the future the news business will focus less on the news flash and more on specialized reporting, and that news providers will monitor ever more systematically their audience and its engagement. The most trusted, enterprising, and ambitious of these news providers will almost certainly be relatively large, and perhaps even oligopolistic.

While the future remains open, much can be learned from the past. The chapters that follow have been written with this goal in mind.

NOTES

1. Andrew Pettegree, *The Invention of News: How the World Came to Know about Itself* (New Haven: Yale University Press, 2014).
2. Alex S. Jones, *Losing the News: The Future of the News that Feeds Democracy* (New York: Oxford University Press, 2009), 3–4. See also Peter Preston, "Without Print Newsgathering, Fighting over Media Plurality Is Academic," *The Guardian*, July 8, 2012, <http://www.theguardian.com/media/2012/jul/08/media-plurality-news-gathering-peter-preston>.

3. James L. Baughman, *The Republic of Mass Culture: Journalism, Filmmaking, and Broadcasting in America since 1941*, 3rd edn (Baltimore: Johns Hopkins University Press, 2006), 160; Michael Schudson, *The Sociology of News*, 2nd edn (New York: W. W. Norton & Co., 2001), 228–9; see also data from Pew Research Center, "In Changing News Landscape, Even Television is Vulnerable," September 27, 2012, <http://www.people-press.org/2012/09/27/in-changing-news-landscape-even-television-is-vulnerable/>.

4. Edward Jay Epstein, *News from Nowhere: Television and the News* (Chicago: I. R. Dee, 2000 [1973]), 142.

5. In keeping with popular convention, we often refer to the United Kingdom as Britain and the United States as America. This convention is not without problems. Yet it has the advantage of brevity, and avoids the thorny issues raised by shifts in political nomenclature. The United States would remain part of British North America until 1776, while Great Britain would not become the United Kingdom until 1801.

6. David A. L. Levy and Rasmus Kleis Nielson, *The Changing Business of Journalism and its Implications for Democracy* (Oxford: Reuters Institute for the Study of Journalism, 2010); Ken Auletta, "Citizens Jain," *The New Yorker*, October 8, 2012.

7. For a sampling of commentary on the so-called "critical juncture" in journalism that has been hastened by the rise of the Internet, see Robert W. McChensey and Victor Picard (eds), *Will the Last Reporter Please Turn Out the Lights: The Collapse of Journalism and What Can Be Done to Fix It* (New York: New Press, 2011).

8. Richard R. John, "Why Institutions Matter," *Common-place*, 9/1 (October 2008), <http://www.common-place.org/vol-09/no-01/john/>.

9. Steve Pincus, *1688: The First Modern Revolution* (New Haven: Yale University Press, 2009), ch. 15.

10. On the rationalist illusion, see Jonathan Silberstein-Loeb, *The International Distribution of News: The Associated Press, Press Association, and Reuters, 1848–1957* (Cambridge: Cambridge University Press, 2014), ch. 4, esp. 92. See also Patricia Hollis, *The Pauper Press: A Study in Working-Class Journalism* (London: Oxford University Press, 1970).

11. Jürgen Habermas, *The Structural Transformation of the Public Sphere: An Inquiry into a Category of Bourgeois Society*, trans. Thomas Burger (Cambridge, Mass.: MIT Press, 1989 [1962]).

12. For a related discussion, see James L. Baughman, "The Reconsideration of American Journalism History," conference paper, American Historical Association, Chicago, January 2012.

13. Richard R. John, *Network Nation: Inventing American Telecommunications* (Cambridge, Mass.: Belknap Press of Harvard University Press, 2010), ch. 4.

14. John, *Network Nation*, ch. 5.

15. For a parallel argument, see George Brock, *Out of Print: Newspapers, Journalism, and the Business of News in the Digital Age* (London: Kogan Page, 2013), chs 3–4.

16. Daniel C. Hallin and Paolo Mancini, *Comparing Media Systems: Three Models of Media and Politics* (Cambridge: Cambridge University Press, 2004).

17. See, for example, Paul Starr, *The Creation of the Media: Political Origins of Modern Communications* (New York: Basic Books, 2004), chs 1–2.

18. Isabel Hofmeyr, *Gandhi's Printing Press: Experiments in Slow Reading* (Cambridge, Mass.: Harvard University Press, 2013).

19. Richard R. John, *Spreading the News: The American Postal System from Franklin to Morse* (Cambridge, Mass.: Harvard University Press, 1995), chs 1–2.

20. Richard R. John and Thomas C. Leonard, "The Illusions of the Ordinary: John Lewis Krimmel's *Village Tavern* and the Democratization of Public Life in the Early Republic," *Pennsylvania History*, 65 (Winter 1998): 87–96.

21. Silberstein-Loeb, *International Distribution of News*, chs 2–3.

22. While the United States government imposed no limitations on radio broadcasting, the AP did. Intent on preserving a level playing field between newspapers that did and did not own their own radio stations, the AP significantly limited the uses to which its members could put its newsfeed. Silberstein-Loeb, *International Distribution of News*, 75–6.

23. "Annual Newspaper Ad Revenue," in Newspaper Association of America, *Newspaper Revenue*, <http://www.naa.org/Trends-and-Numbers/Newspaper-Revenue. aspx>.

2

The Rise of the Newspaper

Will Slauter

In the late seventeenth century, most news—defined as timely reports on public affairs and commerce—did not appear in newspapers. The monarchy, church, and Parliament closely monitored discussions of politics and religion. In most years, the official *London Gazette* (1666–present) remained the only printed newspaper. A tiny elite paid for access to fuller reports found in handwritten newsletters, which were compiled in London by individuals with access to the diplomatic correspondence of the monarchy and free use of the royal post. Merchants also relied on weekly periodicals called price currents for updates on the prices of goods in various markets. But when it came to distributing news in print, periodicals were not as common as separate pamphlets, which could be produced quickly and sold cheaply on the streets, and broadsides, which contained words and images printed on one side of a sheet so that they could be attached to a wall or post for public viewing.

By the late eighteenth century, the business and culture of news had changed substantially. Admittedly, local news still traveled by word of mouth, friends in other places still provided details that could not be found in print, and pamphlets remained important tools of political persuasion. But by 1775 newspapers printed on a regular schedule (weekly, tri-weekly, or daily) could be found in cities throughout England and North America, not to mention Scotland, Ireland, and the West Indies. These newspapers discussed public affairs more openly than their seventeenth-century counterparts, and they contained a range of material that previously appeared in distinct publications: paragraphs of foreign and domestic news, price lists and mortality figures, accounts of crimes and trials, poems and songs, reader correspondence, parliamentary proceedings, political essays, and advertisements. Pamphlets and broadsides continued to be used for late-breaking news or for certain genres, such as the last words of executed criminals. But by 1775 the newspaper had become the primary means of packaging news and selling it to customers.

From the perspective of printers and publishers, periodicals sold by subscription had several advantages over separate publications such as pamphlets
and broadsides: a predictable production schedule, dedicated customers in
known locations, and the promise (though not the guarantee) of steady
income from sales and advertisements. Periodicity—the fact of issuing a
publication on a regular schedule—encouraged the formation of a community
of readers, which in turn attracted advertisers. Selling by subscription locked
customers in and enabled printers to know how many copies to print and
where to deliver them. Newspapers in the late eighteenth century contained
much more than news, and their mix of literary, political, and commercial
material increased their appeal for readers.

Still, it was not inevitable that the newspaper would become the dominant
way of selling news by 1775. The seventeenth and eighteenth centuries constituted a period of experimentation in the form and content of publications
and in their means of distribution. Writers, printers, and distributors of news
adapted to changes in government regulations related to censorship, taxation,
and postal distribution, but their actions also pushed these policies in unfore-
seen directions. To make the newspaper work as a viable medium, individuals
exploited loopholes in tax policy, negotiated deals with postal officials (or
became postmasters), diversified their businesses, and developed relationships
that enabled them to collect news and distribute it to customers.

THE COMMERCIALIZATION OF NEWS IN AN AGE
OF CENSORSHIP AND MONOPOLY

To better understand developments after 1688, the first part of this chapter
provides an overview of the commercialization of news and the development
of periodicity in the early to mid-seventeenth century. Specialists of that
period have pointed out that periodicals are artificial because events of public
concern do not necessarily occur on a predictable schedule. Adherence to a
weekly (and later daily) schedule created the obligation to fill every issue
regardless of whether there was anything new to publish. Accounts received
after an issue had gone to press either had to be held until the following week
or prepared for sale in some other form, such as a broadside or pamphlet.[1]

A variety of broadsides existed in the seventeenth century, from proclamations issued by authority and funeral elegies commissioned by friends of the
deceased to satirical poems and ballads, some of which narrated recent events.
Ballad writers visited public places in search of topical material that they could
put to verse, but rather than providing a straightforward narrative of an event
(such as a fire, an execution, or a battle), they tended to exploit the event to

teach a moral lesson. Ballads and other broadsides could be purchased for about a penny from booksellers, peddlers, or hawkers.[2] Accounts of battles, treaties, crimes, and natural disasters also appeared in pamphlets, which could be produced quickly and sold on the street. The number of pamphlets tended to increase during periods of war, such as during the late 1580s, when England was at war with Spain.[3]

In contrast to broadsides and pamphlets, periodicals required a regular supply of news (to fill each issue) and a systematic means of distributing the final product to customers. Both of these tasks would be greatly facilitated by the development of more extensive and reliable postal routes during the seventeenth century. After 1600, improvements in the royal posts and private courier services across Europe enabled merchants, bankers, diplomats, and others to expect weekly updates from their correspondents in other cities.[4] Regular mail delivery also made it possible for well-connected individuals to issue weekly newsletters to paying subscribers. The newsletters were written rather than printed because they catered to an elite clientele who paid handsomely for access to information that many rulers did not wish to see circulated. But the newsletters were only able to exist in the first place because diplomats and spies leaked information to the compilers, who provided them with other information in return. The compilers recorded news and rumors picked up locally, combined them with reports received from other cities, and mailed the aggregate product to their elite clients. In major trading centers like Venice and Antwerp, some of the news compilers had offices where clerks made copies for local and foreign subscribers; others worked alone with limited means and changed locations to avoid trouble with the authorities. But by around 1620 they could be found in all the courts and trading centers of Europe.[5]

These handwritten newsletters were the basis for the first printed news periodicals. As early as 1605, Johann Carolus of Strasbourg, who already had a business copying incoming newsletters and selling them to local customers, produced a printed version for a wider audience.[6] Printers in other cities soon imitated Carolus, but the main growth spurt came with the Thirty Years' War (1618–48), which generated demand for military news across Europe. These early printed periodicals were often called "corantos" because they provided a "current" of news from various parts of Europe (the first recorded use of the word "newspaper" was not until 1667, and the term was not commonly used before the eighteenth century).[7] The corantos adopted the basic form of the written newsletters (short bulletins arranged by the geographic origin of the news rather than its subject) and they copied many of their reports from the newsletters, which continued to circulate. The first corantos produced in England date to 1621. They were the work of a small group of London printers and booksellers who translated Dutch corantos and printed them for local customers. There is no reliable evidence about circulation, but the print runs were probably in the low hundreds.[8]

The decision to print corantos was risky because English monarchs claimed a prerogative over all affairs of state and discouraged discussion of domestic or foreign policy. In 1620 James I reacted to publications about the European conflict by ordering his subjects "from the highest to the lowest to take heede, how they intermeddle by Penne, or Speech, with causes of State and secrets of Empire, either at home, or abroad."[9] He also persuaded the United Provinces to prohibit the exportation of printed corantos to England. These measures proved ineffective in stopping the flow of news, so the king appointed a licenser to authorize weekly publications by a few select members of the Stationers' Company (the London guild of printers and booksellers). The stationers agreed to avoid discussion of English affairs and to limit themselves to translations of what had been printed on the continent. But Charles I (who became king in 1625) did not appreciate open discussion of foreign affairs either, and after a complaint by the Spanish ambassador about one of the corantos in 1632 the monarch banned them entirely. In 1638 two of the main publishers of news—Nicholas Bourne and Nathaniel Butter—obtained a royal license with the exclusive right to publish translations of foreign corantos. This privilege was meant to limit the production of news to a couple of individuals who promised to avoid printing anything against the monarchy or the church. But with no war to fuel demand for foreign news, their periodicals foundered.[10]

While the monarch used licensing to control news of church and state, Parliament considered it a breach of privilege to publish accounts of its proceedings. Vote counts and summaries of speeches still spread by word of mouth, through scribal newsletters and in "separates," a term used to designate manuscripts containing a single text written up with the intention of being circulated, whether for money or not. During the 1620s, when Charles I struggled against an increasingly vociferous Parliament, enterprising scriveners produced summaries of parliamentary proceedings for paying customers.[11] When the Civil War broke out in 1641–2, scriveners gathered rumors and solicited details from Members of Parliament (who often had their own reasons for leaking information) and sold their reports in stalls near Westminster Hall. Some of these scriveners began issuing "diurnals" (i.e. journals) that provided a day-by-day account of proceedings. By the summer of 1641 printers began reproducing the manuscript diurnals, and shortly thereafter one of the leading scriveners, Samuel Pecke, collaborated with a printer to issue a weekly periodical. He was soon imitated (and copied) by many other "newsbooks." (They were called newsbooks because they were small pamphlets of eight or sixteen pages, and they often had continuous pagination, enabling readers to bind successive issues together in annual volumes.) Printing significantly reduced the cost for the purchaser. Whereas a manuscript diurnal might cost 1s. 6d., many newsbooks sold for a penny (1/18th of the price).[12]

Writers, printers, and booksellers exploited the volatile political situation in the early 1640s to produce a wide range of unlicensed publications devoted to military and political developments. Writers attended trials and criminal executions, where they recorded speeches in shorthand and rushed them into print, usually as small pamphlets or broadsides. The scaffold speech was an important genre that enabled writers to develop many of the skills that would later be associated with reporters: writers attended the event, talked to witnesses, and recorded the words spoken.[13] Reporting parliamentary debates remained more difficult, because the doors were closed to non-members and Parliament sought to keep the press within limits. On several occasions in 1642–3 both Houses of Parliament summoned writers, printers, and booksellers for passages that members deemed "scandalous" and several of them spent time in prison.[14]

In 1643, a parliamentary ordinance specified that all printed works had to be approved by Parliament and registered with the Company of Stationers. To reduce the flow of unlicensed publications, the Stationers' Company worked with officials of the City of London to crack down on the hawkers—men, women, and children—who distributed all sorts of cheap pamphlets, broadsides, and newsbooks. Although individual stationers probably relied on hawkers to reach more customers, the Company blamed them for selling pirated editions and scandalous books with which they did not want to be associated. At the Stationers' request, the Common Council of the City of London ordered the arrest and corporal punishment of anyone found selling books, pamphlets, or papers on the street.[15]

Despite attempts to maintain order by Parliament, the City, and the Stationers' Company, newsbooks flourished until 1649, a year in which fifty-four different titles were published. Weekly newsbooks probably sold 250–500 copies per issue and up to 1000 copies in exceptional cases. Total readership would have been higher because copies were passed around and read aloud in public. Most newsbooks contained no paid advertisements (there were occasional ads for books being sold by the publisher of the newsbook) and so publishers relied entirely on sales for income.[16] After the execution of the King and the creation of the Commonwealth, Parliament again established a strict licensing system in September 1649. The number of authorized news publications shrunk dramatically under the rule of Oliver Cromwell, and few of them dared to criticize the Lord Protector. In the first half of the 1650s there were between eight and fourteen news periodicals circulating at any one time, but in 1655 Cromwell suppressed all but two official publications.[17]

After the Restoration of the monarchy in 1660, Parliament passed "An Act for Preventing the Frequent Abuses in Printing Seditious, Treasonable, and Unlicensed Books and Pamphlets; and for Regulating Printing Presses" (1662). This is often referred to as the Licensing Act because it required all printed matter to be licensed by a royal censor and registered with the

Stationers' Company. But the act regulated all aspects of the trade: it confirmed the Stationers' Company's monopoly, restricted printing to London, and limited the number of presses (each master printer was allowed two presses and over time the number of master printers was to be reduced to twenty).[18]

The secretaries of state had licensing authority over "affairs of state," which included news. In 1663 Charles II granted Roger L'Estrange, a zealous licenser, the exclusive right to print and sell "all Narratives or relacions not exceeding two sheets of Paper & all Advertisements, Mercuries, Diurnalls & books of Publick Intelligence."[19] Granting L'Estrange a monopoly on all sorts of news publications made sense to Charles II, who sought to curtail discussion of the legitimacy of the restored monarchy. But an undersecretary of state named Joseph Williamson soon set in motion a plan to replace L'Estrange's newspapers with an official publication under the direct control of the secretaries of state. In exchange for compensation, L'Estrange agreed to end his news publications early in 1666, though he retained the exclusive right to print advertisements (discussed below). Williamson's official newspaper began as the *Oxford Gazette* in November 1665 (the court was in exile there during part of the "Great Plague"), and changed its name to the *London Gazette* in February 1666.[20]

Williamson hired an editor for the *Gazette*, but he kept the best intelligence for his own subscription newsletter business. Williamson's letters and those of his correspondents traveled postage-free, enabling him to collect news from throughout the kingdom and abroad. Hand-copied newsletters were sent out to paying subscribers and others who received them in exchange for providing intelligence. Local postmasters in particular were expected to summarize information and rumors that they found in the letters under their care. Williamson returned the favor by sending them free copies of the *London Gazette* that they could sell to local customers. Postmasters also distributed copies to inns, taverns, and coffeehouses. In this way, the Post Office was both a means for the monarchy to disseminate its official version of events and a powerful apparatus for collecting intelligence and monitoring personal communications.[21] Charles II responded vigorously to criticism of his policies by issuing several proclamations banning discussion of affairs of state in coffeehouses and other public places; individuals who merely listened to such "licentious talk" or "false news" were liable for punishment unless they reported it to a Justice of the Peace within twenty-four hours.[22]

The *London Gazette*'s monopoly on printed news ended temporarily during the Exclusion Crisis (1678–81), when fears of a Catholic conspiracy (the so-called "Popish Plot") led the emerging Country Party (later to be known as the Whigs) to support the exclusion of Charles II's Catholic brother James from the throne, while the Court Party (the Tories) opposed this exclusion. A number of unlicensed pamphlets, broadsides, and newspapers appeared during this controversy, and their suppression was made more difficult by the lapse of the Licensing Act in 1679. (The Act, first passed in 1662, had to be periodically renewed, and Parliament set this aside while it attempted to exclude Charles II's brother James from the throne.)[23] In the absence of licensing, Charles II sought to use royal prerogative to suppress the newspapers that had appeared in 1679–80. He solicited the opinions of judges, who reported to the Privy Council in May 1680 that the king could legally prohibit any news publication that he deemed a danger to public peace. Charles II immediately issued a proclamation banning the publication of news without prior authorization, but some MPs cited this as an abuse of royal authority designed to usurp the function of Parliament. By the end of 1680, probably with the encouragement of some MPs, several Whig printers again began printing newspapers.[24] Roger L'Estrange defended the monarchy in a periodical called *The Observator in Question and Answer* (1681–7). After the accession of James II in 1685, Parliament renewed the Licensing Act, eliminating the unlicensed papers and leaving the *London Gazette* and L'Estrange's *Observator* as the only newspapers down to 1688. James II's administration also cracked down on the circulation of manuscript newsletters through the post and in coffeehouses.[25]

As James II struggled to keep his grip on power, a number of pamphlets and broadsides appeared, but printed periodicals remained too risky. It was only after the king fled in December 1688 that four unlicensed newspapers were set up, and they did not last long because the new king, William III, sought to limit ongoing discussion of events. In January 1689 the *London Gazette* complained about "divers False, Scandalous and Seditious Books, Papers of News, and Pamphlets, daily Printed and Dispersed, containing idle and mistaken Relations of what passes" and explained that orders had been given "to apprehend all such Authors, Printers, Booksellers, Hawkers and others, as shall be found to Print, Sell, or Disperse the same."[26] In February the monarchy appointed a Messenger of the Press to enforce licensing. The Bill of Rights of 1689 did not guarantee freedom of the press, and Parliament continued to assert its privilege of secrecy. The *London Gazette* remained the only authorized political newspaper.[27]

Nevertheless, the Glorious Revolution could be considered a turning point for two reasons. First, the commercial, fiscal, and military developments that occurred after 1688 generated an increased demand for the kinds of information for which periodicals were ideally suited: regular updates on prices, market conditions, and political circumstances affecting trade.[28] The business press grew and diversified: merchants could now subscribe not only to price currents and stock exchange currents but also to marine lists, which provided information about the arrival and departure of ships in various ports. The public also had access to periodicals containing practical information about agriculture and industry, such as John Houghton's *Collection for Improvement of Husbandry and Trade* (1692–1703). Secondly, after 1688, Whigs in Parliament began to associate licensing with arbitrary rule and monopoly, making it more difficult to defend the Licensing Act when it came up for renewal. Most arguments against pre-publication censorship in the late seventeenth century centered on religious toleration (the idea that freedom of conscience should extend to freedom of expression about religious views), but as party politics developed it became clear that censorship could become a political weapon wielded by the party in power. Meanwhile, the trade restrictions contained in the Licensing Act also came under increased scrutiny. The act limited printing and bookselling to London and to members of the Stationers' Company, a handful of whom claimed a perpetual property right in the most profitable books. When the act came up for renewal in 1693, several printers and booksellers complained to the House of Commons about this disparity within the trade, insisting that licensing enabled a few stationers to monopolize certain categories of works under the pretext of preventing "seditious" publications. Parliament ultimately renewed the Licensing Act, but only for one year and to the end of the next session. By the time the act came up for renewal again in 1695, the philosopher John Locke had prepared a written critique of licensing that highlighted the dangers of both ecclesiastical censorship and trade monopolies, and the MP Edward Clarke used Locke's remarks to campaign against renewal of the existing act. In March 1695 and again in November 1695 Clarke sponsored bills that would have reduced the power of the Stationers' Company and either eliminated licensing or diluted it, but neither of these bills made it out of committee before the end of the session. The result was that the Licensing Act lapsed and no new regulations replaced it.[29]

THE PRODUCTION AND DISTRIBUTION OF NEWS AFTER 1695

In retrospect, the lapse of the Licensing Act in 1695 created a major opening for newspapers, though at the time it was not clear that licensing had ended for good. The Stationers' Company repeatedly petitioned Parliament for some form of press regulation. Because licensing had combined authorization to print and sell a particular work with the exclusive right to do so, the lapse of licensing led printers and booksellers to complain about the spread of "piracy." The term piracy had been used to describe violations of trade customs (such as printing a work registered by another stationer) as early as the mid-seventeenth century, but it became much more common in the years after 1695.[30] Among MPs, meanwhile, the proliferation of newspapers raised the question of whether or not they should be licensed. In 1696, the House of Commons briefly considered a "Bill to prevent the Writing, Printing, and

Publishing any News without License."[31] Yet no such law was passed, and from this point on no monarch asserted a prerogative power over news; such a move would have smacked of arbitrary rule at a time when Parliament was debating how best to regulate printing. Most members of the trade assumed that some form of licensing would be reinstated, and numerous bills were proposed in the ten years after 1695. But licensing had become too controversial to obtain a majority in Parliament, and government now turned to the common law of seditious libel as a way of exercising censorship after publication rather than before. Seditious libel was understood to include any public statement tending to encourage contempt or ridicule of the government (church and state) or its officials.[32]

The end of licensing therefore did not immediately lead to newspapers that were highly critical of the monarch, ministers, or MPs. The newspapers that appeared after 1695 did not avoid domestic politics entirely, but they were more cautious than those of 1641–2 or 1679–80. Three of them—the *Flying-Post*, which became increasingly Whig, the *Post-Boy*, which was associated with the Tories, and the *Post-Man*, which focused on foreign news—appeared three times a week until the early 1730s. The reference to the "post" in all of these titles made clear that newspapers depended on regular mail delivery (now three times a week to and from London) to obtain news and distribute it to customers. Focusing on short bulletins of news and avoiding political commentary, they resembled the early corantos much more than the newsbooks of the Civil War era.[33] Although the tone of the tri-weekly newspapers reflected party politics, they were not free to print parliamentary proceedings. The Lords and Commons considered it a breach of privilege to publish the debates or identify individual members by name and they insisted on this privilege until the 1770s (see next section). But accounts of Parliament did leak out in subscription newsletters, whose writers paid clerks for minutes of proceedings, obtained snippets of news from those who had attended debates, and collected gossip in coffeehouses. Unlike their counterparts in the 1660s and 1670s, these writers did not work directly for the secretaries of state, and so they had to find a balance between serving their elite customers and avoiding trouble with Parliament. John Dyer, who circulated a written newsletter three times a week from at least 1688 until his death in 1713, was arrested several times and brought before the Commons and Lords. Although Parliament watched Dyer closely, they never punished him severely. The longevity of his and other newsletters reveals that elite readers in the early eighteenth century sought out news from a range of manuscript and printed sources.[34]

The early eighteenth century marked a transition period in attitudes toward censorship. The government prosecuted a number of writers and printers for seditious libel, but some political leaders also began to see the benefits of counteracting criticism by commissioning writers to defend their policies.

Robert Harley, an influential minister under Queen Anne (reigned 1702–14), mobilized the talents of Daniel Defoe, Jonathan Swift, and others.[35] Robert Walpole expanded this practice after he became de facto Prime Minister in 1721. By the 1720s, the official *London Gazette* was no match for papers like the *London Journal* (1720–34) or the *Craftsman* (1726–52), which had the active support of opposition leaders. Walpole therefore purchased the *London Journal*, set up new papers to defend his policies, and arranged for copies to be sent postage-free to provincial readers. Meanwhile, the ministry employed an agent to monitor newspapers and pamphlets for seditious material. Printers and press workers were just as vulnerable as writers. For example, during the prosecution of the outspoken Jacobite printer-writer Nathaniel Mist in 1728, several members of his staff were punished, from the compositor who set the type to the woman who sold the paper in the streets.[36]

Printers in England's North American colonies had to worry about the common law of seditious libel, but they also faced royal governors, councils, and assemblies that at various points asserted control over what could be printed.[37] The government of Massachusetts shut down Benjamin Harris's *Public Occurrences* after one issue in 1690 because he took liberties reporting both local and international affairs. Still, Harris had only envisioned a monthly publication: local news spread by word of mouth, news from England rarely arrived more than once a month, and Boston was not yet connected by post to other colonial cities, making it nearly impossible to collect enough news for weekly publication.[38]

The expansion of the post, combined with the end of licensing in 1695, enabled the growth of newspapers in the English provinces and in North America. The Licensing Act had restricted printing to London; within ten years of its lapse there were weekly newspapers in Bristol, Norwich, Exeter, and Boston, Massachusetts.[39] Whereas in English towns printers started newspapers, in Boston postmasters ran the first successful titles. In 1704, the Boston postmaster John Campbell hired the printer Bartholomew Green to produce the *Boston News-Letter* (1704–76, with interruptions), which was an outgrowth of a manuscript newsletter started by his father. As postmaster, Campbell could send and receive letters free of postage (known as a franking privilege), and for fifteen years he used this advantage to gather intelligence and distribute his newspaper to customers. The government did not fund Campbell's paper directly, though it was licensed by the office of the royal governor, which occasionally relied on it to publish official texts. The Postmaster General in London replaced Campbell in 1718, and his successor started the *Boston Gazette* (1719–98), again hiring a printer to do the work. The third Boston paper—the *New-England Courant* (1721–6)—did not enjoy postal privileges. Unlike other publications, it featured prose and verse contributions by a group of local writers, including essays that were critical of clergymen and the colonial government. The authorities responded by sending its printer James Franklin to prison and prohibiting him from continuing the paper (although it continued for a while under James's brother Benjamin Franklin).[40]

Most colonial printers chose to exercise some self-censorship to avoid such trouble with the authorities, not least because they wanted government printing contracts. Indeed, newspapers tended to be part of a larger printing and retailing business. Setting up a printing shop required an investment of a little more than £100 in equipment; presses and type had to be imported from England or purchased or inherited from an existing printer. A successful printing shop combined job printing (any work done for a paying customer), government contracts (for printing laws, notices, currency, etc.), and a newspaper sold by annual subscription.[41] When it came to selling news, printers found that subscription-based periodicals had several advantages over separate publications: a steady weekly production schedule, dedicated customers in known locations, and a regular flow of income from advertisements and subscriptions, although money remained difficult to collect. Between 1700 and 1765, three quarters of colonial printers had a newspaper at one time or another. Of the sixty titles launched during that time, ten lasted less than two years, ten lasted between two and four years, and ten lasted between five and nine years; nineteen of the papers lasted twenty years or more, suggesting that the subscription newspaper had become an important component of a successful printing business.[42]

Printing shops in colonial America were family businesses in which wives and daughters worked alongside nephews and cousins. Some women took charge of printing shops after their husbands' deaths. Elizabeth Timothy of Charleston, for example, managed the business (including the newspaper) from 1738 to 1746, when she passed it on to her son. In Williamsburg, Clementina Rind inherited her husband's shop in 1773 and edited the *Virginia Gazette* until her own death in 1774. About twenty-five women ran printing shops in America before 1820. The family nature of printing businesses in the eighteenth century meant that women often played a greater role in the production and distribution of news than they would in later periods.[43]

In Britain there was no licensing after 1695, but successive governments used taxation to discourage the circulation of the cheapest newspapers (which they associated with more radical ideas) and to raise revenue.[44] The first Stamp Act went into effect in 1712; newspapers printed on a half sheet of paper had to pay a halfpenny tax per copy, and those printed on a whole sheet had to pay a full penny per copy. The logistics were especially difficult for printers in the provinces, because stamped sheets had to be purchased from London in advance of printing, and several papers went out of business in 1712.[45] But printers in London and the provinces quickly found ways to adapt. They noticed that the act did not clearly define "newspaper" and contained no provision for those printed on more than a full sheet of paper. Many printers expanded their publications to 1½ sheets, which they folded so as to create six-page newspapers selling for 1½ *d.* per copy. This tactic enabled them to pay the much lower duty for pamphlets—2*s.* per edition regardless of the number of copies. Other printers evaded the tax entirely, and by the 1720s a range of illegal unstamped publications were being hawked on the streets of London for as little as half a penny. To eliminate the unstamped papers, the government went after the hawkers and street vendors. A 1743 law specified fines and imprisonment for anyone selling unstamped papers, and vigorous enforcement put such papers out of business almost immediately.[46]

The loophole allowing newspapers of more than one sheet to register as pamphlets was closed in 1725, and most of the weeklies scaled back from six pages to four and raised their prices from 1½*d.* to 2*d.* Because space was now more limited, some printers experimented with reducing the size of type and increasing the number of columns from two to three. During the 1730s and 1740s, many newspapers expanded the size of their sheets so as to squeeze more news and advertisements into each issue without paying more tax.[47] The stamp tax was raised again in 1757 (to finance the Seven Years' War), increasing the average price of a newspaper to 2½*d.* That price represented about 5 percent of a London laborer's weekly wages and 10 percent of an agricultural worker's weekly wages. In 1776 the tax rose again (to finance the American War), leading most papers to raise their prices to 3*d.*[48]

Newspapers complained about the duties, but they were largely able to pass the cost on to their elite customers. The decline in total sales after 1712 did not last long, and the tax increases of 1757 and 1776 did not cause significant drops in circulation. But the success of unstamped papers between 1712 and 1743 (when they were suppressed) suggests that newspapers could have reached a wider public if they had not been taxed. In fact, the circulation of individual titles did not increase dramatically during this period. Around 1720 the London dailies probably sold 800 copies each, the tri-weeklies 2500, and the weeklies 3500. By 1775, the morning dailies and evening tri-weeklies dominated with between 2000 and 5000 copies each.[49] Proprietors attempted to appeal to a broader range of customers—female readers, country readers, the beau monde—but before 1776 newspapers depended primarily on a public of merchants, artisans, and shopkeepers earning at least £50 per year.[50]

The laws requiring newspaper stamps also imposed duties on advertisements, but this did not stop ads from transforming the business of news during the eighteenth century. The corantos of the 1620s and 1630s did not contain paid ads, nor did the newsbooks of the 1640s. L'Estrange's official publications in the early 1660s averaged about seven ads per issue. The *London Gazette* originally had a policy against advertisements, which were "not properly the business of a Paper of Intelligence." Over time the *Gazette* came to include paid notices, but during the 1670s, 1680s, and 1690s there were also periodicals entirely devoted to ads and distributed free of charge.

One of these, *The City Mercury: Or, Advertisements concerning Trade* (1675–78?) was published with the authorization (and perhaps the financial involvement) of L'Estrange, who had received a monopoly on advertisements back in 1663. The lapse of licensing in 1695 ended restrictions on who could operate a press as well as who could print advertisements. After 1695 free advertising periodicals in the vein of *The City Mercury* were apparently unable to compete with the tri-weekly and daily newspapers that also contained ads.[51]

The space devoted to advertisements in eighteenth-century English and American newspapers represented a major cultural and economic change. The first daily newspaper, the *Daily Courant* (1702–35), devoted about one half (and sometimes up to two thirds) of its space to advertisements. In the *Daily Post* (1719–46) and the *Daily Advertiser* (1731–98) advertisements took up as much as three quarters of the space, including most of the first page.[52] The success of provincial papers like the *Newcastle Courant* (1711–69) also depended upon their ability to attract advertisers.[53] In colonial America at least a full page (and often two) were devoted to ads for goods and services. A study of the *Pennsylvania Gazette* from 1728 to 1765 revealed that about 45 percent of available printing space was devoted to ads.[54] In most cases ads were submitted directly to the printer by local merchants, shopkeepers, and other individuals selling property, looking for workers, or offering rewards for runaway slaves and servants.[55]

To what extent did ads pay for eighteenth-century newspapers? Financial records from the period are extremely rare, but surviving evidence reveals the basic pattern. For the first eight months of 1707 the *London Gazette* took in £1,135 from sales and £790 (41 percent) from advertisements. The *Gazette* was published less frequently and had fewer advertisements than other London papers, but it charged much more (10s. per notice as opposed to 2s. or 2s. 6d.) and its wide distribution made it the preferred place for announcing auctions, real estate, and lost or stolen goods. Over time the *Gazette* lost ground to the daily and tri-weekly "advertisers" whose titles reflected the importance of ads in attracting readers. In 1775, the *Public Advertiser* raised £560 from sales and £388 (41 percent) from advertisements.[56] The accounts for the *Pennsylvania Gazette* during the period that Benjamin Franklin and David Hall were joint owners (1748–66) reveal a higher proportion of sales receipts (£750 per year on average) to advertising income (£200 per year on average). The *Pennsylvania Gazette* had a much higher circulation than most colonial papers—as many as 2,500 a year compared to an average of 700 or 800—so sales may have comprised a greater proportion of revenue than it did for other papers, but it is important to remember that Franklin and Hall also made money printing ads separate from the newspaper (i.e. handbills or broadsides paid for by local businesses).[57] James Parker, who claimed to have 700 subscribers to his *New York Gazette* in 1769, referred to advertisements as "the Life of a Paper." He also reported that 25 percent of his subscribers never paid their bills, making cash payments for ads all the more important.[58] A detailed study of the *Salisbury Journal* and the *Hampshire Chronicle* showed how newspaper proprietors in English towns also saw advertisements as the main source of profits.[59]

The boundary between news and advertisements was not always clear. Office copies of the *Daily Advertiser* from 1744 (on which an employee recorded the rate charged for each notice) show that "puffs" promoting a product or event were charged the same rate as ads but evaded the tax on advertisements because they were disguised as news.[60] Some newspapers also agreed to print reports for individuals in exchange for payment. When a reader complained about a poorly written obituary in 1765, the editor of the *Gazetteer and New Daily Advertiser* (1764–96) replied, "that paragraph was inserted and *paid for* by a friend of the deceased; and we are no more accountable for the diction thereof, than for any other paragraph or advertisement which people pay to have inserted."[61]

Meanwhile, not all genuine ads were paid for because the financial partners in newspapers often reserved the right to insert notices.[62] In fact, one of the main attractions for the London booksellers, theater managers, and auction houses that invested in newspapers was that they provided an advertising channel for their other products. By the 1720s, group ownership was common for London newspapers, and booksellers tended to dominate the lists of shareholders.[63] This fact helps to explain the preponderance of ads for books, but books were also, along with medicines, the first nationally distributed products. The consortium model of newspaper ownership satisfied three aims: it distributed the financial risk of publication among several partners, created a new sideline revenue stream (in the form of dividends), and enabled booksellers, theater managers, and others to promote their primary products, which were often time-sensitive (a new edition of a book, a play held over for another night, an auction, etc.). In English towns outside of London, group ownership also became more common after the mid-century, but most provincial newspapers remained part of a family business that also included job printing and retail sales of books, stationery, medicine, and household goods.[64]

In terms of distribution, London newspapers increasingly relied on wholesalers, especially the so-called "mercury women," who bought pamphlets and periodicals in bulk, sold some out of their shops and distributed the rest to hawkers (many of whom were also women). Elizabeth Nutt, a widow and mother of printers, oversaw several shops with the assistance of her daughters, and was one of the leading distributors of newspapers in London during the first half of the eighteenth century. Another mercury woman named Anne Dodd also distributed large quantities of pamphlets and newspapers. In 1731, for example, she handled 2,700 out of 10,000 total copies of the *London Journal*. Compared to later periods, when the production and distribution of newspapers became overwhelmingly masculine, in the early to mid-eighteenth century women remained crucial to the dissemination of news.[65]

Improvements in transportation during the eighteenth century facilitated the growth of the newspaper press in London and the provinces. The turnpike network expanded, road conditions improved, and horse and wagon carrier services became cheaper and faster. Many newspaper publishers set up their own distribution networks. The provincial papers in particular relied on booksellers, grocers, schoolmasters, and others to manage delivery. These agents collected payment from subscribers, took in advertisements (for which they received a commission) and supervised delivery by newsmen (for subscribers) and hawkers (for casual buyers). The newsmen sold a range of goods offered by the newspaper proprietor and his agents (books, stationery, medicine, etc.), and the sale of these ancillary products helped ensure delivery of newspapers in more remote areas. If the newsmen had carried only newspapers, they may not have found it worthwhile to visit far-flung customers. Newspaper owners benefited from having dedicated newsmen who made regular contact with their customers; meanwhile, the purveyors of goods and services (such as medicines and insurance) exploited these sales networks and paid to insert ads in the newspapers.[66]

London newspapers relied on the royal post to a much greater extent than their provincial counterparts. To reduce costs, London publishers made deals with postal officials known as Clerks of the Road. In exchange for a fee, the clerks used their franking privileges to send newspapers from London to local postmasters around the country. The postmasters paid the clerks 2*d.* per copy, which they passed on to subscribers. The use of franks therefore benefited the customer (who paid less than if regular postage were charged) and the postal officials (who collected fees, effectively acting as wholesalers). Some postal officials also became shareholders in newspapers, and contemporaries accused them of favoring the distribution of certain titles. Because they were government officials, they also felt pressure to impede newspapers that criticized the administration and favor those that praised it (this clearly happened during the age of Walpole).[67] Members of Parliament also had franking privileges, which they used to send newspapers postage-free to friends and constituents. In an effort to prevent people from forging an MP's signature on newspapers, a 1764 Act allowed MPs to send orders to the Post Office specifying which newspapers they wished to frank. Certain members of the parliamentary opposition exploited this measure to frank large quantities of newspapers on behalf of printers. In the early 1760s, newspapers franked by MPs had made up about 25 percent of those traveling through the mail. By 1782, the proportion was 60 percent.[68] The widespread franking of newspapers had not been intended by Parliament, but it clearly enabled readers throughout the country to obtain newspapers at a significantly reduced cost (postage would have added 2–3*d.* to the cost of each newspaper).[69]

Newspaper distribution worked differently in the American colonies for two reasons. First, newspapers were not affected by stamp and advertising duties, with the exception of a brief period during the Seven Years' War, when Massachusetts and New York temporarily imposed a halfpenny tax on newspapers to raise revenue.[70] Second, the royal post was far less developed in America. Many printers served as local postmasters, but in towns where there was more than one printer, only one of them could be postmaster, and he had a major advantage in terms of obtaining intelligence and ensuring delivery to his own subscribers. There was no uniform rate for sending newspapers through the post, and printers could not always rely on the horse riders to deliver in a timely manner. Riders had limited capacity and would refuse to carry newspapers when they became too burdensome. Moreover, the royal post mainly connected the towns along the coast and only went as far south as Virginia. For all of these reasons, printers (especially those who were not postmasters) often hired their own newsboys (for local delivery) and riders (for more distant subscribers). These ad hoc distribution channels were crucial to newspaper owners throughout the colonial period.[71]

DAILIES, WEEKLIES, AND MONTHLIES: BUSINESS PRACTICE AND JOURNALISTIC CULTURE

Writers, printers, and booksellers experimented with a number of different forms of publication during the early eighteenth century.[72] While editing the official *London Gazette*, Richard Steele launched a tri-weekly publication called the *Tatler* (1709–10). The *Tatler* followed the form of the *Gazette* (two columns of text printed on both sides of a single sheet), but in addition to news and advertisements it contained longer essays on social and literary topics, most of which were written by Steele and Joseph Addison.[73] Steele and Addison also collaborated on the *Spectator* (daily, 1711–12), which combined reader correspondence with essays on cultural and economic issues of the day, and was reprinted numerous times in book form during the eighteenth century. Other essay-based periodicals in the 1710s were more overtly political, such as Jonathan Swift's *The Examiner* (1710–14). All of these periodicals depended upon the talents of particular writers, many of whom benefited from patronage. Addison and Steele had various government appointments and Swift was Dean of St. Patrick's. Robert Harley paid Defoe to write the *Review of the Affairs of France* (1704–13), which largely supported Harley's own policies.[74]

Alongside newspapers and essay periodicals, writers and printers experimented with monthly digests of recent events. Abel Boyer's *Present State of Europe* (1690–1738) compiled reports of foreign affairs and parliamentary proceedings, which remained illegal. Although Boyer was arrested and fined in 1711, he continued to provide occasional accounts of Parliament on and off until his death in 1729. Like Dyer's newsletters, Boyer's monthly periodical tested the limits of acceptable publicity; the former had a restricted circulation and the latter printed debates that were already at least a few weeks old, which may help to explain why these publications were tolerated as much as they were. Boyer provided a model for Edward Cave's *Gentleman's Magazine* (1731–1907), which contained a mix of politics, literature, science, and news, and was the first monthly periodical to use the name "magazine." Cave and his imitators at the *London Magazine* (1732–85) exercised caution in their coverage of Parliament by omitting the names of speakers or veiling them in clever ways. Samuel Johnson, who wrote some of the accounts in the *Gentleman's*, explained that Cave had influence with doorkeepers that enabled his agents to enter the debates or linger in the hallways to gather details. Some MPs also furnished notes or complete speeches, a practice that became more widespread later in the century. In 1738, the House of Commons resolved that it was a breach of privilege to publish accounts of Parliament in any form. The magazines responded by framing accounts as proceedings of a political club or the legislature of an imaginary country, but even these accounts led to fines and reprimands by both Houses of Parliament. By the late 1750s the magazines had discontinued their coverage. Full and regular accounts of Parliament had to await the newspapers of the early 1770s.[75]

By the 1730s, the essay-based periodicals that had thrived in the 1710s and 1720s could not match the range of material now available in the monthly magazines or the freshness of news in the daily and tri-weekly newspapers.[76] Over the course of the 1740s, 1750s, and 1760s, the newspapers backed by booksellers diversified, adding original essays, letters to the printer, and excerpts from books to the traditional mix of news paragraphs and advertisements. By the 1760s, papers like the *London Evening Post* (1727–1806), *Public Advertiser* (1752–94), *Gazetteer and New Daily Advertiser* (1764–96), and *Morning Chronicle* (1769–1865) dominated English journalism. Inspired in part by the magazines, they gathered into one place a range of material that had previously appeared in distinct publications: news reports, political essays, literary criticism, poetry, price lists, and advertisements. In the eighteenth century, the primary unit of news was the paragraph rather than the article. Newspaper columns often contained paragraphs on several topics printed one after the other, without headlines or other marks (besides paragraph breaks) to differentiate one report from another. From the printer's perspective, one advantage of treating the paragraph as the basic nugget of news was that it was relatively easy for printers to select and arrange paragraphs of varying lengths so as to fill a given column with print. Printers scanned other publications looking for paragraphs worth copying, which they combined with any material submitted by merchants, politicians, and interested readers. In addition to letters and essays, readers could submit a single paragraph to the newspapers, some of which set up mailboxes to receive anonymous submissions after hours.[77] Most of the work of selecting and editing material for publication took place in the printing shop, but increasingly this task was given to a separate individual who became known as the "editor." Roger Thompson, who was managing three papers in 1769—the *Gazetteer*, the *General Evening Post*, and the *Craftsman*—may have been the first to hold that title.[78]

For foreign news, London newspapers relied extensively on French and Dutch gazettes as well as the *London Gazette*, whose existing translations could be copied with no expense or risk. Papers in other English towns and in the colonies relied in turn on the London press, so that much of the European news read by people in North America or the English provinces had been filtered through London. Newspapers rarely acknowledged their sources. Many claimed to have (unpaid) correspondents abroad, and some certainly did.[79]

In terms of newsgathering, the most important development during the eighteenth century involved "ship news." Captains and crew who had learned of events during their voyage shared news and rumors with customs officials, insurance brokers, and merchants, who in turn sent them to newspapers. The same ships that brought official government dispatches brought private letters and newspapers, and in the days following a ship's arrival printers struggled to make sense of contradictory reports. The main clearing-house for ship news was Lloyd's coffeehouse in London, home to the Lloyd's association of insurance underwriters. Agents for underwriters greeted ships in each port, noting their port of origin, cargo, and any news relayed by the captain. The underwriters then shared these reports with the master of Lloyd's coffee shop, who recorded each day's news into a large folio volume for immediate consultation by members. The master used the same reports to prepare extracts for publication in *Lloyd's List* (1692 [ms]–present [online]) and *Lloyd's Evening Post* (1757–1805), which other newspapers copied in turn. In an age when most news appeared anonymously, the ship captain's report was a rare example of eyewitness testimony attributed to a named individual.[80]

In colonial seaports, printers who hoped for oral reports from ship captains and the latest newspapers and magazines from London eagerly awaited the arrival of transatlantic ships. The transatlantic voyage could take three months or more, depending on the route and weather conditions. During the winter, few if any ships arrived, which meant a deluge of news in the spring.[81] In the case of important news (such as treaties or Acts of Parliament affecting the colonies), printers sometimes issued broadsides rather than wait for the next issue of their weekly newspapers. Most local news circulated orally or through private letters, but major storms and the last words of executed criminals appeared in small pamphlets or broadsides.[82] The newspapers contained local material in the form of advertisements and occasional reader submissions, but most of the news was copied from newspapers that arrived by ship or post. A few examples of efforts to gather and analyze information of public concern (such as an epidemic) can be found, but these did not appear in newspapers. Instead, such reporting depended upon the initiatives of individual writers, ministers, or civic leaders who gathered information (sometimes using questionnaires) and published it in books or specialized periodicals at their own risk.[83]

Newspapers in the American colonies and the English provinces were managed very differently from their London counterparts. In London, shareholders expected revenue from dividends and a vehicle for advertising their own products or services. Most shareholders were only concerned with the editorial side in so far as it put them at risk for an expensive prosecution for seditious libel.[84] Some booksellers had shares in more than one paper, and some printers were responsible for several papers at once, which further facilitated the reprinting of articles among dailies, tri-weeklies, and weeklies.[85] The political convictions of individual shareholders could not always determine the choices made by the printers and editors managing their papers. In the provinces and in the colonies, a single individual (with the help of family members) often had to solicit advertisers and readers, collect payment from them, compile reports from other newspapers and the occasional submission, and supervise production. He or she had more direct control over insertions, and more reason to worry about offending local readers, advertisers, and officials. Reliance on income from government led to some self-censorship, but such income was rarely enough to buy the loyalty of a printer, who needed printing jobs and advertisements from a range of sources to remain profitable.[86] Benjamin Franklin claimed his *Pennsylvania Gazette* was open to all parties, and from the 1730s he publicly defended the idea that "when Truth has fair Play, it will always prevail over Falsehood."[87] But when presented with a text that might cause controversy or harm his business, Franklin would refuse to insert it in the *Gazette* and propose that the author pay for a separate pamphlet to be distributed without Franklin's name on it. The profitability of Franklin's business depended in part on prudent decisions about what to *exclude* from the newspaper.[88]

Colonial newspapers were not entirely free to report on the activities of royal governors or provincial assemblies because most printers sought government contracts and wished to avoid prosecutions for seditious libel. John Peter Zenger's *New York Weekly Journal* (1733–51) was exceptional because it was financed by a political faction that supported the former Chief Justice of New York, Lewis Morris, in his battle with the governor, William Cosby. The *Weekly Journal* attacked Cosby as tyrannical and argued for the role of a free press in reforming a corrupt government. When the governor sued Zenger for libel in 1735, Zenger's lawyer insisted newspapers should be free to monitor and criticize local officials whose distance from the royal court enabled them to get away with corruption. Legal precedents made clear that in libel cases truth was irrelevant, and the role of the jury was supposed to be limited to deciding whether or not the defendant had printed the text. Still, the jury was persuaded by the arguments of Zenger's lawyer and blocked the conviction. The Zenger trial revealed officials could not always count on a jury to side with them, but it did not lead to any change in the law. Attitudes toward freedom of the press remained ambiguous in the eighteenth century. Almost no one argued for pre-publication censorship, but few celebrated the idea of a totally unrestrained press.[89]

Although colonial newspapers continued to copy news from London, during the 1740s and 1750s they began to contain more reports from other cities in North America, including discussions of crime, disease, religion, the role of women, and the danger of slave revolts and Indian raids.[90] After 1760, the increase in the number of printers in the larger towns (Boston, New York, and Philadelphia) and conflict with Britain led to more differentiation of newspapers along political lines, with printer-editors taking more outspoken positions to attract readers.[91] But the main turning point came with the Stamp Act of 1765, not to be confused with the stamp duty on newspapers still operating in Britain. The 1765 Act was part of a series of measures by which the crown sought to get the American colonists to help pay Britain's debt after the Seven Years' War. Although it imposed duties on a range of paper items from playing cards to legal documents, it promised to be especially burdensome for newspaper printers, who feared that they would not be able to pass the cost of the stamp on to their customers. Opposition to the Act politicized the press, and while some printers still avoided controversy, most felt pressure to choose sides. By the outbreak of war in 1775, it became nearly impossible for printers to remain neutral. The use of verbal and physical violence against printers who did not support independence revealed that liberty of the press now meant something different from lack of prior restraint: rather than being open to all sides, radical leaders expected printers to advance the cause of "liberty" and they went after those who did not.[92]

Between 1763 and 1776, the number of newspapers in the English colonies doubled from twenty-one to forty-two, but this growth did not eliminate political pamphlets, which also surged during this period. Pamphlets enjoyed a symbiotic relationship with newspapers: many of them began as essays in newspapers, and others enjoyed a much wider circulation thanks to excerpts or full reprints in the newspapers.[93] Thomas Paine's *Common Sense* (1776) was the most influential pamphlet of the age, but its influence depended in large part on the way it was reprinted and commented on in newspapers.[94] Newspapers also featured a new genre—the exposé—which drew heavily on pamphlet culture by revealing facts that tarnished an individual's reputation or rallied readers behind a cause.[95]

In London, extensive coverage of parliamentary debates in the 1770s further reinforced the newspaper's importance as a venue for public opinion. Magazines again took the first step by publishing tentative accounts early in 1770, and by the end of that year several daily and tri-weekly newspapers were also printing the debates. In February 1771, the House of Commons summoned the printers or editors of eight papers for violating standing orders against publication. While some MPs argued that accounts should be prohibited because they tended to misrepresent speeches, others argued that the public had a right to be informed. Some took a middle course, suggesting that newspapers be allowed to print accounts, but only after the session had ended. The radical leader John Wilkes used his position as Alderman of London to mobilize constables and magistrates to help three of the printers resist arrest and publicly challenge the authority of the House of Commons. Once it became clear that Wilkes had the upper hand, the Commons dropped the charges, giving the newspapers tacit permission to print debates. After a similar struggle with Wilkes in 1774, the Lords also abandoned their long-held privilege.[96]

It took several years for newspapers to develop full and regular accounts, but by the outbreak of the American Revolution, parliamentary debates took up a significant amount of space in most London newspapers. Not all papers produced original versions; several simply copied the accounts provided by other newspapers.[97] In addition, the Houses of Parliament still reserved the right to exclude "strangers," the term used for non-members who observed from the "Strangers' Gallery." Even when reporters were admitted, they were not guaranteed a seat or officially permitted to take notes until some time in the 1780s.[98] There is some evidence that shorthand was used, but no reporter in the 1770s claimed to be providing a verbatim transcript. William Woodfall, a highly respected writer for the *Morning Chronicle*, described his typical account as "a mere skeleton of the arguments urged upon the occasion" and warned readers not to expect "the exact phraseology used by the speakers."[99]

Investments in direct newsgathering remained limited. A few newspapers had editors who received a salary from the shareholders or were given an ownership stake in exchange for their efforts, but most relied on material copied from other newspapers or unpaid contributions by merchants, politicians, and other well-connected readers.[100] Apart from any salary paid to an editor, the money spent acquiring news went to subscriptions and postage to obtain newspapers printed in other cities and countries. The cost of procuring foreign gazettes and paying translators led many papers to rely on the reports found in other papers, especially the *London Gazette*.[101] The lack of copyright for news paragraphs and essays appearing in periodicals, and the low incidence of payment for original submissions clearly reduced the cost of obtaining "copy."[102] Outlays for stamp and advertising duties, printing, and paper dwarfed those associated with collecting and editing the news throughout this period.[103] Indeed, the high cost of production and government taxation during this period was offset by the negligible amount spent on reporting.

CONCLUSION

On the eve of the Glorious Revolution there was one official newspaper printed in London and none in the English provinces or North American colonies. By the outbreak of the American Revolution there were twenty-one newspapers in London, about forty-two in the American colonies, and approximately fifty in English towns outside London.[104] These papers were no longer subject to pre-publication censorship but they remained vulnerable to prosecution for seditious libel. Despite Zenger's victory there was no change in the law during this period and most newspaper owners sought to avoid a prosecution. Yet there was an important advance in the freedom to publish parliamentary debates, whose regular inclusion after 1770 marked a shift in newspapers' focus on foreign affairs toward more coverage of national (and imperial) politics. Pamphlets continued to be important forums for debate and often had a symbiotic relationship with newspapers. Broadsides were still used to provide late-breaking news, but by 1775 newspapers had become the primary means of commercializing news. Periodicity proved crucial for attracting readers and advertisers, and sale by subscription enabled publishers to know approximately how many copies to print and where to send them.

The fact that news periodicals flourished in England despite the duties on newspapers and advertisements confirms that their owners developed effective strategies for attracting readers and advertisers among the merchant and political elite. Government appointments and political subsidies helped finance some newspapers and essay-based periodicals during the early eighteenth century, but in the middle decades of the century the "advertisers" and "evening posts" came to dominate the trade. Most of these publications were owned and controlled by shareholders who counted on regular dividend payments and remained largely independent of political pressure.[105] In the English provinces and the American colonies, most newspapers were part of a printing and retail business run by a family or a small partnership. They also depended on a combination of subscription and advertising revenue to be successful. Apart from a few writers covering Parliament, there were no reporters. Newspapers depended on a shared custom of copying, which kept newsgathering costs low and ensured that news could spread from one place to another. In the colonies, printers who served as postmasters exploited this advantage to collect and distribute news, but like their rivals who were not postmasters, they also had to build business relationships and distribution networks to ensure the success of their newspapers. In England proprietors made deals with the Clerks of the Road, postmasters, and MPs to take advantage of their franking privileges.

The custom of copying and the exploitation of postal privileges made economic sense for the owners and printers of newspapers, but they also had important political consequences. When the press on both sides of the

Atlantic became more politicized in the 1760s and 1770s, writers exploited the fact that newspapers copied from each other to disseminate their messages to a wider audience.[106] While some planted stories or mislabeled sources in an attempt to advance political or financial goals, others cherished the ability to assume a depersonalized voice in debates about culture, society, and government.[107] The fact that so many paragraphs and essays were copied or submitted by unpaid correspondents needs to be understood in light of the culture and business of journalism at the time. The active participation of readers and the freedom with which printers and editors republished existing articles were part of what made the growth of the newspaper press possible in the eighteenth-century English Atlantic world.

NOTES

1. C. John Sommerville, *The News Revolution in England: Cultural Dynamics of Daily Information* (New York: Oxford University Press, 1996); Joad Raymond, "News," in *The Oxford History of Popular Print Culture*, vol. 1: *Cheap Print in Britain and Ireland to 1660*, ed. Joad Raymond (Oxford: Oxford University Press, 2011), 377–97; Andrew Pettegree, *The Invention of News: How the World Came to Know about Itself* (New Haven and London: Yale University Press, 2014), 8–11.
2. Angela McShane, "Ballads and Broadsides," in Raymond (ed.), *The Oxford History of Popular Print Culture*, vol. 1, 339–62.
3. Joad Raymond, *Pamphlets and Pamphleteering in Early Modern Britain* (Cambridge: Cambridge University Press, 2003), 12–17; Andrew Pettegree, *The Book in the Renaissance* (New Haven: Yale University Press, 2010), ch. 7.
4. Paul Arblaster, "Posts, Newsletters, Newspapers: England in a European System of Communications," *Media History*, 11/1–2 (2005): 21–36.
5. Brendan Dooley, *The Social History of Skepticism: Experience and Doubt in Early Modern Culture* (Baltimore: Johns Hopkins University Press, 1999), ch. 1; Mario Infelese, "News Networks between Italy and Europe," in *The Dissemination of News and the Emergence of Contemporaneity in Early Modern Europe*, ed. Brendan Dooley (Farnham: Ashgate, 2010), 51–67; Pettegree, *Invention of News*, 107–16.
6. Johannes Weber, "The Early German Newspaper—A Medium of Contemporaneity," in Dooley (ed.), *The Dissemination of News and the Emergence of Contemporaneity*, 69–79.
7. "newspaper, n." *OED Online*. Oxford University Press, September 2014. On the danger of treating early news publications as "forerunners" of newspapers, see Joad Raymond, "Newspapers: A National or International Phenomenon?" *Media History*, 18/3–4 (2012): 249–57.
8. Carolyn Nelson and Matthew Seccombe, "The Creation of the Periodical Press 1620–1695," in *The Cambridge History of the Book in Britain*, vol. 4: *1557–1695*, ed. John Barnard and D. F. McKenzie (Cambridge: Cambridge University Press, 2002), 533–50; Sommerville, *News Revolution*, 19–22; Pettegree, *Invention of News*, 182–95.

9. "A Proclamation against Excesse of Lavish and Licentious Speech in Matters of State (1620)," in *Censorship and the Press, 1580–1720*, vol. 1: *Background, 1557–1579; 1580–1639*, ed. Geoffrey Kemp and Cyndia Susan Clegg (London: Pickering & Chatto, 2009), 201–2.

10. Nelson and Seccombe, "Creation of the Periodical Press," 535–7; Raymond, "News," 380–3.

11. Harold Love, *Scribal Publication in Seventeenth-Century England* (Oxford: Clarendon Press, 1993), 10–18.

12. Joad Raymond, *The Invention of the Newspaper: English Newsbooks, 1641–1649* (Oxford: Clarendon Press, 1996), 106–7; Raymond, "News," 396–7.

13. Michael Mendle, "News and the Pamphlet Culture of Mid-Seventeenth-Century England," in *The Politics of Information in Early Modern Europe*, ed. Brendan Dooley and Sabrina Baron (London: Routledge, 2001), 57–79.

14. Jason McElligott, "1642," in *Censorship and the Press, 1580–1720*, vol. 2: *1640–1660*, ed. Geoffrey Kemp and Jason McElligott (London: Pickering & Chatto, 2009), 34–5.

15. Jason McElligott, "1643," in *Censorship and the Press*, ed. Kemp and McElligott, vol. 2, 56–62.

16. Raymond, *Invention of the Newspaper*, 233–4.

17. Nelson and Seccombe, "Creation of the Periodical Press," 537–43; Raymond, *Invention of the Newspaper*, 73–8.

18. Michael Treadwell, "The Stationers and the Printing Acts at the End of the Seventeenth Century," in *The Cambridge History of the Book in Britain*, ed. Barnard and McKenzie, vol. 4, 755–78.

19. "L'Estrange to bee Surveyor of the Printing Presse &c (1663)," in *Censorship and the Press, 1580–1720*, vol. 3: *1660–1695*, ed. Geoffrey Kemp (London: Pickering & Chatto, 2009), 50–1.

20. James Sutherland, *The Restoration Newspaper and its Development* (New York: Cambridge University Press, 1986), 8–11.

21. Susan E. Whyman, *The Pen and the People: English Letter Writers 1660–1800* (Oxford: Oxford University Press, 2009), 49–52.

22. "Proclamation[s] to Restrain the Spreading of False News, and Licentious Talking of Matters of State and Government (1672, 1674)," in *Censorship and the Press*, ed. Kemp, vol. 3, 155–8.

23. Treadwell, "The Stationers and the Printing Acts," 769–70.

24. Mark Goldie, "Restoration Crisis, 1679–81," in *Censorship and the Press*, ed. Kemp, vol. 3, 169–72; Sutherland, *Restoration Newspaper*, 10–18.

25. Steve Pincus, *1688: The First Modern Revolution* (New Haven: Yale University Press, 2009), 151–2, 166–8.

26. Quoted in Sutherland, *Restoration Newspaper*, 23.

27. Nelson and Seccombe, "Creation of the Periodical Press," 547–9; Mark Goldie, "Introduction," in *Censorship and the Press, 1580–1720*, vol. 4: *1696–1720*, ed. Mark Goldie and Geoff Kemp (London: Pickering & Chatto, 2009), ix–x.

28. On the fiscal, military, and commercial developments, see Pincus, *1688*, ch. 12.

29. Mark Goldie, "The Printing Act in Question, 1692–3," in *Censorship and the Press*, ed. Kemp, vol. 3, 347–50; Mark Goldie, "The Rejection of Licensing," in *Censorship and the Press*, ed. Kemp, vol. 3, 413–21.

30. Adrian Johns, *Piracy: The Intellectual Property Wars from Gutenberg to Gates* (Chicago: University of Chicago Press, 2009), 23–4, 41–3.
31. Ronan Deazley, *On the Origin of the Right to Copy: Charting the Movement of Copyright Law in Eighteenth-Century Britain (1695–1775)* (Oxford: Hart Publishing, 2004), 18.
32. Victoria Gardner, "Liberty, License and Leveson," *History Today*, 63/2 (February 2013): 3–4; Goldie, "Introduction," in *Censorship and the Press*, ed. Goldie and Kemp, vol. 4, ix–xxv; Philip Hamburger, "The Development of the Law of Seditious Libel and the Control of the Press," *Stanford Law Review*, 37/3 (February 1985): 661–765.
33. Martin Conboy, *Journalism: A Critical History* (London: Sage, 2004), 56–8.
34. Alex Barber, "'It is Not Easy What to Say of Our Condition, Much Less to Write It': The Continued Importance of Scribal News in the Early 18th Century," *Parliamentary History*, 32/2 (2013): 293–316.
35. J. A. Downie, *Robert Harley and the Press: Propaganda and Public Opinion in the Age of Swift and Defoe* (Cambridge: Cambridge University Press, 1979).
36. Michael Harris, *London Newspapers in the Age of Walpole: A Study of the Origins of the Modern English Press* (Cranbury, NJ: Associated University Presses, 1987), 136–47.
37. Richard D. Brown, "The Shifting Freedoms of the Press in the Eighteenth Century," in *A History of the Book in America*, vol. 1: *The Colonial Book in the Atlantic World*, ed. Hugh Amory and David Hall (New York: Cambridge University Press, 2000), 366–76.
38. Ian K. Steele, *The English Atlantic, 1675–1740: An Exploration of Communication and Community* (New York: Oxford University Press, 1986), 146–7.
39. G. A. Cranfield, *The Development of the Provincial Newspaper 1700–1760* (Oxford: Clarendon Press, 1962), 10–13.
40. Charles Clark, *The Public Prints: The Newspaper in Anglo-American Culture, 1665–1740* (New York: Oxford University Press, 1994), 77–108, 129–39.
41. Joseph Adelman, *Revolutionary Networks: The Business of Printing and the Production of American Politics, 1763-1789* (forthcoming).
42. Stephen Botein, "'Meer Mechanics' and an Open Press: The Business and Political Strategies of Colonial American Printers," *Perspectives in American History*, 9 (1975): 127–225, esp. 143–7; Charles Clark and Charles Wetherell, "The Measure of Maturity: The *Pennsylvania Gazette*, 1728–1765," *William and Mary Quarterly*, 3rd ser., 46/2 (April 1989): 279–303, figures at 280.
43. Karen Weyler, *Empowering Words: Outsiders and Authorship in Early America* (Athens, Ga.: University of Georgia Press, 2013), 165–203. See also the work of Paula McDowell, cited in n. 65, and Conboy, *Journalism*, 41–2.
44. Hannah Barker, *Newspapers, Politics and English Society 1695–1855* (Harlow: Longman, 2000), 3–4, 66; Downie, *Robert Harley*, 150–9.
45. C. Y. Ferdinand, *Benjamin Collins and the Provincial Newspaper Trade in the Eighteenth Century* (Oxford: Clarendon Press, 1997), 12–13.
46. Harris, *London Newspapers*, 19–30.
47. Harris, *London Newspapers*, 22–5.
48. Barker, *Newspapers, Politics and English Society*, 39.

49. Michael Harris, "London Newspapers," in *The Cambridge History of the Book in Britain*, vol. 5: *1695–1830*, ed. Michael Suarez and Michael Turner (Cambridge: Cambridge University Press, 2009), 413–33, estimates at 422–4.

50. Uriel Heyd, *Reading Newspapers: Press and Public in Eighteenth-Century Britain and America* (Oxford: Voltaire Foundation, 2012), 83–95. Heyd argues that readership was expanding, but his evidence comes from the way newspapers marketed themselves. Harris insists that there was no major change in the customer base, at least within London ("London Newspapers," 416). On access to cultural products more generally see Robert Hume, "The Economics of Culture in London, 1660–1740," *Huntington Library Quarterly*, 69/4 (December 2006): 487–533.

51. R. B. Walker, "Advertising in London Newspapers, 1650–1750," *Business History*, 15/2 (July 1973): 112–30.

52. Walker, "Advertising in London Newspapers," 122–3.

53. Victoria Gardner, "John White and the Development of Print Culture in the North East of England, 1711–1769," in *Book Trade Connections from the Seventeenth to the Twentieth Centuries*, ed. John Hinks and Catherine Armstrong (New Castle, Del.: Oak Knoll Press, 2008), 71–92.

54. Clark and Wetherell, "The Measure of Maturity," 284–8.

55. On ads for runaways, see David Waldstreicher, *Runaway America: Benjamin Franklin, Slavery, and the American Revolution* (New York: Hill and Wang, 2004), 17–24.

56. Walker, "Advertising in London Newspapers," 116–18, 130.

57. Estimates from Botein, "'Meer Mechanics' and an Open Press," 148–9. On Franklin's business, see James N. Green and Peter Stallybrass, *Benjamin Franklin: Writer and Printer* (Newcastle, Del.: Oak Knoll Press, 2006), ch. 3.

58. Botein, "'Meer Mechanics' and an Open Press," 148–9.

59. Ferdinand, *Benjamin Collins*, 74.

60. Walker, "Advertising in London Newspapers," 123. The printer's copy of the *Edinburgh Evening Courant* from 1752 contains similar evidence (Heyd, *Reading Newspapers*, 110–11).

61. *Gazetteer and New Daily Advertiser*, London, March 13, 1765, p. 4.

62. Richmond P. Bond and Marjorie N. Bond, "The Minute Books of the St. James's Chronicle," *Studies in Bibliography*, 28 (1975): 17–40.

63. Michael Harris, "The Management of the London Newspaper Press during the Eighteenth Century," *Publishing History*, 4 (1978): 95–112; Harris, *London Newspapers*, chs 4–5.

64. Victoria Gardner, *The Business of News in England, 1760–1820* (London: Palgrave, forthcoming), ch. 2.

65. Paula McDowell, *The Women of Grub Street: Press, Politics, and Gender in the London Literary Marketplace 1678–1730* (Oxford: Clarendon Press, 1998), 25–6, 55–61; Harris, *London Newspapers*, 38–40.

66. R. M. Wiles, *Freshest Advices: Early Provincial Newspapers in England* (Columbus: Ohio State University Press, 1965), ch. 3; Gardner, *Business of News in England*, ch. 2; Ferdinand, *Benjamin Collins*, ch. 2.

67. Michael Suarez, "Introduction," in *The Cambridge History of the Book in Britain*, ed. Suarez and Turner, vol. 5, 12–17; Harris, *London Newspapers*, 43–4.

68. Kenneth Ellis, *The Post Office in the Eighteenth Century: A Study in Administrative History* (London: Oxford University Press, 1958), 49–53.

69. Whyman, *The Pen and the People*, 66–7.

70. Arthur Schlesinger, *Prelude to Independence: The Newspaper War on Britain 1764–1776* (New York: Vintage, 1965 [orig. 1958]), 65.

71. Joseph Adelman, "'A Constitutional Conveyance of Intelligence, Public and Private': The Post Office, the Business of Printing, and the American Revolution," *Enterprise and Society*, 11/4 (2010): 1–44.

72. On the importance of this "experimental" phase in the history of journalism, see Conboy, *Journalism*, 54–60.

73. Richmond P. Bond, *The Tatler: The Making of a Literary Journal* (Cambridge, Mass.: Harvard University Press, 1971).

74. Downie, *Robert Harley*; Hume, "The Economics of Culture in London," 521–2.

75. Fredrick Seaton Siebert, *Freedom of the Press in England 1476–1776: The Rise and Decline of Government Control* (Urbana: University of Illinois Press, 1965), 347–54.

76. Harris, *London Newspapers*, 121, 184–5.

77. For more on the paragraph, see Will Slauter, "The Paragraph as Information Technology: How News Traveled in the Eighteenth-Century Atlantic World," *Annales: Histoire, Sciences sociales.* [English version], 67/2 (April–June 2012): 253–78.

78. Robert Haig, *The Gazetteer, 1735–1797: A Study in the Eighteenth-Century English Newspaper* (Carbondale, Ill.: Southern Illinois University Press, 1960), 86–9, 92–3, 162–3.

79. Sutherland, *Restoration Newspaper*, 125–6, 139–43.

80. John McCusker, "The Business Press in England Before 1775," in John McCusker, *Essays in the Economic History of the Atlantic World* (London: Routledge, 1997), 145–76; Will Slauter, "News and Diplomacy in the Age of the American Revolution," PhD dissertation (Princeton University, 2007), ch. 1.

81. Steele, *English Atlantic*, 10, 51, 61, 113–14, 151, 295.

82. On the importance of oral and epistolary networks see Richard D. Brown, *Knowledge is Power: The Diffusion of Information in Early America, 1700–1865* (New York: Oxford University Press, 1989).

83. David Paul Nord, "'Plain and Certain Facts': Four Episodes of Public Affairs Reporting," *Journalism History*, 37/2 (Summer 2011): 80–90.

84. Bond and Bond, "The Minute Books of the St. James's Chronicle," 32–6.

85. Harris, "London Newspapers," 425–6.

86. Botein, "'Meer Mechanics' and an Open Press," 164–95.

87. Quoted in Botein, "'Meer Mechanics' and an Open Press," 182.

88. Clark and Wetherell, "The Measure of Maturity," 291; Green and Stallybrass, *Benjamin Franklin*, 57–61.

89. Brown, "Shifting Freedoms," 368–71.

90. David Copeland, *Colonial American Newspapers: Character and Content* (Newark: University of Delaware Press, 1997).

91. James N. Green, "English Books and Printing in the Age of Franklin," in *The Colonial Book in the Atlantic World*, ed. Amory and Hall, 248–98, esp. 291.

92. Brown, "Shifting Freedoms," 374–5.

93. Charles Clark, "Early American Journalism: News and Opinion in the Popular Press," in *The Colonial Book in the Atlantic World*, ed. Amory and Hall, 347–66, esp. 361–5.

94. Trish Loughran, "Disseminating *Common Sense*: Thomas Paine and the Problem of the Early National Bestseller," *American Literature*, 78/1 (March 2006): 1–28.

95. Thomas C. Leonard, *The Power of the Press: The Birth of American Political Reporting* (New York: Oxford University Press, 1986), ch. 1.

96. Peter Thomas, "The Beginning of Parliamentary Reporting in Newspapers, 1768–1774," *English Historical Review*, 74/293 (October 1959): 623–36.

97. Will Slauter, "A Trojan Horse in Parliament: International Publicity in the Age of the American Revolution," in *Into Print: Limits and Legacies of Enlightenment. Essays in Honor of Robert Darnton*, ed. Charles Walton (University Park: Penn State University Press, 2011), 15–31.

98. Arthur Aspinall, "The Reporting and Publishing of the House of Commons' Debates, 1771–1834," in *Essays Presented to Sir Lewis Namier*, ed. Richard Pares and A. J. P. Taylor (London: Macmillan, 1956), 227–57.

99. Quoted in Thomas, "Beginning of Parliamentary Reporting," 636.

100. Michael Harris, "Journalism as a Profession or Trade in the Eighteenth Century," in *Author/Publisher Relations during the Eighteenth and Nineteenth Centuries*, ed. Robin Myers and Michael Harris (Oxford: Oxford Polytechnic Press, 1983), 37–62; Jeremy Black, *The English Press in the Eighteenth Century* (London: Croom Helm, 1987), 87–104; J. A. Downie, "Periodicals, the Book Trade and the 'Bourgeois Public Sphere,'" *Media History*, 14/3 (2008): 261–74.

101. Harris, *London Newspapers*, 161–2.

102. On copyright, see Will Slauter, "Upright Piracy: Understanding the Lack of Copyright for Journalism in Eighteenth-Century Britain," *Book History*, 16 (2013): 34–61.

103. See the *Public Advertiser*'s accounts for 1765–71 (British Library Add. 38,169).

104. Harris, "London Newspapers," 424; Botein, "'Meer Mechanics' and an Open Press," 215–16.

105. Hannah Barker, *Newspapers, Politics, and Public Opinion in Late Eighteenth-Century England* (New York: Oxford University Press, 1998), 4, 46–53.

106. William Warner, "Communicating Liberty: The Newspapers of the British Empire as a Matrix for the American Revolution," *ELH*, 72/2 (Summer 2005): 339–61; Slauter, "The Paragraph as Information Technology."

107. Michael Warner, *Letters of the Republic: Publication and the Public Sphere in Eighteenth-Century America* (Cambridge, Mass.: Harvard University Press, 1990).

3

News in the Age of Revolution

Joseph M. Adelman and Victoria E. M. Gardner

In 1794 Joseph Gales, owner of the *Sheffield Register*, his wife Winifred, and their four children embarked on a long and perilous journey from Sheffield to Philadelphia.[1] Britain was convulsed by the turmoil of the French Revolution and Gales stood accused of plotting to arm those committed to parliamentary reform. As his wife later wrote, his choice was stark; he could "risk the tender mercies of a packed jury, and prejudiced judges if he should be indicted for printing libels or imprisoned to give evidence . . . [under] the suspension of Habeas Corpus, precluding Bail—or . . . leave his family, friends, and country!"[2] Before he could be arrested, Gales fled to Hamburg while Winifred stayed behind to sell the business. Such was the threat of mobs that armed men stood guard outside their Sheffield house every night until she and their children had left the town.[3] The journey to Hamburg and then to the United States was arduous and frightening; storms threatened their vessels and the Royal Navy boarded them, searching for foreigners and traitors. Once safely in Philadelphia, Gales immediately rekindled his career by establishing the *Independent Gazetteer*. The onset of yellow fever in 1797 forced another move, this time carrying just two cases of type to North Carolina, where he began the *Raleigh Register* on a borrowed press at the behest of local Republicans. The paper met with success financially, enabling Gales in 1805 to purchase the *National Intelligencer* in Washington for his son, Joseph Jr. It became the official newspaper of the Republican party for two decades, and Gales Jr. edited it until his death in 1860.[4]

In less than a decade, Joseph Gales Sr. traversed not only an ocean, but also much of the Anglo-American world as a printer, first in provincial England, then successively in the United States capital, in a small Southern city, and finally by providing financial backing for his son to venture anew when Washington became the American capital. The Gales family certainly traveled further than most newspaper proprietors in this period, but their story echoes that of their compatriots in their efforts to make a commercial living amidst political turmoil that rocked the Anglo-American world. Gales's skills may have transferred easily across the Atlantic, but he faced divergent attitudes towards the freedom and funding of news as each country sought to deal with an increasingly powerful press.

During the Age of Revolution, the press in Britain and the United States grew at a rapid rate as the demand for news—and the expectation that it would be easily and readily available via the newspaper press—became a central feature of the political culture of both countries. Readers sought access to legislative debates, the machinations of executive and administrative power, and the latest and most accurate commercial information to support and sustain economic life. As each state sought to project power and influence at home and abroad, those seeking to shape politics increasingly turned to the newspaper press and control of its market.

Despite a shared heritage and surface commonalities, the newspaper presses in Britain and the United States increasingly diverged over the period 1775–1815. Comparative studies of the period, however, are few and far between. Those that do compare the two identify politics and culture as the major points of differentiation, in part the result of a growing sense of political and cultural "Other."[5] Examining the political economy of news, this chapter demonstrates that on both sides of the Atlantic there was a growing expectation of the public's right to news and political information. Prioritizing newspapers above other forms of print as the most appropriate vehicles to do so, the governments of both countries legislated on the press and on postal networks, the chief communications systems on which news distribution relied. In the United States, an independent press was a cornerstone of the fledgling nation and government actively encouraged its expansion. In Britain, the readership of newspapers was controlled by stamp duties while free newspaper postage was granted with the cursory approval of individual MPs. We argue that these regulatory frameworks had a significant and divergent impact on the press of each country. In Britain, duties created high barriers to entry, thus limiting competition but enabling considerable financial prosperity through advertising income for the successful. Paradoxically, this commercial power in turn freed most British newspapers from political subsidies, leaving politicians struggling to influence content. In America, codified press freedom facilitated comparatively low barriers to entry, and thus an almost limitless market. However, as a result, the large number of newspaper printers had radically lower chances of commercial success than their British counterparts, necessitating political sponsorship.

Arguing that "news" became situated in newspapers in the period 1775–1815, and that press legislation had the opposite effect in Britain and America from that which legislators intended, this chapter first examines the expansion of each country's newspaper press. It considers changes to the newspaper trade as politicians, printers, and readers alike came to recognize the newspaper as the key carrier of news, political information, and opinion. In prioritizing the newspaper press over other forms of print, and providing it with some freedoms, the governments of both countries recognized its importance in politics, providing means of controlling it too. Thus, in the second section, this article considers the legislative decisions made in each country and determines how these shaped the press–politics nexus. In the final section, we review the role of the post, which was recognized in each country as a crucial aspect of news delivery and therefore political influence, with each country's government legislating accordingly.

NEWS AND NEWSPAPERS

In the United States and Britain, a close relationship developed between political comment and opinion, "news" (defined here as "time-sensitive pieces of information") and newspapers over the later eighteenth century: more than in the periods preceding or following it. Enlightenment attitudes towards the freedom of knowledge and the liberty of citizens encouraged a focus on the newspaper press as the appropriate forum for the political education of citizens and the formation and expression of public opinion as a force on politics. Thus, despite the profound importance of pamphlets during the War of Independence and the French Revolution, especially Thomas Paine's *Common Sense* (1776) in America and the *Rights of Man* (1791–3) in Britain, both countries saw a decline in the pamphlet in favor of the newspaper by the turn of the nineteenth century. The number of newspapers rose sharply and newspaper offices exhibited signs of embryonic professionalization.

In size, circulation, and finance, the London press was by far the largest in Britain and America, broadly followed by British provincial and Atlantic seaboard titles, and then the remainder of the American press. In 1770 there were seventeen London newspapers, rising to twenty-three titles by 1790 and fifty-five by 1820 (by then comprising morning and evening dailies, tri-weeklies, bi-weeklies, and weekly Sundays).[6] London titles also had by far the greatest circulations. In 1775, the *Daily Advertiser* and the *Gazetteer* each had a circulation of around 5,000. Britain's concentrated geography meant that many London newspapers circulated nationally; a significant proportion of the *London Evening Post* and the *General Evening Post*, the largest evening tri-weeklies, was destined for the country.[7]

These circulations were impressive, bearing in mind that stamp duty was placed on every copy of a newspaper. Imposed in 1712 at ½*d.* on every copy of every newspaper and regularly increased throughout the eighteenth century, stamp duty reached 4*d.* before being reduced to 1*d.* in 1836 and repealed altogether in 1855. The duty was raised by a fiscal-military state experiencing almost constant warfare, and newspapers were taxed alongside other "luxury" goods.[8] Despite nineteenth-century campaigns against the "taxes on knowledge," which emphasized the pernicious nature of the legislation, the primary purpose of the taxes appears to have been to raise revenue, although it had a beneficial and not-unintended side effect in limiting newspaper purchase to a "respectable" middling readership. Even so, papers were freely available in taverns, inns, coffeehouses, public houses, and pot houses; they were read out loud in victualing establishments and village squares; and they were passed around families, friends, and clubs who convened specially for the purpose.[9] Estimates of the number of readers per newspaper therefore range from ten to forty, but the middle class made up the core of newspaper readers.[10] At the very least, taxing the newspaper alongside other middle-class luxuries suggests that the government identified the newspaper with a middling and upper readership.

The expansion of the British press was achieved through advertising, for the cover price of a newspaper barely covered stamp duty and production costs. Despite three increases in advertisement duty between 1776 and 1815, advertisements were placed in newspapers in ever-increasing quantities. As a result, in 1774, for example, London's *Public Advertiser* produced £1,740 in profit and the *Morning Post*, £1,500. By the early nineteenth century, the *Morning Chronicle* allegedly produced £12,000 a year.[11] In the context of the British and American press, however, London was atypical.

Towns elsewhere in Britain also gained newspapers in the eighteenth century. These were produced in printing offices which combined newspaper printing with other print jobs and book and stationery sales, similar to American offices. In 1770 there were forty-two English provincial weeklies, which grew to sixty weekly provincial titles by 1790 and 120 by 1820 in sixty-two towns.[12] There existed a handful of Scottish newspapers and in 1808 the first English-language Welsh newspaper was established. A successful provincial newspaper could expect a circulation of around 2,000 and this remained steady throughout the period.[13] Potential growth in readership instead came in the form of multiple titles so that by 1820, thirty-three towns in England had at least two titles while larger towns like Liverpool and Manchester laid claim to five apiece.[14] As with the London press, British provincial newspapers were sustained by buoyant and growing advertising columns, so that a successful provincial proprietor could make upwards of £200 per annum from a printing and newspaper business combined: hardly London profits, but a comfortable income for a middling provincial tradesman and his family.[15] With limited circulation and more modest profits, British provincial newspapers were similar to the American press, although its expansion far outstripped that of Britain.

In the United States, where there was no sustained regime of taxation on newspapers, the newspaper press experienced rapid growth facilitated by the massive expansion of the post office, the spread of transportation networks, and improvements in transportation technology, including early canals and steamboats.[16] During the Revolutionary War, the steady growth in newspapers that had occurred over the course of the eighteenth century slowed to a crawl, but as soon as the war ended in 1783, their number increased dramatically. In 1780 there had been just thirty-eight newspapers but within a decade they had nearly tripled, reaching 106 in 1790. New newspapers were founded at a remarkable rate during the early republic, doubling roughly every ten years until 1820, when they reached 582. The rate of growth was far faster than in Britain and easily outpaced rapid population growth in the new United States.[17] The growth was dramatic both in the interior of the new nation, particularly the trans-Appalachian west, and in the major Atlantic seaports. By the early nineteenth century, growing cities such as Boston, New York, and Philadelphia each boasted a dozen daily newspapers.

Although the American press grew at a rapid rate, unlike their British counterparts, most American printers could not fund their publications through subscriptions or advertisements. During the colonial period and early republic, Americans subscribed to newspapers by the thousands, and advertisers flocked to their pages, but printers and publishers faced enormous difficulties in getting subscribers and advertisers to pay, as many ignored requests for payment. Printers fulminated against such recalcitrant subscribers, advertising frequently in their own newspapers with threats or pleas for payment.[18] In 1785, for example, James Johnston, publisher of the *Gazette of the State of Georgia*, noted that some of his subscribers had "been ... in arrears for two years," and asked them to pay in full, either in cash or with "rice, indigo, deer skins, beeswax, or tallow, or any thing for family use."[19] Most printers relied on government work, which could provide a steady source of income for those who earned contracts. As early as the 1760s, however, newspapers in the rapidly growing Atlantic seaports became sustainable through circulation and advertising revenue alone. Additionally, the political climate of the imperial crisis encouraged printers to align their newspapers more closely with political factions.[20] In the early republic, growth continued apace as new state governments encouraged press expansion. Governors, legislatures, and other political leaders frequently solicited for printers to come to new capitals or commercial centers, both to serve communities and to provide better access to news and information about the world beyond them. As this chapter later explores, this led to a closer relationship between printers and political parties.

For news markets that could support multiple newspapers, the most obvious form of differentiation was political. In London, newspapers had begun to carve up the readership in this way in the early eighteenth century. In other British towns and in the United States, where the market was often smaller and printers either received considerable government printing work or (in the

United States) were entirely dependent on it, printers were more circumspect, invariably professing neutrality.[21] That perspective shifted during the Revolutionary era. In Britain, as more newspapers were produced in individual towns, and as increasingly contentious debates over the war in America took place in Parliament and through the press, newspapers were more explicit in their political affiliations. In America, most printers continued to declare their neutrality, even when they had underlying political leanings or affiliations. Isaiah Thomas, a staunch Patriot funded in part by John Hancock, emblazoned his *Massachusetts Spy* in 1772 with the epigraph, "Open to ALL Parties, but *Influenced* by None"—a common motto on both sides of the Atlantic.[22] As political tensions rose during the 1770s it slowly became profitable to display a political affiliation (mostly for Patriots) or costly to do so (almost always for Loyalists). The republican rhetoric of the era furthermore pitched the press as the "bulwark of liberty," the last guard against encroaching tyrannical power.[23] In those locales with a vibrant and competitive political print culture—especially Boston, New York, and Philadelphia—partisan journalism could be a profitable avenue for a printer in the early republic, just as it was in London and in Britain's larger towns. With Americans focused intensely on politics and the ways in which the new government under the Constitution would take shape, opportunities abounded for editors to publish essays, letters, and vitriol in the pages of their newspapers. In Boston, for instance, the *Centinel* and the *Chronicle* established their reputations in the 1780s and 1790s through their political rivalry. The two papers engaged directly with one another in debate for over fifteen years, developing deep commercial and political bases from which to draw.[24] Partisanship paid because it enabled the segmentation of the reading and advertising market.

The growing specialization of newspapers as *the* form of print delivering news and political communication in both countries was also evident in the specialization of roles in the later eighteenth-century newspaper trade, both in the emergence of distinct occupations as printers, publishers, and editors and in the separation of newspaper trade positions from those of the wider print trade. On the whole, British and American printers still collated news from a variety of sources: other newspapers and printed sources, manuscript letters, and oral reports brought directly to them or relayed from others. In this sense, newsgathering was passive, for printers did not go out into the world to seek news.[25] Thanks to extraordinary profits, London was again atypical in the precocious segmentation of printing-house occupations. Since the 1720s, bookseller consortia had owned London newspapers. These consortia increasingly required editors to collate paragraphs written by hacks or taken from the European papers.[26] By the end of the century, editorships at large London papers were lucrative and held some social prestige. William Jerdan, editor of the *Sun*, for example, was earning over £500 per annum in 1813.[27] Salaried parliamentary reporters were also employed and these roles encouraged closer communications with politicians. The kinds of salaries attained by London editors placed them within the middling professional echelons of London society, while reporters and editors had growing opportunities to mix socially and communicate with Members of Parliament.[28] In provincial towns, as in London, growing advertising revenues enabled proprietors to shift the focus of their businesses from multiple book trade activities, of which newspaper production was one, to newspaper production as the central activity of the business. It also enabled those at the larger offices to hire editors.

In North America during the colonial era, a single person served as printer, publisher, and editor, but increasingly the printer performed only the mechanical work of setting type and pulling the press while someone with a higher socioeconomic status and often better political connections took over editorial duties. Editors emerged shortly before the Revolutionary War, particularly at literary publications such as magazines. In 1775, for instance, Robert Aitken, the printer and publisher of the *Pennsylvania Magazine*, hired Thomas Paine, who had only recently arrived in Philadelphia, as editor. In that capacity he composed some of his first pro-American essays, hinting at the political arguments he would develop more fully in *Common Sense* in January 1776.[29] After the war, the separation of occupational roles expanded to newspapers, and editors were hired to conduct the day-to-day tasks of compiling and composing, which is evidence of the growing importance placed on newspapers as a form of political communication. By the early 1800s, most major-city newspapers functioned with separate editors and printers. By contrast, in backcountry regions, the role of the printer remained something more akin to the work of colonial printers: a situation that remained unchallenged until later in the nineteenth century.[30] In this way, the production of newspapers was diverging from the production of other forms of print as newspaper owners and politicians alike recognized the advantages of the newspaper as a medium for political communication.

REGULATING NEWSPAPERS

As newspaper publishing became increasingly specialized, governments and readers turned to newspapers for political information and opinion. By the mid-eighteenth century, the British press regularly referred to "public opinion" and "the people," but the "public" to whom press and politicians referred was the subject of changing debate. For many, especially politicians, "the people" meant the political nation, that is, neither the political elite nor the 75 percent of the population who lived in poverty but the emergent middle classes.[31] As the American and French Revolutions inspired a new awareness of political representation, radical politician John Jebb argued that the political nation consisted of all adult males.[32] This was a wider definition than most would have recognized. In Britain, the public's right to news had long been established, although who that public included was contested. Indeed, in a country that celebrated freedom of the individual in its unwritten constitution, successive governments had to strike a balance between the economic demands of a commercially successful sector (which could benefit politicians and parties by shaping public opinion) and the political goal of restricting the flow of information to a respectable press and public.

As the newspaper sector grew numerically and commercially, and as politicians and readers alike recognized the importance of at least acknowledging public opinion through the press, the British press won important new privileges. From 1764, newspapers inadvertently gained the right to free postage, as long as an MP franked them. In 1771, newspapers gained the right to publicize parliamentary proceedings. When the House of Commons in Westminster attempted to arrest printers who had reported parliamentary debates, John Wilkes MP offered the printers shelter in the City of London, a separate jurisdiction. The "Printers' Case" resulted in the lapse of the ban on reporting proceedings from Parliament, which afforded the public unprecedented access to both Houses and invited press comment in new editorials and letters to the editor. The new transparency of parliamentary reports brought politicians and reporters into closer contact via interactions in the House of Commons and through correspondence, for politicians sent copies of their speeches to London and provincial newspapers.[33] The move also had an effect inside Parliament, for committing reports to paper and to consumption out of doors meant that politicians changed their oratorical style inside Parliament as they began to speak "within the context of a culture of print."[34] All parties and factions were generally represented in the press, but opposition MPs supporting parliamentary reform particularly favored newspapers. No doubt aware of the press's potential, the speeches of Charles James Fox, leading proponent of the French Revolution both before and after Louis XVI's execution, have been aptly described as having been "made with the public in mind."[35] New privileges enabled a new relationship with Parliament, therefore, but in each case politicians retained as much control over the information leaving the Commons as possible.

Thanks to parliamentary debates, editorials and letters to the editor commenting on politics increasingly became a regular feature of newspapers. Perceptions that letters in newspapers were more effective fora for propaganda contributed to the decline in Britain of essay papers and political pamphlets. As early as 1756, Lord Hardwicke recommended that if the Ministry wished to rebut the onslaught against it concerning the loss of Minorca, it should place information in newspapers, for "these short diurnal libels do more harm than large pamphlets because they spread amongst the common people."[36] Letters in newspapers were thus considered a more pervasive—and persuasive—means of reaching the public. In addition, by controlling the supply of information to newspapers over which they had regulatory control, politicians could influence what appeared in them.

The question as to whether advertising freed the British press from the constraints imposed by political subsidies has been long debated.[37] Direct political subventions for the press were a feature of the relationship between press and politicians in the later eighteenth century, but they declined in number. The government spent nearly £5,000 per annum on the press during the early years of the French Revolution—a sizeable sum but far less than the amount Walpole's ministry spent in the 1730s.[38] Individual editors received more substantial amounts. In 1781, Henry Bate Dudley of the *Morning Herald*, accused by the *London Evening Post* of being "a prostituted hireling and betrayer of his country," was paid as much as £3,000 for backing Lord North during the Prime Minister's continued unpopularity.[39] As Hardwicke suggested in 1756, and in accordance with normal practice, government and politicians, like members of the public, paid to insert favorable paragraphs in newspapers.[40] Indeed, most attempts to control the now-sizeable and profitable press (with significant powers of comment over politicians) were ad hoc and often specific to individual publications. For example, a particular MP might grant his local newspaper advertising or printing contracts, in much the same way that they did in the United States. Thus, the bigger issue facing politicians was the collective power of the press, which had increased its influence with the rise of commercial news agents and had curtailed the ability of successive governments to control of the press as a result of the governments' need for tax revenue.

Politicians legitimized the place of the press in society through their willingness to work with print and to use Parliament as a forum for the discussion of public opinion.[41] Yet British newspapers gained greater power to comment on politics because those in the press had made them central to political life. Politicians needed the press for publicity now that their speeches were printed, and for the revenue that stamp and advertising duties provided to a state almost constantly engaged in warfare. It is estimated that newspapers brought in around £140,000 in stamp duties in 1792–3. Crudely adding advertisement duty of £63,578 onto stamp duty adds nearly one third again to the overall taxes paid by newspapers, now totaling £203,578.[42] In 1787, therefore, Edmund Burke proclaimed, in the words of nineteenth-century social critic Thomas Carlyle, that "there were Three Estates in Parliament; but, in the Reporters' Gallery yonder, there sat a Fourth Estate more important far than them all."[43] Parliament legitimated the press as the ideal carrier of news and opinion and acknowledged its power as a check on Parliament in part because the press shaped public opinion.[44]

If the freedom of the press in Britain was determined by the commercial success of and legislative decisions about the press, in the United States its freedom was rooted in political ideology. During and after the Revolutionary War, delegates in eight states (including the semi-independent Vermont) embedded protections for the "liberty of the press" as part of the declarations of rights in their new state constitutions.[45] Although the Federal Constitution did not define any rights retained by the people, the Bill of Rights as ratified in 1791 included a provision for the freedom of the press. Congress and the states gave their blessing to the idealization of the press as a quasi-institutional check on the power of government and therefore as an oppositional force to the workings of government.[46]

The meaning of press freedom, however, was unclear. Political leaders disagreed vehemently on the role of newspapers in the political sphere. On the one hand, many political leaders saw newspapers as crucial to the proper functioning of a republic, not least because the political ideologies that under-pinned the Revolution, including republicanism, assumed a citizenry informed by news consumption and the press as an oppositional force to blunt the possibility of government corruption.[47] Education—in particular, instruction in reading—was a crucial component of a republic, granting its citizens the ability to participate in public life (and for women, to educate their children for active participation in politics).[48] On the other hand, those in power, as well as many elites, saw the press as dangerous and seditious. Americans saw the press as a cherished institution that deserved protection and a blight that obfuscated more than it informed.[49]

Printers and publishers viewed print as a force that could unify the country and encourage the development of a national identity. Most famously, Noah Webster sought to make the English language more American through his popular spelling book by expunging extraneous unpronounced letters from words and by changing spellings to eliminate pernicious French influence.[50] Mathew Carey sought to create a national literature through his *American Museum* (1787–92), intended to be a repository and showcase for American science and *belles lettres*. Others followed, seeking to create a set of elite publications that would foster American literature. In creating distinctively American productions, they also required Americans to write, edit, print, and publish the material, thus matching cultural ideals with the commercial motivation to promote American manufactures.[51]

After the Revolutionary War, press and party politics in America were highly integrated. With a view toward national politics, printers rallied vigor-ously in favor of a more centralized national government. During the debates over ratifying the Constitution of 1787, nearly all printers sided with the federalists in support of the new Constitution. Yet print was crucial for the anti-federalists—so much so that it was likely the only thing that brought any coherence to the disparate anti-Constitution arguments.[52] In fact, those who opposed the Constitution argued that the failure of their enterprise lay not in the rejection of their ideas and arguments but in the censoring of their publications. Opponents of the Constitution alleged specifically (though without much evidence) that the Post Office, headed by federalist Ebenezer Hazard, was systematically excluding their pamphlets and newspapers from the mails, thereby preventing their arguments from receiving a full public airing.[53] William Goddard, the stalwart proponent of a free and open postal system, threatened to establish a new postal system to replace the Continental Post Office, but never did.[54]

Once the Constitution was ratified and the new federal government set to work in New York and then Philadelphia, printers rushed to gain federal printing contracts and to provide a printed forum for political debates concerning the operations of government. Political leaders of all stripes likewise sought out publications that could and would popularize their political arguments and help them to sway public opinion in their favor. Within a decade after the ratification of the Constitution, this symbiotic relationship between newspaper editors and political leaders energized new political parties that centered around newspapers and their editors.[55] Printers and newspaper editors thus became the foremost proponents of party politics and found new methods to support their journalism through patronage positions within government. For all the talk of press independence, newspaper printers relied heavily on political patronage.

The acceptable limits of political debate again became a source of conflict in the late 1790s as Britain and America navigated the turmoil wrought by the French Revolution and subsequent European wars. Events in France, especially the Terror of 1793–4, became a flashpoint for the development of the political press. Initially celebrated by many Britons as the end of a tyrannical government and the introduction of a constitutional monarchy similar to that in Britain, by 1790 the French Revolution divided popular politics and the press. Radical groups sought to capitalize on inspiration from across the Channel, promoting parliamentary reform through new societies, such as the Sheffield Society for Constitutional Information (SSCI, est. 1791), of which Joseph Gales of the *Sheffield Register* was a founding member. In response, popular loyalism flourished too and new conservative associations sprung up to combat the radical threat. Press support was important to both sides but the main means of debate was through pamphlets. In what was the last major outpouring of political pamphlets, printed debates began in earnest with Edmund Burke's *Reflections on the Revolution in France* (1790) and Thomas Paine's response, *Rights of Man* (1791–3), followed by a raft of publications on both sides, including works by Hannah More, William Godwin, and others seeking to sway popular opinion. Sales of Paine's *Rights of Man* may have reached 1.5 million. This figure, although contested, is indicative of its popularity.[56] Newspapers were viewed as dangerous but the conservative cause fully embraced pamphlets as a means of reaching the working-class population. Indeed, popular conservatism played a significant role in neutralizing radicals.[57]

Although the authorities lacked evidence to prosecute suspected publishers for their allegedly radical tendencies, they could monitor and arrest them for other reasons. Newspaper proprietors active in radical groups or engaged in the promotion, sale, and distribution of the *Rights of Man*, including Richard Phillips of the *Leicester Herald* (1792–5) and London-based *Monthly Magazine* (1796–1829), were arrested and imprisoned. As the beginning of this essay describes, Joseph Gales, SSCI founder-member and proprietor of the *Sheffield Register* (1787–94), escaped to America to avoid arrest for treason. James Montgomery, Gales's successor at the renamed *Sheffield Iris* was prosecuted and imprisoned twice, once for publishing a poem that celebrated the fall of the Bastille and once for criticizing a Sheffield magistrate's forcible response to a protest. Montgomery was under no illusion as to the real reason behind his imprisonment in 1795. "The prosecution," wrote Montgomery, "is levelled against the Iris; they are determined to crush it."[58] Ultimately governments determined that the newspaper press was to be retained in respectable hands and read by respectable readers. Even radicals appear to have selected pamphlets over newspapers: it has recently been suggested that Thomas Paine cut his teeth on the *Sussex Weekly Advertiser; Or, Lewes Journal* (1746–1920), between 1768 and 1774, the year that he left for America. In the United States and in Britain, however, it is significant that Paine selected the pamphlet as his preferred form of political communication.

Legislation that touched the press in the 1790s largely focused on eliminating radicalism. This included the Habeas Corpus Suspension Act (1794), which enabled the arrest and imprisonment of individuals without trial, and the Treasonable Offences Act (1795), which extended the crime of treason to include speaking and writing. An increase in stamp duty in 1797 was justified by emphasizing the luxury status of newspapers. Parliamentarians argued that raising the stamp duty was beneficial to the lower orders because newspapers were a luxury item. The rise would thus not affect them. On the contrary, Sheridan argued for the Opposition that the increase was "frivolous and vexatious" and "a vital blow struck at the liberty of the press."[59] The increase passed but a rise in the advertisement duty, which was mooted, was dropped, which suggests that the proposed Act was aimed at members of the radical, rather than the respectable, press.

The Newspaper Regulation Act (1798) further underlined the difference between the radical and respectable press. The only act to affect the entire press directly, it required newspaper proprietors, printers, and others connected to the trade formally to register their interests. Furthermore, in the case of articles intending to "excite hatred and contempt" of King, constitution, or Parliament that had been copied from the foreign press, it placed the burden of proof on the defendant, which contradicted common practice in other areas of the criminal law. Those convicted for violating the Newspaper Regulation Act could face six to twelve months' imprisonment. Furious debates in

Parliament focused on the role of the press within the constitution. Joseph Jekyll, who opposed the Newspaper Regulation Act, argued that the government was "attempting to undermine the freedom of that Censorial Power vested in the People, and which was now one of the best remaining securities for the Liberties of the People."[60] The freedom to discuss public men and measures, reformer Francis Burdett argued, was "now the only check on bad Administration, and the only prop to support the tottering fabric of the Liberties of the People." On the contrary, the Attorney General, in proposing the motion, argued that the Act, "far from abridging the Liberty of the Press, was meant to restore it."[61] Freedom of the press was not in doubt but the definition of an acceptable press was. For the Attorney General, restoring freedom of the press involved removing the more pernicious, radical elements of it. The motion was carried, marking a watershed in the relationship between Parliament and the press. In the early decades of the nineteenth century, the relationship between the press and Parliament became increasingly confrontational.

In the United States, the French Terror divided newspaper editors like no event before. For cosmopolitan republicans like Thomas Paine, who saw the rise of movements for liberty and freedom spreading to Europe, and for Jeffersonian Republicans like Benjamin Franklin Bache, the Revolution was a triumphal epoch in human history that justified bloodshed. For their counterparts with Federalist inclinations, including editors John Fenno, Noah Webster, and William Cobbett, the Terror represented a frightening turn in what they already saw as an unsettling revolution against proper authority. The Terror of 1793–4 in France signaled a firm split among American newspapers along partisan lines. Commercial relationships continued, but after that time printers and editors were much less likely to make political connections beyond like-minded men.[62]

By 1797, when John Adams took office as President, Federalists argued that Republican attacks on both Adams and Washington had transgressed the appropriate bounds of press freedom. With war against France looming in 1797 and 1798, Congress acted to curtail the allegedly seditious activities of Republican editors through the Sedition Act, which made it illegal to criticize President Adams, Congress, or the government in print. The law was aimed explicitly at the burgeoning oppositional Republican newspaper network.[63] Congress's response seems bizarre and obviously unconstitutional to modern eyes, but made sense in the context of contemporary anxieties about the durability of the republic.[64] During the three years the law was in force, many of the most notable Republican printers and newspaper editors were arrested, indicted, and tried under the law, including William Duane, Matthew Lyon, and James Callender. Yet the Act ultimately did little to staunch the expansion of the Republican press in the lead-up to the presidential election of 1800.[65] The Sedition Act expired in 1801 as Thomas Jefferson took office as President, but the Republican ascendancy did not end the conflicts over acceptable actions within the newspaper press. Republicans used state libel laws to impose similar strictures on the speech of their adversaries.[66]

Debates over the limits of free speech during wartime arose again in 1812, when martial fever struck the United States after President James Madison and Congress declared war on Great Britain. In a reversal of their earlier roles, the war provided Republican newspaper publishers with an opportunity to trumpet their commitment to the new nation and to rally the people to the cause. For Federalists who opposed the war, their position immediately made them vulnerable to charges of anti-patriotism and exposed newspaper editors to attacks not seen since those against Loyalists during the Revolutionary War. Nowhere was this problem more acute than in Baltimore, a staunchly pro-Republican and pro-war city. Baltimore was home to the *Federal Republican*, published by Alexander Contee Hanson, Jr., which, in the face of brutal opposition, "became the nation's most virulent detractor of Jefferson and Madison's anti-British foreign policy and the resulting War of 1812."[67]

Within a few days of the declaration of the 1812 war, Hanson faced the moral economy of the crowds.[68] On June 22, 1812, a mob attacked and destroyed Hanson's office and destroyed his printing press.[69] Undeterred, Hanson quickly established a new place of business in a three-story brick building and sought out protection from a force of loyal Federalists, including two former Continental Army generals, Henry Lee and James Lingan. Republicans attacked again a few days later, injuring Hanson and Lee and killing Lingan, which shut down the *Federal Republican*. Even the aftermath of the riots was riven by partisan bickering, as "Republicans insisted that the Federalists exaggerated the Baltimore violence or had brought it upon themselves" and "Federalists... denounced the riots as the poisonous consequences of democracy and immigration."[70] The rioters stained the reputation of both Baltimore and the Republicans, turning Maryland into a Federalist stronghold during the war; Hanson was elected to Congress.[71] In this way, the later eighteenth century represented a critical period for the definition of news and newspapers in the United States and Britain. In both countries news and political opinion was funneled into the press. In the United States, the press became part of the political status quo in part because certain individuals simultaneously acted as printers and politicians. In Britain, the press became a broadly accepted element of political life, but politicians and respectable publishers restricted its size as well as access to political opinion.

THE PRESS AND THE POST

Legislative attitudes towards the control of press content in Britain and America were remarkably similar to those applied to its distribution. Decisions regarding the availability of newspapers via postal networks were informed by, and consolidated, the funneling of political information into newspapers over the later eighteenth century. In the United States, the Post Office Act of 1792 was pivotal in creating a system that subsidized the national circulation of newspapers. Long before the passage of the Post Office Act, decisions regarding the post office explicitly reflected concerns about the availability of news. Prior to the 1770s, many printers served as postmasters. Most notably, from 1753 until 1774, Benjamin Franklin served as Deputy Postmaster General for North America. Between the 1750s and 1790s, in fact, at least sixty-seven master printers served as local postmasters either in the British imperial post office or the new United States Post Office, although the practice of appointing printers to the position declined sharply after 1792.[72] Postal officials in the British colonies also attempted to regulate newspaper circulation, but often created confusion and conflict in the process. The British Post Office in North America informally permitted printers to exchange single copies of their newspapers for free to facilitate news circulation. The practice was a matter of custom rather than law, and in towns in which a printer was also the postmaster he could mistreat the publications of his rivals. Post riders frequently extorted printers or neglected their delivery duties, which frustrated printers and readers. Consequently, a parallel system of news delivery developed. Some printers hired their own post riders to make runs and the public generally sought out cheaper means to avoid the exorbitant rates of the British Post Office.[73]

In 1774, printers and anti-imperial activists mounted a charge to overthrow the British Post Office, which underscored its importance to their protest efforts.[74] William Goddard, publisher of Philadelphia's *Pennsylvania Chronicle* and Baltimore's *Maryland Journal*, felt aggrieved at his treatment at the hands of the postmaster of the Philadelphia imperial post office, who slowed the delivery of newspapers between Goddard's two offices. Goddard first hired his own rider to travel the hundred miles between Philadelphia and Baltimore, but that failed to solve the problem. In the midst of the imperial crisis, Goddard used the timing of the slight against him by the imperial Post Office to launch a campaign to establish a "Constitutional Post." The proposal promised to benefit the commercial interests of Goddard, other printers, and colonial merchants. According to the plan he outlined, the "Constitutional Post" would provide news more readily to their businesses by establishing and making public for the first time "Terms on which Newspapers are to be carried" and posting them publicly.[75] Goddard then sought to enhance his own commercial prospects by linking his position to broader arguments about taxation, censorship, and intercolonial unity. In 1774, the idea barely got off the ground, but in July 1775 the Second Continental Congress picked up on the idea of an independent American post office. The Second Continental Congress created a Continental Post Office with Benjamin Franklin at its head. The creation of a Continental Post Office was noteworthy given that the only other national institutions in existence at the time were Congress itself and the Continental Army.[76] Debate continued during and after the Revolutionary War about the role of the post office, but the Confederation Congress made few changes to the British model on which the Continental Post Office was based.

Three years after Congress first met under the Constitution, it passed the Post Office Act of 1792. The Act reinforced the freedom of the press by prioritizing free carriage of information through the mails. The Post Office Act was one of the most significant pieces of legislation in the early years of Congress. In establishing regulations for the operations of the Post Office, the Act settled the century-long quarrel over how the post should function in American society. The Act accomplished three main goals.[77] First, it facilitated the circulation of newspapers by allowing them into the mails at favorable rates (and conversely setting high rates for letters, a policy that persisted into the 1840s).[78] The postal subsidy consolidated the position of the newspaper as the principal medium for the distribution of news and political information. Second, the Act prohibited government officials from censoring the mails. Although the law was occasionally breached, the Act established an expectation, if not a standard, for the sanctity of the post. In Britain, there was no such law. Third, the Act established procedures to expand the Post Office. In the early republic, the Post Office expanded rapidly and haphazardly. Congressmen eager to please their constituents used their powers to erect post offices in their districts. In 1790, two years before Congress passed the Act, the Post Office comprised seventy-five post offices situated almost entirely along the Atlantic seaboard. By 1810, nearly 2,300 post offices existed around the nation, making it the country's most sprawling federal institution. This large network of post offices facilitated the distribution of thousands of newspapers each week.

In addition to the indirect benefit of cheap rates to circulate newspapers, the Post Office offered two other advantages to newspaper printers and editors. First, the 1792 Act permitted editors to exchange newspapers for free. This provision greatly supported the proliferation of newspapers around the country. Second, positions in the Post Office enabled printers to gain better access to news through franking privileges. For instance, in 1790, Daniel George wrote from Maine to his colleague Isaiah Thomas, surprised to discover that Thomas was the postmaster of Worcester, Massachusetts. George had been "racking and cracking my brains, in devising means to convey my letters to you without expence." Now that he knew Thomas could frank his letters, George let him know that he would write more frequently, providing Thomas with better news from Maine.[79] Over the ensuing decades, postal officers, Congress, and the public debated just how much service the Post Office should provide and at what cost, but the 1792 Act set a strong precedent for an expansive postal system to integrate the new nation. The newspaper press was central to that integration. It informed national identity and educated the public in politics. To promote and support the Post Office became synonymous with defending the public's right to news and information.

In Britain too, decisions about the post office informed the national distribution of news and encouraged the use of newspapers for the supply of political information and opinion over other forms of print. Typically, legislators sought to balance their own interests—raising revenues, self-publicizing, and retaining supervision over information networks—with the demands of a commercially successful sector. For most of the century the press made a significant contribution to Post Office finances. The six Clerks of the Road (one for each of the main roads from London) purchased London newspapers in bulk at reduced cost and transported them over the mails for free, making a profit on their sale to local postmasters.[80] The Clerks operated as national news agents. MPs could also send newspapers to friends and constituents gratis. In the 1760s, the six Clerks made a combined revenue of around £6,000 per annum, although they had to pay officers and assistants out of their earnings.[81] Laws enacted in 1757 (banning the sale of cheap papers by hawkers to the provinces) and 1764 (formalizing the Clerks' prerogatives) protected the Clerks' privilege, which was essentially a private transaction between government-employed officials and newspaper owners. Pursuant to the law of 1764, MPs could designate a newspaper for free circulation (rather than signing the envelope in which each newspaper was sent), the effect of which was to allow for the passage of unlimited copies and editions of each title for a limited period of time.

So-called "Members' Orders" swiftly became the means by which the majority of newspapers were sent over the mails and provided another new means by which newspaper proprietors and MPs were in contact in the later eighteenth century.[82] By 1782, Members' Orders accounted for about 60 percent of the three million newspapers sent through London per annum. Some MPs were perhaps anxious for constituents to read their now-published speeches, or they viewed their permission to frank, which had to be renewed on a regular basis, as a means of encouraging individual titles' loyalty. Indeed, permission to frank placed MPs in a supervisory role over individual publications, however cursory, and some withdrew support if a newspaper became too radical. Justifying free carriage via MPs, and therefore the loss incurred by the Clerks, the press emphasized its continuing contribution to the Exchequer, in the form of "numerous Orders, readily granted, under the Persuasion of increasing Stamp Revenue."[83] In 1787 a separate Newspaper Office was formed to cope with the rapid increase in newspapers sent over the mails, which reached 4.6 million in 1790, 6.4 million in 1793, and 8.6 million in 1797.[84] As a result, the Clerks' incomes fell drastically. In 1787, for example, Edward Barnes, Clerk of the Chester Road for seventeen years, earned £193 5s. 10d. in 1787 from the circulation of newspapers, compared to a career high of around £600.[85] By

1792, it was estimated that the circulation of newspapers was bringing in around one third of its pre-1764 levels. With incomes falling, the abolition of the Clerks' franking privileges as an emolument was considered in Parliament, but despite falling revenues the privilege was not abolished until 1836. That year, the stamp duty was reduced to 1*d*. The penny charged for the stamp included postage.[86]

The Postmasters-General argued that the removal of the Clerks' privileges would reduce their incomes, but by the 1790s retaining control over the distribution of newspapers for the purposes of surveillance was thought to be more important. Francis Freeling, Secretary of the Post Office, instructed postmasters to send him the names of subscribers to radical titles, including the *Cambridge Intelligencer*, which had a national circulation and threatened to spread radical ideas.[87] Local postmasters also interfered with the distribution of newspapers. Readers in Leeds, Halifax, and Wakefield all reported verbal abuse from postmasters when collecting the *Sheffield Iris*, and 150 subscribers cancelled their subscriptions to the paper.[88] Subscribers of the *Manchester Gazette* similarly complained that their newspapers went undelivered. Those that did arrive were torn, soiled, or partially burned.[89] Fewer printers were postmasters in Britain compared to the United States. In Manchester, however, James Harrop of *Harrop's Manchester Mercury*, was appointed postmaster thanks to his paper's anti-radical stance.[90] Whereas the Post Office appeared therefore to have increasingly diverted its commercial distribution of newspapers from the Clerks, and to have placed growing emphasis on the economics of the press in official reports, surveillance over the mails and the tampering of information passing through it increased in the 1790s.

By the early nineteenth century, as campaigns for the removal of stamp duties became more vocal and the franchise grew, if only somewhat, there was a sea change in attitudes towards the role of the Post Office in the delivery of newspapers. Commercial news agents usurped the income of the Clerks of the Road. In 1833, Henry Parnell, Whig MP for Dundee, presented a petition from over 200 "news venders, agents, and dealers" who complained about the Clerks' and postmasters' influence that was "unlike the officers of any other department under Government, and contrary to every sound principle of trade."[91] With the abolition of the Clerks' privilege, the stamp duty was reduced to 1*d*., which now included free passage over the mails.

The commercial news agents to whom Parnell referred had increased in number in response to the growth of newspapers and advertisements. William Tayler of Warwick Court, Newgate Street, for example, specialized in the provision of national advertisements and London newspapers to the provincial press and the provision of provincial advertisements to the London press.[92] Acting as a national broker for news, Tayler also played a representative role, for in 1797 he had a hand in coordinating proprietors' protests at proposed advertising duty hikes.[93] In 1836 the news agents' function of representing the press reached a more formal footing with the establishment of the Provincial Newspaper Society at the behest of John Buller, agent at one of London's largest provincial news agencies, R. F. White and Son, who became its first President.[94] The society aimed to promote the general interests of the provincial press, strengthening its position in business and lobbying Parliament on press legislation. Members' initial concerns were the encroachment of the London papers caused by the reduction in stamp duties and the rise of the railways. Later successes included reform of the libel laws in 1843 and of the laws on the reporting of defamatory remarks in 1881. The society in turn formed the majority of the first committee of the Press Association (PA), established in 1868. The role of commercial agents in centralizing and representing the press thus had its roots in the eighteenth century.

CONCLUSION

As two decades of warfare that had entangled both Britain and the United States wound down in 1815, newspaper proprietors and politicians continued to clash over circulation and content. Yet in both nations, significant changes in press content, in its commercial power, and in the socioeconomic status of its members had resulted in the creation of a national press infrastructure. Publishing, writing, and editing became discrete occupations. An explosion of newspapers on both sides of the Atlantic marked the period from 1775 to 1815. In the United States, newspapers spread away from the coast and, aided by developing communications networks, expanded across the country. In Britain, the press continued to expand into some new areas, but growth of this more mature press (in a considerably smaller country) was characterized by the appearance of multiple titles in the same towns. Communications networks, especially the postal service, were crucial not simply to the expansion in the number of titles in both countries, but in underpinning a national news network.

The press in Britain and America capitalized on the Age of Revolution as the opportunities for reporting and for political engagement abounded. As America and then France sought to create modern nations, newspapers formed the centerpiece of free communication. Politicians on both sides of the Atlantic sought to direct news and political opinion into the press, and to regulate news dissemination via the post. They did so, however, for different reasons. In the United States, a nationally recognized but commercially dependent press became, with the Post Office, the core element of a system to circulate information broadly across the nation to educate and inform the citizenry. As the key vehicle for news and information, the press also became a constituent feature of party politics. Politicians in Britain recognized that its legislatively constrained but commercially powerful newspaper press was a permanent feature in national life. In Britain, political pressure was brought to bear on the press obliquely. Taxation, libel laws, pressure from individual MPs, and manipulating the supply of information through postal networks were some of the restrictive mechanisms politicians deployed to control the press. These indirect methods of restraint reflected the competing compulsions politicians felt to cooperate with the press and to establish a clear distinction between respectable and radical papers. As a result, a fissure appeared in the British press. Nineteenth-century radical proprietors drew a distinction between their publications and the rest, which they considered to be part of the establishment. Although the reasons and consequences were different, in the Age of Revolution newspaper publishers on both sides of the Atlantic solidified the press as an agent of national political life underwritten by government and party.

NOTES

1. Joseph M. Adelman and Victoria E. M. Gardner are joint first authors of this chapter.
2. Winifred Gales, *Recollections*, 65 (scan 87), Gales Family Papers, 1815–1939, University of North Carolina at Chapel Hill, online at: <http://www.lib.unc.edu/mss/inv/g/Gales_Family.html>, accessed June 10, 2013.
3. Winifred Gales, *Recollections*, 94 (scan 105).
4. Jeffrey L. Pasley, *"The Tyranny of Printers": Newspaper Politics in the Early American Republic* (Charlottesville: University of Virginia Press, 2001), 155; Donald A. Ritchie, *Press Gallery: Congress and the Washington Correspondents* (Cambridge, Mass.: Harvard University Press, 1991), 7–34.
5. Hannah Barker and Simon Burrows, *Press, Politics and the Public Sphere in Europe and North America, 1760–1820* (Cambridge: Cambridge University Press, 2001); Uriel Heyd, *Reading Newspapers: Press and Public in Eighteenth-Century Britain and America* (Oxford: Voltaire Foundation, 2012). Comparative scholarship on the late eighteenth-century press reinforces scholarship on the history of the press in each country: both have privileged political and cultural explanations for change and minimized the importance of economic factors. On the British press, see Hannah Barker, *Newspapers, Politics, and Public Opinion in Late Eighteenth-Century England* (Oxford: Clarendon Press, 1998); Barker, *Newspapers, Politics and English Society, 1695–1855* (Harlow: Pearson, 2000); Bob Harris, *Politics and the Rise of the Press: Britain and France, 1620–1800* (London and New York: Routledge, 1996); Kathleen Wilson, *Sense of the People: Politics, Culture and Imperialism in England 1715–1785* (Cambridge: Cambridge University Press, 1995). On the American press, see Marcus L. Daniel, *Scandal and Civility: Journalism and the Birth of American Democracy* (New York: Oxford University Press, 2009); Pasley, *"The Tyranny of Printers"*; David Waldstreicher, *In the Midst of Perpetual*

Fetes: The Making of American Nationalism, 1776–1820 (Chapel Hill: OIEAHC, University of North Carolina Press, 1997); Rosalind Remer, *Printers and Men of Capital: Philadelphia Book Publishers in the New Republic* (Philadelphia: University of Pennsylvania Press, 1996).

6. Michael Harris, "London Newspapers," in *The Cambridge History of the Book in Britain*, vol. 5: *1695–1830*, ed. Michael F. Suarez and Michael L. Turner (Cambridge: Cambridge University Press, 2009), 424; Jeremy Black, *The English Press in the Eighteenth Century* (Philadelphia: University of Pennsylvania Press, 1987), 14; Ian R. Christie, "British Newspapers in the Later Georgian Age," in *Myth and Reality in Late-Eighteenth-Century British Politics, and Other Papers* (Berkeley and Los Angeles: University of California Press, 1970), 314.

7. Harris, "London Newspapers," 424, 427.

8. Lyn M. Oats and Pauline Sadler, "Political Suppression or Revenue Raising? Taxing Newspapers during the French Revolutionary War," *Accounting Historians Journal*, 31 (2004): 93–128; Lyn M. Oats and Pauline Sadler, "Variations on a Theme: Stamp Duty in the Eighteenth Century," in *Studies in the Histories of Tax Law*, vol. 4, ed. John Tiley (Oxford: Hart Publishing, 2012), 67–85. On the relationship between the tax, middle-class consumables, and war, see Patrick O'Brien, "The Political Economy of British Taxation, 1660–1815," *Economic History Review*, 41 (1988), 1–31, and J. V. Beckett and Michael Turner, "Taxation and Economic Growth in Eighteenth-Century England," *Economic History Review*, 43 (1990): 377–403.

9. Heyd, *Reading Newspapers*, 18–22; Barker and Burrows, *Press, Politics*, 101–8; Christie, "British Newspapers," 325; C. Y. Ferdinand, "Newspapers and the Sale of Books in the Provinces," in *The Cambridge History of the Book in Britain*, vol. 5, ed. Suarez and Turner, 444.

10. Heyd, *Reading Newspapers*, 22.

11. Christie, "British Newspapers," 319.

12. Victoria Gardner, "Newspaper Proprietors and the Business of Newspaper Publishing in England, 1760–1820," DPhil dissertation (University of Oxford, 2009), 23–4.

13. See the declarations in *York Chronicle*, June 14 and 21, 1776, and *Nottingham Journal*, January 6, 1781. The *Salisbury Journal* declared in 1780 that it had a circulation of 4,000; few other newspapers boasted such a large circulation: C. Y. Ferdinand, *Benjamin Collins and the Provincial Newspaper Trade in England* (New York: Oxford University Press, 1997), 19.

14. Gardner, "Newspaper Proprietors," 37.

15. Victoria E. M. Gardner, "John Fletcher (1756–1835) and the *Chester Chronicle* Account Books," in *Periodicals and Publishers: The Newspaper and Journal Trade 1740–1914*, ed. John Hinks and Catherine Armstrong (New Castle, Del. and Winchester: British Library and Oak Knoll, 2009), 97–120.

16. Allan R. Pred, "Urban Systems Development and the Long-Distance Flow of Information through Preelectronic U.S. Newspapers," *Economic Geography*, 47 (1971), 498–524.

17. Pasley, *"The Tyranny of Printers,"* 401–5; Andie Tucher, "Newspapers and Periodicals," in *A History of the Book in America*, vol. 2: *An Extended Republic: Print, Culture, and Society in the New Nation, 1790–1840*, ed. Robert A. Gross and Mary Kelley (Chapel Hill: University of North Carolina Press, 2010), 391, 393.

18. The same frustrations were evident in British papers, yet the cost of pre-stamped paper was so high that printers struck most wayward subscribers off their books: Gardner, "John Fletcher."

19. *Gazette of the States of Georgia*, May 26, 1785.

20. Stephen Botein, "Printers and the American Revolution," in *The Press and the American Revolution*, ed. Bernard Bailyn and John B. Hench (Worcester, Mass.: American Antiquarian Society, 1980), 11–57.

21. Stephen Botein, "'Meer Mechanics' and an Open Press: The Business and Political Strategies of Colonial American Printers," *Perspectives in American History*, 9 (1975): 127–225; James N. Green, "English Books and Printing," in *A History of the Book in America*, vol. 1: *The Colonial Book in the Atlantic World*, ed. Hugh Amory and David D. Hall (Cambridge: Cambridge University Press, 2000), 255–7.

22. See, for example, *Massachusetts Spy*, June 11, 1772.

23. Richard D. Brown, *The Strength of a People: The Idea of an Informed Citizenry in America, 1650–1870* (Chapel Hill: University of North Carolina Press, 1996), 49–84.

24. John B. Hench, "The Newspaper in a Republic: Boston's *Centinel* and *Chronicle*, 1781–1801," PhD dissertation (Clark University, Worcester, Mass., 1979).

25. Clark, *The Public Prints*, 211.

26. On group ownership, Harris, *London Newspapers*, ch. 4.

27. Christie, "British Newspapers," 322.

28. See, for example, Charles Knight's description of his work experience at the *Globe* in the early nineteenth century: Charles Knight, *Passages of a Working Life during Half a Century: With a Prelude of Early Reminiscences* (London: Bradbury and Evans, 1864), vol. 1, 105–22.

29. *The Pennsylvania Magazine: Or, American Monthly Museum* (Philadelphia: Robert Aitken, 1775–6). On Paine's political argumentation in the *Pennsylvania Magazine*, see Eric Foner, *Tom Paine and Revolutionary America* (New York: Oxford University Press, 1986), 72–3.

30. Jack Larkin, "'Printing is something every village has in it': Rural Printing and Publishing," in Gross and Kelley (eds), *An Extended Republic*, 148. See also Milton W. Hamilton, *The Country Printer: New York State, 1785–1830* (New York: Columbia University Press, 1964).

31. Barker, *Newspapers, Politics, and Public Opinion*, 2–3.

32. Barker, *Newspapers, Politics, and Public Opinion*, 3.

33. P. D. G. Thomas, "The Beginning of Parliamentary Reporting in Newspapers, 1768–1774," *English Historical Review*, 74 (1959), 623–36.

34. Christopher Reid, "Whose Parliament? Political Oratory and Print Culture in the Later Eighteenth Century," *Language and Literature*, 9/2 (2000), 126; Christopher Reid, *Imprison'd Wranglers: The Rhetorical Culture of the House of Commons 1760–1800* (Oxford: Oxford University Press, 2012).

35. Jürgen Habermas, *The Structural Transformation of the Public Sphere: An Inquiry into a Category of Bourgeois Society*, trans. Thomas Burger (Cambridge, Mass.: MIT Press, 2003), 66.

36. Harris, *Politics and the Rise of the Press*, 38.

37. Arthur Aspinall, *Politics and the Press 1780–1850* (London: Home and Van Thal Ltd, 1949), 66–102; Lucyle Werkmeister, *The London Daily Press, 1772–1792*

(Lincoln, Neb.: University of Nebraska Press, 1963), 4–5; compare Barker, *Newspapers, Politics and Public Opinion*; Karl Schweizer and Rebecca Klein, "The French Revolution and Developments in the London Daily Press to 1793," *Publishing History*, 18 (1985): 85–97; Ivon Asquith, "Advertising and the Press in the Late Eighteenth and Early Nineteenth Centuries: James Perry and the Morning Chronicle, 1790–1821," *Historical Journal*, 18/4 (1975): 703–24.

38. Aspinall, *Politics and the Press*, 68–9.
39. Hannah Barker, "Dudley, Sir Henry Bate, Baronet (1745–1824)," *Oxford Dictionary of National Biography* (Oxford: Oxford University Press, 2004), <http://www.oxforddnb.com/view/article/8152>, accessed November 5, 2012; *London Evening Post*, February 24, 1780.
40. Will Slauter, "The Paragraph as Information Technology: How News Traveled in the Eighteenth-Century Atlantic World," *Annales: Histoire, Sciences sociales*, 67/2 (2012): 253–78 (259–61).
41. Jeremy Black, "Parliament, the Press and Foreign Policy," *Parliamentary History*, 25/1 (2006): 9–16.
42. Stephen Dowell, *A History of Taxation and Taxes in England*, 4 vols. (London, 1884), vol. 2, 206–7; Victoria Gardner, *The Business of News in England, 1760–1820* (London: Palgrave Macmillan, forthcoming 2014), ch. 1.
43. Edmund Burke, quoted by Thomas Carlyle, *Heroes, Hero-Worship and the Heroic in History* ([1841], reprinted London and New York: J. M. Dent and Sons, 1948), 392.
44. Schweizer, "Parliament and the Press," 4.
45. The states were: Massachusetts, Vermont, Pennsylvania, Maryland, Virginia, North Carolina, South Carolina, and Georgia.
46. Charles E. Clark, "The Press the Founders Knew," in *Freeing the Presses: The First Amendment in Action*, ed. Timothy E. Cook (Baton Rouge: Louisiana State University Press, 2005), 33–50. See also Potter Stewart, "Or of the Press," *Hastings Law Journal*, 26 (1975): 631–8; Timothy E. Cook, *Governing with the News: The News Media as a Political Institution* (Chicago: University of Chicago Press, 1998).
47. On republicanism in revolutionary America, see Bernard Bailyn, *The Ideological Origins of the American Revolution* (Cambridge, Mass.: Belknap Press of Harvard University Press, 1967); Gordon S. Wood, *The Creation of the American Republic, 1776–1787* (Chapel Hill: IEAHC, University of North Carolina Press, 1969); Robert E. Shalhope, "Toward a Republican Synthesis: The Emergence of an Understanding of Republicanism in American Historiography," *William and Mary Quarterly*, 3rd ser., 29/1 (1972), 49–80; idem, "Republicanism and Early American Historiography," *William and Mary Quarterly*, 3rd ser., 39/2 (1982), 334–56.
48. See, for example, Cathy N. Davidson, *Revolution and the Word: The Rise of the Novel in America*, expanded edn (New York: Oxford University Press, 2004), 121–50.
49. Brown, *Strength of a People*, 86.
50. Noah Webster, *Dissertations on the English Language: With Notes, Historical and Critical . . .* (Boston: Isaiah Thomas and Co., 1789), 394–5.
51. See Catherine O'Donnell Kaplan, *Men of Letters in the Early Republic: Cultivating Forms of Citizenship* (Chapel Hill: OIEAHC, University of North Carolina Press,

2008); Carl Robert Keyes, "A Revolution in Advertising: 'Buy American' Campaigns in the Late Eighteenth Century," in *Creating Advertising Culture: Beginnings to the 1930s*, vol. 1: *We Are What We Sell: How Advertising Shapes American Life... And Always Has*, ed. Danielle Sarver Coombs and Bob Batchelor (Santa Barbara, Calif.: Praeger, 2014), 1–25.

52. John K. Alexander, *The Selling of the Constitutional Convention: A History of News Coverage* (Madison, Wis.: Madison House, 1990); Saul Cornell, *The Other Founders: Anti-Federalism and the Dissenting Tradition in America, 1788–1828* (Chapel Hill: OIEAHC, University of North Carolina Press, 1999). See also Jackson Turner Main, *The Anti-Federalists: Critics of the Constitution, 1781–1788* (Chapel Hill: IEAHC, University of North Carolina Press, 1961).

53. See, for example, *Independent Gazetteer* (Philadelphia: Eleazer Oswald), January 16, 1788, in John P. Kaminski and Gaspare J. Saladino (eds), *The Documentary History of the Ratification of the Constitution*, 21 vols (Madison: State Historical Society of Wisconsin, 1976–present), 543.

54. William Goddard to Mathew Carey, February 28, 1788; *Maryland Journal*, February 29, 1788; both in Kaminski and Saladino (eds), *Documentary History*, 553.

55. Pasley, *"Tyranny of Printers."*

56. Marcus Wood, "Radical Publishing," in Suarez and Turner (eds), *The Cambridge History of the Book in Britain*, vol. 5, 838.

57. See, for example, Mark Philp (ed.), *The French Revolution and British Popular Politics* (Cambridge: Cambridge University Press, 1991); Emma Vincent Macleod, "British Attitudes to the French Revolution," *Historical Journal*, 50/3 (2007); 689–709.

58. James Montgomery to Joseph Aston, October 29, 1795, Sheffield Archives, SLPS 37/1-2.

59. Quoted in Lynne Oats and Pauline Sadler, "Stamp Duty, Propaganda and the French Revolutionary and Napoleonic Wars," in John Tiley (ed.), *Studies in the History of Tax Law* (Portland, Or.: Hart, 2004), vol. 1, 253–4.

60. *The Sun*, June 14, 1798.

61. *The Sun*, June 14, 1798.

62. Seth Cotlar, *Tom Paine's America: The Rise and Fall of Transatlantic Radicalism in the Early Republic* (Charlottesville: University of Virginia Press, 2011); Daniel, *Scandal and Civility*; Pasley, *"Tyranny of Printers."*

63. On the passage of the Sedition Act and its effect on the newspaper press, see Pasley, *"Tyranny of Printers,"* 105–31.

64. Joanne B. Freeman, "Explaining the Unexplainable: The Cultural Context of the Sedition Act," in Meg Jacobs, William J. Novak, and Julian E. Zelizer (eds), *The Democratic Experiment: New Directions in American Political History* (Princeton, NJ: Princeton University Press, 2003), 20–49.

65. Pasley, *"Tyranny of Printers,"* 125–8.

66. Freeman, "Explaining the Unexplainable," 39–41.

67. Pasley, *"Tyranny of Printers,"* 245.

68. The term "moral economy of news" comes from Charles G. Steffen, "Newspapers for Free: The Economies of Newspaper Circulation in the Early Republic," *Journal of the Early Republic*, 23 (Fall 2003): 381–419 (quote at 382). On the concept of

"moral economy" more generally, see E. P. Thompson, "The Moral Economy of the English Crowd in the Eighteenth Century," *Past and Present*, 50 (1971): 76–136.

69. For a detailed account of the Baltimore riots, see Alan Taylor, *The Civil War of 1812: American Citizens, British Subjects, Irish Rebels, and Indian Allies* (New York: Alfred A. Knopf, 2010), 177–9; John Nerone, *Violence Against the Press: Policing the Public Sphere in U.S. History* (New York: Oxford University Press, 1994), 67–71; Paul A. Gilje, *Rioting in America* (Bloomington: Indiana University Press, 1996), 60–3.

70. Taylor, *Civil War of 1812*, 178.

71. Nerone, *Violence Against the Press*, 70.

72. Richard R. John, *Spreading the News: The American Postal System from Franklin to Morse* (Cambridge, Mass.: Harvard University Press, 1995), 120–1.

73. William Smith, *The History of the Post Office in British North America, 1639–1870* (Cambridge: Cambridge University Press, 1920; New York: Octagon Books, 1968), 25, 51–4; Konstantin Dierks, *In My Power: Letter Writing and Communication in Early America* (Philadelphia: University of Pennsylvania Press, 2009).

74. For a full account of the movement, see Joseph M. Adelman, "'A Constitutional Conveyance of Intelligence, Public and Private': The Business of Printing, the Post Office, and the American Revolution," *Enterprise & Society*, 11/4 (2010): 709–52.

75. *The PLAN for establishing a New American POST-OFFICE* (Boston: n.p., 1774).

76. May 29, 1775, *Journals of the Continental Congress*, ed. Worthington Chauncey Ford, 34 vols (Washington: Government Printing Office, 1904–37), vol. 2, 71; July 26, 1775, vol. 2, 208–9.

77. John, *Spreading the News*, 51.

78. See also Richard B. Kielbowicz, "The Press, Post Office, and Flow of News in the Early Republic," *Journal of the Early Republic*, 3 (1983): 255. On the shift in postal policy that led to an increase in the circulation of personal letters, see David Henkin, *The Postal Age: The Emergence of Modern Communications in Nineteenth-Century America* (Chicago: University of Chicago Press, 2006), 42–62.

79. Daniel George to Isaiah Thomas, October 10, 1789, Isaiah Thomas Papers, American Antiquarian Society, Worcester, Mass.

80. For more detail, see Kenneth Ellis, *The Post Office in the Eighteenth Century: A Study in Administrative History* (London: Oxford University Press, 1958); Howard Robinson, *The British Post Office: A History* (Princeton: Princeton University Press, 1948); Susan Whyman, *The Pen and the People: English Letter Writers, 1660–1800* (Oxford: Oxford University Press, 2009), ch. 2.

81. Estimates vary: Harris, "London Newspapers," 46–7 suggests £3–4,000 per annum whereas Ellis, *The Post Office*, suggested £4–6,000. One report from 1806 estimates £6,400, stating that "the situation before the … [1764] Act was such, that the North and Chester roads cleared above fourteen hundred pounds per annum, and the other four roads full nine hundred pounds": "Reports of the Commissioners Appointed by Act Geo. III. Cap. 19 to Enquire into the Fees, Gratuities, Perquisites and Emoluments … " (1806), 814.

82. Ellis, *The Post Office*, 52; Robinson, *The British Post Office*, 148.

83. Seventeenth Parliament, First Report of the Commissioners, 29.

84. Robinson, *The British Post Office*, 148, n. 21.
85. Examination of Mr Edward Barnes, Reports of the Commissioners (1806), 811, 812.
86. See for example, Eighteenth Parliament of Great Britain: 1st session (September 27, 1796–July 20, 1797), Seventh Report from the Committee on Finance, Collection of the Public Revenue: Post Office, p. 196. Historians generally argue incorrectly that Parliament rescinded the Clerks' privilege in 1792: Michael Suarez, "Introduction," in Suarez and Turner (eds), *Cambridge History of the Book*, vol. 5, 12–17; Barker, *Newspapers, Politics and English Society*, 43; Black, *The English Press*, 70. Confusion may have arisen over the wording of the Postmaster Generals' directive: payment to "other Officers and Clerks in the Office" was "to be discontinued, that is, those other than the six Clerks of the Road": Seventeenth Parliament, First Report of the Commissioners, 29.
87. M. J. Smith, "English Radical Newspapers in the French Revolutionary Era, 1790–1803," PhD dissertation (University of London, 1979), 188–9.
88. James Montgomery to William Todd, August 3, 1795, Sheffield City Archives, Montgomery MS. MD 2104/58, Sheffield, UK.
89. Smith, "English Radical Newspapers," 200.
90. C. Roeder, "Beginnings of the Manchester Post Office," *Transactions of the Lancashire and Cheshire Antiquarian Society*, 22 (1904): 30–4.
91. Commons Sitting of Friday, June 28, 1833. Hansard, 3rd ser., vol. 18.
92. Michael L. Turner, "Distribution: the Case of William Tayler," in Suarez and Turner (eds), *The Cambridge History of the Book*, vol. 5, 466–78.
93. Gardner, "Newspaper Proprietors," 119–21.
94. Gallop, "Chapters in the History," 184; H. Whorlow, *The Provincial Newspaper Society, 1836–1886: A Jubilee Retrospect* (London: Page, Pratt & Co., 1886).

4

The Victorian City and the Urban Newspaper

David Paul Nord

In 1893 the crusading English journalist W. T. Stead came to Chicago. Stead had risen to fame in the 1880s exposing the mysteries and corruptions of London. Now he set his sights on Chicago, the city he took to be second only to London in importance in the English-speaking world—but also the wickedest city in the world. Driven by his usual manic energy, Stead hoped to see everything and meet everyone. One Chicagoan he sought out was Melville Stone, the founder of the *Chicago Daily News*. Though they differed in many ways, the two men immediately became friends, in part because they had played similar roles in the history of newspapers in Britain and America.[1] In the 1880s W. T. Stead and Melville Stone had been leading architects of what the English (and some Americans, too) called the "new journalism."

The "new journalism" is an appropriately elastic label for what was happening in the newspaper business in Britain and America at the end of the nineteenth century. By the late 1880s British commentators had already begun to write the term with capital letters—the New Journalism—as if it were a formal title.[2] (I'll follow their style.) What they had in mind was a flowering of new forms and practices associated with increasing commercialization and popularization of the daily newspaper. To put it simply, they wrote about changes in four areas: *format* (more lavish use of headlines, subheads, illustrations, and news on page one); *business organization* (cheap price, modernized advertising and circulation management, more reporters and reporting, more evening and Sunday papers); *content* (more interviews, more human interest stories, more sports and entertainment, more features for women, more cable news, more investigations and crusades, more sensationalism, more punch); and *technology* (faster printing and typesetting machinery, half-tone photo reproduction, telegraph, telephones, and typewriters).[3]

So, where did the New Journalism come from? The British viewed it as an American import, and in a way it was. British and American newspapers had always been close cousins, and many of the specific styles of the New Journalism had been brewing in America since the birth of the New York "penny press" of the 1830s and 1840s.[4] But perhaps more interesting than simple borrowing—and more important for the history of journalism—are similarities in the American and British contexts in which the New Journalism arose. Nineteenth-century observers and later historians have explored some of those contextual similarities, including technological innovation, democratization in politics and education, and shared political culture.[5] But the similarity that W. T. Stead and Melville Stone discussed in 1893 is the one that interests me: *urbanization*. What drew these New Journalists together was their fascination with a remarkable city—Chicago—and a shared experience with modern urban politics, economics, and daily life.

A new ethos of urbanism is not usually listed as a signature characteristic of the New Journalism, but I believe it should be. I have made this claim about US newspapers, arguing that the modern daily newspaper was born in the 1870s in the industrial cities of the American Midwest: Detroit, Cleveland, St. Louis, and Chicago.[6] These newspapers were the first genuinely *urban* mass media in America. They recognized that the rise of the modern city had changed the nature of community life. This realization was partly cultural, but it was fundamentally political and economic. As business firms themselves, newspapers were direct contributors to the growth of commerce and manufacturing in mid-nineteenth-century cities; they were also ardent advocates of private enterprise. But in the late nineteenth century, the empirical realities of industrialization, rapid population growth, and environmental degradation in their cities led many urban newspapers to question the ideology of economic liberalism and individualism and to offer instead a more social, more collectivist understanding of modern urban political economy and community—an understanding that would come to be labeled "progressive." A similar trajectory can be traced in urban politics and urban journalism in Victorian Britain. Before the New Journalism made its flashy debut in London and New York in the 1880s and 1890s, newspapers in industrial cities such as Manchester and Birmingham were incubating a new urban ethos not unlike that of Chicago and other burgeoning cities of the American Midwest.

THE NEW INDUSTRIAL CITY

The New Journalism may have been invented in America, but the industrial city emerged first in Britain, and its most striking manifestation was Manchester. Manchester has been called the "shock city" of the early nineteenth century, the city that displayed the most astonishing features of its time, both positive and negative. On the positive side, Manchester was the first modern industrial city, whose mechanized cotton mills and massive warehouses symbolized what came to be called the Industrial Revolution. By 1840 Manchester had a population of a quarter million and was a major world supplier of manufactured textiles. On the negative side, the rapid population growth and dramatic increase in the use of coal for steam power (a million tons a year by the late 1830s) precipitated environmental catastrophe, transforming Manchester's waterways into open sewers, its skies into dense shrouds of smoke, and its workers' housing into fetid slums.[7] One of the city's most famous visitors in the 1830s, Alexis de Tocqueville, vividly captured the contradiction. In Manchester, he wrote, "humanity attains its most complete development and its most brutish; here civilization works its miracles, and civilized man is turned back almost into a savage."[8] This was the "paradox of progress." And Manchester, far from being exceptional, became the "template of the modern city," including America's own great shock city, Chicago.[9]

At the heart of the shock city lay, not just physical and economic change, but an economic and political idea: liberalism. The entrepreneurs who created these cities believed in private property and private business enterprise. Of course, liberty and property had long been watchwords of English and American political philosophy, but this was a more radical commitment to the liberty of property. Shock cities were largely private cities, built by private capital for private profit. And, again, Manchester set the pace.[10] In the 1830s and 1840s, Manchester businessmen, led by Richard Cobden and John Bright, organized the nationwide free trade movement that secured the repeal of duties on grain imports (corn laws) and laid the foundation of the Radical wing of the new Liberal Party. For these economic radicals, liberalism meant private enterprise, free trade, and individual liberty.[11]

Cobden and his friends were dubbed the Manchester School of political economy, and for the rest of the century the term "Manchester School" was increasingly associated—by its critics, especially—with the economic principle of laissez-faire. But this is misleading. Cobden's great cause was free trade— that is, the abolition of import duties, which he believed stunted commerce, misdirected capital investment, created monopolies, corrupted government, and provoked international war. For Cobden, the ancient Saxon tradition of individual liberty, the birthright of all Englishmen, was simply equality before the law: "Equal Laws," as Cobden put it.[12] He did believe that industry should usually be left to its own instincts, and he venerated the memory and the economic principles of Adam Smith. But like Smith, Cobden and his disciples did not oppose government action in principle; rather they opposed the corruption and special privilege that government action often fostered.[13] In short, the "professors" in the Manchester School were not adherents of a strict laissez-faire ideology, but they were champions of private enterprise as the engine of economic progress, morality, and civilization.

The Manchester liberals imagined that they spoke for "the people" in general, not just for the rising middle class. Cobden and Bright and their colleagues believed that private enterprise and free trade would benefit the working class as well as the bourgeoisie because everyone except the favored few suffered in a political regime of sinecure, monopoly, and corruption.[14] But, despite the liberals' sanguine hopes, the rapid population growth and industrial development of Manchester in the early nineteenth century produced deep class divisions and residential segregation, which economic liberalism could neither explain nor address. And Manchester became a center of working-class unrest and labor radicalism as well as middle-class liberalism.[15]

For Richard Cobden, the ideals of radical liberalism—individualism, private enterprise, low taxes, government restraint, religious liberty, and international peace—were most fully realized in the United States. Unlike Britain, America had no feudal residuum to purge: no landed aristocracy, no ecclesiastical hierarchy, no government-contrived monopolies. Or so Cobden believed.[16] In America, as in Britain, the idea of laissez-faire did gain a foothold in economic theory, but actual practice was another matter. State and local governments routinely managed economic markets and subsidized favored businesses. The federal government tinkered with tariffs, currency, banking, and communications policy throughout the century.[17] Though Cobden's holy grail of international free trade had its champions in America, the United States remained more protectionist than Britain. And in the American West, new cities such as Chicago depended on government subsidies in the form of land grants and harbor and transportation projects.[18]

But as he gazed westward, Cobden was not entirely deluded. A free trade zone of continental proportions did emerge in the United States, abetted by governmental regimes overwhelmingly favorable to the growth of private business. The invention of the limited-liability corporation coupled with the adoption of general incorporation statutes in most states energized entrepreneurship in America.[19] Equal access to capital and trade, unimpeded by favoritism and corruption—not strict laissez-faire—is the essence of liberal (Smithian) political economy. It is precisely what Cobden meant by "Equal Laws" and "No Monopoly."[20] Not in lieu of but because of government policy, the rapid growth of American cities such as Chicago was largely the work of private enterprise. Indeed, the new industrial cities in the United States grew more wedded to private enterprise and private decision-making as the century progressed.

Chicago, America's own shock city, provides a dramatic example of government subsidy giving way to expanding privatism. Like many frontier cities, Chicago first took life in the imaginations of real estate speculators. The town site was soggy marshland near the southern shore of Lake Michigan. This was a miserable place to build a great city, but boosters knew that the site held enormous potential as a transportation hub. The small, sluggish Chicago River that emptied into Lake Michigan had its source just a few miles from the Des Plaines River, which lay in the watershed of the Illinois and Mississippi rivers. In other words, as low and muddy as it was, Chicago stood at the apex of the most important mid-continental divide in North America.[21] The city builders believed that if the Indians were removed, if government lands in the surrounding countryside were settled, if the river harbor were dredged, and if a canal were constructed to connect the Great Lakes with the Mississippi River, then Chicago would blossom into the great emporium of the West. At the end of the Black Hawk War in 1833, all of these things seemed to be happening, and the greatest boom in land speculation in American history began. In the new town of Chicago, lots that had cost $33 in 1829 sold for $100,000 in 1836.[22]

That first bubble burst in the Panic of 1837, but the early speculators were right about Chicago's future. The Illinois and Michigan Canal was completed and opened for shipping in 1848, and it did establish Chicago's regional commercial supremacy. But the water that would drive Chicago's greatest growth was neither lake nor canal; it was steam. In the 1850s some 20,000 miles of railroad track were laid in the United States, more than 2,500 miles in Illinois. And Chicago became the hub of a giant wheel of rail-borne commerce that spread out across the American heartland.[23] Soon factories as well as locomotives began to blacken Chicago's skies with the smoke of coal-fired steam engines. Though Chicago would not rival Manchester in manufacturing output until the decades after the Civil War, already in the 1850s the city was, according to the *Chicago Tribune*, on its way to a "brilliant future" in manufacturing.[24]

Though the founding of Chicago required government subsidy, the spectacular growth of Chicago, like that of Manchester, was the product of thousands upon thousands of private decisions. And the entrepreneurs preferred it that way. In the 1840s, as Chicago became a fragmented chaos of conflicting land uses, public decision-making became more privatized. Private subscriptions and special assessments replaced general public works, and as a result decisions about public infrastructure moved to the private sector. This was a "segmented system" of government, a system in which decisions were made by property owners who had a direct financial interest in the outcome.[25] In mid-century Chicago, there was no general public interest, only a jumble of private interests.

In Chicago, as in Manchester, private entrepreneurial energy powered an enormous boom in industrial output, in population growth, and in the production of millionaires. But, also like Manchester, Chicago paid a steep price in poverty, disease, class conflict, and environmental degradation. Because of the privatization of government through Chicago's "segmented system," the city was unable to deal effectively with city-wide infrastructure investments such as waterworks and sewerage, or with city-wide hazards such as smoke pollution and epidemic disease. In neither Manchester nor Chicago did property owners or politicians fully grasp the economic concept that

would later be called "negative externalities." But the crises of industrial
urbanization were teaching this economic concept, as yet unnamed, in a
rough and ready way. City dwellers could see it, drink it, and breathe it. By
the 1860s, the "paradox of progress" was as obvious to Chicagoans as it had
been to Alexis de Tocqueville in Manchester thirty years before. In a commentary on the putrid, poisonous stench of the Chicago River in 1865, one observer
wrote: "It may seem paradoxical to say that which is the very cornerstone of a
city's prosperity should also prove the most important drawback to that
prosperity.... Without the river, the city of Chicago would never have existed;
with the river the citizens ... [find] it all but impossible to exist."[26]

THE COMMERCIAL NEWSPAPER

Among the myriad manufacturing firms that sprouted up in the industrializ-
ing cities of Britain and America was the daily newspaper. Though the
newspaper itself was an eighteenth-century British export to America, in the
nineteenth century America far surpassed the mother country in the growth of
newspapers, especially dailies. The widespread diffusion of newspapers in the
United States was due in part to the sheer physical size of the country. The
metropolitan dailies of New York were always far less dominant in America
than were the major London papers in England. Differences in tax policy
played a role as well. The Americans never taxed newspapers, advertisements,
or newsprint, while the British taxed all three—rather heavily after the violent
suppression of an 1819 working-class demonstration in Manchester known as
Peterloo. The policy goal was to prevent the proliferation of cheap seditious
papers aimed at a restive working class.[27] Both countries subsidized newspaper distribution through their postal networks, but the British linked that
subsidy to the newspaper stamp-tax system: stamped papers were carried by
post for free. This policy increased the geographical market for the London
dailies. For example, by 1850 the increasingly dominant *Times* could go to
press at 4 a.m. in London and still be delivered in Manchester by 2 p.m. the
same day, thanks to fast mail trains. Yet by raising the per-copy price of all
newspapers, the stamp tax actually protected established provincial papers in
cities such as Manchester from London competition and from local competition as well. Because of the tax, daily newspapers were simply too expensive for
most readers. Therefore, nearly all the provincial papers remained weekly
or twice-weekly publications, which could be larger in size than a daily yet
priced only slightly more. Meanwhile, local competition was also discouraged
because an upstart competitor needed immediate and substantial per-copy
revenue from either circulation or advertising to cover the tax. For many years
radical liberals such as Richard Cobden and John Bright pressed for the

abolition of the newspaper taxes, which they derided as "taxes on knowledge," an especially egregious affront to liberal principles of free trade and reason. The liberal argument gradually carried the day in Britain. The newspaper stamp tax was reduced in 1836 and eliminated in 1855. The tax on advertisements was dropped in 1853, and the newsprint duty was abolished in 1861.[28]

With the end of the so-called "taxes on knowledge," the daily newspaper blossomed in English provincial cities. In the fifteen years after 1855, seventy-eight new dailies were founded, with fifty-nine surviving in 1870. The United States, however, remained far ahead of Britain, with 254 dailies by 1850, 574 by 1870, and 971 by 1880.[29]

In both countries these newspapers were thoroughly commercial enterprises, but they were "commercial" in two different ways. First, they were businesses like other businesses in the nineteenth century: They manufactured and sold a consumer product. They were part of an industrial revolution that is better understood as an evolution—that is, they were traditional artisanal shops gradually transformed by new technologies, new capital investment, and new business strategies. Beyond selling a product themselves, they were commercial in another way: they were major promoters of commerce in their cities. They were the voices of the commercial class. Of course, this was not true of all newspapers in either Britain or America. Noncommercial and even anti-commercial newspapers, such as labor, religious, and associational papers, flourished too.[30] But the provincial newspapers that contributed most to the creation of the modern twentieth-century metro daily were commercial in both of these ways: as commercial products and as champions of commercial culture. And, again, Manchester and Chicago illustrate the pattern.

Manchester and Chicago spawned many newspapers that represented great diversity in politics, interests, and classes. But the two most successful newspaper businesses in the second half of the nineteenth century were the *Manchester Guardian* (founded 1821) and the *Chicago Tribune* (founded 1847). These two newspapers nicely illustrate the evolution of the commercial newspaper into what I call, in the next section of this chapter, the urban newspaper.

The *Manchester Guardian* and the *Chicago Tribune* prospered because they sold two products that people wanted to buy: news and advertising. Their founders and early managers were entrepreneurs who understood how to run a newspaper business in a growing commercial city. Both papers established early reputations for prowess in news. John Edward Taylor and Jeremiah Garnett, founders of the *Guardian* and proprietors through the 1850s, were journalists as well as business managers and political operators.[31] So were Joseph Medill, who joined the *Tribune* in 1855 and emerged as the paper's guiding light after 1874, and Horace White, who held the editorship in the late 1860s and early 1870s.[32] As the two newspapers evolved over the course of the nineteenth century, journalism was important, but more important was savvy business management.

For both the *Guardian* and the *Tribune*—and for most British and American newspapers—the 1850s and 1860s were years of dramatic change in business operations. Key decisions involved growing advertising revenue along with circulation, while budgeting for timely capital investments in machinery, especially printing presses. Making advertising pay was paramount, and from the beginning the proprietors at both papers lavished attention on that part of the business. At the *Guardian* John Taylor insisted that every issue carry at least a hundred ads, and by 1840 the paper had nearly doubled that benchmark number in each of its twice-weekly editions, far outstripping its rivals.[33] At the *Tribune* Joseph Medill was an astute advertising manager from the moment he came on the paper in 1855. He modernized the *Tribune*'s commercial advertising by introducing a rate system to encourage retail advertisers to update their copy at least once a week, a strategy pioneered by James Gordon Bennett Sr. in New York. The idea was to endow advertising with real news value. And it worked. By the 1860s the *Tribune* was the advertising leader in Chicago.[34]

More ads, more copies, and more pages required more capital. In the 1850s the traditional print shops of the *Guardian* and the *Tribune* were transformed into modern manufacturing plants. In 1850, for example, the *Tribune* struck off 1,200 copies daily on an Adams flat-bed press powered by one old pony. Over the next decade, the paper installed a succession of fast steam-powered Hoe cylinder presses, as circulation climbed above 24,000 by 1860. The American Civil War was a huge boon for newspapers in the northern cities, and the *Tribune* invested heavily in presses and other equipment.[35] Meanwhile, in Manchester the *Guardian* was driven to the brink of failure by its own success. In 1855, when the newspaper stamp tax ended, the Manchester *Examiner* immediately switched to daily publication, and the *Guardian* followed suit. To handle the new daily schedule—with a circulation of 9,000–10,000 on Wednesdays and Saturdays and 5,000–6,000 on the other days—the *Guardian* partners ordered a new Hoe press from New York. But this press proved inadequate even before it arrived because the *Guardian*'s daily circulation jumped to more than 20,000 when it dropped its price to a penny to meet competition from the *Examiner*. The *Guardian* desperately needed larger, faster presses immediately, and the managers struggled to raise the money to pay for them. In the end, the new daily *Guardian* weathered the fiscal storm of 1858 and settled into steady prosperity in the 1860s, with a circulation of around 40,000 by the end of that decade.[36]

For the *Guardian* and *Tribune*, the printing press was merely the centerpiece of an increasingly technological operation. Throughout the rest of the century, the newspapers were early adopters of a panoply of machines and gadgets, ranging from linotypes to typewriters to telephones. But the most important piece of new technology after 1850 was the electric telegraph. The telegraph allowed provincial newspapers to compete in news with the large metropolitan dailies in London and New York, even in the age of rail. The *Guardian* and the *Tribune* took to the telegraph as quickly as possible, both publishing their first telegraphic dispatches in 1847.[37] But while the telegraph protected provincial papers from competition from London and New York newspapers, it enslaved them to the telegraph companies and wire-news monopolies that developed in Britain and America in the 1850s and 1860s. In Britain the private telegraph companies set up their own "intelligence departments" to provide news at monopoly rates. In America the distribution of telegraph news fell under the control of the New York newspapers through the device of the New York Associated Press.[38] In the 1850s the young John Edward Taylor of the *Guardian* (son of the founder) and Joseph Medill of the *Tribune* were leaders in the struggles against the metropolitan telegraph news monopolies. Indeed, they were key founders of telegraph news cooperatives that continue today: the Press Association (PA) in Great Britain and the Western Associated Press (later the modern Associated Press) in the United States.[39] Taylor's and Medill's decade-long struggle with national monopolies in their own business reinforced their broader understanding of political economy. On both sides of the Atlantic, anti-monopoly remained a central tenet of economic and political liberalism.

The aim of the *Guardian* and *Tribune* managers, however, was not merely to build their own businesses; it was to promote business in their cities. Of course, all businessmen were interested then, as now, in the general business climate: what was good for the city was good for them. Newspapers served this interest directly by providing business news, current prices and market data, and advertising. But newspapers differed from other businesses. They were not just private manufacturing firms. Their fundamental product—publication—required that they do their business in the public realm. While other businesses made things, newspapers made things public. And this necessarily meant politics and government. For newspapers such as the *Guardian* and *Tribune*, all economy was political economy.

From its earliest days, the *Manchester Guardian* made clear its devotion to public issues of political economy. In their prospectus, the founders promised close attention to "the condition of trade and its prospects, particularly as far as regards that most important branch, the Cotton Manufacture." The senior partner, John Edward Taylor, had come from the cotton trade and knew it well. More generally, the founders pledged to "assist in the diffusion of just principles of Political Economy." Subjects would include debates on the national debt, the currency, taxation, and other issues that might arise from "the conflicting views and wishes of the Commercial and Agricultural Interests." And "particular attention will be paid to all subjects of local interest": commercial proceedings, courts of law, and public meetings. The *Guardian* further promised to uphold the twin journalistic principles of "spirited discussion of political questions, and the accurate detail of facts."[40] These two

public functions of journalism—the forum function and the fact function—
were Enlightenment legacies revered by both British and American journalists
in the eighteenth and nineteenth centuries and are still alive, barely, today.[41]

At the heart of *Guardian*'s mission, was "a sincere and undeviating attachment to rational Liberty."[42] Of all the political terminology in the *Guardian*'s
prospectus, "rational liberty" was perhaps the most important. This was the
mantra of an emergent Manchesterian liberalism in both politics and journalism. In politics, rational liberty meant civil and religious liberty and liberty of
property—that is, free trade and anti-monopoly. In its early decades the
Guardian became the "cotton lords' bible," as both its detractors and supporters dubbed it; and that role drew the paper into the heart of the free trade
movement of the 1830s and 1840s, a movement that was born in Manchester.[43] Both Taylor and Jeremiah Garnett were early members of the leadership
council of the Anti-Corn Law League and early supporters of the League's
champions, Richard Cobden and John Bright. The newspaper never wavered
from the liberal doctrine of free trade.[44]

Though the *Guardian* was a founding member of the Manchester School of
political economy and an early contributor to the formation of the Liberal
Party, it was neither a slavish organ of the Anti-Corn Law League nor a
dependable supporter of many of the policies and tactics of the Radical (left-
leaning) wing of the Liberal Party. Like most Liberals, the *Guardian* was wary
of organized labor, but the paper was much more wary than Cobden and
Bright of the extension of the ballot to working men beyond the tepid reforms
of 1832. Furthermore, the paper split with Cobden and Bright over foreign
policy, especially their opposition to the Crimean War of 1854–5.[45] Essentially, the *Manchester Guardian* at mid-century remained steadfast in the mod-
erate (Whig) wing of the Liberal Party: devoted to commercial interests and
private enterprise, skeptical of democracy, and little concerned with what
Friedrich Engels, a most unusual Manchester businessman of that era, called
"the Condition of the Working Class in England."[46] In other words, to borrow
the terminology of class that Engels would later help to popularize, this was a
newspaper for the bourgeoisie, not the proletariat.

The term "rational Liberty" carried meaning for English journalism as well
as English politics. Liberal newspapermen such as Taylor and Garnett drew on
ideas about the civic virtue of press liberty dating back to John Milton in the
seventeenth century. They believed, as the *Guardian*'s prospectus declared, in
facts and in rational discussion. And they believed in the public function of
publication. Indeed, in the Victorian era most provincial English newspapers
aligned with the Liberal Party because of the liberal faith in education,
public information, and reason in the conduct of public affairs. The liberal
philosopher Jeremy Bentham insisted that the key to good government was
"publicity." "In an assembly elected by the people," he wrote, "publicity is
absolutely necessary to enable the electors to act from knowledge." Faith in

publicity—that is, in publication of public information—is fundamentally a journalistic ideal, for the business of newspapers is to make things public.[47] In its early decades, the *Manchester Guardian* sometimes found itself at odds with the business elites it so eagerly supported. The problem? Too much publicity, too much journalism: the paper's copious reporting on local government meetings and local institutions sometimes annoyed the oligarchs who were accustomed to conducting the public's business, as well as their own, in private.[48] This focus on the public realm of life in Manchester would gradually help steer the *Guardian* leftward in the late nineteenth century, toward a more collectivist New Liberalism—an urban liberalism—under the long editorship of Charles Prestwich Scott.

The *Chicago Tribune* was also thoroughly enthralled with the political economy of its city. From its founding in the 1840s the *Tribune* was the self-proclaimed "business-man's newspaper," much as the *Guardian* was the cotton lords' bible. The *Tribune*'s devotion to business meant publication of vast troves of economic information and obsessive attention to public policy, particularly those policies that touched on industry and on the prerogatives of private property: taxes, tariffs, and currency. Like the *Guardian*, the *Tribune* embraced the liberal economic principles of individual liberty, private enterprise, and anti-monopoly—but with a characteristic American twist. In its early decades the *Tribune* embraced that peculiar American frontier individualism that was hardly individualism at all: boosterism.[49]

Boosterism was the political economy of growing a city from the ground up—or in the case of Chicago from the mud up. Private enterprise was vital to the work, but so was government. At its founding, Chicago had one virtue only: location. To make that location pay, federal and state government aid was required—for defense, for harbor improvements, and for building the Michigan and Illinois Canal. Local government aid was needed for streets, bridges, and other public works. Furthermore, the federal government held vast tracts of land, and the prime task of the frontier booster was to convert that public land into private property.[50] The role of a booster newspaper was to promote government policies that would support the boosters' effort to harness public resources for private profit and to advertise the success of that effort locally and nationally. This the *Tribune* did with gusto.[51]

Except for this frontier booster ethos, the *Tribune*'s proprietors shared much with their cousins in Manchester, including a philosophical preference for what English liberals sometimes called "sedate government."[52] Horace White, editor of the *Tribune* in the 1860s and early 1870s, was a liberal free trader and equal rights enthusiast in the Cobden–Bright mold. In fact, he was a self-professed Cobdenite. He studied the works of Richard Cobden and Adam Smith; he corresponded with John Bright and John Stuart Mill; he joined the Cobden Club of London; he founded the Chicago chapter of the American Free Trade League; and he filled the newspaper with excerpts from the writings of English and continental liberal theorists.[53] White also helped to link the *Tribune* to Cobdenite liberalism in another important way: he hired Henry Demarest Lloyd. Lloyd had begun his brilliant journalistic career in New York in 1869 as a field agent and editor for the Free Trade League and as the writer of free-trade letters to the *New York Evening Post* under the pseudonym "No Monopoly." White recruited Lloyd onto the *Tribune* in 1872 precisely because of their shared enthusiasm for free trade, anti-monopoly, and Manchester School liberalism.[54] In the political turmoil of 1872, White and Lloyd helped foment the Liberal exodus from the regular Republican Party.[55]

Unlike White, Joseph Medill was a loyal Republican partisan. When he gained sole control of the *Tribune* in 1874, he vowed to bring it back into the party fold, even if that meant support for protective tariffs. But Medill maintained the *Tribune*'s fundamental economic liberalism, including opposition to monopolies and support for open entry and equal rights in business enterprise. Medill greatly admired White's protégé Henry Demarest Lloyd and kept him on the editorial page for nearly a decade after White's departure. Throughout the late 1870s and early 1880s, Lloyd used the *Tribune* (along with national magazines) to rail against the "lords of industry": the combinations and monopolies that cornered markets, fixed prices, suppressed workers' wages, and redistributed wealth from honest industry to corrupt corporate oligarchs and speculators. He larded his articles with references to English economists, from Adam Smith to Richard Cobden.[56] For Lloyd, Medill, and the *Chicago Tribune*, the archetypal "lord of the pool" was railroad magnate Jay Gould. Gould's 1881 takeover of Western Union, the telegraph monopoly, only further stoked their anti-monopoly fervor.[57]

Lloyd and Medill criticized monopolists at the local level as well, including the city's major meatpackers and the Union Stockyards. But in general Medill solidified the *Tribune*'s status as the businessman's paper and the tireless booster of private enterprise. And he championed sedate government in Chicago. In 1876 Medill declared that the great public works of the city were largely completed, and now was the time for government retrenchment. The *Tribune* supported the "segmented system" of special assessments for infrastructure repairs and crusaded against taxes and the "tax-eaters" who levied them. For Medill and the *Tribune* in the 1870s and 1880s, the raison d'être of local government was the protection of private property.[58]

By mid-century, property qualifications for voting in America had generally been abandoned, and both Horace White and Joseph Medill accepted the fact that universal white male suffrage was here to stay. But a grudging acceptance of democratic participation by the working class did not deter either editor from denouncing the ignorant rabble who polluted the politics of their city. Both condemned mobocracy and pleaded for government by businessmen, the best men. Under Medill, the *Tribune* grew increasingly anti-Catholic, anti-Irish, and anti-foreign in general. It resolutely condemned strikes and other actions of organized labor as depredations on private property.[59] In 1877, when the great railroad strike spilled into Chicago, Medill lectured the strikers on the laws of labor economics: "If these men think that they can't take the wages offered them, they can step out and let others take their place who feel that they can live upon the wages." Only when violence broke out did the paper see a role for government intervention. Federal, state, and local force must suppress the mob. The orders must be "shoot to kill"—for "a bullet in time saves nine."[60]

Though the *Tribune* was as horrified as the *Guardian* by the specter of a rising proletariat, the paper shared with the *Guardian* a faith in facts, in citizen education, and in politics by public discussion—that is, a faith in journalism. Medill despised the "tax-eaters and jackals" in local government as much as the "ruffians and communists" in the streets of Chicago, but he kept the public conversations going. He never doubted that the issues his newspaper railed about were public issues requiring public engagement. For a newspaper, whether in Britain or America, everything fell into the public realm. Joseph Medill would never move as far left as C. P. Scott at the *Manchester Guardian*, but even at the stalwart Republican *Chicago Tribune*, the scale and complexity of the modern industrial system, the communal imperative of urban life, and the public nature of the newspaper business itself would gradually nudge the old man to the brink of what would come to be called progressivism.[61]

THE URBAN NEWSPAPER

Eighteen-seventy-one was a year of transition for the *Manchester Guardian* and the *Chicago Tribune*. At the *Guardian*, C. P. Scott, the 24-year-old nephew of founder John Edward Taylor, began an association with the newspaper that would last sixty years, almost all of those years as editor. By the early twentieth century, Scott had transformed the *Guardian* from the organ of the local cotton lords into a newspaper of national and international significance. Meanwhile, in Chicago, change came in a more sudden and harrowing fashion. In 1871 the Great Chicago Fire consumed the commercial heart of the city, including the *Tribune*'s supposedly fireproof building. Both city and newspaper quickly rose from the ashes, and Joseph Medill assumed control of the paper in 1874. By the time of his death in 1899, Medill had built the *Tribune* into what it had always aspired to be: the leading newspaper of the American heartland. As the two newspapers reached outward, however, they remained rooted in their cities. Indeed, both the *Guardian* and the *Tribune*— as well as many other newspapers of the late Victorian era—were fundamentally shaped by the cities they helped to shape. These businessmen's papers, these quintessentially commercial papers, these paragons of private enterprise were gradually drawn into a more public, more communal, more collectivist understanding of life in the modern city. They became what I call urban newspapers.

When C. P. Scott assumed the editorship of the *Manchester Guardian* in 1872, four decades had passed since the publication of James Phillips Kay's shocking exposé, *The Moral and Physical Condition of the Working Classes in the Cotton Manufacture in Manchester.*[62] During those forty years, daily life in Manchester—and in other English industrial cities—had become only slightly less appalling for the poor. And during those forty years, the *Guardian*, like the commercial elite it served, held firm to the belief that the poor were largely to blame for their own misery. This was a tenet of the liberal faith in free markets and free labor. It was a faith that Scott would gradually abandon. By the end of the century, the *Guardian* was prepared to assert that capitalism, not moral failure or natural law, was the cause of the misery of the poor and of the social and environmental crisis of the city.

Scott was the key catalyst of change, but even before he arrived, the *Guardian* had come to appreciate the limits of private enterprise in a modern industrial city. Indeed, the Manchester manufacturers and Liberal Party politicians had as well. Though they opposed national-level legislation dealing with sanitation and health, they could plainly see that some local government action in the realm of disease control was necessary.[63] The business and political elites of Manchester also promoted local government enterprises such as gas lighting, water supply, flood control, and canal construction. Discussions of public infrastructure projects dominated local politics for decades and dotted the pages of the newspapers, including the *Guardian*. Manchester even gained a reputation as an early pioneer of "municipal socialism," although historians have sometimes argued that "municipal capitalism" would be the more apt term for public ownership of utilities. But whether it is labeled socialism or capitalism, it was not private enterprise, much less laissez-faire.[64]

In July 1872, just six months after Scott had taken over as *Guardian* editor, the city suffered a catastrophic flood—one of a long, unhappy series—and flood-control infrastructure schemes once again animated the city council and filled the newspapers with news.[65] The new *Guardian* editor had other urban problems on his mind as well. Under Scott, for the first time, the *Guardian* took an interest in poverty and the deprivation of the working class. In early 1873 Scott published several "social investigations" of housing and family health in Manchester, in nearby cities and towns, and in the mining districts. These were systematic reporting projects—enterprise stories, as they would be called today—which went beyond the usual stenographic accounts of public meetings, government actions, and court proceedings.[66]

Scott, however, was cautious in both politics and journalism. Only gradually did the *Guardian*'s local news reports on labor and poverty seep into the leaders (editorials) of the newspaper. But seep in they eventually did, and 1889 was a watershed moment for Scott, for the *Guardian*, and for the city of

Manchester. In that year, the city council, dominated by middle-class Liberals, finally decided to take seriously the wretched health conditions of Manchester's slums. This was the culmination of grass-roots organizing from the bottom up, coupled with the publication of a new statistical study of mortality rates in Manchester and an outpouring of public discussion in the streets and in the newspapers. And the *Guardian* was in the thick of it. The events of 1889 transformed the environmental politics of the city.[67] The year 1889 also marked a high point of the eight-hour-day movement in Britain, punctuated by a massive dock strike in London. And for the first time, the *Guardian*, under Scott's leadership, came down on the side of organized labor.[68] In reports and leaders written by W. T. Arnold, the *Guardian* argued that trade combinations were essential tools for working men negotiating with the combinations of powerful employers.[69]

Throughout the 1890s, C. P. Scott moved the *Guardian* leftward. As a result, the paper played a major role in what Scott's biographer calls the "modern-ization of liberalism," which he defines as the abandonment of the "gospel of laissez-faire."[70] Of course, neither the *Guardian* nor the Manchester School had ever professed allegiance to strict laissez-faire. But, still, the leftward turn of the *Guardian* in the 1890s was striking in its growing skepticism of unrestrained private enterprise. During a lockout of union coal miners in 1893, for example, the *Guardian* not only supported the miners, it came out in favor of the principle of a "living wage." The paper dismissed the employers' invocations of economic law and the sanctity of individual labor contracts. "The idea that wages—in other words, the living, the comfort, and the civilization of the great mass of men—is to be the one elastic and squeezable thing in a business, has got to go," wrote Scott's chief lieutenant C. E. Montague. If the settlement of industrial disputes required government intervention, then so be it—for gov-ernment is "nothing less than the community itself."[71] The *Guardian* also supported more active government at the local level. In 1894 Scott used the paper to promote the Manchester Liberal Party's ambitious Progressive Muni-cipal Programme, which called for municipal control of tramways, improved housing for the working class, strict sanitation enforcement, more progressive property taxation, and an eight-hour day for municipal workers.[72]

A key figure in this transformation was L. T. Hobhouse, a young Oxford sociologist whom Scott had admired from a distance and then brought onto the *Guardian* staff in 1897. Hobhouse's first book, *The Labour Movement*, published in 1893, had impressed both Scott and Montague. In that early manifesto of the New Liberalism, Hobhouse had endorsed trade unionism, cooperation, and municipal and state socialism. "What really unites these movements is the general character of the means they adopt for the further-ance of their ends," he wrote. "In one form or another all three alike are introducing the principle of collective control of industry by the community in the interests of all its members."[73] Many years later, in a memorial tribute to

C. P. Scott, Hobhouse recalled why Scott had hired him: "The reason he gave was his belief that the relations of Liberalism and Labour must govern the future of politics, and that the problem was to find the lines on which Liberals could be brought to see that the old tradition must be expanded to yield a fuller measure of social justice, a more real equality, an industrial as well as a political liberty."[74] It was through daily journalism at the *Guardian* that Hobhouse worked out his theory that social democracy, spearheaded by government, was necessary to fulfill the liberal promise. In a torrent of some forty-five articles and leaders in the *Guardian* during an engineers' strike in 1897, Hobhouse argued that the power of organized capital must be counterbalanced by organized labor and by the intervention of the state.[75]

Though Scott flirted with socialism, he remained true to liberalism, but a liberalism of sympathy, open-mindedness, and cross-class community as well as of individual liberty. In contrast to Marxian socialists and to the organizers of the emerging Labour Party, New Liberals such as Scott, Hobhouse, and J. A. Hobson, another famous *Guardian* writer, rejected a class-based politics, imagining instead a broad-based community of "the people." The role of government was to ensure that all people, including the downtrodden, had access to the kind of individual freedom that Liberals had always revered.[76] In a sense, the traditional Cobdenite liberal believed that liberty was the prerequisite of equality; the New Liberal believed that equality was the prerequisite of liberty. As Hobhouse memorably declared in his book *Liberalism*, "liberty without equality is a name of noble sound and squalid result." In the industrial age, "individualism, when it grapples with the facts, is driven no small distance along Socialist lines," he wrote, for "to maintain individual freedom and equality we have to extend the sphere of social control."[77] In labor relations this meant policies to equalize the imbalances of power between employer and worker. In cities it meant policies such as the taxation of "unearned income" from rising land values to support health and housing programs as well as public infrastructure. This is the perspective and these are the policies that C. P. Scott understood to be the essence of a New Liberalism for the twentieth century.[78]

In important ways, C. P. Scott's New Liberalism was journalistic in origin and style. It grew from his experiences in the city of Manchester and from his daily work on the *Guardian*. He believed in facts, not ideology. He retained the classic liberal faith in knowledge and education and in "the people." The function of a newspaper was to bring disparate classes together by reporting the news and providing a forum for rational discussion. Factual information, he believed, was the necessary basis of sympathy and community.[79] Scott certainly believed that newspapers owed their readers interpretation as well as facts, which is why he hired thinkers like Hobhouse and Hobson. But his most famous quotation on newspaper work is this one: "Comment is free, but facts are sacred."[80] In the early twentieth century, Scott explored the possibility of launching a London edition of the *Guardian*. In the end, though, during Scott's reign, the *Guardian* remained in Manchester, the city of its birth. "The public has its rights," Scott said on his eightieth birthday. "The paper which has grown up in a great community, nourished by its resources, reflecting in a thousand ways its spirit and its interests, in a real sense belongs to it."[81]

Back in Chicago in 1871, just ten weeks before the fire, the *Chicago Tribune* was celebrating the completion of a major public works project: the famous "deep cut," which reversed the flow of the Chicago River, sending Lake Michigan water into the Illinois River via the Illinois and Michigan Canal. The goal was to protect Lake Michigan, the source of the city's drinking water, from disease-laden sewage that fouled the river. The project was enormous though not enormous enough to do the job completely, especially during spring rains when the river would, as usual, flush its noxious waters into the lake.[82] For the next three decades, until an entirely new sanitary canal was opened in 1900, the *Tribune* and other Chicago newspapers were as heavy laden with sewage stories as the river was with sewage. In other words, as in Manchester, public works dominated the politics and the journalism even of the emblematic American private city, Chicago. However, the immediate urban catastrophe of 1871 was not sewage but fire. And perhaps the most curious outcome of the Great Fire was the election of Joseph Medill as mayor of Chicago.

Though a shrewd political operator within the Republican Party, Medill was a failure as mayor. He was elected on a nonpartisan reform ticket that reflected the broad civic spirit that flourished briefly in Chicago after the fire. Mayor Medill pushed for fireproof building codes and other reconstruction initiatives, but his experience left him more, not less, skeptical of the role of government in the political economy of the city. As mayor he sought to cut the city's budget and to shut down the saloons and gambling dens that he believed supported corrupt ward politicians. The aldermen blocked most of Medill's moves, and the petulant mayor resigned before his term was complete. He set off on a European vacation, pondering his future and plotting a return to the *Tribune*.[83] Medill's mayoral fiasco taught him little new; rather, it confirmed his prejudices: a mania for low taxes and businesslike government; a contempt for foreigners; and an abiding hatred of the grafters, bummers, loafers, and ward heelers on the city council.

When Medill regained control of the *Tribune* in 1874, he declared war on the city council, which he called "the fountain head of all the corruption that has disgraced the city of Chicago for years."[84] In the first six months of 1876, the *Tribune* carried 115 major editorials calling for retrenchment and lower taxes in local government and 119 attacking local government officials for extravagance or corruption. And this was an ordinary, unexceptional six months. Day after day, year after year, decade after decade, the *Tribune* fulminated against the "spendthrift reckless demagogues who think that

Governments are instituted for no other purpose than to confiscate private property."[85] For Medill and the *Tribune*, corrupt politicians were in the same category as labor unions: they were insatiable predators on other people's property. And yet, despite the paeans to private property, economic law, and government retrenchment, Medill's *Tribune* gradually came to accept—even to encourage—a range of progressive public policies. Joseph Medill was no C. P. Scott, and the *Chicago Tribune* never became an organ of a "new liberalism" in America. But the empirical reality of industrial capitalism—especially its impact on life in the city—just as it led Scott, toward a practical progressivism. By the end of the century the old liberal dogmas of private enterprise, anti-monopoly, competition, and individualism no longer seemed adequate.

The post-1874 *Tribune*—Medill's *Tribune* at last—had no place for Horace White, who decamped to New York to edit the *Evening Post*. Medill's rift with White, however, had been over partisan politics, not economic theory. White's bolt to the Liberal Republicans in 1872 had been more than Medill, the party stalwart, could stand. Medill's economic liberalism was largely consonant with White's and even with White's more radical protégé, Henry Demarest Lloyd, whom Medill kept on the paper after White's departure and made chief editorial writer in 1880.[86]

By the mid-1880s, however, Lloyd's views on political economy had advanced beyond Medill's traditional liberalism of anti-monopoly and private enterprise. In the *Tribune* and in his magazine articles, Lloyd began to articulate a new understanding of political economy in America much like that of Scott, Montague, and Hobhouse in England. He wrote that classical economic theory had failed. Smith's and Cobden's liberalism had relied on free trade and competition, but modern capitalism was all about combination, not competition. The age of competition and the "cant of individualism" had passed. "Laissez-faire theories of politics and political economy are useless in the treatment of the labor question, in the regulation of railroads, sanitary and educational government, and a multitude of similar questions," he wrote. Indeed, these theories are not merely useless; "they are murderous."[87] Lloyd, the erstwhile cheerleader for free trade and competition as the antidote to monopoly, now believed that the tendency to monopoly in some industries was irresistible. What was needed was not competition, but social combination. The choice was either unregulated monopoly or social control of monopoly by government. As Lloyd put it, "When capitalists combine irresistibly against the people, the Government, which is the people's combination, must take them in hand."[88]

Lloyd's flirtation with socialism had little support at the *Tribune* and none among the business elite of Chicago; and so in 1885 Medill eased Lloyd out the door. Meanwhile, Medill had joined a capitalist combination in his own industry: the Daily Newspaper Association of Chicago, organized in 1884.

The association's purpose was the same as that of the trusts and combinations that Lloyd (and Medill) had lambasted: to fix prices, to deter competition, and to present a united front against the demands of the newspaper unions.[89] Yet the departure of Lloyd and the paper's own increasingly ruthless business practices merely slowed the *Tribune*'s own flirtation with a new, more progressive liberalism. This evolution in the *Tribune*'s understanding of political economy can be seen in two key areas: the clash between capital and labor and the regulation of public utilities.

The clash between capital and labor in Chicago grew violent in the late nineteenth century. Three especially traumatic confrontations were the great railway strike of 1877, the eight-hour movement and Haymarket affair of 1886, and the Pullman strike of 1894.[90] In each of these cases, the *Tribune*— and most of the newspapers in the city—denounced the strikers and sensationalized the violence. That is the whole story as told in historical surveys of Chicago journalism, and it certainly is an important part of the story.[91] But there were nuances in the journalism of these labor uprisings that offer insight into the political role of newspapers in cities.

In 1877, for instance, the *Tribune* under Medill and Lloyd viewed the general public—the consumers of railway services—as the most important of the players in the great railway strike. The public interest—that is, the interest of the whole community—trumped the private interests of both the workers and the corporations. Though it poured most of its vitriol on the strikers, the *Tribune* conceded that the railroad workers had legitimate grievances. And the paper denounced the management of the great railway corporations, especially the despised monopolist Jay Gould.[92] The *Tribune* argued that a peaceful, equitable, even natural balance between the interests of labor and capital could be achieved. During the 1877 strike, the *Tribune* urged again and again that a national system of arbitration was needed. The paper believed in discussion and negotiation and in the efficacy of facts and information in the rational settlement of conflict. The *Tribune* also advocated pensions and disability programs funded jointly by employers and employees. Such rational, organizational arrangements would be good for both capital and labor and for the public at large.[93]

The Haymarket affair and the Pullman strike sorely tested the *Tribune*'s faith in conflict resolution through peaceful, organizational means. In 1886 the newspapers of the city, with the *Tribune* leading the pack, launched hysterical attacks on the "anarchist menace" and on the "Socialistic, atheistic, alcoholic European classes" that had imported anarchism to Chicago.[94] On the broader issue of the eight-hour day, however, the *Tribune* argued for careful deliberation on the basis of facts and hard information. The paper now supported labor unionism—reluctantly—as long as unions eschewed strikes and violence in favor of arbitration. Arbitration still seemed to the *Tribune* the most rational, fact-based method for settling industrial disputes. If there were no fundamental conflict between capital and labor, as the *Tribune* believed, then arbitration would benefit everyone, especially the general public.[95]

The *Tribune* took a similar stance during the 1894 Pullman strike. While continuing to denounce strikes and secondary boycotts—and immigrants— the paper also railed against George Pullman for his stubborn refusal to negotiate with his employees. The *Tribune* conceived of a common interest between capital and labor, and again the watchword was arbitration. The controlling interest, however, must be the public interest. Through the act of publication itself, the *Tribune* asserted that the issues at stake were no longer private matters. Indeed, for a newspaper everything is public.[96]

The other great issue of urban political economy for the *Chicago Tribune* in the late nineteenth century was public-utility regulation. On this subject, Joseph Medill was no doctrinaire laissez-faire ideologue. He believed that in some modern industries, such as railroads and telegraph, competition was no longer an adequate deterrence to monopoly. Though he had fired Henry Lloyd for straying too far left, he shared Lloyd's fundamental insight into modern corporate capitalism: "The cat must be killed or belled," Lloyd had quipped. Medill opposed killing the beast, but he agreed that belling (regulation) was sometimes needed.[97] Yet, philosophically, Medill remained opposed to socialism and municipal ownership and steadfastly committed to private enterprise for most public services. In 1890, for example, he ran a series of editorials lambasting the cooperative theories of the Bellamy Nationalists and trumpeting the virtues of private enterprise. "No greed, no surplus; no surplus, no railroads," the paper explained to its readers.[98]

For practical reasons, too, Medill resisted government control of utility services at the local level throughout the 1880s and 1890s. Chicago's special woes involving water—floods, stagnant sewage, waterborne disease—led the city to take control of water-related utilities by the 1850s. And newspapers, including the *Tribune*, usually supported public waterworks projects and drainage schemes. But as the local politicians—the "pump-house gang"— learned to siphon surplus funds from the water and sewer departments for personal and partisan gain, Medill's *Tribune* increasingly insisted on private enterprise in other urban utilities: gas, electricity, and street railways. Medill was appalled by the prospect of more vital public services falling into the hands of the "boodlers, bummers, and tax-eaters, . . . the jackals, cormorants, and incorrigible pap-suckers" who ran city government. As late as 1895, Medill still argued for a version of the old "segmented system" for controlling municipal services: Give veto power to the property owners directly affected.[99]

By the late 1890s, however, Medill had changed his tune, partially and grudgingly. He had grown so disgusted by the arrogant greed of the privately owned utility monopolies in Chicago—especially the street railway company—that he came to accept, at least theoretically, the concept of municipal ownership. The *Tribune* still argued that the city government was too corrupt to manage day-to-day operations of the utilities, but now the paper declared that the city, not private capital, should own the systems.[100] Though hardly a full-throated endorsement of municipal socialism, this was a remarkable transformation for the erstwhile champion of private enterprise.

As a solution to the problem of political corruption, the *Tribune* had little faith in structural reforms of government but much faith in information and education. "As the political system of managing municipalities has come to stay," the paper declared, "the only thing to do is to make the best of it and to see that all possible is done to make the voters intelligent and honest." To help fashion intelligent and honest voters, the *Tribune* published an astonishing amount of information on public utilities and political economy. Statistics on water-flow rates in the South Branch of the Chicago River, the fine points of the single-tax theory, the specifics of municipal governments in Great Britain—everything warranted detailed description and commentary. In 1898–9 the *Tribune* carried an average of 154 stories per week on local government and public affairs, 44 percent of which were about local public-utility matters.[101]

Like C. P. Scott in Manchester, Joseph Medill was moved by the circumstances of modern industrialism and urban life to support positions emblematic of an emerging municipal progressivism, including belief in a general public interest, a public-interest standard in political economy, preference for fact-based and public-mediated modes of conflict resolution, and support for public control, even public ownership, of local utility monopolies. Unlike Scott, Medill remained philosophically an economic liberal (a conservative, as Americans would now say), and the *Tribune* remained skeptical of labor unions and most progressive reforms. But given the philosophical differences of the two editors, the similarities in the civic values of their newspapers are revealing. They suggest the pragmatic nature of urban newspaper politics as well as the editors' shared understanding of the political role of journalism. For both Scott and Medill, the most fundamental political values were civic and journalistic. No matter how frustrated they became with local politics, no matter how wary of democracy and the working class, they never lost faith in information and public deliberation—that is, faith in both the fact function and the forum function of journalism. They never doubted the civic virtue of newspaper publication, of "publicity." They never doubted what Delos Wilcox, the American progressive reformer and utility expert, called "the authority of facts."[102]

THE NEW JOURNALISM

The *Manchester Guardian* and the *Chicago Tribune* are never mentioned among the progenitors of the New Journalism at the end of the nineteenth century. In an age of growing sensationalism, human-interest stories, flashy headlines, and lavish illustrations, the *Guardian* and the *Tribune* remained traditional commercial newspapers, their proprietors more interested in a "quality" readership than in a mass audience. But these two provincial newspapers offer revealing case studies of the origins of the New Journalism precisely because they themselves were not practitioners of it in its full flower. Even these staid businessmen's papers were drawn into a new understanding of political economy by the "collectivism of urban life."[103] Public works, public order, public utilities, public health—all things public—were fundamental to the journalism of these new urban newspapers as well as to the politics of the New Liberalism in Britain and municipal progressivism in America. The idea that there exists a general public—not just individuals or classes—that can be organized and moved by published facts and information is a journalistic faith that lay at the core of the modern metropolitan daily newspaper, including the more famous exemplars of the New Journalism.

Though the *Tribune* is seldom linked to the rise of the New Journalism, the city of Chicago is. Indeed, one of the first in the wave of newspapers that created the New Journalism in the United States was the *Chicago Daily News*, an evening penny paper launched in December 1875 by Melville Stone. The *Daily News* was built on the business model of the cheap consumer product aimed at a mass market. It was physically small, condensed in style, lively and entertaining. And it was successful. Stone's partner, Victor Lawson, was unusually adept at growing circulation and managing advertising on modern business principles, including the use of sworn circulation figures and fixed advertising rates. Like Joseph Medill a generation earlier, Lawson understood that ads could and should be news, and he used both news and advertising to create a true mass medium in Chicago. By the 1880s the *Daily News* had a circulation of 150,000, when no other Chicago newspaper had topped 100,000. By 1895 the circulation of the *Daily News* hit 200,000.[104]

The *Chicago Daily News*, however, was not simply a mass media product; it was a genuinely urban newspaper from the outset. Though Melville Stone was in some ways an ordinary liberal businessman, he always believed that the city was a community rather than a marketplace, a belief reinforced by the Great Fire. "No class in society can afford to ignore another," the paper declared in 1876; "we are far too interdependent."[105] In its first year of publication, the *Daily News* advocated a variety of public works, not only to provide necessary public services, but to create jobs for the unemployed. During the great labor uprisings of the late nineteenth century, the paper condemned strikes, violence, and anarchism, just as the *Tribune* did, but the *Daily News* was much more sympathetic to organized labor, though always tough in negotiations with its own union workmen. Moreover, though Stone and Lawson hated political corruption as much as Joseph Medill did, they made the *Daily News* an early supporter of municipal ownership of public utilities, especially street railways. In the 1890s, year after year, the paper devoted from 25 to 35 percent of its local government and public affairs stories to public-utility matters.[106]

By the late 1890s, despite considerable ideological differences, the *Tribune* and the *Daily News* held similar positions on many local public issues, in part because they had come to share a similar understanding of the nature of modern urban life and of the civic function of the modern newspaper. Both papers perceived that the clash of capital and labor and the interdependence of citizens in great cities required public intervention and public enterprise. And both papers imagined that these public policies depended upon journalism—that is, the application of facts and information. This is the core of the urban newspaper and of urban progressivism—and a vital element of the New Journalism as well.

Newspaper entrepreneurs in other Midwestern cities quickly adopted the format, style, and business model pioneered by the *Chicago Daily News* and also by the *Detroit Evening News*, a lively two-cent paper that James Scripps had launched in 1873. In 1878 Scripps's younger brother E. W. carried the new model to Cleveland. In the 1880s and 1890s, E. W. Scripps built a national chain of small, afternoon papers notable for both their modern management strategies and for their support of labor unions and their commitment to the community life of their cities.[107] Also in 1878, Joseph Pulitzer, soon to be the undisputed master of the New Journalism in America, merged two St. Louis papers to create the *St. Louis Post-Dispatch*. In the 1870s Pulitzer was an economic liberal in the mold of Horace White, committed to free trade, private enterprise, individual liberty, and anti-monopoly. Like his contemporaries in Chicago, the liberal Pulitzer was skeptical of labor unions and municipal government enterprise in the early years. But over time, through years of struggles with utility corporations and with capital–labor conflict, the *Post-Dispatch* moved in the direction of a progressive liberalism: utility regulation, public works, municipal reform, and some sympathy for organized labor. Moreover, like the newspapers of Chicago, the *Post-Dispatch* brimmed with facts and information. In 1894–5 one of every three stories on government or public affairs was about municipal utilities.[108]

In 1883 Pulitzer took this new Midwestern formula to New York, by purchasing and renovating the *New York World*. The *World* employed the full panoply of New Journalism innovations: sensational writing, crusades, human interest, entertainment, interviews, bold headlines, copious illustrations, and modern business practices.[109] While the *Post-Dispatch* in St. Louis remained essentially a businessman's paper, the *World* reached out to everyone in New York, including the working class, new immigrants, and the poor. The traditional liberal Pulitzer became more of a "new liberal" in New York, supporting unions and labor legislation as well as anti-monopoly crusades, public works, and utility regulation. "The keystone of *The World*'s arch of triumph is public service," the paper proclaimed on the fifth anniversary of the

Pulitzer regime.[110] Perhaps the most innovative aspect of "public service" for the *World* was direct personal service to readers, in the pages of the newspaper and through personal correspondence. The Pulitzer manuscripts collection for the 1880s is replete with handwritten pleas from ordinary readers seeking information, guidance, and assistance.[111] One great purpose of a newspaper, Pulitzer believed, was to help citizens navigate life in the modern city.

It was newspapers such as the *Chicago Daily News* and the *New York World* that impressed the British and inspired the New Journalism that emerged in London in the 1880s. Important early exemplars of this New Journalism in England were the *Pall Mall Gazette*, which W. T. Stead took over in 1883, and the *Star*, which the radical Liberal activist T. P. O'Connor founded in 1888.[112] Stead is often credited with bringing the New Journalism to England, but in a moment of uncharacteristic modesty, he was willing to share top billing with O'Connor. "He and I may fairly claim to have revolutionized English journalism," Stead wrote in a profile of his old friend. "We broke the old tradition and made journalism a living thing, palpitating with actuality, in touch with life at all points."[113]

The innovations that Stead and O'Connor borrowed from the Americans touched mainly on design, genre, and tone. New design elements included more illustrations, headlines, and subheadings. New journalistic genres included interviews, sensational investigations, and crusades. Stead believed that the interview was perhaps the most novel American form to be imported by the *Pall Mall Gazette*. But the genre that created the most buzz in English journalism circles was the investigative exposé. Stead's sensational reporting on poverty and sexual crime in London rivaled Pulitzer's *World* at its most lurid.[114] O'Connor believed that tone was the key element: "clear, crisp, sharp," sometimes humorous, always personal. From personality profiles to gossip to hard news, he declared, "you must strike your reader right between the eyes."[115]

Beyond format and style, Stead's *Pall Mall Gazette* and O'Connor's *Star* shared another characteristic with their American cousins as well as with some of their more stodgy British brethren, such as the *Manchester Guardian*: they were urban newspapers. At the *Pall Mall Gazette*, the subject of Stead's first major crusade in 1883 was urban slum housing. In some ways that series, "The Bitter Cry of Outcast London," was standard New Journalism sensationalism.[116] But the series was also a serious study of political economy in the Victorian city. It was an exploration of the failure of what Stead labeled "laissez-faire" in urban working-class housing markets, of the interdependence of classes in the urban community, and of the relationship between "Socialism and Freedom." Like Henry Demarest Lloyd, Stead argued that "there is no choice for us between Individualism and Socialism," because the industrial system was already a kind of "anarchic Socialism." And like L. T. Hobhouse, Stead believed that the driving force of political economy in the city was empirical necessity, not ideology. Under modern conditions, he wrote, government intervention "is necessary and salutary, and is a safeguard, not a danger, to individual freedom."[117] Stead also believed in the power of facts and information. On the same day that the "Bitter Cry" series began, Stead ran an article that described—more in the style of the *Manchester Guardian* or the *Chicago Tribune* than of the New Journalism—a proposed sewage treatment plant on the lower Thames, complete with engineering diagrams and statistics.[118]

At the *Star*, T. P. O'Connor and his chief lieutenant, H. W. Massingham, punched their readers between the eyes with politics as well as entertainment. They promoted labor unionism, Irish Home Rule, electoral reform, and other national-level policies of the left wing of the Liberal Party. But the paper's forte was the local political economy of its own city. "We regard the organization of London Radicalism as the first great work of the *Star*," the editors declared. And so it was. For the *Star*, as for the *Manchester Guardian*, 1889 was a watershed year. The paper reported on the eight-hour movement and the great dock workers' strike, and it successfully promoted an agenda of municipal socialism for the new London County Council, which held its first election in 1889.[119] Thirty years later Massingham said that one of the *Star*'s signal achievements was the creation of the London Progressive Party, a cross-class coalition of liberals, radicals, labor unionists, and socialists. Indeed, it was Massingham at the *Star*—so they say—who first applied to this new style of urban politics the term "Progressive."[120]

THE LONDONER IN CHICAGO

Then in 1893, at the height of his fame, W. T. Stead came to Chicago. He was invited by his American collaborator, Albert Shaw, a scholar and journalist with whom Stead had founded an American edition of Stead's left-leaning magazine, *Review of Reviews*, in 1891. A doctoral graduate of Johns Hopkins, Shaw had studied municipal government in the United States and Britain, and had forged links between progressive reformers and journalists on both sides of the Atlantic. As a journalist, Shaw had worked for both W. T. Stead and Melville Stone, and it was Shaw who brought the two famous editors together in Chicago in 1893. Shaw loved Stead, but like Stone he was chagrined by the relentless flogging of vice, crime, and corruption in Stead's famous exposé *If Christ Came to Chicago*, which Stead quickly dashed off and published in 1894.[121] But Shaw must have been delighted to read the book's final substantive chapter, which was a remarkably expansive prescription for activist government, cross-class community, municipal socialism, and progressive reform in Chicago.

In this chapter, titled "In the Twentieth Century," Stead imagined a future Chicago transformed into a paradise of civic spirit and public enterprise. It was a dazzling vision. First, Stead predicted public works on the grandest scale: a Great Lakes oceanic canal, making Chicago the greatest seaport in the world; a giant drainage canal that would cleanse the city while generating clean, cost-free electric power; neighborhood heating plants; public markets, public baths, immense lakefront parks. Second, he imagined a sweeping expansion of municipal ownership of utilities: gas, electricity, street railways, telegraph, telephone, subway tunnels, pneumatic tubes, hot air ducts, even department stores—plus free transit, free libraries, free reading rooms, free higher education, free medical care. Third, Stead foresaw a revolution in labor relations, mediated by government: the eight-hour day, no child labor, public works for the unemployed. The mission of the municipal government of the future would be to "knit together the caste- and class-severed units of the city's population into a homogeneous whole," Stead wrote. "If Christ came to Chicago it seems to me that there are few objects that would more command his sympathy and secure his help than efforts to restore the sense of brotherhood to man and to reconstitute the human family on a basis adjusted to modern life."[122] Stead was no doctrinaire socialist. Rather, he was a journalist and a Christian who simply believed that a city had a communal duty to its citizens.[123]

Albert Shaw, who had a wry sense of humor, was probably amused by his mentor's utopian hyperbole. But in a book that Shaw produced a year later, though deploying the more measured idiom of the New Liberalism of England and municipal progressivism of America, he made roughly the same point: it was urban life, not a revolution in fundamental political values, that was driving change in both politics and journalism in cities. Shaw wrote:

> Superficially regarded, the activities of the modern city would seem to have a strong and rapid socialistic trend, because so many subjects of common interest are passing under the direct control of municipal authorities. But in point of fact, when strictly analyzed, modern municipal collectivism does not so very seriously transgress the valuable old principles of individual freedom and private initiative.... A close analysis would reveal the fact that a very large part of the list of modern undertakings commonly deemed socialistic might properly be regarded as extensions of individualism.[124]

In other words, as a Hobhouse or a Lloyd or even a W. T. Stead might say, in the modern city, collectivism was the necessary foundation of individual liberty. It was the culmination, not the repudiation, of liberalism. And, most importantly, this new, progressive liberalism was driven by facts and information, not ideology. In Shaw's words:

> If one grasps the idea that the cheerful and rational acceptance of urban life as a great social fact demands that the City Government should proceed to make such

urban life conduce positively to the welfare of all the people whose lawful interests bring them together as denizens of great towns, he will understand the point of view from which this book has been written.[125]

And, I will add, he or she will understand the civic and economic values—the principles of political economy—of the urban newspaper in late Victorian Britain and America.

NOTES

1. Melville E. Stone, *Fifty Years a Journalist* (Garden City, NY: Doubleday, 1921), 200–4.
2. Matthew Arnold, "Up To Easter," *Nineteenth Century*, 21 (May 1887), 638; T. P. O'Connor, "The New Journalism," *New Review*, 1 (October 1889), 423–34; W. T. Stead, "Government by Journalism," *Contemporary Review*, 49 (May 1886), 653–74.
3. Historians and textbook authors in both countries have also adopted the term "new journalism" for this era and have produced various lists of innovations, although they also tend to see a good deal of continuity with previous eras. See, for example, Frank Luther Mott, *American Journalism*, 3rd edn (New York: Macmillan, 1962), ch. 26; Ted Curtis Smythe, *The Gilded Age Press, 1865–1900* (Westport, Conn.: Praeger, 2003), ch. 5; Joel H. Wiener (ed.), *Papers for the Millions: The New Journalism in Britain, 1850s to 1914* (Westport, Conn.: Greenwood Press, 1988); Dennis Griffiths, *Fleet Street: Five Hundred Years of the Press* (London: British Library, 2006), ch. 6; and Martin Conboy, *Journalism in Britain: A Historical Introduction* (London: Sage, 2011), 12–19.
4. Joel H. Wiener, *The Americanization of the British Press, 1830s–1914: Speed in the Age of Transatlantic Journalism* (New York: Palgrave Macmillan, 2011); Marion T. Marzolf, "American 'New Journalism' Takes Root in Europe at the End of the 19th Century," *Journalism Quarterly*, 61 (Autumn 1984): 529–30; W. T. Stead, *The Americanization of the World* (London: H. Markley, 1902), 110–11. See also Joel H. Wiener and Mark Hampton (eds), *Anglo-American Media Interactions, 1850–2000* (New York: Palgrave Macmillan, 2007). On the American "penny press" of the 1830s and 1840s, see Paul Starr, *The Creation of the Media: Political Origins of Modern Communications* (New York: Basic Books, 2004), ch. 4.
5. Jean K. Chalaby, "Journalism as an Anglo-American Invention: A Comparison of the Development of French and Anglo-American Journalism, 1830s–1920s," *European Journal of Communication*, 11 (September 1996): 303–26.
6. David Paul Nord, *Communities of Journalism: A History of American Newspapers and their Readers* (Urbana: University of Illinois Press, 2001), chs 5–7.
7. Asa Briggs, *Victorian Cities* (New York: Harper & Row, 1963), 92–3; Alan Kidd, *Manchester*, 3rd edn (Edinburgh: Edinburgh University Press, 2002), ch. 2. See also Simon Gunn, "Urbanization," in *A Companion to Nineteenth-Century Britain*, ed. Chris Williams (Oxford: Blackwell Publishing, 2004), ch. 14.

8. Alexis de Tocqueville, quoted in Briggs, *Victorian Cities*, 110–11.

9. Harold L. Platt, *Shock Cities: The Environmental Transformation and Reform of Manchester and Chicago* (Chicago: University of Chicago Press, 2005), 7, 11–12.

10. Tristram Hunt, *Building Jerusalem: The Rise and Fall of the Victorian City* (New York: Metropolitan Books, 2005), 146–50; Briggs, *Victorian Cities*, 100–1, 122–3. I borrow the term "private city" from Sam Bass Warner, Jr., *The Private City: Philadelphia in Three Periods of its Growth* (Philadelphia: University of Pennsylvania Press, 1968).

11. G. R. Searle, *The Liberal Party* (New York: Palgrave, 2001), 10–14.

12. Richard Cobden, *To the Manufacturers, Millowners, and Other Capitalists, of Every Shade of Political Opinion, Engaged in the Various Branches of the Cotton Trade, in the District of Which Manchester is the Centre* (Manchester, England: J. Gadsby, 1841), 6. See also William D. Grampp, *The Manchester School of Economics* (Stanford, Calif.: Stanford University Press, 1960); and Daniel T. Rodgers, *Atlantic Crossings: Social Politics in a Progressive Age* (Cambridge, Mass.: Belknap Press of Harvard University Press, 1998), ch. 3.

13. Cobden, *To the Manufacturers*, 6; Grampp, *Manchester School*, 103; Robert Kelley, *The Transatlantic Persuasion: The Liberal-Democratic Mind in the Age of Gladstone* (New York: Knopf, 1969), 74–6, 197.

14. Searle, *Liberal Party*, 13–14; Eugenio F. Biagini, *Liberty, Retrenchment and Reform: Popular Liberalism in the Age of Gladstone, 1860–1880* (Cambridge: Cambridge University Press, 1992), 11–12, 50–1; Matthew Roberts, *Political Movements in Urban England, 1832–1914* (New York: Palgrave Macmillan, 2009), 71–3.

15. Platt, *Shock Cities*, 63–8; Kidd, *Manchester*, ch. 5; Martin Hewitt, *The Emergence of Stability in the Industrial City: Manchester, 1832–67* (Aldershot, UK: Scolar Press, 1996), 294–8.

16. Samuel H. Beer, *Modern British Politics: Parties and Pressure Groups in the Collectivist Age* (New York: W. W. Norton, 1982), 37; John Morley, *The Life of Richard Cobden* (Boston: Roberts Brothers, 1881), 23–7, 635. See also Stephen Meardon, "Richard Cobden's American Quandary: Negotiating Peace, Free Trade, and Anti-Slavery," in *Rethinking Nineteenth-Century Liberalism: Richard Cobden Bicentenary Essays*, ed. Anthony Howe and Simon Morgan (Aldershot, UK: Ashgate, 2006), 208–26. John Bright idealized America even more than Cobden. See Bill Cash, *John Bright: Statesman, Orator, Agitator* (London: I. B. Tauris, 2012), 93–4, 152–3.

17. William J. Novak, *The People's Welfare: Law and Regulation in Nineteenth-Century America* (Chapel Hill: University of North Carolina Press, 1996), 1–17; William J. Novak, "The Myth of the 'Weak' American State," *American Historical Review*, 115 (June 2008): 752–72; Gary Gerstle, "The Resilient Power of the States across the Long Nineteenth Century," in *The Unstable American State*, ed. Lawrence Jacobs and Desmond King (New York: Oxford University Press, 2009), 61–87.

18. Daniel Walker Howe, *What Hath God Wrought: The Transformation of America, 1815–1848* (New York: Oxford University Press, 2007), 561–2; John Lauritz Larson, *Internal Improvement: National Public Works and the Promise of Popular Government in the Early United States* (Chapel Hill: University of North Carolina Press, 2001), 3–7.

19. Charles Sellers, *The Market Revolution: Jacksonian America, 1815–1846* (New York: Oxford University Press, 1993), 51–2; Ronald E. Seavoy, "Laissez-Faire: Business Policy, Corporations, and Capital Investment in the Early National Period," in *Encyclopedia of American Political History*, ed. Jack P. Greene (New York: Scribner's, 1984), vol. 2, 734–6. See also John Lauritz Larson, *The Market Revolution in America: Liberty, Ambition, and the Eclipse of the Common Good* (New York: Cambridge University Press, 2010).

20. Cobden, *To the Manufacturers*, 6–7. See also Kelley, *Transatlantic Persuasion*, 197.

21. Dominic A. Pacyga, *Chicago: A Biography* (Chicago: University of Chicago Press, 2009), 18–20; Donald L. Miller, *City of the Century: The Epic of Chicago and the Making of America* (New York: Simon & Schuster, 1996), ch. 4.

22. William Cronon, *Nature's Metropolis: Chicago and the Great West* (New York: W. W. Norton, 1991), 29.

23. Cronon, *Nature's Metropolis*, 65–72.

24. *Chicago Tribune*, January 29, 1857, quoted in Pacyga, *Chicago*, 21.

25. Robin L. Einhorn, *Property Rules: Political Economy in Chicago 1833–1872* (Chicago: University of Chicago Press, 1991), 8–9, 17, 60; Platt, *Shock Cities*, 131–2. "Segmented system" is Einhorn's term.

26. *Chicago Times*, January 2, 1865, quoted in Platt, *Shock Cities*, 134. See also Carl Smith, *City Water, City Life: Water and the Infrastructure of Ideas in Urbanizing Philadelphia, Boston, and Chicago* (Chicago: University of Chicago Press, 2013), ch. 2.

27. Joel H. Wiener, *The War of the Unstamped: The Movement to Repeal the British Newspaper Tax, 1830–1836* (Ithaca, NY: Cornell University Press, 1969), 4–5; Mark Hampton, *Visions of the Press in Britain, 1850–1950* (Urbana: University of Illinois Press, 2004), 31–2.

28. The influence of tax policy on the newspaper business in Britain is a major theme in journalism history. See, for example, Hampton, *Visions of the Press*, 63–4; Aled Jones, "The Press and the Printed Word," in *Companion to Nineteenth-Century Britain*, ed. Williams, 370–4; and Ivon Asquith, "1780–1855," in *Newspaper History: From the Seventeenth Century to the Present Day*, ed. George Boyce, James Curran, and Pauline Wingate (London: Constable, 1978), 112–13. On the Manchester newspaper market, see David Ayerst, *The Manchester Guardian: Biography of a Newspaper* (Ithaca, NY: Cornell University Press, 1971), 94–6.

29. Alan J. Lee, *The Origins of the Popular Press in England, 1855–1914* (London: Croom Helm, 1976), 67–8, 274–8; US Department of the Interior, Census Office, *The Newspaper and Periodical Press*, prepared by S. N. D. North (Washington: Government Printing Office, 1884), 187.

30. Nord, *Communities*, ch. 4.

31. William Haslam Mills, *The Manchester Guardian: A Century of History* (New York: Henry Holt, 1922), 37–8; Ayerst, *Manchester Guardian*, 64.

32. Wayne Klatt, *Chicago Journalism: A History* (Jefferson, NC: McFarland, 2009), 12–13, 25–6; Lloyd Wendt, *Chicago Tribune: The Rise of a Great American Newspaper* (Chicago: Rand McNally, 1979), 63, 72–3, 88, 206–12, 247–51.

33. Ayerst, *Manchester Guardian*, 81, 128.

34. Wendt, *Chicago Tribune*, 57, 96, 213, 226.

35. Wendt, *Chicago Tribune*, 30, 139, 153, 197, 265–7. See also Richard Junger, *Becoming the Second City: Chicago's Mass News Media, 1833–1898* (Urbana: University of Illinois Press, 2010), 21–2.

36. Ayerst, *Manchester Guardian*, 117–19, 128–32, 134, 226.

37. Ayerst, *Manchester Guardian*, 97–9, 136; Wendt, *Chicago Tribune*, 26–7, 180; Junger, *Becoming the Second City*, 20.

38. Wiener, *Americanization*, 67–8; Richard R. John, *Network Nation: Inventing American Telecommunications* (Cambridge, Mass.: Belknap Press of Harvard University Press, 2010), 146–9; Menahem Blondheim, *News Over the Wires: The Telegraph and the Flow of Public Information in America, 1844–1897* (Cambridge, Mass.: Harvard University Press, 1994), ch. 5; Jonathan Silberstein-Loeb, *The International Distribution of News: The Associated Press, Press Association, and Reuters, 1848–1947* (New York: Cambridge University Press, 2014), chs 2 and 4.

39. Ayerst, *Manchester Guardian*, 142–8; Wendt, *Chicago Tribune*, 198, 218, 274, 293–4.

40. *On Saturday, the 5th of May, 1821, will be Published, Price Seven-pence, No. 1 of a New Weekly Paper, to be entitled The Manchester Guardian* (Manchester: J. Pratt, 1821). A facsimile of this broadside appears in the front matter of *C. P. Scott, 1846–1932: The Making of the "Manchester Guardian"* (London: Frederick Muller, 1946).

41. Nord, *Communities*, 5–7.

42. *On Saturday, the 5th of May, 1821.*

43. H. D. Nichols, "The *Guardian* before Scott," in *C. P. Scott, 1846–1932*, 19; Ayerst, *Manchester Guardian*, 63–4.

44. Mills, *Manchester Guardian*, 83; Ayerst, *Manchester Guardian*, 72.

45. Nichols, "*Guardian* before Scott," 19, 22–3, 27–8; Mills, *Manchester Guardian*, 84, 91–6; Ayerst, *Manchester Guardian*, 72–3, 96, 125–7.

46. Friedrich Engels, *The Condition of the Working Class in England in 1844*, trans. Florence Kelley Wischnewetsky (New York: J. W. Lovell, 1887). This book, first published in German in 1845, was not published in English translation until 1887. On Engels in Manchester, see Hunt, *Building Jerusalem*, 38–44.

47. Jeremy Bentham, "Of Publicity," in *The Works of Jeremy Bentham*, ed. John Bowring (Edinburgh: William Tait, 1843), vol. 2, 310–12; Lee, *Origins*, 23; Hampton, *Visions*, 8–9.

48. Nichols, "*Guardian* before Scott," 20–1.

49. Nord, *Communities*, 117, 137; Junger, *Becoming the Second City*, 17–20, 34–5.

50. On Chicago in its early booster era, see Cronon, *Nature's Metropolis*, chs 1–2; Einhorn, *Property Rules*, ch. 2; Pacyga, *Chicago*, ch. 1; and Miller, *City of the Century*, chs 3–4.

51. Klatt, *Chicago Journalism*, 16; Junger, *Becoming the Second City*, 29–36.

52. Dedication to John Bright, in Morley, *Life of Richard Cobden*, v.

53. Joseph Logsdon, *Horace White: Nineteenth Century Liberal* (Westport, Conn.: Greenwood, 1971), 142–3, 167, 173–5; Wendt, *Chicago Tribune*, 211–14; *Chicago Tribune*, August–September 1869, passim. See also Horace White, "Preface to First Edition," in M. Frederic Bastiat, *Sophisms of Protection* (New York: Putnam, 1877), xii.

54. Richard Digby-Junger, *The Journalist as Reformer: Henry Demarest Lloyd and "Wealth Against Commonwealth"* (Westport, Conn.: Greenwood Press, 1996), 23–4, 39–40; John L. Thomas, *Alternative America: Henry George, Edward Bellamy, Henry Demarest Lloyd and the Adversary Tradition* (Cambridge, Mass.: Harvard University Press, 1983), 23–4.

55. Logsdon, *Horace White*, 211–12, 238–9; Digby-Junger, *Journalist as Reformer*, 40.

56. Wendt, *Chicago Tribune*, 250–1, 271–95; Digby-Junger, *Journalist as Reformer*, 58–64; *Chicago Tribune*, December 30, 1881. See Henry Demarest Lloyd, "The Story of a Great Monopoly," *Atlantic*, March 1881, 317–34; Henry Demarest Lloyd, "The Political Economy of Seventy-Three Million Dollars," *Atlantic*, July 1882, 69–81; Henry Demarest Lloyd, "Making Bread Dear," *North American Review*, 86 (August 1883), 118–36; Henry Demarest Lloyd, "Lords of Industry," *North American Review*, 87 (June 1884), 535–53. These early magazine articles were collected after Lloyd's death in Henry Demarest Lloyd, *Lords of Industry* (New York: Putnam, 1910).

57. Wendt, *Chicago Tribune*, 271–4; John, *Network Nation*, 130–1, 149, 179–80. Lloyd's article "The Political Economy of Seventy-Three Million Dollars" is mainly about Jay Gould.

58. Nord, *Communities*, 117–18.

59. Logsdon, *Horace White*, 266–7, 273; Junger, *Becoming the Second City*, 25–6, 101–3, 106–8.

60. Nord, *Communities*, 137; *Chicago Tribune*, July 1877, passim.

61. Nord, *Communities*, 146–7, 153, 159, 161, 165.

62. On Kay and his 1832 report, see Hunt, *Building Jerusalem*, 13–15; and Briggs, *Victorian Cities*, 99.

63. Hunt, *Building Jerusalem*, 299–303.

64. Hunt, *Building Jerusalem*, 316; Platt, *Shock Cities*, 70–4. After 1870 Birmingham surpassed Manchester as the leading exemplar of "municipal socialism," under the charismatic Mayor Joseph Chamberlain. See Hunt, *Building Jerusalem*, ch. 8; and Briggs, *Victorian Cities*, ch. 5. See also Joseph Chamberlain, "Favorable Aspects of State Socialism," *North American Review*, 152 (May 1891): 534–48; and Julian Ralph, "The Best-Governed City in the World," *Monthly Magazine*, 81 (June 1890): 99–111.

65. Platt, *Shock Cities*, 224–6.

66. Ayerst, *Manchester Guardian*, 170.

67. Platt, *Shock Cities*, 320–9; Kidd, *Manchester*, 124–7; John C. Thresh, *An Inquiry into the Causes of Excessive Mortality in No. 1 District, Ancoats* (Manchester, England: Heywood, 1889). The first volume of another important statistical study—this one about London—also appeared in 1889. See Charles Booth, *Life and Labour of the People in London*, 9 vols (London: Macmillan, 1892–7).

68. L. T. Hobhouse, "Liberal and Humanist," in *C. P. Scott*, 85; Ayerst, *Manchester Guardian*, 255–6; Peter Clarke, *Liberals and Social Democrats* (Cambridge: Cambridge University Press, 1978), 63.

69. *Manchester Guardian*, August 27, September 2, September 6, 1889.

70. J. L. Hammond, "C. P. Scott, 1846–1932," in *C. P. Scott*, 40; J. L. Hammond, *C. P. Scott of the Manchester Guardian* (New York: Harcourt, Brace, 1934), 63, 72.

71. *Manchester Guardian*, October 3, 1893, November 18, 1893. See also Peter Weiler, *The New Liberalism: Liberal Social Theory in Great Britain, 1889–1914* (New York: Garland, 1982), 58–9.

72. James Robert Moore, "Progressive Pioneers: Manchester Liberalism, the Independent Labour Party, and Local Politics in the 1890s," *Historical Journal*, 44 (December 2001): 1004; James R. Moore, *The Transformation of Urban Liberalism: Party Politics and Urban Governance in Late Nineteenth-Century England* (Aldershot, UK: Ashgate, 2006), 172, 214.

73. L. T. Hobhouse, *The Labour Movement* (London: T. F. Unwin, 1893), 45–6; Ayerst, *Manchester Guardian*, 258–60. See also Peter Clarke, *Lancashire and the New Liberalism* (Cambridge: Cambridge University Press, 1971), 171–2.

74. Hobhouse, "Liberal and Humanist," 85–6.

75. Hammond, *C. P. Scott of the Manchester Guardian*, 72–4.

76. Searle, *Liberal Party*, 58–60; Clarke, *Liberals and Social Democrats*, 65; Rohan McWilliam, *Popular Politics in Nineteenth-Century England* (London: Routledge, 1998), 42–3, 67–8, 79.

77. L. T. Hobhouse, *Liberalism* (New York: Henry Holt, 1911), 86, 100; L. T. Hobhouse, *Democracy and Reaction* (London: T. F. Unwin, 1904), 214–17. See also J. A. Hobson, *The Crisis of Liberalism: New Issues of Democracy* (London: P. S. King & Son, 1909), 133–5.

78. Hobhouse, *Liberalism*, 98–9; Clarke, *Liberals and Social Democrats*, 63–6; Clarke, *Lancashire*, 170–3. See also Moore, *Transformation of Urban Liberalism*, ch. 9.

79. C. P. Scott, "The Function of the Press," *Political Quarterly*, 2 (1931): 59–60; Hobhouse, "Liberal and Humanist," 90. See also Hampton, *Visions*, ch. 3; and Mark Hampton, "The Press, Patriotism, and Public Discussion: C. P. Scott, the *Manchester Guardian*, and the Boer War, 1899–1902," *Historical Journal*, 44 (March 2001): 177–97.

80. *Manchester Guardian*, May 5, 1921; also in C. P. Scott, "The *Manchester Guardian*'s First Hundred Years," in *C. P. Scott*, 161. This maxim still appears at the top of the *Guardian*'s opinion section.

81. C. P. Scott, quoted in Hammond, *C. P. Scott of the Manchester Guardian*, 300. See also Clarke, *Lancashire*, 157. In 1964, three decades after Scott's death, the *Guardian* moved to London.

82. Platt, *Shock Cities*, 176–7, 188–9; Cronon, *Nature's Metropolis*, 249–50; Pacyga, *Chicago*, 105–6; Miller, *City of the Century*, 425–30.

83. Einhorn, *Property Rules*, 235–6; James L. Merriner, *Grafters and Goo Goos: Corruption and Reform in Chicago, 1833–2003* (Carbondale: Southern Illinois University Press, 2004), 39–41; Wendt, *Chicago Tribune*, 243–4.

84. *Chicago Tribune*, March 17, 1875.

85. Nord, *Communities*, 118; *Chicago Tribune*, March 16, 1876.

86. Wendt, *Chicago Tribune*, 264, 271–5; Digby-Junger, *Journalist as Reformer*, 61–70.

87. Lloyd, "Political Economy of Seventy-Three Million Dollars," 69, 72, 74–5.

88. Lloyd, "Making Bread Dear," 134; Lloyd, "Lords of Industry," 550–3. Lloyd admired Charles Francis Adams, Jr. and his idea that some businesses are "natural monopolies." See Thomas K. McCraw, *Prophets of Regulation: Charles Francis*

Adams, Louis D. Brandeis, James M. Landis, Alfred Kahn (Cambridge, Mass.: Harvard University Press, 1984), 7–10; and Rodgers, *Atlantic Crossings*, 107–8.

89. Digby-Junger, *Journalist as Reformer*, 68–70; Thomas, *Alternative America*, 147–8. On the Daily Newspaper Association of Chicago, see Jon Bekken, "'The Most Vindictive and Most Vengeful Power': Labor Confronts the Chicago Newspaper Trust," *Journalism History*, 18 (1992): 11–17.

90. Pacyga, *Chicago*, chs 3–4; Miller, *City of the Century*, ch. 13. See also Carl Smith, *Urban Disorder and the Shape of Belief: The Great Chicago Fire, the Haymarket Bomb, and the Model Town of Pullman* (Chicago: University of Chicago Press, 1995); and Richard Schneirov, *Labor and Urban Politics: Class Conflict and the Origins of Modern Liberalism in Chicago, 1864–1897* (Urbana: University of Illinois Press, 1998).

91. Junger, *Becoming the Second City*, ch. 4; Klatt, *Chicago Journalism*, ch. 2.

92. Nord, *Communities*, 138–9.

93. Nord, *Communities*, 140. In his first major magazine article, Lloyd argued for arbitration in railroad labor disputes. See Lloyd, "The Story of a Great Monopoly," 44.

94. Nord, *Communities*, 141–2; *Chicago Tribune*, May 6, 1886, May 7, 1886.

95. Nord, *Communities*, 142.

96. Nord, *Communities*, 143–5.

97. Lloyd, "The Story of a Great Monopoly," 43–4. Medill endorsed some of Lloyd's proposals for national railroad regulation, and he favored federal ownership of the telegraph. See Wendt, *Chicago Tribune*, 262–4; and John, *Network Nation*, 130–1.

98. Nord, *Communities*, 158; *Chicago Tribune*, February 9, 1890 (quote), March 19, 1894, August 5, 1894. See also David Paul Nord, *Newspapers and New Politics: Midwestern Municipal Reform, 1890–1900* (Ann Arbor, Mich.: UMI Research Press, 1981), ch. 4.

99. Platt, *Shock Cities*, 175; Nord, *Communities*, 152, 158; *Chicago Tribune*, January 4, 1895, March 5, 1895.

100. Nord, *Communities*, 161; Nord, *Newspapers and New Politics*, 90. See also Georg Leidenberger, *Chicago's Progressive Alliance: Labor and the Bid for Public Streetcars* (DeKalb: Northern Illinois University Press, 2006), chs 2–3.

101. *Chicago Tribune*, December 14, 1890; Nord, *Communities*, 159; Nord, *Newspapers and New Politics*, 141.

102. Delos E. Wilcox, "The American Newspaper: A Study in Social Psychology," *Annals*, 16 (July 1900): 56.

103. Rodgers, *Atlantic Crossings*, 112.

104. Nord, *Communities*, 119–20; Charles H. Dennis, *Victor Lawson: His Time and His Work* (Chicago: University of Chicago Press, 1935), chs 9–10. For a general discussion of newspaper business practices in this era, see Gerald J. Baldasty, *The Commercialization of the News in the Nineteenth Century* (Madison: University of Wisconsin Press, 1992).

105. Nord, *Communities*, 121; *Chicago Daily News*, April 1, 1876, April 17, 1876, May 10, 1876. See also Stone, *Fifty Years*, 53–4, 152–4.

106. Nord, *Communities*, 123–4, 138, 144, 156–8; Nord, *Newspapers and New Politics*, 41–4, 92, 141. On Lawson's dealings with the *Daily News*'s own unions, see Bekken, "'Most Vindictive,'" 14.
107. Smythe, *Gilded Age Press*, 74, 82–4. See also Gerald J. Baldasty, *E. W. Scripps and the Business of Newspapers* (Urbana: University of Illinois Press, 1999).
108. Nord, *Newspapers and New Politics*, 33–4, 97–9, 141; Julian S. Rammelkamp, *Pulitzer's Post-Dispatch, 1878–1883* (Princeton, NJ: Princeton University Press, 1967), 10–11, 82–5, 236, 273; James McGrath Morris, *Pulitzer: A Life in Politics, Print, and Power* (New York: Harper, 2010), 190–1.
109. Smythe, *Gilded Age Press*, ch. 6. See also George Juergens, *Joseph Pulitzer and the New York World* (Princeton, NJ: Princeton University Press, 1966).
110. *New York World*, May 10, 1888; Morris, *Pulitzer*, 219, 271, 296–7.
111. Joseph Pulitzer Papers, Butler Library, Columbia University, New York, 1886–7 folders.
112. Griffiths, *Fleet Street*, 116–26; Joel H. Wiener, "How New Was the New Journalism?" in *Papers for the Millions*, ed. Wiener, 47–72; Laurel Brake, "The Old Journalism and the New: Forms of Cultural Production in London in the 1880s," in *Papers for the Millions*, ed. Wiener, 1–24; John Goodbody, "The *Star*: Its Role in the Rise of the New Journalism," in *Papers for the Millions*, ed. Wiener, 143–63; Ray Boston, "W. T. Stead and Democracy by Journalism," in *Papers for the Millions*, ed. Wiener, 91–106.
113. W. T. Stead, "Character Sketch: Mr. T. P. O'Connor, M.P.," *Review of Reviews*, November 1902, 478–9.
114. W. T. Stead, "Character Sketch: The 'Pall Mall Gazette,'" *Review of Reviews*, February 1893, 153–5; Stead, *Americanization*, 110–13; Raymond L. Schults, *Crusader in Babylon: W. T. Stead and the Pall Mall Gazette* (Lincoln: University of Nebraska Press, 1972), chs 2 and 5.
115. "Prospectus," *Star*, January 17, 1888; Stead, "Character Sketch: Mr. T. P. O'Connor," 479; O'Connor, "New Journalism," 423, 434.
116. *Pall Mall Gazette*, October 16, 1883. On the "Bitter Cry" series, see Schults, *Crusader in Babylon*, 49–57; and Drew Gray, *London's Shadows: The Dark Side of the Victorian City* (London: Continuum, 2010), 119–23.
117. *Pall Mall Gazette*, October 16, 1883, November 5, 1883, November 7, 1883.
118. *Pall Mall Gazette*, October 16, 1883.
119. Goodbody, "The *Star*," 143–55; Alfred F. Havighurst, *Radical Journalist: H. W. Massingham, 1860–1924* (Cambridge: Cambridge University Press, 1974), 18–28.
120. *Star* (London), May 6, 1920; Havighurst, *Radical Journalist*, 27–8.
121. Albert Shaw, "William T. Stead," *American Review of Reviews*, June 1912, 689–98; Stone, *Fifty Years*, 201–2; Rodgers, *Atlantic Crossings*, 132–3. Shaw's article is a remembrance: Stead died on the Titanic, April 15, 1912.
122. W. T. Stead, *If Christ Came To Chicago!* (Chicago: Laird & Lee, 1894), part 5, ch. 6. Quotes are on pp. 408–9.
123. Schults, *Crusader in Babylon*, 55–6; Miller, *City of the Century*, 533–9.
124. Albert Shaw, *Municipal Government in Great Britain* (New York: Century, 1895), 6–8.
125. Shaw, *Municipal Government*, 3.

5

International News in the Age of Empire

James R. Brennan[1]

The gathering and distribution of international news became a global business during the nineteenth century. Dramatic rivalries between major metropolitan newspapers seeking scoops during periods of world crisis, although famous, were rare. International news was expensive to collect and transmit, and direct competition favored only the deep-pocketed in the short run and no one in the long run. Less visible but more consequential were the cooperative institutional arrangements that protected and subsidized news from market competition. Cooperation in the production of news was the norm. These contractual arrangements were a form of technology that, like telegraphy and mechanical composition, aided news production during this period.[1]

Newspaper subscribers and advertisers paid for most of the news produced by Britain and America during this period, including international news that forms the focus of this chapter. But the methods and systems of payment were products of negotiation, conflict, and collusion. First-movers were often rewarded, as production costs and communication bottlenecks for international news generated high barriers to entry for newcomers. Between 1840 and 1918, news was increasingly paid for and supplied by international news agencies, which benefited from economies of scale. Two distinct models of international newsgathering emerged in Britain and the United States, each anchored in its distinctive political economy. For Britain, international news was originally the product of London newspaper interests, which were deeply intertwined with, and at times indistinguishable from, the information and analysis produced by and for Britain's Foreign Office. To counter London's dominance, the country's provincial press and its leading international news agency, Reuters, pioneered a model of newsgathering predicated on cooperation. For newspaper publishers in the United States, where the content of international news was less visibly defined by how it related to the state's imperial and diplomatic interests than in Britain, the cost of gathering international news could be spread over a larger domestic market, but the size of the American market raised the costs of coordinating cooperation. The story of how the AP became the country's main international news provider reflects the high coordination costs associated with establishing cooperation in the United States.

This chapter also examines three developments that shaped the news business during this period: differing strategies to manage the problem of exclusivity; market segmentation and the innovation of novel genres of international news; and the construction of imperial and anti-colonial news networks. Managing exclusivity presented a recurrent dilemma in the cooperative sharing of news. News organizations recognized that expanding access to their news reports spread the costs of collection more widely, yet they simultaneously recognized that maintaining exclusivity in news distribution increased the value of the news reports to those in receipt of them. News outlets excluded from receiving the news reports patronized rival news suppliers. By controlling which news outlets received their news, news associations regulated competition for international news.[2] Ambitious latecomers, however, could sidestep established cooperative arrangements by reinventing the form and content of international news provided they had enough money to do so. Well-capitalized metropolitan dailies crafted new genres of international news during the second half of the nineteenth century. They sought to make news from around the world more accessible to a mass readership. Foreign correspondents became actors in a story of growing Anglo-American power abroad. This growth in power, particularly in British colonies, was assisted by imperial propaganda efforts of governments and white settlers to generate political solidarities. This, in turn, moved anti-colonial activists to question imperial rule through similarly global networks of news circulation.

DOMESTIC FOUNDATIONS OF THE INTERNATIONAL NEWS BUSINESS, 1840–1880

The distinctive features of the domestic market in Britain and the United States shaped the way in which news from abroad was supplied in the two countries. During the 1830s and 1840s, newspaper publishers in growing American urban centers changed from small to medium-sized enterprises.[3] The costs of starting a newspaper remained relatively low. In 1835, James Gordon Bennett required only $500 to start the *New York Herald*. The *Herald* was the first paper in the United States to sell for a penny. During the 1830s and 1840s, however, most newspapers in the United States principally provided national news.[4] Press coverage was frequently partisan. In Britain during the 1830s, the Radical press flourished. Weekly Radical provincial newspapers thrived by evading stamp duty. Although they were prohibited without a stamp from circulating by post, they were also comparatively inexpensive to produce and were circulated by volunteers. An independent-minded editor usually controlled and produced the content of these Radical publications.[5] In Britain and the United States, among metropolitan newspapers with large circulations, the growing costs incurred through wide adoption of steam-powered rotary presses had yet to dislodge the influence of the "sovereign editor" over newspaper content.

In the decades that preceded the penetration of the telegraph and rise of mass-circulation dailies, the political economy of American news was based on commercial foundations of subscriptions and advertisements, supplemented by government and party subventions. In Jacksonian America, newspaper subventions came from three sources: franking and postal exchange privileges; direct political patronage from local, state, and national governments through lucrative printing contracts, editorial jobs, and subscriptions; and cooperative news-sharing between partisan newspapers, in what was termed the "party-press system."[6] This last practice was a postal exchange system in which party papers were exchanged to take advantage of free newspaper postage, creating what was in effect a national partisan news service comprised of clipped and pasted news items from across the country. Between 1820 and 1846, roughly half of the news in the nation's newspapers was clipped from other papers. William Lloyd Garrison's abolitionist newspaper *The Liberator* (1831–65) wielded influence not through its numbers of direct subscribers, who amounted to only four hundred, but through its exchange lists with two hundred other newspapers.[7] In Britain, the stamp duty—which a newspaper had to pay to circulate by post—ensured that the "respectable" press would be both narrow in readership and closely monitored by government. During the Napoleonic wars, the stamp duty acted as a lever of political control and patronage. The duty accounted for nearly two thirds of the *Times*'s total expenses, while party leaders in Westminster secretly paid the paper to offset the amount the duty consumed. When the paper turned down direct Treasury loans in 1803, it had inaugurated its ostentatious campaign for "Fourth Estate"-style independence.[8] Before 1850, direct payouts from government and political parties were critical sources of income for smaller newspapers across Britain. The Radical "unstamped" press lacked access to postal circulation, but was compensated by the price advantage afforded to it in comparison to considerably more expensive "stamped" newspapers like the *Times*.[9]

Major technological and political changes altered this arrangement in the 1850s. Leading newspapers were defined by their ability to acquire exclusive scoops. Speed of transmission often determined who had the news first. Before the telegraph, obtaining the news first in the United States was often as much a matter of technique as capital. Publishers devised ever more inventive ways to rush to shore the news reports arriving aboard transatlantic steamships. James Gordon Bennett (*New York Herald*) and Daniel Craig (*Boston Daily Mail*), for example, used a relay system of carrier pigeons, which led frustrated rivals to take shots at their competitors' avian advantages.[10] The telegraph raised the costs of acquiring exclusives, and thereby magnified the potential wastefulness of duplicated reporting for newspapers. As telegraph companies consolidated during the 1850s, New York City dailies similarly combined to form an association, the New York Associated Press (NYAP), to negotiate exclusive contracts with telegraph providers; this arrangement provided the foundation for a new "national news apparatus."[11] Craig, who was appointed NYAP's director in 1851, locked in these advantages by having NYAP serve as a clearinghouse for domestic and international news, offering Midwestern newspapers an affordable international news report, while pressuring reluctant subscribers with threats to withhold reports or to sell them to rivals at discounted rates. The association's subsequent history underscores the main strategic dilemma that faced news cooperatives—either to adopt an inclusive policy to spread both news and its costs more widely, or to adopt an exclusive policy to increase the value of news reports to members. NYAP alternated between both strategies, but those newspapers that found themselves excluded from NYAP embraced or created rival associations.[12]

Outside the Northeast, New York's predominance—premised on its seaboard position and hub of financial and telegraphic activity—generated resentment. After touring western cities in 1851, following a loss of NYAP subscribers, Craig found that most editors regarded their telegraphic news expenditure as they would "regard a contribution to an unjust and unlawful tax-gatherer—a species of imposition which it is not quite safe to resist."[13] By the late 1850s, NYAP items occupied at least two columns daily in many American newspapers. After further consolidating their position during the Civil War, the NYAP faced a new wave of rivals. In 1866, Bennett's *New York Herald* attempted to launch its own international news business, while newspapers in the western part of the country formed a rival Western Associated Press (WAP). Western Union sought to establish its own news service, but abandoned the idea to avoid congressional scrutiny and threats of nationalization. In 1867, the NYAP struck a wary truce with the WAP and with Western Union that lasted until the early 1890s.[14] A collusive relationship based on powerful mutual interests developed that further entrenched their respective dominant positions. If the NYAP patronized Western Union exclusively, Western Union benefited. A single combined news service reduced transmission costs for Western Union by relieving it of having to transmit multiple reports across its network.[15] In return, NYAP users paid on average 6.6 cents per message in 1870; non-press users paid 71 cents.[16] Yet even at these favorable rates, Western Union consumed three quarters of NYAP-WAP's revenues.[17]

In Britain, state regulatory changes more visibly affected the news business. The 1855 abolition of newspaper stamp duty, or "taxes on knowledge" as its opponents termed it, helped to create conditions for mass-circulation newspapers. A series of interrelated developments soon followed—lower newsstand and subscription prices, increased newspaper sales, and the invention of new printing press technologies such as rotary offset lithography and linotype.[18] Between 1858 and 1914, the number of newspapers increased from 151 to 478 in London, and from 274 to 2,205 across Britain and Ireland.[19] The abolition of the stamp duty coincided with a shift toward newspapers that sought to cater to middle-class readerships.[20] The first beneficiary of the post-stamp duty dispensation was the *Telegraph*, founded in 1855; by 1862 it had a daily circulation of 140,000.[21] The *Times* had accounted for three quarters of all London newspaper circulation in 1855, but its circulation rapidly fell behind its new rival. By 1876, the *Telegraph* had reached a circulation of 250,000, the largest of any newspaper in the world.[22] The decades following the stamp duty's abolition witnessed rising readerships, rising profitability, and rising costs in starting a newspaper. The costs to launch a London daily rose from £20,000 in 1855 to £50,000 in 1867; and from £150,000 in 1870 to £300,000 by 1906–8.[23]

The nationalization of telegraphy in Britain leveled the playing field between London and provincial newspapers. The first mover to collect and distribute foreign news in Britain was Reuters, established in 1851 to conduct a centralized "wire service" to distribute copy to provincial papers and thereby avoid wasteful duplication costs that these papers might otherwise have to bear individually.[24] Reuters secured exclusive rights to sell international news to the Electric and International Telegraph Company, which resold the news to the provincial press. Reuters retained rights to sell directly to newspapers published in London.[25] Key elements of this arrangement survived after the Post Office purchased the country's domestic telegraph lines in 1868. In 1868, provincial newspaper publishers anxious to take control of their own news supply, and with encouragement from the Post Office, formed an inclusive cooperative called the Press Association (PA). Members of the association benefited from the reduction in costs that cooperation produced. The PA signed a ten-year contract with Reuters in 1870 for exclusive rights to sell Reuters' foreign news outside London. In return, the PA paid Reuters a £3,000 annual subscription (£8,000 after 1884) and granted Reuters exclusive rights to sell the PA's news reports abroad. This relationship restricted Reuters' ability to develop a domestic news service, but also enabled both to counter rivals effectively, such as the short-lived Dalziel News Agency. By 1889, 160 British dailies in the PA enjoyed an affordable Reuters news service that was in effect subsidized by London newspapers, each of which had to pay £1,600 for the same Reuters subscription, or nearly a fifth the rate paid by the entire PA.[26] Wealthier London newspapers resented Reuters for its favorable treatment of provincial rivals, and because "the agency functioned to minimize the advantages of substantial independent reportorial strength overseas for any given newspaper."[27] In practice, the so-called "advantages" that London newspapers enjoyed in overseas reporting were redeployed rather than minimized. Reuters provided London newspapers with defensive coverage of international news that enabled them to invest individually in more specialized reporting.

INVENTING INTERNATIONAL NEWS, 1840-1880

In the American press, international news dropped precipitously following independence in 1776. Newspaper content underwent a national westward reorientation. In 1705, foreign news comprised 80 percent of the *Boston News-Letter*; in 1856 it consumed 27 percent of the *Boston Post*. In the 1830s, national rather than international news provided the core content of the New York-centered American penny press. Domestic news items appealed to a great mass of readers in the growing metropolis and in turn convinced local advertisers to purchase space in newspapers as a way in which to market their goods.[28] Timely international news declared a paper's prestige but not necessarily its profitability. During the 1830s and 1840s, James Gordon Bennett's *New York Herald* pioneered international newsgathering through a network of stringers. These efforts distinguished the *Herald* from other penny-press publications and positioned it to attract upmarket readers who viewed international news coverage as a mark of excellence.[29] Horace Greeley's more genteel *New York Tribune* (established in 1841) outpaced the *Herald* by placing a premium on top journalists. The *Tribune* boasted the period's most prestigious roster of foreign correspondents, which included Henry James, Margaret Fuller, Karl Marx, and George Washburn Smalley. Smalley pioneered the concept of the functioning foreign bureau during his years in London.[30]

As a recognizable genre, international news—as opposed to the mere reporting of international events—had been pioneered by the *Times*, whose international coverage was primarily concerned with the "general course of diplomatic activity and general state of British overseas interests, wherever and whatever they might be."[31] In practice this meant reliance on a network of correspondents, invariably based in capital cities—the *Times*'s first foreign bureau was established in Paris in 1848—with access to impressive diplomatic contacts from which most of its information came. International news was first introduced to the *Times* to lighten the paper from the tedium of Parliamentary reporting. The demand for international news grew in tandem with British global influence during the mid-nineteenth century. As in the United States, timely news exclusives were a top priority—the *Times* spent as much as £10,000 a year on overland mail costs before the advent of telegraphy.[32] Telegraphy imposed considerable additional costs. In 1857, the *Times* quickly realized its financial vulnerability to the new technology when the paper paid £5,000 for telegrams to maintain adequate coverage of the Indian Mutiny.[33] As Britain's leading provider of international news, the *Times* also had political influence. The *Times* sent the first dedicated war correspondent, William Howard Russell, to the Crimean War (1853–6). Russell made his reputation reporting the graphic experience of soldiers and criticizing the decisions of military leadership. In part through Russell's visceral reporting, the *Times* gained a powerful voice that enabled its editorials to shape government policy. Breakfasting with Lord Palmerston on his return from Crimea, Russell was disconcerted to be asked by the Prime Minister what the famous reporter would have done had he been commander-in-chief of the army.[34] Lord John Russell considered the power wielded by the *Times* with regard to "the most secret affairs of the State . . . mortifying, humiliating, and incomprehensible."[35] Indeed, repeal of the stamp duty in 1855 was partly designed to clip the newspaper's wings—the repeal removed an expensive barrier (the stamp) to national distribution by mail that had afforded the *Times* an effective national monopoly for decades. Abolition of the stamp encouraged competition.[36]

Owing to its more diplomatically connected staff and lengthier dispatches, the *Times* retained its influential niche in international news reporting and commentary for several decades after the advent of international telegraphy. But telegraphy had widened press participation in international news, and further segmented the newspaper market by delivering a new genre of international news reporting. The high expense of telegraphy intensified the distinction between short-item or spot "reporting" and lengthier "appreciating" (interpretive commentary), which was rooted in parliamentary reporting but expanded with the expansion of gathering international news by telegraph.[37] The leading provider of a shorter and more modular international news report designed precisely to widen press participation in international news was Reuters. The company owed its early successes abroad to its exclusive contracts with cable companies, as well as "to its ability to plug in to existing networks of merchants in Europe and the Empire and tap them for news."[38] During the 1860s and 1870s, Reuters followed the progress of transoceanic cables, opening offices in Alexandria, Bombay, Cape Town, and Sydney.[39] Russell's letters from Crimea had taken up to twenty-two days to reach London, and the long personal dispatch could not convey "breaking news" like the telegraphed message. For leading newspapers, access to breaking international news could not be ignored, and Reuters' service became a necessary if defensive product for newspapers to receive. In 1858, even the *Times*, which had haughtily rejected earlier overtures from Reuters, reluctantly subscribed to the agency's service of foreign telegrams to supplement the discursive dispatches it received from its far-flung correspondents.[40] Reuters offered a "situationer" service of expansive explanatory pieces, but "hard news," reported in Reuters' short and factual style, remained its principal news product.[41]

As the network of international telegraph cables expanded, newspapers increasingly relied on telegraphy to gather foreign news. Expensive transmission costs kept messages short. The advent of "cablese"—the truncated language of cabled news reporting—did not give birth to "objective reporting" so much as it sharpened divisions of journalistic labor. Bennett's *New York Herald*, the earliest and most aggressive American investor in transatlantic cabled news, relied on its foreign news editor "to make every five words a hundred in print" by converting curt cables into a "magniloquent verbosity" of plausible detail and imagination.[42] The number of the world's telegraphic transmissions rose from 29 million in 1868 to 329 million by 1900.[43] Costs dropped dramatically—the press rate per word of North Atlantic cable traffic fell from $10 in 1866 to $0.75 by 1884.[44] As rates dropped, newspapers and agencies increased the quantity of cabled matter.[45] Like other capital-intensive industries of the age, the global telegraph system developed through a mixture of competition, cooperation, and collusion between international cable companies.[46] Likewise, in the 1860s, Reuters, Wolff (Germany), and Havas (France) formed a cartel agreement, the so-called "Ring Combination," pursuant to which the agencies allocated to each other geographic regions of the world in which they could sell their news reports exclusively. Press barons, such as James Gordon Bennett, Jr., decried the "telegraph monopoly ring" as an affront to competition in newsgathering.[47] Several short-lived news agencies challenged the "Ring Combination," but none enjoyed enduring success, excepting the American-based United Press (established in 1907) and, to a lesser extent, William Randolph Hearst's International News Service (established in 1909). The members of the "Ring Combination" enjoyed first-mover advantages that deterred the establishment of directly competing organizations, but there was room for alternative news services that appealed to differing demands and sectors of the newspaper market. Members of the news agency cartel shared their news with each other, which reduced the costs incurred in gathering news and increased the quantity of news available to subscribers at a fraction of the price it cost to collect. Combination had the disadvantage of making each news agency dependent on one another.[48] News reports reflected the national biases and political priorities of the main members. Variable quality in the news reports of the several members of the cartel created opportunities for rival services to meet unmet demand.

INTO AFRICA: NEWS, PROPAGANDA, AND EMPIRE

During the nineteenth century, international news reporting in Britain's newspapers grew in tandem with its expanding Empire. During the mid-nineteenth century, the norms and conventions of local British settlers and officials shaped imperial news coverage. For example, the alarmist Cape newspaper reporting of the Xhosa cattle killing in 1857, which badly caricatured Xhosa motives and actions in outrageously racist ways even by mid-Victorian standards, became the authoritative account in British newspapers.[49] Newspapers in Britain and across the white dominions of Australia, Canada, New Zealand, and South Africa labored to create and celebrate "Britishness," while pro-imperial journalists in search of work moved freely between metropole and dominion, almost like "roving actors."[50] These developments piqued interest in international news among businessmen and consumers, and coincided with the rise of so-called "new imperialism." According to this view of imperialism, British "civilization" was unsuited to African and Asian peoples. Hardening racial attitudes coincided with an increase in the quantity of news and other information available for public consumption, and a quickening of the pace with which it was circulated. As the historian John Darwin vividly put it, "a tidal wave of print formed the backwash of empire." The literate urban consumer, "with new tastes and interests shaped by marketing and the printed word, was a key figure in the remaking of late-Victorian society."[51]

In the second half of the nineteenth century, the metropolis and the wider world were being created and discovered. Victorian readers could closely follow the "opening up" of the African continent. Earlier in the century, reporting Africa had been an odd mixture of business reporting, abolitionist propaganda, and scientific exploration. By 1870, resources to finance African newsgathering had shifted and newspaper publishers eclipsed the Royal Geographical Society in setting the information-gathering agenda. In a media gimmick event that came to symbolize the absurd peak of Victorian high manners on the "dark continent," James Gordon Bennett, Jr., in partnership with the *Daily Telegraph*, commissioned Henry Morton Stanley to find David Livingstone. Stanley's quest marked the apogee of Bennett's "new era in journalism,"[52] in which celebrity, caricature, and open-ended promises of future commercial potential shifted the British reading public's view of Africa.[53] Livingstone's quasi-canonization and burial at Westminster Abbey after his death in 1874 inspired British (and American) readers to bring Christianity, commerce, and civilization to the still-uncharted swathes of sub-Saharan Africa. "Africa" formed a reportorial blank canvas upon which journalists could wax grandiloquent about the continent's potential, while hard-headed businessmen sought ways to secure reliable information regarding commodities. The instrumental value of news developed alongside major infrastructural investment. Sub-Saharan Africa was the last place to be connected by submarine telegraph to Europe. Driven by the pursuit of diamonds and gold, between 1879 and 1887 the (British) Eastern Associated Company of John Pender laid cables that connected the continent. Only in South Africa were precious minerals discovered in abundant quantity, and few people aside from the "Randlords" could afford cable fees of $40 per word from Durban to London. British loans and the guarantee of government cable traffic had broadly subsidized Pender's network in Africa, to secure military communication and security needs demanded by the expanding British Empire.[54]

Reporters increasingly became part of the story. The fame and fortune that Stanley gained from his Africa trips during the 1870s raised the visibility and status of foreign correspondents. Where reporters for the *Times* and other newspapers had previously often been anonymous, Stanley became a household name. Anonymity had privileged the authority of the paper over its correspondents.[55] Foreign correspondents had already enjoyed the highest status within the journalism profession, but many had to make do with piecework and short-term contracts.[56] The first professional association of foreign reporters, the Council of Foreign Press, was founded in Paris in 1879; the more enduring Foreign Press Association was founded in London in 1888 and helped to establish a diplomatic credentialing process.[57] The field continued to attract more than its share of adventurers and chancers in Africa. During the 1880s and 1890s, as the scramble for Africa reached a fevered pitch, international newsgathering increasingly blurred popular entertainment with hard-nosed diplomatic reporting. In 1884–5, the failure of the Anglo-Egyptian occupation of Khartoum, during which messianic Muslim rebels murdered General Charles "Chinese" Gordon, marked not only the success of a local Islamist rebellion, but also one of Victorian Britain's greatest real-time dramas, for which Reuters demanded greater subscription rates from its London-based newspaper customers to match the high costs of international coverage.[58]

DOMESTIC FOUNDATIONS: COMMERCIAL NEWS IN THE AGE OF THE PUBLISHER, 1880–1900

In the late nineteenth century, the American and British appetite for international news underwent radical transformations, which reflected the rise of retail consumer culture that overturned the existing business model of newspapers in both countries. Newspaper circulation increased enormously, as did the costs of starting a newspaper. Marked by the industry-standard adoption of linotype in the 1890s, production costs increased roughly tenfold from previous compositor techniques, yet this was offset, indeed it was driven, by massive increases in circulation.[59] Newspaper start-up costs rose twentyfold between 1850 and 1900, in conjunction with concentration of press ownership.[60] The tastes of a growing mass readership altered the supply of international news. For example, in 1883, Reuters instructed its reporters to focus on all types of sensational disturbances "[i]n consequence of the increased attention paid by the press to disaster &c."[61]

For the *Times* of London, long-reputed the world leader in international news, these were decades of comparative decline and displacement. The paper had struggled to retain its leadership in international news during a period when its circulation fell from between 60,000 and 70,000 in the late 1870s to 35,000 in 1899.[62] In both form and content, international news in the *Times* remained linked to the reporting and concerns of the Foreign Office. In 1891, the *Times* appointed its former correspondent Donald Mackenzie Wallace to lead the paper's newly established foreign department. The foreign department housed an extensive library and "Intelligence Department" to provide reporters and editors with greater historical and political context than their less bookish competitors could muster. International news in the *Times* primarily concerned diplomacy in Europe.[63] Wallace, a diplomat rather than a journalist by training and temperament, instructed reporters "to put themselves into intimate relations with ministers, to ascertain the policy of governments and opinions of influential persons."[64] Wallace hired his reporters directly from the ranks of the Colonial Office.[65] Through this approach, the *Times* carved out a notably non-sensationalist niche for international news that catered to the interests and tastes of political elites and cosmopolitan-minded professionals.

The market in international news was growing and segmenting. Alfred Harmsworth's *Daily Mail* (1896) best embodied the industry's shift to increased volume, brevity, range, and accessibility in newspaper content. He charged a halfpenny when most others charged a penny (and the *Times* charged three pence), while announcing circulation figures on the paper's masthead, which surpassed one million during the heyday of the South African War (1899–1902). In comparison to the bold headlines and graphics of New York papers, the *Daily Mail* looked conservatively presented, but in its lively yet brief treatment of news, descending from high politics to the trivial, Harmsworth's paper won over Britain's lower middle class, which previously had found dailies uninteresting and expensive. The key virtues of the *Daily Mail* were brevity and simplicity, presented in a layout through which the busy reader could gain an outline of the day's news in sixty seconds.[66] Harmsworth produced a newspaper that was both populist and aspirational. As he put it, the *Daily Mail* was for people "who like to think they earned £1,000 a year."[67] Although newspapers such as W. T. Stead's *Pall Mall Gazette* were animated by the spirit of reform, Harmsworth's newspapers were more representative of the British press, which lacked the emotional involvement and muckraking zeal of American popular journalism.[68] The *Daily Mail* covered a wide range of subject matter. As Harmsworth observed, previous journalism dealt only with a few aspects of life, "[w]hat we did was to extend its purview to life as a whole."[69] High-minded and self-styled "Fourth Estate" figures such as C. P. Scott believed

Harmsworth's paper corroded the quality of British political discourse, yet paradoxically Harmsworth was, by dint of his enormous wealth and comparative detachment from party politics, the "only truly independent newspaperman of the day."[70] Within a few years of its founding, the *Daily Mail* had created a British overseas news organization third only to the *Times* and Reuters. Operating with the conviction that international news could serve as a staple of popular journalism, the newspaper lavished attention on the British Empire in a signature jingoist and monarchist fashion.[71]

The American newspaper was always a marriage between a profit-seeking business and an influence-seeking political enterprise. Yet by the late nineteenth century, "the business side began to dominate the marriage."[72] In the 1880s, Joseph Pulitzer's *New York World* initiated the practice of selling advertising space on the basis of certifiable circulation, which helped to usher in a tighter relationship between space-hungry advertisers and revenue-hungry newspapers. The ratio of editorial matter to advertising changed over the 1880s from 70:30 to 50:50, while advertising revenues grew from 44 percent of total newspaper income in 1880 to 55 percent in 1900.[73] Pulitzer's newspaper also pioneered a new reportorial division of labor, between "legmen" who covered events and "rewrite men" who transformed details into story form—much like Britain's emerging division between "reporter" and "subeditor" that developed in the 1890s.[74] The presentation of news reflected these shifts in production. The inverted pyramid, a system of ordering facts in descending order of importance, grew more popular during the latter half of the nineteenth century. This was encouraged in part by the cost of telegrams, which encouraged brevity and which broke down developing stories into smaller and more frequent segments.[75] Demand for steady editorial copy led to the creation of "beats" and the "space system" to scoop up probable "metro" news events, planned events, and self-marketing. Newspapers could not afford to wait for news to happen, and increasingly sought out "lifestyle" items that could better link advertisers with consumers.[76]

CONSOLIDATING INTERNATIONAL NEWS IN THE BRITISH EMPIRE AND UNITED STATES, 1880–1902

Demand for international news and the quantity sent via cable spiked during periods of armed conflict, but its costs were distributed unevenly. Telegraph companies were generally the chief economic beneficiaries of reporting foreign wars.[77] Wire services like Reuters tended to spend more than they earned during times of war. Subscription income was largely fixed but the costs of coverage increased. A popular slogan at Reuters was that "the boring years paid for the exciting years." Such were the costs of excitement that in 1885 Reuters introduced a war surcharge, which added 50 percent to subscription charges to make its revenue more responsive to fluctuations in the costs of newsgathering.[78] Reuters had not grown rich on supplying international news. Between 1869 and 1915, Reuters' news business generated on average less than 2 percent of total company profits.[79] Other services, in particular its global remittance service, proved far more lucrative. "I am sorry to have again to make the admission that news gathering and distribution is an unremunerative business," Baron Reuter reported to shareholders in 1908, and added that without these other services, "we could not possibly afford for news telegrams what we at present spend."[80] Government protection and favorable contracts, particularly within the Asian and African regions of the British Empire, did provide profitable news markets for Reuters. The agency received limited but important subsidies overseas, including an inflated subscription from the Khedive of Egypt.[81] India proved the most profitable part of the Empire for Reuters, owing first to its favorable subscription terms with the Raj, and later to its control over the supply of domestic news in India.[82] Reuters in effect charged the colonies and dominions of the British Empire to supply international news to the British provincial press. By 1919, the South African press paid Reuters £24,000 for its news subscription, the London press paid £22,500, and the PA continued to pay a mere £8,000.[83]

Over the late nineteenth century, a domestic nationwide news system took shape in the United States through the creation and sale of exclusive regional memberships, which were effectively franchises, in contrast to the inclusive practices of Britain's PA. The two major American news associations, the NYAP and WAP, leveraged their size to lease cable lines at more favorable rates to provide large and reliable daily services to subscribers. The quality and seeming indispensability of their news product enabled the allied NYAP-WAP to sell exclusive regional franchises to newspapers for huge sums.[84] Excluded local rivals in turn combined to establish the United Press Association (UPA) in the 1880s, which provided a less timely and more error-prone service. This also generated wasteful expenses for newspapers by duplicating much of the NYAP-WAP product. Peace between the rivals was reached through a secret stock-sharing arrangement between leading figures in the UPA and NYAP.[85] The arrangement was revealed in 1891 as a scheme by which NYAP and WAP directors had conspired to dilute the costs of UPA copy, which was composed of pilfered Reuters material combined with rewritten copy from its own subsidiary, the Cable News Company. The copy was then sold as a product below the price of what NYAP-WAP were required to charge, with stock pool owners taking the difference. In 1893, a reformed Associated Press of Illinois (today's AP) finally put paid to UPA by striking an exclusive ten-year contract with Reuters.[86] Before this, the United States had been a sort of neutral territory for the cartel of Reuters, Havas, and Wolff, the so-called

"Ring Combination." Several agencies jointly exploited the United States, but Reuters, which supplied an English-language service, took the lead in transmitting news and brokering exclusive arrangements with NYAP and WAP. The 1893 agreement made the AP a junior partner of the Ring Combination. Pursuant to its agreement with the European agencies, the AP held exclusive rights to distribute in the United States news supplied by the Combination. In turn, the AP paid the Combination an annual subscription and provided other members of the cartel with its news reports for distribution throughout the world. By the First World War, the AP dramatically increased its operational autonomy and established a major presence in the cartel's domain of South America. The AP spent $274,514 to cover the Spanish American War, a sum that Baron Reuter freely admitted no European institution could match.[87]

Against the backdrop of the AP's global expansion, international news-gathering by American institutions was characterized by dramatic episodes of expensive, even profligate competition between newspaper rivals. The rivalry between William Randolph Hearst's *New York Journal* and Joseph Pulitzer's *New York World* in the late 1890s, culminating in their rival coverage of the Spanish–American War, deservedly stands at the center of many newspaper history accounts of this period. Its lavish reportorial contest is an exception to the era's general practice of providing international news through cooperation. Pulitzer purchased the *New York World* from Jay Gould in 1883, and immediately set about creating the most vibrant and influential newspaper in the United States. Pulitzer's journalism aimed to combine reformist crusades with growing circulations. Reviled by their more stately rivals as "yellow journalism," Pulitzer's *New York World* and Hearst's *New York Journal* were sensational, self-congratulatory, and occasionally inaccurate. They formed an activist genre in the way that their competitor, the *New York Times*, formed a counter-activist genre. The tagline of Hearst's *Journal* was "the journalism that acts." Most threatening to Pulitzer's *World* was Hearst's seemingly limitless resources, which he spent liberally in pursuit of circulation.[88] Immediately after acquiring the *New York Journal* in 1895, Hearst undercut the rival dailies of Pulitzer and James Gordon Bennett, Jr. by charging one cent to their two cents; he next raided the newsroom of Pulitzer's *World* by offering higher pay. Pulitzer retaliated by exercising his AP membership privileges to blackball Hearst from gaining access to AP reports. Only by having fortunately acquired another New York newspaper with an AP subscription, which he quickly merged with the *Journal*, did Hearst successfully avoid this tactic that had been employed to put several dozen other newspapers out of business.[89]

Hearst's *Journal* combined racy coverage of local crime with jingoistic and xenophobic reporting on America's own "small wars" of empire. Hearst sent twenty reporters to Manila, Havana, and San Juan to cover the 1898 war with Spain in what became, when measured by the number of deployed reporters and telegraph costs, the greatest foreign war coverage up to that point in American history.[90] Many of these correspondents were already or became national celebrities. Hearst employed Richard Harding Davis, James Creelman, and Stephen Crane; Pulitzer's roster included Sylvester Henry Scovel and Edwin Harden. Correspondents entered the war they were covering, from shooting at Spanish defenses, to collecting intelligence for the United States military, and capturing towns and challenging senior army officers.[91] The cost of covering the war left both papers in debt—a debilitating debt for Pulitzer, who by late 1898 had effectively quit the circulation race with Hearst and shifted his commitments to making the *New York World* more truthful.[92] During the war, American news providers demonstrated their enterprise and ability to gather news. Indeed, the press regularly surpassed the American government in its ability to acquire intelligence, commandeer scarce boats, and boost the morale and appetite of readers, sometimes with invented stories.[93]

Two interrelated developments in Anglo-American international news had emerged by the end of the nineteenth century. To cater to the tastes of a broader mass reading public, editors pressed more vigorously for stories of heroic conflict. To exercise control over unfolding political and military events, government officials intervened more vigorously in the flow of international news. Particularly in the British Empire, the distinction between news and political advertising grew more nebulous. Imperialist publicity angered editors if it exceeded their commercial needs, but much of the copy produced by international news agencies was generally sympathetic to empire.[94] The relationship between the British government and Reuters in particular was often implicitly cooperative. This could involve informal arrangements for trading information, such as the exchange of Reuters telegrams for "the first crack" at the British Indian Government's official news; or straightforward financial exchange, such as payment of inflated "Government subscriptions" in British colonies that were in effect imperial subsidies, including payments directly from the Foreign Office.[95] Because of its wide distribution, government officials were often inclined to brief Reuters first, to avoid accusations of bias that might accompany granting access to a particular newspaper. As news agency of the British Empire, Reuters aimed to perform a public service. Reuters' staff members regarded themselves as similar to senior home and colonial servants.[96] The biographies of Reuters correspondents "read more like those of Foreign Office bureaucrats than Fleet Street journalists, and perhaps it is more useful to think of them as such."[97]

In the British Empire, the "small wars" of the late Victorian period were the stuff of both political intelligence and popular theater. "A new breed of professional war correspondents," which included all the leading London newspapers as well as Reuters, covered the Sudanese campaign of General Herbert Horatio Kitchener, which sought to avenge Gordon's death.[98] By

1899, circuits of imperial propaganda had formed between the British and dominion press, which celebrated Britain–Dominions trade, exchange of peoples, and growing markets for newspapers and wire services.[99] Editorial pressures to provide items that paying newspapers would print dampened the flow of imperialist publicity. There had to be some "real news" to make the more staid (but ubiquitous) imperial propaganda digestible.[100]

Such arrangements were put to the test during the South African War (1899–1902), which marked the zenith of British imperial news. The war revealed the coziness between foreign journalists and government officials, particularly among the young set of officials in Lord Milner's "Kindergarten," which administered South Africa's postwar reconstruction.[101] Howell Arthur Gwynne, Reuters' correspondent, flattered General Kitchener in his reports and then benefited from privileged access to the General.[102] Winston Churchill, having already acquired the status of celebrity journalist for his reporting in Cuba and Afghanistan, went to South Africa on a generous contract with the *Morning Post*, seeking to parlay journalistic heroics into a parliamentary seat. His daring escape from prison became a bestseller, for which he earned over £10,000. By blurring the lines between reporter and combatant, Churchill risked not only his own life but those of hundreds of other journalist noncombatants.[103] Censorship was far more rigorous in the South African War than in any previous Victorian battle; censors scuttled reports from disfavored journalists, Boer atrocity stories were encouraged, and British misdeeds—most noticeably the advent of civilian concentration camps—went largely unreported. Most reporters were "either crushed by censorship, joined the atrocities campaign, or were incompetent and wrote nonsense."[104]

The growing market for international news was segmenting to meet popular tastes. During the South African War, the *Times* fought a defensive battle to retain the paper's unique prestige in international reporting, and scrambled to field reporters to compete with Reuters' hundred-odd reporters and stringers.[105] While the content of the *Times*'s international news remained more sophisticated than its competitors, the genre that it had pioneered—characterized by the institutional sensibilities of Whitehall—was being crowded aside by the defensive "spot coverage" of Reuters that all newspapers relied on, and by the more sensationalist coverage of its London rivals. Comparatively less elitist, deferential, and civil-service-minded *Daily Mail* writers included the novelist Edgar Wallace and Lady Sarah Wilson.[106] In sharp contrast to the *Times*, Harmsworth's ideal of international news was anti-diplomatic. His reporters were instructed to avoid rather than court local officials.[107] The peg of a good *Daily Mail* international story often rested on narrating exotic adversities faced by individual Britons abroad, independent of larger diplomatic considerations or context. Moreover, the core element of *Daily-Mail*-style imperial news stories—the exploits of white British derring-do in the face of darker, threatening races benighted by impoverishment and ignorance—was effortlessly transposed onto the "darker" areas of Britain's own cities. London's East End led the way as a "playground for journalists" to make sensational reports on urban crime, depravity, and exploitation, in which they became important actors in the story themselves and "dramatized their efforts in civilizing the poor."[108]

ANTI-COLONIAL INTERNATIONAL NEWS, IMPERIAL COOPERATION, AND THE FIRST WORLD WAR

Britain had played the leading role in establishing global news circuits over the nineteenth century, often as a constituent part of its imperial expansion. In India, Reuters developed an unusually profitable news business, owing largely to its control of domestic news through its part ownership of the Eastern News Agency, as well as to its direct subsidies from the British Raj.[109] British officials had complacently assumed that the combination of Reuters and "British pipes"—that is, British-owned telegraph services—would be sufficient to control the provision of international news to India.[110] But the same news circuits that carried imperial propaganda to India could also carry anti-colonial messages, often inadvertently. By simply reporting the range of contemporary political debates, Reuters' cable service in the 1880s and 1890s was filled with information about Irish and radical agitation in and out of Parliament. *Review of Reviews*, W. T. Stead's internationalist-minded monthly news summary launched in 1891, circulated widely in India and was eagerly appropriated by Indian newspaper editors. Previously such editors had to depend on conservative Anglo-Indian newspapers for their foreign news, but with Stead's *Review* they could now learn directly of Egypt's nationalist struggles, Japan's rise to power, and Gandhi's political campaigns in South Africa.[111] The Indian National Congress and nationalist-minded newspapers drew inspiration from these unintended bounties of the Empire's news circuits. "Greater range and density of communications," Christopher Bayly observes, "unless tightly policed by the state, could allow marginal or heterodox voices to make themselves heard or to organize clandestinely."[112]

Moreover, in this age of empire and mass-circulation newspapers, alternative models of providing international news existed beyond the corporate organizations of London and New York. In his farm-cum-press commune of Phoenix Settlement just outside Durban, South Africa, Mohandas Gandhi pioneered the communal production of the *Indian Opinion* as "a strategy to produce a moral community" independent of both market and state forces.[113] Relying on his own writers, a far-flung international network of letter contributors, and occasional items taken from Reuters and major South Asian newspapers, the weekly *Indian Opinion* under Gandhi's editorship (1903–14) provided a model of nationalist journalism in which funding consisted of limited advertising, generous patronage from wealthy nationalists in both India and South Africa, and a dedicated and politically engaged readership.[114] The unworldly nature of Gandhi's business model was precisely its point—a rejection of capital-intensive technologies and corporate information networks where possible, a banning on wage labor, and general reluctance to shape content to advertising. His indifference to copyright extended both to liberal "borrowings" from a variety of print sources circulating in South Africa, as well as aggressive efforts to convince readers to republish *Indian Opinion* items wherever possible across the globe. The newspaper's masthead defiantly announced "no rights reserved"—to observe copyright laws would be to accept the constraints of the market and the state. Advertising was scaled back in 1909, and dispensed with entirely in 1912 except for what he deemed socially useful objects such as pamphlets and books.[115] Gandhi's aim was to encourage slow-paced communal production of newspapers for slow reading, in conscious resistance to what he viewed as the "industrial reading" of imperial rule and industrial capitalism, in which ever faster information bombarded readers and reading "became calibrated to machine-driven rhythms."[116] Few subsequent "nationalist" presses fully embraced Gandhi's formidable example, but many anti-colonial newspapers across the British Empire made do by "borrowing" Reuters copy and supplementing it from news-sharing networks operating across the globe, particularly after the First World War.[117]

More conventional newspaper publishers in Britain and its white Dominions of Canada, Australia, New Zealand, and South Africa looked on the British Empire as a promising arena for greater political and economic cooperation. The first Imperial Press Conference was convened in London in 1909 with the financial backing of British newspaper proprietors concerned with rising cable bills that accompanied rising news copy from the Dominions, in hopes of reducing imperial press cable rates.[118] Out of the conference formed the Empire Press Union, which successfully lobbied for a reduction in cable transmission costs for the press within much of the empire by 25 percent, and worked to circulate parliamentary and official news to international journalists.[119] In practical terms, the 1909 conference highlighted economic differences between British and Dominion news interests—the latter, particularly Australians, feared that sharp reductions to cable rates would undermine news combination monopolies at home. The subsequent cable rate reductions did not significantly increase the supply of Reuters's services to Britain, but did help British newspapers to commission more international news from their own correspondents.[120] The Imperial Press Conference did salve political differences between imperialist and Dominion nationalists, and prepared its participants to engage better with the rising propaganda of emerging belligerents on the continent of Europe.

The First World War transformed the institutional arrangements of the international news business. The Ring Combination lay in tatters, as did Reuters' profits. The company's lucrative private telegram and money remittance services depended on Reuters' word-saving cable codes. Following the outbreak of war, the Admiralty disallowed use of these codes for security reasons, and the business model that had in effect cross-subsidized Reuters' news collection became defunct. Seeking out new revenues as well as the chance to dispose of its poorly performing bank, the company approached the Foreign Office to finance a leveraged buyout in 1915. The company's new director, Roderick Jones, eventually restructured Reuters as a private company the following year, with the Foreign Office secretly acquiring shares and the ability to nominate one director and veto any other. Only after the war was Jones able to fulfill his larger plan of selling Reuters to the PA.[121] During the war, Reuters relied on government grants, which it received in return for distributing propaganda under its "Agence Reuters" logo.[122] With the distinction between news and propaganda growing indiscernible, the AP became more concerned about of the shortcomings of the "Ring Combination" and its surviving members. Immediately after the war, the AP aggressively expanded its international news coverage, particularly to confront stiff competition from the UP, which expanded its coverage unburdened by cartel agreements.[123]

The war also transformed the nature of international reporting. In 1914, General Kitchener banned reporters from the battlefield, and the Defence of the Realm Act (DORA) ensured that British international news prioritized national morale and discouraged honest reporting. British newspapers offered their unconditional support for the war effort. The reporter's job was to provide "colorful stories of heroism and glory calculated to sustain enthusiasm for the war and ensure a supply of recruits for the front," as well as to cover up the mistakes of high command and safeguard the reputation of generals. Under such conditions, journalists lost enterprise and instead prioritized the happiness of officers, in effect becoming their own censors.[124] The nature of trench warfare meant that reporters were removed from sites of battle—this, combined with strict censorship, limitations on accredited reporters, and a telegraph system under wartime stress, meant that the British public, like that of Germany and France, was left uninformed. Particularly unsatisfied were member newspapers of the PA, which was limited to one Reuters' account of a given day's war news.[125] Readers did not learn the full extent of the wartime casualties until after Versailles. The dominant genre of war reporting was the "atrocity story." In one famous and fictitious example, British papers reported the existence of German "corpse factories" in which dead soldiers were boiled to make glycerin for ammunition.[126] Colorful, exploitative, and easily managed for propaganda purposes, atrocity stories symbolized the descent of the quality and rigor of international news during the First World War.

The breakdown of globalization that accompanied the First World War created a global media landscape rich in paradox. Whereas a single cartel arrangement had governed Reuters' relations in Europe before the war, after 1918 it contracted sixteen separate agreements with (mostly new) national news agencies.[127] The great technological innovation of the postwar media world—the advent of mass radio broadcasting in the 1920s—promised instantaneous access to news across the globe, yet its development depended on the particular and often arbitrary institutional arrangements that emerged within each given country. While the new technology was undoubtedly disruptive, the news organizations that used the medium relied on forms of protection—from government monopoly and license fees (BBC) to copyright law (AP and UP)—to ensure a steady supply of news.

CONCLUSION

Large organizations that cooperated to protect the supply of news, primarily by sharing the costs of its gathering and distribution, drove the international news business in nineteenth-century Britain and America. The era's hallmark developments—the advent of telegraphy and the emergence of mass dailies— expanded the possibilities and volume of international news. The literary legacy of this expansion is the emergence of distinct newspaper subgenres that accompanied market segmentation—the diplomatic letter came to share space at the newsagent's shop with the reporter-adventurer tale, the jingoist political item, the humanitarian revelation, and the foreign atrocity story. In the United States, newspapers, their associations, and communication companies created cooperative frameworks for gathering, selling, sharing, and disseminating international news along comparatively exclusive lines. Although the AP's exclusion of local competitors encouraged rivals, when those rivals grew strong the AP grew more inclusive.[128] The best-resourced news organizations were located in major cities, particularly New York. Long habituated to being first with international news, these newspapers sought to generate exclusive items as America's interest in events abroad increased, most notably during the Spanish–American War. Yet competition among metropolitan newspapers proved expensive to the point of debilitation, and most newspapers concluded that it was a better use of resources to share international news, if only as a defensive tactic to retain an individual newspaper's prestige. The result was an increase in the supply of international news across the United States. In Britain, the state played a more formative role. Domestically, it abolished the stamp duty and opened the nation's news market to greater competition; it also nationalized the country's telegraphy and thereby leveled access to international news among provincial newspapers. The British

Empire in turn helped to offset the expenses that the press within the British Isles incurred in gathering news from abroad. A tendency toward cartelization—most explicitly in the formation of the "Ring Combination"— reveals not the strangling of a free market in news, but a practical solution to address the high costs and risks of gathering international news.

NOTES

1. On technology, see James W. Carey, *Communication as Culture: Essays on Media and Society* (Boston: Unwin Hyman, 1989); on liberal politics, see Kevin Williams, *Read All About It: A History of the British Newspaper* (London: Routledge, 2010), and Michael Schudson, *Discovering the News: A Social History of American Newspapers* (New York: Basic Books, 1978); on industrial production, see Oliver Boyd-Barrett and Terhi Rantanan, "The Globalization of News," in *The Globalization of News*, ed. Oliver Boyd-Barrett and Terhi Rantanan (London: Sage Publications, 1998), 1–14, and Gerald J. Baldasty, *The Commercialization of News in the Nineteenth Century* (Madison, Wis.: University of Wisconsin Press, 1992).
2. Jonathan Silberstein-Loeb, *The International Distribution of News: The Associated Press, Press Association, and Reuters, 1848–1947* (New York: Cambridge University Press, 2014), ch. 1.
3. Christopher B. Daly, *Covering America: A Narrative History of a Nation's Journalism* (Amherst: University of Massachusetts Press, 2012), 83; Williams, *Read All About It*, 17–20.
4. John Nerone and Kevin G. Barnhurst, "News Form and the Media Environment: A Network of Represented Relationships," *Media, Culture and Society*, 25 (2003): 118.
5. Williams, *Read All About It*, 77, 86–94.
6. Baldasty, *Commercialization of News*, 19–21.
7. Silberstein-Loeb, *International Distribution of News*, 12; John Nerone, "Newspapers and the Public Sphere," in *A History of the Book in America*, vol. 4: *The Industrial Book, 1840–1880*, ed. Scott E. Casper, Jeffery D. Groves, Stephen W. Nissenbaum, and Michael Winship (Chapel Hill: University of North Carolina Press, 2007), 233–5.
8. Martin Walker, *Powers of the Press: The World's Great Newspapers* (London: Quartet Books, 1982), 29–31; Williams, *Read All About It*, 84.
9. Williams, *Read All About It*, 93.
10. Robert Desmond, *The Information Process: World News Reporting to the Twentieth Century* (Iowa City: Iowa State University, 1978), 82–101.
11. Richard A. Schwarzlose, *The Nation's Newsbrokers*, vol. 1: *The Formative Years, from Pretelegraph to 1865* (Evanston: Northwestern University Press, 1989), 209.
12. Silberstein-Loeb, *International Distribution of News*, 18–19, 24.
13. Menahem Blondheim, *News over the Wires: The Telegraph and the Flow of Public Information in America, 1844–1897* (Cambridge, Mass.: Harvard University Press, 1994), 97.

14. Blondheim, *News over the Wires*, 6, 146–52.
15. Silberstein-Loeb, *International Distribution of News*, 19.
16. Richard John, *Network Nation: Inventing American Telecommunications* (Cambridge, Mass.: Belknap Press of Harvard University Press, 2010), 145.
17. Oliver Boyd-Barrett, *The International News Agencies* (London: Constable, 1980), 135.
18. James Curran and Jean Seaton, *Power without Responsibility: Press, Broadcasting and the Internet in Britain* (London: Routledge, 2010), 26.
19. Williams, *Read All About It*, 99.
20. Martin Conboy, *Journalism: A Critical History* (London: Sage Publications, 2004), 109.
21. Dennis Griffiths, *Fleet Street: Five Hundred Years of the Press* (London: British Library, 2006), 96–7.
22. Williams, *Read All About It*, 102, 106.
23. Curran and Seaton, *Power without Responsibility*, 26. In constant prices from 1855, £47,380 was worth £327,400 in 1870; <www.measuringworth.com>.
24. On Reuters' origins, see Donald Read, *The Power of News: The History of Reuters* (Oxford: Oxford University Press, 1999), 12–17.
25. Silberstein-Loeb, *International Distribution of News*, 99–100.
26. Silberstein-Loeb, *International Distribution of News*, 101–9.
27. Oliver Boyd-Barrett, "Market Control and Wholesale News: The Case of Reuters," in *Newspaper History from the Seventeenth Century to the Present Day*, ed. George Boyce, James Curran, and Pauline Wingate (London: Constable, 1978), 195.
28. John Maxwell Hamilton, *Journalism's Roving Eye: A History of American Foreign Reporting* (Baton Rouge: Louisiana State University Press, 2009), 45.
29. Hamilton, *Journalism's Roving Eye*, 47.
30. Hamilton, *Journalism's Roving Eye*, 59, 69–75.
31. Lucy Brown, *Victorian News and Newspapers* (Oxford: Clarendon, 1985), 210.
32. Conboy, *Journalism*, 116.
33. Walker, *Powers of the Press*, 37.
34. Phillip Knightley, *The First Casualty: The War Correspondent as Hero and Myth-Maker from the Crimea to Iraq* (Baltimore: Johns Hopkins University Press, 2004), 15.
35. Williams, *Read All About It*, 109.
36. Walker, *Powers of the Press*, 34–7.
37. Anthony Smith, "The Long Road to Objectivity and Back Again: The Kinds of Truth We Get in Journalism," *Newspaper History from the Seventeenth Century to the Present Day*, ed. George Boyce, James Curran, and Pauline Wingate (London: Constable, 1978), 167.
38. Silberstein-Loeb, *International Distribution of News*, 165.
39. Roland Wenzlhuemer, *Connecting the Nineteenth-Century World: The Telegraph and Globalization* (New York: Cambridge University Press, 2013), 90.
40. Williams, *Read All About It*, 114; Michael Palmer, "The British Press and International News, 1851–1899: Of Agencies and Newspapers," in *Newspaper History from the Seventeenth Century to the Present Day*, ed. George Boyce, James Curran, and Pauline Wingate (London: Constable, 1978), 208.
41. Palmer, "The British Press and International News," 211.
42. Joseph I. C. Clarke, *My Life and Memories* (New York: Dodd, Mead, 1925), 125. I thank Andie Tucher for this reference.

43. Armand Mattelart, *Mapping World Communication: War, Progress, Culture,* trans. Susan Emanuel and James A. Cohen (Minneapolis: University of Minnesota Press, 1994), 11.

44. Robert W. Desmond, *Windows of the World: The Information Process in a Changing Society, 1900–1920* (Iowa City: University of Iowa Press, 1980), 79.

45. Dwayne R. Winseck and Robert M. Pike, *Communication and Empire: Media, Markets and Globalization, 1860–1930* (Durham: Duke University Press, 2007), 148.

46. Winseck and Pike, *Communication and Empire,* 90.

47. Desmond, *Information Process,* 166–8. The "reserved territories" for Reuters were Britain and the British Empire, the United States (until 1893 when the modern AP took over), Holland, Spain, China, Japan, and South America (with Havas until 1890). For Agence Havas: France and the French Empire, Belgium and its colonies, Italy, Spain, Switzerland, Angola, Libya, Italian colonies, Indo-China, South Africa (with Reuters, then exclusively after 1890), Mexico (until 1893). For Wolff: Prussia/Germany, German Empire, Austria–Hungary, Norway, Sweden, Russia, Poland, Romania, Bulgaria.

48. Silberstein-Loeb, *International Distribution of News,* 198–203.

49. Simon J. Potter, "The English Press," in *Newspapers and Empire in Ireland and Britain: Reporting the British Empire, c.1857–1921,* ed. Simon J. Potter (Dublin: Four Courts Press, 2004), 44–7.

50. Simon J. Potter, *News and the British World: The Emergence of an Imperial Press System, 1876–1922* (Oxford: Clarendon Press, 2003), 17.

51. John Darwin, *The Empire Project: The Rise and Fall of the British World-System, 1830–1970* (Cambridge: Cambridge University Press, 2009), 100–1.

52. Hamilton, *Journalism's Roving Eye,* 80.

53. See generally Dorothy Hammond and Alta Jablow, *The Africa that Never Was: Four Centuries of British Writing about Africa* (New York: Twayne Publishers, 1970), 49–73.

54. Winseck and Pike, *Communication and Empire,* 103, 106, 110; Jill Hills, *The Struggle for Control of Global Communication: The Formative Century* (Urbana: University of Illinois Press, 2002), 70–6.

55. Conboy, *Journalism,* 126.

56. Alan J. Lee, *The Origins of the Popular Press in England, 1855–1914* (London: Croom Helm, 1976), 111.

57. Desmond, *The Information Process,* 311–12.

58. Silberstein-Loeb, *International Distribution of News,* 111.

59. Lee, *Popular Press in England,* 81.

60. John M. Mackenzie, "The Press and the Dominant Ideology of Empire," in *Newspapers and Empire in Ireland and Britain: Reporting the British Empire, c.1857–1921* ed. Simon J. Potter (Dublin: Four Courts Press, 2004), 25.

61. Read, *The Power of News,* 100.

62. Jacqueline Beaumont, "*The Times* at War, 1899–1902," *The South African War Reappraised,* ed. Donal Lowry (Manchester: Manchester University Press, 2000), 67–8.

63. Brown, *Victorian News and Newspapers,* 242.

64. *The Times, The History of the Times,* vol. 3: *The Twentieth Century* (London: Times Publishing Co., 1947), 132.

65. Walker, *Powers of the Press*, 40.

66. G. A. Cranfield, *The Press and Society: From Caxton to Northcliffe* (London: Longman Group Ltd, 1978), 219–20; Williams, *Read All About It*, 9.

67. Curran and Seaton, *Power Without Responsibility*, 42.

68. Francis Williams, *The Right to Know: The Rise of the World Press* (London: Longmans, Green and Co., 1969), 75.

69. Quoted in Colin Seymour-Ure, "Northcliffe's Legacy," in *Northcliffe's Legacy: Aspects of the British Popular Press, 1896–1996*, ed. Peter Catterall and Colin Seymore-Ure (New York: St. Martin's Press, 2000), 12.

70. George Boyce, "The Fourth Estate: The Reappraisal of a Concept," in *Newspaper History from the Seventeenth Century to the Present Day*, ed. George Boyce, James Curran, and Pauline Wingate (London: Constable, 1978), 31.

71. Chandrika Kaul, "Popular Press and Empire: Northcliffe, India and the Daily Mail, 1896–1922," in *Northcliffe's Legacy: Aspects of the British Popular Press, 1896–1996*, ed. Peter Catterall and Colin Seymore-Ure (New York: St. Martin's Press, 2000), 49, 56; Palmer, "The British Press and International News," 217–18.

72. Michael Schudson, "Persistence of Vision: Partisan Journalism in the Mainstream Press," in *A History of the Book in America*, vol. 4: *Print in Motion: The Expansion of Publishing and Reading in the United States, 1880–1940*, ed. Carl F. Kaestle and Janice A. Radway (Chapel Hill: University of North Carolina Press, 2009), 140.

73. Schudson, *Discovering the News*, 93.

74. Daly, *Covering America*, 115; Williams, *Read All About It*, 147.

75. Blondheim, *News over the Wires*, 38.

76. Ted Curtis Smythe, *The Gilded Age Press, 1865–1900* (Westport Conn.: Praeger, 2003), 150–4; Baldasty, *Commercialization of News*, 94–6, 140.

77. Brown, *Victorian News and Newspapers*, 15.

78. Gerben Bakker, "Trading Facts: Arrow's Fundamental Paradox and the Origins of Global News Networks," in *International Communications and Global News Networks*, ed. Peter Putnis, Chandrika Kaul, and Jürgen Wilke (New York: Hampton Press, 2011), 25.

79. Silberstein-Loeb, *International Distribution of News*, 188.

80. Jonathan Fenby, *The International News Services* (New York: Schocken Books, 1986), 37.

81. Read, *Power of News*, 66.

82. Read, *Power of News*, 87; Milton Israel, *Communications and Power: Propaganda and the Press in the Indian Nationalist Struggle, 1920–1947* (Cambridge: Cambridge University Press, 1994), 100–1; Silberstein-Loeb, *International Distribution of News*, 175.

83. Silberstein-Loeb, *International Distribution of News*, 128.

84. Silberstein-Loeb, *International Distribution of News*, 39–41.

85. Silberstein-Loeb, *International Distribution of News*, 42–3.

86. Schwarzlose, *The Nation's Newsbrokers*, vol. 2: *The Rush to Institution, from 1865 to 1920* (Evanston: Northwestern University Press, 1990), 131–81; Desmond, *Information Process*, 360–2.

87. Terhi Rantanen, "Foreign Dependent and Domestic Monopoly: The European News Cartel and U.S. Associated Presses, 1861–1932," *Media History*, 12 (2006), 23–30. The AP would only become an equal contractual partner in 1927.

88. James McGrath Morris, *Pulitzer: A Life in Politics, Print, and Power* (New York: HarperCollins, 2010), 322.

89. David Nasaw, *The Chief: The Life of William Randolph Hearst* (Boston: Houghton Mifflin, 2000), 98–110; see also Silberstein-Loeb, *International Distribution of News*, 50.

90. Joel H. Wiener, *The Americanization of the British Press, 1830s–1914* (London: Palgrave Macmillan, 2011), 198–9.

91. W. Joseph Campbell, *The Spanish–American War* (Westport, Conn.: Greenwood Press, 2005), 2.

92. Morris, *Pulitzer*, 345.

93. For a lively account, see Joyce Milton, *The Yellow Kids: Foreign Correspondents in the Heyday of Yellow Journalism* (New York: Harper and Row, 1989).

94. Alex Nalbach, "'The Software of Empire': Telegraphic News Agencies and Imperial Publicity, 1865–1914," in *Imperial Co-Histories: National Identities and the British and Colonial Press*, ed. Julie F. Codell (Madison: Teaneck, 2003), 69.

95. Nalbach, "'The Software of Empire'," 71–6.

96. Donald Read, "The Relationship of Reuters and Other News Agencies with the British Press, 1858–1984: Service at Cost or Business for Profit?" in *Northcliffe's Legacy: Aspects of the British Popular Press, 1896–1996*, ed. Peter Catterall and Colin Seymore-Ure (New York: St. Martin's Press, 2000), 154–5.

97. Silberstein-Loeb, *International Distribution of News*, 167.

98. Simon J. Potter, "The English Press," in *Newspapers and Empire in Ireland and Britain: Reporting the British Empire, c.1857–1921*, ed. Simon J. Potter (Dublin: Four Courts Press, 2004), 49.

99. Potter, *News and the British World*, 212.

100. See John MacKenzie, *Propaganda and Empire: The Manipulation of British Public Opinion, 1880–1960* (Manchester: Manchester University Press, 1984).

101. Potter, *News and the British World*, 112.

102. Silberstein-Loeb, *International Distribution of News*, 167.

103. Knightley, *First Casualty*, 70–1; William Manchester, *The Last Lion*, vol. 1: *Winston Spencer Churchill: Visions of Glory, 1874–1932* (New York: Little, Brown, 1983), 292, 328–31.

104. Knightley, *First Casualty*, 77–80, quotation at 80.

105. Jacqueline Beaumont, "*The Times* at War, 1899–1902," in *The South African War Reappraised*, ed. Donald Lowry (Manchester: Manchester University Press, 2000), 67–8.

106. Kenneth O. Morgan, "The Boer War and the Media (1899–1902)," *Twentieth Century British History*, 13/1 (2002): 2.

107. Brown, *Victorian News and Newspapers*, 212–13.

108. Brad Beaven, *Visions of Empire: Patriotism, Popular Culture and the City 1870–1939* (Manchester: Manchester University Press, 2012), 65.

109. Silberstein-Loeb, *International Distribution of News*, 175.

110. Milton Israel, *Communications and Power: Propaganda and the Press in the Indian National Struggle, 1920–1947* (Cambridge: Cambridge University Press), 103.

111. C. A. Bayly, "Informing Empire and Nation," in *Information, Media and Power through the Ages*, ed. Hiram Morgan (Dublin: University College Dublin Press, 2001), 184, 191–2.
112. Bayly, "Informing Empire and Nation," 190.
113. Isabel Hofmeyr, "Indian Ocean Lives and Letters," *English in Africa*, 35 (2008): 15.
114. Uma Mesthrie, "From Advocacy to Mobilization: *Indian Opinion, 1904–1914*," in *South Africa's Alternative Press: Voices of Protest and Resistance, 1880s–1960s*, ed. Les Switzer (Cambridge: Cambridge University Press, 1997), 99–126.
115. S. N. Bhattacharya, *Mahatma Gandhi: The Journalist* (Bombay: Asia Publishing House, 1965), 113, 118.
116. Isabel Hofmeyr, *Gandhi's Printing Press: Experiments in Slow Reading* (Cambridge, Mass.: Harvard University Press, 2013), 18.
117. For examples, see James R. Brennan, "Politics and Business in the Indian Newspapers of Colonial Tanganyika," *Africa*, 81 (2011): 42–67; Uma Mesthrie, *Gandhi's Prisoner: The Life of Gandhi's Son Manilal* (Cape Town: Kwela Books).
118. Potter, *News and the British World*, 135–41.
119. Bayly, "Informing Empire and Nation," 196; Chandrika Kaul, *Reporting the Raj: The British Press and India, c.1889–1922* (Manchester: Manchester University Press, 2004), 37.
120. Potter, *News and the British World*, 142, 157.
121. Jonathan Silberstein-Loeb, "Foreign Office Control of Reuters during the First World War: A Reply to Professor Putnis," *Media History*, 16 (2010): 281–93; Read, *The Power of News*, 131.
122. Donald Read, "The Relationship of Reuters and Other News Agencies," 155–6.
123. Silberstein-Loeb, *International Distribution of News*, 204–6.
124. Knightley, *First Casualty*, 100–3, quotation at 103.
125. Silberstein-Loeb, *International Distribution of News*, 127.
126. Knightley, *First Casualty*, 111–16.
127. Silberstein-Loeb, *International Distribution of News*, 204.
128. Silberstein-Loeb, *International Distribution of News*, 226.

6

Broadcasting News in the Interwar Period

Michael Stamm

In December 1901, a new development in journalism crossed the Atlantic when radio pioneer Guglielmo Marconi made a wireless telegraphic transmission from England to Newfoundland. The substance of the message was simple (it consisted only of the letter "s"), but emboldened by the achievement and the acclaim that it brought, Marconi continued seeking ways to move more information over greater distances. By early 1903, Marconi had improved his transmitters and commenced sending longer wireless messages to ships traveling across the Atlantic. The goal of these experiments was not just to transmit information across the ocean via wireless. Rather, it was to use wireless telegraphy on the Atlantic Ocean in the same way that land-based newspaper publishers had been using wired telegraphy for over half a century: Marconi's dispatches were to be set in type and printed for the "public" traveling on ships. The Marconi Wireless Telegraph Company partnered with Cunard Line, a leading transatlantic ship company, and installed onboard wireless systems and printing equipment. In February 1903, Marconi himself made the trip from England to New York on the *Etruria* to participate in a public demonstration of his innovations. As the ship traveled west and began receiving wireless dispatches from the shore, the ship's purser relayed these messages to the onboard printer, who in turn "set up the first Marconi newspaper." The operation was modest but successful, and the company continued to experiment with the process and expand the network of participating ships.[1]

By the following summer, Marconi Wireless was ready to produce what it called the "first complete daily newspaper to be printed at sea." In June 1904, Marconi again personally made the transatlantic trip as part of a demonstration on the Cunard ship *Campania*. With information sent to the ship from transmitters on shore, onboard printers produced an eight-page newspaper entitled the *Cunard Daily Bulletin*. A glowing report claimed that the paper featured "all the latest news by wireless telegraphy" and functioned "the same as a daily on land." Passengers were reported to be "eagerly buying the paper at five cents a copy." *Editor & Publisher*, the leading trade journal for the American newspaper business, was impressed, remarking that "journalism enters pastures new." With the aid of wireless, the "mid-sea daily" was a novel way to get news to readers and "another step in the marvelous progress characteristic of the publishing business."[2]

Though performed in public, Marconi's experiments were proprietary demonstrations. His corporation owned the only equipment capable of sending and receiving the wireless messages, and the *Cunard Daily Bulletin* had no onboard rival. In effect, the "local" shipboard newspaper publisher retained a monopoly on news distribution in the wireless age. This experimental scenario changed dramatically over the following fifteen years, as inventions by Marconi and others advanced wireless technology from point-to-point wireless telegraphy into point-to-mass sound broadcasting. This development troubled newspaper publishers in Great Britain and the United States, with some believing that, to put it in the terms of Marconi's transatlantic experiments, radio might undermine rather than enable the success and even the existence of the established daily newspaper cousins of the *Cunard Daily Bulletin*. What would happen to the newspaper, many would wonder on both sides of the Atlantic, if the public heard the news directly over the airwaves?

These concerns about the newspaper's continued viability in the radio age would prove unfounded. The printed daily newspaper would remain the dominant mass medium in Great Britain and the United States during the interwar period. But, in many significant respects, its evolution and development in both countries from the 1920s to the 1940s would be structured by its relationship to the emerging new medium of radio. After 1920, radio broadcasting gradually but clearly initiated a number of significant changes in the methods and channels of news distribution, and this introduced new understandings of what "news" was as a product. Broadcasting began separating news distribution into overlapping but distinct acts: the communication of facts about past events, and the communication of live accounts of ongoing events. For example, the result of a baseball game in 1915 would be unknown to those who did not attend the game until they read the newspaper. Though there were exceptions for those who heard through word of mouth, the result and account of the game were for most obtained through newspapers printed after the event. By 1925, in comparison, a radio listener might hear a broadcast that reported the score of a game he or she had not attended, and some might even have heard the game live over the airwaves. In this later period, broadcasters were able to provide both a factual report of the game and mediated access to it as it happened. Newspapers lost the monopoly on the mass distribution of factual news, and they were by nature precluded from presenting live accounts of particular events. After radio, these two forms of news—fact and live account—would present distinct forms of competition with the newspaper, and the degree to which each would be distributed via radio had to do with specific industry and policy choices made on each side of the Atlantic.

Throughout the early twentieth century, debates about radio's usefulness and legitimacy in Great Britain and the United States featured prominently in the public culture of both countries.[3] Policymakers were confronted by the same two basic problems of allocating a scarce amount of usable spectrum space and establishing standards regulating the content of the broadcasting that was done on it. They would arrive at fundamentally different solutions, which in turn would structure distinct national markets for news. This chapter will trace the effects of these policy solutions on news distribution in Great Britain and the United States between roughly 1920 and 1945. The basic argument is threefold: first, in both countries, broadcasting augmented but did not supplant a news market based on the sale of printed newspapers. Second, the activities of newspaper publishers individually and collectively as members of cooperative newsgathering associations strongly influenced the development of significantly different systems of news broadcasting. Third, in both countries, the state played a central role in structuring and defining the terms of competition in the new multimedia market for news. Radio redefined what news was as a product, and newspaper publishers and policymakers in turn shaped the distinct markets for that product in the United States and Great Britain.

THE CREATION OF BRITISH BROADCASTING

In March 1919, after years of experimentation, Guglielmo Marconi built a transmitter in Ireland that was capable of broadcasting sound to the United States. As radio subsequently developed in Britain, many newspapers found it to be a topic of significant public interest, and it provided material for numerous published news stories. Some newspapers went so far as to create radio "events" that they could cover, and the *Daily Mail* was responsible for what is considered the first major public demonstration of broadcasting in Great Britain, the June 15, 1920 broadcast of Dame Nellie Melba singing opera. Marconi Wireless conducted a series of well-publicized broadcasts in the following months, and by February 1922 was doing short regular broadcasts at the permission of the Post Office.[4]

These broadcasts continued as British policymakers began debating policies to structure the country's broadcasting system, while other firms such as Metropolitan-Vickers Electrical Company and Western Electric Company began planning broadcasting facilities. By May 1922 the Post Office had received more than twenty applications for permission to operate radio stations. Officials within the Post Office grew increasingly anxious about maintaining order in broadcasting, especially after Assistant Secretary F. J. Brown traveled to the United States and returned to report on what he perceived as the "chaos" on the America airwaves emerging in the absence of a clear regulatory structure. The *Daily Mail* remained an enthusiastic radio supporter, and by June was reported to be planning its own broadcasting operations. By August, frustrated by its inability to get permission to broadcast, the paper announced that it would begin using a transmitter in The Hague to air programming that could reach British listeners. Seeking to exert control over the nascent radio system before it became disorderly, British policymakers began developing a regulatory mechanism through the auspices of the Post Office, which had authority over telecommunications in Britain since the Telegraph Act of 1868 had given it a monopoly on transmitting telegrams over the wires. In 1904, the British government expanded postal authority over communications to include wireless telegraphy. When broadcasting was developed, the Postmaster-General quickly assumed control on the principle that its previous regulatory powers naturally extended to cover it.[5]

By mid-1922, Post Office officials made it clear to radio manufacturers and aspiring broadcasters that they rejected a system of multiple competing broadcasters in favor of one structured around a single new broadcasting corporation. Many expected this to be an expensive creation, with the cost of the transmission infrastructure estimated to be over £100,000. The Post Office aimed to induce the manufacturers to cooperate to form this single broadcasting corporation, and the subsequent constitution of the original British Broadcasting Company as a licensed monopoly thus represented a harmonization of public and private interests. For the state, the formation of the BBC in this way was motivated by concerns about public finance and the assertion of cultural and political authority over an emerging form of mass communication. For the manufacturers, this offered a path to market power through the control of the sale of radio sets, as the Post Office offered the inducement of giving the BBC the exclusive privilege to sell legal radio sets in Britain, thus protecting domestic manufacturers from competition from the much cheaper sets available from Austria and Germany.[6]

With state and industry goals aligned after negotiations in the summer of 1922, the British Broadcasting Company was officially formed in late 1922, and the Post Office granted the BBC the exclusive privileges of both broadcasting in Britain and selling officially licensed receiving sets. While not mandating that the BBC broadcast any particular kinds of content, the license did place specific limitations on the amount and type of news broadcasting that the BBC could do, barred advertisements, and generally required that the BBC would air "a programme of broadcast matter to the reasonable satisfaction of the Postmaster-General." In its original form, the BBC was a private company owned by British manufacturers of radio sets and equipment. Shares were available to any domestic company wishing to subscribe, though the majority were held by six large firms (Marconi, General Electric, British Thomson-Houston, Metropolitan-Vickers, Western Electric, and Radio Communication), representatives of which formed the board of directors under the chairmanship of former Postmaster-General Lord Gainford. Legally protected from foreign competition, British manufacturers aimed to profit from set sales, and revenues for their broadcasting system were to come from annual license fees paid by the listeners on each receiving set, half of which went to the Post Office and half to the BBC. For listeners, the BBC was essentially a voluntary subscription service, with the annual license originally selling for 10 shillings. Listeners provided direct financial support for the system, creating a reciprocal relationship between the BBC and its audience. Whatever their vision for the BBC, managers would always have to contend with a public composed of people understanding themselves to be not only listeners but also patrons.[7]

NEWS BROADCASTING ON THE BRITISH AIRWAVES, 1922–7

At the time of the BBC's creation, British newspaper publishers wielded considerable political influence. As one political scientist puts it, prior to World War I, press baron Lord Northcliffe "controlled... a larger share of national newspaper circulation than Rupert Murdoch in the 1990s," and with no competition from other media. Northcliffe retained this standing after the war, with one English financier going so far as to call him in 1919 "the most powerful man who has lived since Oliver Cromwell's day." Publishers and press representatives like Northcliffe did not hesitate to deploy their influence in the period leading up to the BBC's creation, especially as they lobbied to insulate their newspapers from what they perceived to be competition from broadcasting. In June 1922, H. C. Robbins, the general manager of the Press Association (PA), a London-based news association serving the provincial press, claimed that newsgathering was a "very costly matter," and he aimed to make sure that news collected by PA members was not broadcast without its permission or control. Lord Riddell of the Newspaper Proprietors' Association, the trade group representing the national newspapers, also wanted clear assurances that the BBC would not "lift" printed news to read on the air, believing that hearing broadcast news would induce many listeners to eschew the later purchase of printed newspapers.[8]

Because of strong pressure from these press representatives, the BBC at its founding was specifically limited in the amount and type of news broadcasting that it could do. The Company reached an agreement with the major news agencies (Reuters, PA, Exchange Telegraph, and Central News) giving it a daily bulletin of between 1,200 and 2,000 words from which staffers could develop a half-hour newscast that would air no earlier than 7:00 p.m. and be credited to the agencies at the outset of the program. The BBC agreed to forego any independent newsgathering, and payment for the agency news was to begin at £4,000 per year and to increase as the number of listener licenses did. In effect, publishers were able to use their considerable influence to prevent the BBC from fully developing its news broadcasting and, as the state licensed a monopoly broadcaster, it also protected the interests of a cartel of leading publishers and news agencies by limiting competition from broadcast news. London-based press critic Herbert Ridout remarked that the arrangement for news broadcasting on the BBC meant that it was "hardly likely to present any serious opposition to the daily newspapers," with the lone weekly exception being the Sunday evening news report, since there were no evening papers that day and thus a "gap of 24 otherwise newsless hours between Sunday morning and the next day." This interval gave the BBC the occasional role of breaking-news reporter, for example on Sunday, February 4, 1923, when the negotiations at the Conference of Lausanne temporarily collapsed and the BBC's report preceded the Monday morning newspapers. In the following few years, many at the BBC remained dissatisfied with reporting breaking news only by these dictates of chance, and they would remain perpetually at odds with the press and its Post Office supporters as they tried to expand the BBC's news broadcasting.[9]

After the initial BBC charter went into effect, the company faced the lingering challenge of ensuring that listeners actually obtained the licenses that provided the revenue for the system. At the outset, the most pressing financial problem was not that radio took sales away from newspapers, as some publishers had feared, but instead that listeners had unlicensed receiving sets that were not generating revenues to support the system. Some of these sets were built by amateurs who thus were not only avoiding the cost of purchasing a commercially manufactured set, but who were also by the terms of the BBC charter exempt as self-identified "experimenters" from paying license fees as listeners. Others violated the law by purchasing comparatively inexpensive foreign-manufactured sets that BBC staffer C. A. Lewis called "pirate" equipment. What Lewis called the "wholesale evasion of the regulations" quickly led to an alarming lack of revenue, and the system was threatened with financial collapse.[10]

This issue of motivating listeners to purchase revenue-generating licenses was the primary problem facing the ten-member panel convened in 1923 by Member of Parliament Sir Frederick Sykes to recommend modifications to the emerging system. Throughout deliberations extending over thirty-four sessions, the Sykes Committee was guided by the belief that, because of its social significance, broadcasting should stay under public control rather than be allowed to fall into private hands. The Sykes Report noted that "we consider that the control of such a potential power over public opinion and the life of the nation ought to remain with the State, and that operation of so important a national service ought not to be allowed to become an unrestricted commercial monopoly." As it conducted its investigation, the Sykes Committee devoted significant attention to the issue of news broadcasting, and press representatives continued to lobby for the BBC to be barred from engaging in significant programs of news distribution. Lord Riddell of the Newspaper Proprietors' Association argued that publishers needed protection from the competition posed by broadcast news, and Riddell wanted this protection to include limits on both the broadcasting of factual news reports and the broadcasting of live accounts of events. Were the BBC to broadcast reports of unpublished news such as "racing and football results," it would "seriously interfere with the sale of newspapers." Any "publican" with a radio set would thus be "able to supply the requirements of his customers, who would be eagerly waiting in the bar for the results." The broadcasting of live events such as the King's speech would likewise "probably have a most prejudicial effect on the newspapers," Riddell claimed, as it would upset the practical monopoly that newspapers had on distributing the content of most political addresses to the public. Papers such as the *Times* routinely printed the full text of political speeches, and Riddell was concerned that radio would not only supplant that function of the newspaper but that it would also erode the speech's value as the source of a news report, as some consumers might not feel compelled to purchase a newspaper in order to read about a speech that they had already heard.[11]

After their lobbying, press representatives found that the final report of the Sykes Committee supported most of their suggestions. The committee was impressed by the testimony of the press associations and sympathetic to the claim that they "spend very large sums in the collection and distribution of news." The Sykes Committee felt that the current arrangement worked for all parties, though it did suggest that "there should be a gradual extension of the broadcasting of news, under proper safeguards, and that more latitude should be given for the broadcasting of special events without regard to the hour." The Sykes Committee's overall assessment of British Broadcasting was glowing, and the report also offered a strong endorsement of the work done to date by John Reith, who had become the BBC's first General Manager upon its formation. Throughout his sixteen-year tenure at the BBC, Reith waged a persistent campaign to elevate popular tastes and attitudes. Broadcasting, Reith wrote in 1924, was "an ally of immense potency in the campaign for a general intelligence and a higher culture," and he saw the BBC's fundamental mission as "being to bring the best of everything into the greatest number of homes." Broadcasting, Reith argued, could provide "direct information on a hundred subjects to innumerable men and women, who thereby will be enabled not only to take more interest in events which were formerly outside their ken, but who will after a short time be in a position to make up their own minds on many matters of vital moment, matters which formerly they had either to receive according to the dictated and partial versions and opinions of others, or to ignore altogether." To fulfill this mission of better informing the public, Reith wanted "greater freedom" to broadcast both more news reports and "direct transmissions of ceremonies and functions of great interest, in particular those at which important speeches are delivered." Reith suggested that this would have only a positive influence on newspaper circulation, believing that "the spirit of wireless and the method of the newspaper are distinctly complementary, and that interest in one undoubtedly stimulates interest in the other."[12]

By September 1924, Reith's persistence had resulted in a modest expansion in news content, as the BBC and press representatives signed an agreement allowing the BBC to broadcast significant daytime public events as long as they provided only a "preliminary announcement and a microphone record of the occasion without any further description or comment." The early results were mixed. That year, Reith arranged a widely heard and praised broadcast of King George's speech from the Empire Exhibition, but part of the compromise that the BBC had made about not providing "further description or comment" also resulted in some unintentionally avant-garde sound transmissions. For the 1926 Epsom Derby, for example, the company was only permitted to broadcast the live sound of the race and could not have a commentator offer the results, leaving listeners to imagine what transpired at the horse race from the muffled and distant sounds of hooves. But Reith had succeeded in establishing the BBC as a provider of news in the form of live accounts, and the organization would continue to develop these capacities.[13]

These limitations on news continued until the BBC's license was set to expire on December 31, 1926, but two events during that year dramatically changed the terms of the debate about news broadcasting: the hearings of the Crawford Committee and the General Strike. Under the chairmanship of David Lindsay, the Earl of Crawford and Balcarres and a former member of the House of Commons, the Crawford Committee began meeting in 1925 to consider whether to extend or modify the original BBC charter, and its meetings took place amidst a rising clamor from the public for more news reports, especially sporting results. With many more Britons paying for licenses after the Sykes Report (the number of licenses rose from 597,000 at the end of 1923 to 1.6 million at the end of 1925), many wanted to be able to hear breaking news and more live accounts of events and resented that they could not.[14]

During the Crawford Committee hearings, press representatives continued to claim that a BBC actively engaged in news broadcasting would spell ruin for their businesses. Though sympathetic to some press concerns, Reith rejected this line of thinking by arguing to the Committee that publishers were standing in the way of progress. In "other countries," Reith claimed, "the

Press is already employing the microphone to distribute the news simultaneously with the event," and he believed that publishers interested in best
serving the public should support the expansion of the BBC's news reporting.
Reith had an ally in the Earl of Crawford, who in his diary expressed private
disdain for the popular press in Britain in noting that the country "would be all
the better for a violent purging of these sheets." In its official report, and in
more measured terms, the Crawford Committee was publicly supportive of
Reith's argument that the BBC should do more news broadcasting, writing
that radio news reports might actually "lead interested people to study the
longer and more vivid descriptions recorded in the press." In addition to
advocating more news broadcasting, the Crawford Committee also made the
broader recommendation that basic structures of ownership and control of
British broadcasting be reconstituted. The Committee argued that the British
Broadcasting Company, a licensed private firm owned by equipment manufacturing companies, should be replaced by a new "public corporation" that
would "act as a Trustee for the national interest in Broadcasting." The state
could reach a financial settlement with current BBC shareholders "without
serious difficulty" as it created the new publicly owned but independently
managed broadcasting service.[15]

The Crawford Committee report was published on March 5, 1926, after
which the BBC awaited parliamentary approval of the recommendations. In
the interim, one of the most important events in the BBC's early history took
place: the General Strike from May 3–12. The General Strike started with
grievances related to the coal industry, but the Trades Union Council called
upon workers in other industries to strike, including those in newspaper
publishing. To keep the public informed during the strike while newspaper
circulation was radically curtailed, the "news agencies temporarily abandoned
all the restrictions placed on the content and timing of BBC news bulletins."
On the second morning of the strike, the BBC established its own "emergency
news staff," which worked around the clock gathering news and writing
bulletins that were broadcast at 10 a.m. and at 1, 4, 7, and 9:30 p.m. Britons
widely praised the BBC's service during the General Strike, for example the
ordinary citizen who wrote to the *Times* about the "unwearying and incom-
parable service to the public" that the BBC had provided.[16]

The BBC's service during the General Strike was a watershed moment in its
history, and it helped to secure the approval of the Crawford Committee's
recommendations, which went into effect on January 1, 1927. With that, the
BBC's initials now stood for British Broadcasting Corporation, and although
the BBC remained the sole domestic broadcaster and had the same personnel
and facilities, British radio was different in some fundamental respects. The
state bought out the radio manufacturers that had owned and operated the
British Broadcasting Company. Foreign-manufactured sets were now permitted in Britain, but the BBC maintained a monopoly on the authority to collect

license fees from listeners. Most importantly, the new BBC was transformed into a public corporation, as the Crawford Committee had recommended, and in this respect it was similar in nature to the UK's Central Electricity Board, also established in 1926. With "no shareholders apart from the state," the new BBC operated under the trusteeship of a royally appointed Board of Governors, but it was granted a significant degree of autonomy. While Parliament did hold ultimate authority over it, and although the Post Office issued its license, the new BBC was, as one contemporary described it, "made subject to political control only of an indirect and spasmodic nature." The reconstituted BBC was initially a much less active news broadcaster than many of its listeners wanted, and staffers within the BBC began immediate efforts to meet these whetted public appetites for the broadcasting of news reports and live events. The BBC's aim, as John Reith put it, was to act as a "public utility service," and he understood news broadcasting to be an important part of this.[17]

By 1927, the British had established and legitimized a national broadcasting system. In structuring the country's broadcasting system, the British government also structured the multimedia marketplace for news by protecting the entrenched interests of newspaper publishers and news agencies. Publishers in the foundational period of British broadcasting succeeded in staving off what they feared would be ruinous competition from radio and, in creating a monopoly broadcaster, the British state simultaneously preserved the monopoly position that the country's newspaper press had on the news business. This was distinctly different from the competitive multimedia news marketplace that emerged in the United States.

CREATING THE AMERICAN SYSTEM
OF BROADCASTING, 1920–7

The initial phase of broadcasting in the United States had many parallels with the British experience. As in Britain, many of the early and significant broadcasting demonstrations were either sponsored or done by newspapers. In August 1920, for example, the *Detroit News* station WWJ gave returns for local elections, and in November 1920, WWJ and Pittsburgh station KDKA broadcast presidential election results. Not long after these initial demonstrations, however, radio in the United States developed significant differences with Great Britain, and particularly in the way in which news broadcasting was done. As the BBC noted, prior to the foundation of the original Company, "certain people in the newspaper world had contemplated entering the new field and operating stations in conjunction with their existing activities. When it was known that a single organization was to be formed, the newspapers

united to protect themselves against any damage which it might do to them."
In the United States, in contrast, newspapers across the country obtained
broadcast licenses throughout radio's formative period. Speaking for many
publishers, press baron William Randolph Hearst noted in 1924 that he was
"very much interested in radio," as he believed that there might be a tremendous opportunity "for radio in connection with newspapers and news services." Hearst and numerous other publishers seized the opportunity denied to
British publishers and acquired broadcast licenses. As they did so, they
remained as active and influential as their British counterparts in the policy-
making processes structuring early radio. However, given the different kinds
of broadcasting systems emerging, they made very different kinds of demands
on the state. In Britain in the 1920s, publishers excluded from operating their
own stations supported public spectrum ownership and the creation of a
monopoly broadcaster because it allowed them a more effective means of
controlling the competition posed by news broadcasts. In the United States,
publishers supported a system of public spectrum ownership and dispersed
and private station ownership, as this gave them the opportunity to operate
their own stations in conjunction with their newspapers. As in Britain,
American publishers aided in creating a system along the lines that they
promoted, but one of the most important distinctions in the United States
was most publishers did not seek the limitations on news broadcasting that
their British counterparts had.[18]

When broadcasting initially developed in the United States after the First
World War, it was under the authority of the Department of Commerce, and
the rapidly increasing number of broadcasting stations after 1920 prompted
Secretary of Commerce Herbert Hoover to develop newly effective policy
mechanisms to regulate it. Hoover, like many observers of early broadcasting,
believed that some degree of federal control was necessary to manage what
seemed to be incipient chaos. To this end, Hoover held four national radio
conferences between 1922 and 1925, aiming to create what he believed to be a
better national broadcasting policy. In broadcasting, as in other industries,
Hoover was driven by the desire to "draw on the energy and resources of
private enterprise yet deploy these within the context of purposeful planning
and coordination." Throughout the radio conferences, Hoover expressed a
shared belief with the British that the spectrum was and should remain a
public resource. But, unlike the British, Hoover believed that this resource was
best utilized by multiple licensed private parties rather than a single one, and
his aims in creating American radio policy were grounded not in a desire to
create or sanction monopolistic control of broadcasting but rather to decen-
tralize station ownership as much as possible. As he remarked in a radio
address in 1924, "What we must safeguard is that there shall be no interference
with free speech, that no monopoly of broadcasting stations should grow up
under which any person or group could determine what material will be

delivered to the public." Hoover was also clear that he believed news broadcasting to be an important function of radio. As he noted in his opening statement at the first national radio conference, radio offered a "great . . . possibility for service, for news, for entertainment, for education."[19]

Under Hoover's stewardship, the core aim of broadcast policy in the United States became managing competition between multiple private broadcasters. This was a significant departure from the structure of British broadcasting, which entrusted decisions about programming to one regulated organization. In the United States, programming choices, including those about the amount of news reporting, would be left in the hands of individual broadcasters. This was in principle supported by many Americans expressing anxiety about the kind of centralized control of broadcasting that the BBC was employing. As the inventor Hudson Maxim remarked in 1924, "I distrust the wisdom of allowing radio broadcasting to be controlled by any private monopoly, but I also distrust the wisdom and the ability and the justice of federal control of radio. The solution seems to lie between the devil of private monopoly and the deep sea of perilous paternalism."[20]

Hoover's early efforts to regulate the American broadcasting system avoided the creation of a new administrative commission in favor of keeping regulatory control with the Department of Commerce. However, these efforts failed as a number of American broadcasters began disobeying license and frequency assignments and challenging the regulatory system in court. Some wanted to broadcast at higher wattages to reach larger audiences, while others rejected the operating assumption that the Commerce Department had the authority to license them to specific frequencies so as to manage interference and competition. A 1926 court case in Chicago, Illinois, in which a broadcaster successfully sued to claim private property rights in its frequency threatened to overturn the basic principle of public spectrum ownership, and Congress finally stepped in to create an administrative body with clear regulatory powers.[21]

In the law that emerged, the Radio Act of 1927, Congress vested regulatory control over broadcasting in the Federal Radio Commission (FRC) and gave it the power to authorize the frequency and power allocations of licensed broadcasters. Licensees were required to apply periodically to renew their licenses and, when doing so, had to demonstrate that they had conducted themselves on the air in the "public interest, convenience, or necessity." This ambiguous phrase was taken from public utility law and proved perpetually controversial. Indeed, one FRC General Counsel later remarked that it meant "about as little as any phrase that the drafters of the Act could have used and still comply with the constitutional requirement that there be some standard to guide the administrative wisdom of the licensing authority." The standard in the United States was in some respects as broad and vague as that in Britain, where the BBC was charged with presenting "a programme of broadcast matter to the reasonable satisfaction of the Postmaster-General," but there were two crucial differences in the United States. First, the Radio Act of 1927 contained no restrictions on news broadcasting. And second, while the British Postmaster-General applied its standard to one broadcaster, the American FRC was charged with assessing the conduct of approximately six hundred stations.[22]

NEWS BROADCASTING ON THE AMERICAN AIRWAVES, 1920–9

As a result of policy made in the 1920s, the market for broadcast news in the United States was much more open and competitive than it was in Britain. In the United States, stations were permitted to broadcast whatever news they liked. Many broadcasters aired news reports and accounts of live events—content that British publishers had successfully limited on the early BBC. News broadcasting remained a staple on American radio throughout the 1920s, though far less abundantly than it would be in the 1930s. Typically, early news broadcasts resembled those of WEAF and WJZ. In 1924, these New York City stations began broadcasting farm reports based on material that they received from the New York Bureau of Farms and Markets. WJZ also partnered with the New York Stock Exchange to give the daily quotations of some sixty stocks, and it also broadcast daily news summaries provided to it by the *New York Evening Post* and the *Wall Street Journal*.[23]

If a particular station happened to be owned by a newspaper, as many were, news broadcasting could be an effective means of cross promotion and a way to reach the local public through multiple channels. In Texas in early 1923, for example, the program director of the *Fort Worth Star-Telegram* station WBAP noted that his company "serves, in a large measure, an agricultural population," and thus the station provided a "complete daily system of broadcasts of cotton, grain, cattle and other quotations of vital interest to the farmers and ranchers." Newspapers around the country employed similar multimedia strategies, including urban mass circulation dailies like the *Milwaukee Journal* (owner of WTMJ) and *St. Louis Post-Dispatch* (owner of KSD), as well as smaller papers like Indiana's *South Bend Tribune*, which owned station WSBT. In every case, as one WSBT staffer remarked in 1923, having a radio station providing some news reporting was "a very attractive means of letting the public know that the paper is on the job and up to the minute."[24]

Stations neither owned by nor partnered with newspapers presented different problems to the publishing business, and some stations regularly "lifted" content from newspapers. As some publishers saw it, such sharp practices came in the wake of the United States Supreme Court's decision in *International News Service v. Associated Press*. In that case, the court held that by taking the news reports of the Associated Press, a nationwide news organization, and reselling them before they had lost their commercial value, INS, a competitor of the AP, engaged in unfair competition.[25] Some publishers similarly disapproved of broadcast news, believing that the reading on the air of news taken from newspapers constituted a "form of news republication" that the *INS* case had made illegal. Some in the AP opposed news broadcasting even on stations owned by fellow members because of radio's immediacy and geographic reach. The AP was a cooperative news agency built around the sharing of news between members prior to publication. The benefits to member newspapers of making their news reports available before printing them were twofold. First, they were able to access the news gathered locally and individually by other AP members. And second, AP members had the exclusive privilege of printing these reports within the territory immediately surrounding their places of publication. Were broadcasts by a station owned by an AP member to reach into the territory in which another member's paper circulated, as they could in many places, listeners in the latter area might get the news before the member could publish the paper, thereby denying it the privilege of exclusivity and violating the cooperative agreement upon which the AP was based.[26]

Broadcasting thus presented a considerable threat to some publishers, and especially those that spent significant amounts of money gathering news to print. The AP claimed to have spent nearly $4,000,000 "gathering and distributing news for its member newspapers" in 1918, and the increased appetite for foreign news stimulated by the First World War continued in peacetime. After the war, the AP successfully relied on the favorable ruling in *INS* to sue broadcasters alleged to have broadcast the AP's news reports without permission. But the issue that ultimately divided AP members was broadcasting by members themselves, as some influential AP members owned radio stations and believed that news broadcasting was an adjunct to publishing and a way of promoting the sale of printed newspapers.[27]

The differing stances taken by the AP in the 1924 and 1928 presidential elections show the challenges that the association faced in maintaining unity in its ranks among those who owned radio stations and those who did not. In 1924, many stations, including some owned by AP members, wanted to broadcast election returns, and the AP barred its members from doing so. The *Chicago Tribune*, an influential member, chafed under the restrictions. "Perhaps it would seem more canny," the *Tribune* argued, "to preserve in darkness the news that Coolidge has been elected or that there is a deadlock over the presidency until it could be revealed to the interested public at the news stands on the morning after. But this is the era of radio." One AP competitor, United Press, took a similarly proactive stance toward radio.

The UP, a commercial news agency not bound by the cooperative arrangements of the AP, simply sold news to subscribing newspapers, and its leadership was keen to sell to radio broadcasters as well. As UP president Karl Bickel believed, radio was a "factor in the business of news transmission . . . And it is not the intention of the United Press to stick its head in the proverbial sand bank like the proverbial ostrich, and cry out that it is not here and that it must not be a factor simply because we do not like it or do not see how we can adjust ourselves to it."[28]

Ultimately, the UP took the lead ahead of the AP in helping broadcasters air coverage of the 1924 election. The UP provided news to nearly thirty stations, including the one owned by the *Chicago Tribune*. Stations owned by William Randolph Hearst broadcast returns from reports gathered independently by staff members. Other papers operating radio stations took similar actions, and some broadcast returns that they had received directly from the offices of political parties. In the wake of the election, some AP members were reported to be "embarrassed" at the organization's stance on news broadcasting. Subsequent AP activities did little to mollify them, as the AP reportedly took "stenographic reports" of election night broadcasts from around the country in a hunt for unauthorized use of its news, and the association subsequently cited seven member newspapers for broadcasting returns from the AP reports on their stations. All of the accused denied the charges, claiming that the news that they aired came "from other sources," which, if true, put members in the frustrating position of having to pay for the same news twice while still being sanctioned by the AP for broadcasting it. Many forward-looking publishers publicly supported the *Chicago Tribune*'s stance. The *Appleton Post-Crescent* implied that the AP was taking an anachronistic attitude toward news distribution. In a post-election editorial, the paper called the *Tribune*'s stance the "right one" and stated that newspapers could easily weather whatever competition radio presented. "People will continue to read the newspapers for the complete account of the day's news," the *Post-Crescent* asserted, "irrespective of whether a portion of it is broadcast or not. It will be futile to resist or attempt to resist the use of so valuable a medium for public information as radio. To do so would be analogous to the early attempts to bar the introduction of machinery in industry."[29]

This attitude toward radio became increasingly common in the United States in the mid-1920s. During the 1928 presidential campaign, the AP shifted its position on broadcasting. *Editor & Publisher* called it a "transformation from hostility to open friendliness." For the 1928 elections, the AP, along with INS and the UP, agreed to supply the National Broadcasting Company with returns, and papers around the country announced partnerships with local stations to broadcast news. This conception of radio would have been a "radical" move for the AP in 1924, as one industry observer described it. By 1928, however, many in the press understood the deal to be, as *New York*

World managing editor William Preston Bearall said, a "definite supplementary service of untold value to the public."[30]

Although some newspaper publishers throughout the 1920s remained skeptical about the benefits of radio news broadcasts, few were opposed to the broadcasting of live events, and these proved to be a less controversial way for stations to attract listeners. This was a particularly significant transatlantic contrast. American radio stations were much more active and aggressive than the BBC was in broadcasting live events. Absent the BBC's limitations on broadcasting live events, American radio gave listeners much greater access to the raw material of printed newspapers than British broadcasting. This was especially true of sporting events, which provided frequent and significant programming comparatively early in American radio's history. The first broadcast of a baseball game was in 1921, and the World Series was a radio staple by 1923. Broadcasters sought any sporting event that might spark public interest, including horse races, boxing matches, and football games. Perhaps unsurprisingly, radio proponents and broadcasting executives attempted to assure publishers that live event broadcasts did not threaten newspaper sales. In 1925, radio executive David Sarnoff remarked "In the broadcasting of public events radio makes every listener a participant. The man who has 'attended' a political convention by radio reads the newspaper accounts of the convention with added zest . . . The same is true in the field of sports, as in the broadcasting of a major prize fight, or World Series baseball game."[31]

One prominent example of this practice took place on September 22, 1927, when the *New York Telegram* and twenty-five other papers associated with Scripps Howard Newspapers arranged to broadcast the fight between John Dempsey and Gene Tunney from Chicago's Soldier Field. At a cost of $100,000, the broadcast went over seventy stations across the country. Scripps Howard papers aggressively publicized the fight. Company vice-chairman William W. Hawkins commented later how pleased he was with the broadcast and how he believed that this kind of multimedia news reporting should be expanded. "The more successful radio is, the more successful the newspapers will be," Hawkins claimed. The fight broadcast, Hawkins argued, created a "direct real interest in the event on the part of the millions of people, who otherwise would have had merely a mild interest, if any at all. Having heard the fight reported over their radios, they were anxious to read the reports of the expert newspaper sporting writers from the ringside. Their interest and curiosity had been whetted by the radio."[32]

With circulations and advertising revenues continuing to rise in the 1920s, the reaction to radio from publishers and news agencies in the United States was occasionally hostile but mostly favorable. Indeed, many publishers became broadcasters. To these publisher-broadcasters, multimedia news reporting was a prudent business strategy, and they resisted efforts aimed to prevent them from broadcasting news. Across the Atlantic, British publishers and news agencies had an incentive to collude in preventing news broadcasting as they were precluded from operating their own radio stations. In the United States, many publishers actively sought to become broadcasters, and this lowered the incentive to collude against radio news broadcasting. However, differing stances among some American publishers toward broadcasting did create divided loyalties, especially among AP members, and this provoked one final and futile spasm of opposition to radio during the early years of the Great Depression.[33]

SELLING AMERICAN NEWS IN A DEPRESSION ECONOMY, 1929-38

In much of its formative decade, American radio broadcasting developed in a prosperous economy, but its evolution in the following decade took place in a climate of economic collapse. Financially, newspapers were hit hard during the Great Depression, as advertising revenues declined from $800 million in 1929 to $490 million in 1932. Although revenues rebounded to $600 million by 1937, publishers faced a major loss of revenue during the Depression. Meanwhile, radio advertising revenues more than tripled from $40 million in 1929 to $145 million in 1937. After the Depression began, the combination of competition over advertising revenue and news distribution made many publishers increasingly anxious about their businesses, and some began to retreat from the conciliatory and cooperative attitudes that they had displayed toward radio during the 1928 election.[34]

As some United States publishers sought to limit competition from broadcasting during the Depression, they did so in a distinctly different way than their British counterparts. Whereas British publishers in the 1920s sought to restrict the broadcasting of both live events and subsequent news reports of them, in the United States press hostility to news broadcasting rarely focused on the broadcasting of live events; rather, publishers directed their ire toward spot news reports, especially items they believed were taken directly out of newspapers. Anti-radio publishers in the United States aimed to protect their monopoly on factual news, and they sought to restrict Americans' abilities to get breaking news from anyone but them. As one commentator wrote in *Harper's*, publishers and broadcasters were "coming to blows over the privilege of telling you and me what happened to-day in Tokio and Timbuctoo and New York City; over the right to recount what the president plans to tell Congress and what the captain of the lightship said to the captain of the liner who sank his craft. They are going to fight, in brief, over the privilege of purveying news."[35]

In some ways, this line of thinking reflected not just Depression economics but also the growing importance of radio as a news source. In 1933, driven by these related anxieties, publishers initiated what became known as the Press–Radio War, the culmination of which was the Biltmore Agreement. Named for the New York hotel in which it was negotiated, the agreement was a trade pact between representatives of the American Newspaper Publishers Association, the major wire services (AP, UP, and INS), the National Association of Broadcasters, and the CBS and NBC radio networks. The networks agreed to limit their daily news broadcasting to two five-minute reports based on material provided to them by a new press-controlled private agency called the Press–Radio Bureau. While using this material, the networks were prohibited from giving their morning reports before 9:30 a.m. and the evening reports before 9:00 p.m.[36]

During the Press–Radio War of the early 1930s, the arguments made by American publishers and news agencies against radio mirrored—almost exclusively without them acknowledging it—those that their British counterparts had made about the BBC in the 1920s. In both cases, publishers and news agencies wanted to protect their monopolies on the sale and distribution of factual news reports, and few outside publishing circles were happy with the arrangement. Perhaps most significantly, influential American policymakers in the 1930s were extremely dissatisfied with the limited amount of news that now would be presented on participating stations, and many strongly opposed the Biltmore Agreement. Senator Clarence Dill, one of the primary architects of American broadcasting policy, argued that broadcasters owed the public news if they wanted to fulfill their public interest obligations as licensees. Broadcasting news was for American stations "not only their full right. It is their duty. It is a part of that public service which they are bound to give if they are to justify the use of the radio frequencies the government has granted them," and Dill threatened to encourage the revocation the licenses of stations colluding with the press to limit broadcast news.[37]

Just as important as Dill's threat was activity in the private sector, in particular the creation of new wire services established to sell news to radio broadcasters. Most prominently among them, former CBS news staffer Herbert Moore in February 1933 established a radio news organization called Transradio Press aimed at providing news to the many independent stations that were not participating in the agreement. (Only those owned by and affiliated with the networks were.) Moore quickly gathered a small but globally dispersed collection of correspondents into what he called a "new and militant organization," and by June was "producing a daily volume of 30,000 words of fully authenticated, genuinely world-wide flash and bulletin news." By the end of 1933, Transradio had 150 stations subscribing and a potential audience of fifty million for its news reports. Transradio was not the only company to break into this sector. In New England, the owners of the stations comprising the Yankee Network invested significant sums in news-gathering operations, and both UP and INS began selling news to broadcasters in 1935. By that point, pressure from the state and activities in the private sector had broken what one journalist called the "news-strangulation program imposed upon broadcasters by the publishers." Though the Great Depression continued, attempts by publishers to limit competition from radio had been thwarted by pressure from the public and private sectors, and the market for broadcast news continued to develop in the United States. By 1935, one journalist noted that, in New York City, "At several points on the dial, at several hours of the day, the air is supersaturated with news in a variety of forms."[38]

NEWS BROADCASTING ON THE BRITISH AIRWAVES, 1927–36

As American broadcasting was expanding dramatically, so too was the BBC. It grew from a company with 773 employees and 2.2 million license holders in 1927 to an institution with 5,000 employees and 9 million license holders in 1939. After the success of the 1926 General Strike broadcasts, John Reith sought to capitalize on the increased public demand for broadcast news, remarking that "We are anxious to take a lead in ordinary times, as we were through force of circumstances bound to take it in the Emergency." Reith's efforts began to show results in the early years of the new BBC. Though the new BBC still received its news from the news agencies, its daily supply had increased to 5,000 words (at the increased annual fee of £14,000), and the Corporation was allowed to do its first nightly news broadcast at the earlier time of 6:30 p.m. and also to do another at 9:00 p.m. It was granted the ability to broadcast some live events and the capacity to provide context and commentary, though the number of these sorts of broadcasts initially was fixed at a maximum of four hundred per year. By 1929, at an annual cost of £16,000, the BBC was receiving the complete wire services from Reuters and the PA, and it was able to begin editing its own broadcasts based on that news. An increased supply of news to the BBC contributed to an increase in the quantity of news aired. Between 1927 and 1930, the percentage of the broadcast day devoted to news doubled from 4.5 to 9 percent. Still, the amount of news that the BBC aired in its early years remained low compared to other sorts of broadcasting, particularly music, which remained the most popular type of programming. Between 1927 and 1930, the BBC aired an average of 78.5 hours of programming per week, with music amounting to an average of 58 percent of the broadcast content over the period.[39]

Although relationships between the BBC and the press improved and the broadcasting of live accounts increased after 1927, some tension lingered when it came to the broadcasting of news reports. As the BBC noted in 1930, the "general attitude of the Press to broadcasting cannot be described as ever having been cordial, although it has fluctuated between definite hostility and mere watchfulness." Many in the press still considered the BBC a threat to their print sales and, as was the case in the United States, the Depression inflamed these concerns and prompted obstructionist practices. The use of one such tactic began in late 1931, when publishers convinced some government ministers to forbid the broadcasting of news bulletins from government agencies. By that point, the BBC generally received agency news releases late in the day, which afforded time to assemble particularly significant news items for its evening broadcast, thereby scooping the morning papers. What the BBC found after 1931 was that many of these government news releases now came with a "Not For Broadcasting" note, and many in the BBC began to believe that these "embargoes" were deliberate attempts to curtail their ability to provide breaking news reports before the newspapers.[40]

As the BBC navigated these challenges and began broadcasting more news, it generally did so with a very different tone than the popular press, in particular the so-called New Journalism, which had developed in the popular press starting in the 1880s. The term originated with the critic Matthew Arnold, who would later be the most significant influence on John Reith's philosophy of broadcasting. In 1887, Arnold remarked that, though this emerging new style of journalism was "full of ability, novelty, variety, sensation, sympathy . . . [and] generous instincts," it was also defined by the fact that "its one great fault is that it is *feather-brained*." In practice, publishers of the New Journalism aimed for entertainment over enlightenment, a journalistic philosophy that, combined with low prices, attracted wide readership.[41] Some editors celebrated their creation of a new kind of popularly appealing journalism. As Frank Harris, editor of the *Evening News*, remarked, "Kissing and fighting . . . were the only things I cared for at thirteen or fourteen, and those are the themes the English public desires and enjoys today."[42] One could scarcely go further away from the conception Reith had of the BBC's role. Broadcasting, Reith believed, should elevate popular tastes rather than reflect or pander to them, as Harris suggested, and his alignment with Arnold's conception of the New Journalism shaped the kind of news that the BBC broadcast.

Under Reith's leadership, and with increased news reporting capabilities and permissions after 1927, the BBC calibrated the tone and content of its news in opposition to New Journalism. While noting that it still received its news from the newspapers and news agencies, the BBC reminded listeners that a "great many stages have to be gone through before the announcer reads the news to the listening public." BBC representatives described themselves as performing a curatorial function for the news and noted that "One of the most valuable assistants in this task of preparing the bulletins is an extremely large waste-paper basket," into which staffers deposited news agency reports that were "clearly unsuitable for broadcasting." Such inappropriate material included "the long reports of murder trials" and "the accidents which have no outstanding significance." There were always innumerable items that could appropriately "find a place in the columns of a newspaper but must, from considerations of time and policy, be omitted from a broadcast news bulletin." Ultimately, the BBC claimed, the "maintenance of a high standard in the selection of news is of the greatest importance." The application of these editorial policies created an occasional gap between the kind of news the BBC aired and the kind of news the mass public wanted. In one infamous episode demonstrating this disjuncture, the BBC on Good Friday in 1930 reported that, after its news editors looked over the day's bulletins, it regretted to inform listeners that "there is no news tonight." Some in the press quickly seized on this statement, with the *Sunday Chronicle* remarking that "The BBC could have announced the death of Lady Glanely, the fire at Lord Haddo's mansion, the mountaineering accident to Professor Julian Huxley and the motor collision involving Lady Diana Cooper, among other items." Surveys of contemporary public opinion showed that some audience members preferred the news of the *Sunday Chronicle* to that of the BBC. In 1933, for example, the *News Chronicle* surveyed 20,000 readers and found the most popular stories to be ones about "accidents, crime, divorce and human interest," with demand for public affairs reporting much less robust.[43]

Although some listeners might have wished for more colorful broadcasts, other listeners who disliked the tone and content of the popular press held the news reports of the BBC in high esteem. The consistent presentation of "serious" broadcast journalism also garnered the BBC official approbation. The initial charter of the BBC had been for a ten-year term, and when the Ullswater Committee began considering its renewal in 1935, members lauded the BBC's news broadcasting despite acknowledging that the Corporation was "dependent for the bulk of its news on four commercial agencies which are primarily designed to cater for the Press." Committee member Clement Attlee, at the time an MP, was particularly supportive of a change in this arrangement. "In my view," Attlee argued, "it would be desirable that in course of time the B.B.C. should build up its own news service or take over the existing agencies." This, he believed, could better "enable the B.B.C. to give the public fair and impartial information."[44]

After the Ullswater Committee renewed the charter, the BBC did begin to expand its news programming along some of the lines that Attlee had suggested. The BBC had started a separate News Department in 1934 with an initial staff of five, and this expanded to thirty-one by the end of 1938. Perhaps the most important of these new hires was Richard Dimbleby, an ambitious young reporter who advocated a host of new practices for the BBC, for example having correspondents at the ready to go to the scene of an ongoing event. In writing to the BBC in 1936 in hopes of securing employment, Dimbleby suggested that employing live eyewitness accounts from the field would allow the news to be "presented in a gripping manner, and, at the same time, remain authentic." Dimbleby's initiative resulted in a job at the BBC and, not long after he started, World War II offered him and other British broadcast journalists the opportunity to provide unprecedented service to the country.[45]

CONCLUSION: THE MARKETS FOR NEWS IN CRISIS AND WARTIME, 1936–45

During the Second World War, news broadcasting became an essential part of everyday life in Britain and the United States. The Second World War was, as historian Susan Douglas reminds us, "a war that people *listened* to," and this was true on both sides of the Atlantic. Through widely heard and celebrated broadcasts in Britain and the United States, broadcast journalists became trusted sources for reports about breaking news about the war from around the world. In wartime Britain, the political scientist Sir Ernest Baker noted that, for many listeners, it was the BBC's "news that matters—matters above everything else." Baker believed that the BBC was conducting itself admirably in its reporting, and he remarked that there was "little but praise to be given to its collection and presentation of news. It seems to most of us well done— honestly done—objectively done. To turn on the nine o'clock news is to turn on a cold douche from the fountain of truth." Others praised the BBC for providing listeners with the live auditory experience of the war directly from the battlefront. One critic gave particular praise to reporter Charles Gardner for his "most memorable broadcast . . . from the cliffs of Dover during the Battle of Britain. Above his voice listeners could hear bombs exploding, anti-aircraft guns firing, aircraft engines roaring, and the excited voices of gunners." Assessments of wartime radio in the United States were similarly laudatory, and many praised American broadcasters for providing "every lis- tener the running story of the war" from around the world. One observer noted in the *Washington Post* that the "long distance voices in London or Cairo, Moscow or Melbourne, Algiers or Calcutta have been as clear as if uttered in New York or Hollywood . . . The radio reporter and domestic commentators have become institutions of the American scene. Radio has proven its ability to render efficient public service under wartime conditions."[46]

This increased importance of news broadcasting in Britain and the United States represented a convergence of histories that had moved down divergent paths from the early 1920s to the mid-1930s. Starting around 1935 in both countries, news broadcasting in Britain and the United States became both more plentiful in quantity and legitimate in standing, and few of the arguments in favor of limiting it seemed tenable as the war in Europe loomed. For the next decade, broadcasters in the two countries were united in purpose, and many of the journalists risking their lives to provide listeners with news shared goals, values, and practices as reporters. However, during this period, the institutions providing this broadcast news in Britain and the United States still operated within the distinct regulatory regimes that had been developing since the early 1920s. In Britain, representatives at the BBC had sought to provide news coverage back to the founding of the original Company in 1922, and they had encountered consistent opposition from newspaper publishers and news agencies wishing to retain control of the market for news. Prevented from broadcasting themselves, British publishers and news agencies colluded to convince state officials to limit the amount of news that the BBC could broadcast so as to minimize competition from the new medium. Over time, the BBC succeeded in chipping away at press control over the news and, by the mid-1930s, the modified Corporation had established its own news department and begun broadcasting more news. The Ullswater Committee's recommendations for further expansion of news reporting provided additional state support for doing this. In the United States, broadcasters had provided news since the earliest days of the medium, though they had dramatically expanded their capabilities over time. There had been periodic challenges from the press to restrict news broadcasting, most notably from the AP after the 1924 election and during the early stages of the Press–Radio War in 1933. However, these attempts to restrict news broadcasting had proven unsuccessful, due both to the absence of state-imposed limitations on broadcast news and the fact that, unlike in Britain, newspapers were not barred from broadcasting. With so many American newspapers operating stations, the idea of limiting news broadcasting came to be seen by publishers as a self-sabotaging notion. And, as the Ullswater Committee had provided a policy nudge to the BBC's expanded news broadcasting after 1935, in the United States this came in the form of threats from Senator Clarence Dill during the same year to pursue license revocations for stations colluding with publishers to limit radio news.

By the time of the Munich Crisis in 1938, broadcasters in the United States and Britain had used the momentum generated by this respective political support to develop the personnel and practices that they would use to great acclaim during the Second World War. The events leading up to the Munich Crisis began in March 1938 when Germany occupied Austria, and tensions across Europe peaked later in the year when Germany threatened to annex Czechoslovakia. Over the course of eighteen days in September, European leaders met in Munich, where they eventually tried to appease Hitler by agreeing to allow Germany to take Czechoslovakia's Sudetenland. All the while, American listeners were kept abreast of breaking news. According to one estimate, as the networks covered the crisis, NBC broadcast 443 news bulletins comprising 58 hours of broadcast time, and CBS added 54.5 hours of news during the period. This coverage came at great expense, according to the networks, which claimed to have spent $160,000 on it and also refunded another $35,000 to advertisers when they preempted sponsor announcements with news. Foregoing profits for public service proved to be a temporary sacrifice, however. Before long, news broadcasting came to be seen as a good investment and, in the American media, war news became good business. One broadcast executive claimed to have produced eight regular daily news-casts before the crisis, with five or six usually sponsored. Given the explosion in popularity of broadcast news, he now found that he not only had sponsors for all his station's newscasts, but a waiting list. By the time war broke out in Europe the following year, American radio was ready to provide news and generate substantial profits doing so. By the end of the war, almost one fifth of all network programming was news, most of it sponsored.[47]

Likewise, the BBC readily adapted to the needs of war reporting. During the Munich Crisis, the BBC not only aired numerous breaking news reports but also used the event as a means to break away from the group of commercial news services it had been bound to since its founding in 1922. Not long after the conclusion of the crisis, the BBC began subscribing to a wider range of news agency reports from which to develop its daily broad-casts. In September 1939, over vigorous protest from Roderick Jones of Reuters that the existing relationship between the BBC and the news agencies should be maintained, the BBC began purchasing international news from British United Press, a Canada-based subsidiary of United Press of America. In 1942, the BBC also began purchasing news from the AP, giving it additi-onal content from which it could select to report on its expanding newscasts.[48]

Beyond purchasing the content of additional commercial news agencies, the BBC also dramatically expanded its own news apparatus to meet the chal-lenges of reporting the war. News Department director John Coatman brought a number of respected print journalists to the BBC and, by the start of war in September 1939, the BBC news staff was assembling roughly 1.5 hours of news per day, with the two most prominent of the ten daily newscasts airing at 6 and 9 p.m.[49] According to estimates, the 9 p.m. broadcast reached nearly half of the population, and public demand for news broadcasts proved insatiable. As a BBC spokesman remarked during the war, "Once the News was not of very great importance... Now it occupies the peak hours and has swept culture into the background." In July 1939, the BBC commissioned a study of listener attitudes, and the researchers found high levels of interest across all segments of the population. They were surprised to note that, even though their questionnaire to children did not ask any specific questions about attitudes toward news, one in eight young respondents "mentioned it of their own accord as one of the most interesting things they had ever heard." In one group interview, when an adult participant claimed to dislike broadcast news, an "old lady" turned to her in surprise. "Not listen to the News! Why, if we *was* going to war, the first you'd know of it would be the Germans marching up the street!"[50]

Richard Dimbleby, hired by the BBC in 1936, pioneered methods of field recording as he had promised and had become adept at doing remote broadcasts of breaking news. Dimbleby developed a method of using a microphone and an amplifier to allow him to use ordinary telephones as a way of reaching directly to the BBC studios, and he also experimented with mobile recording equipment. A fire at the Crystal Palace in late 1936 was one of Dimbleby's first major scoops, as it started late in the evening after the last papers had gone to press. In March 1937, Dimbleby reported on floods in East Anglia to great acclaim. By the time war broke out, Dimbleby and the BBC had the personnel and the technology to provide audio coverage of the war, and he did so from throughout Europe, North Africa, and the Middle East. One of his most celebrated broadcasts took place in January 1943, when Dimbleby became the first BBC reporter to go on an aerial bombing raid, this one to Berlin. In his subsequent broadcast account of the flight, Dimbleby described the plane taking fire from the Germans as it reached the city, remarking that, "As we turned in for our first run across the city, it closed right around us. For a moment it seemed impossible that we could miss it, and one burst lifted us in the air as though a giant hand had pushed up the belly of the machine."[51] Dimbleby's January broadcast was eleven months before Edward R. Murrow's famous broadcast of an account of his own trip on a bombing run over Berlin. As Dimbleby had, Murrow used radio to bring his audience both a report of the facts of war and a sense of the experience of war. Always a master of simile and the use of visual cues, Murrow told American audiences that, as he came toward the city, the "small incendiaries were going down like a fistful of white rice thrown on a piece of black velvet." The experience, Murrow narrated, led him to see that "Berlin was a kind of orchestrated hell, a terrible symphony of light and flame."[52]

For British and American audiences, the 1943 radio accounts of bombing raids over Berlin by Dimbleby and Murrow were important and exhilarating listening experiences, and they were potent demonstrations of the powerful appeal that broadcast journalism could have. But they were ultimately but two of thousands of reports broadcast on both sides of the Atlantic during a time of great stress and strain. Though the British experienced the horrors of war at a closer physical proximity than did Americans, the fact that broadcasters and broadcast journalists expended tremendous amounts of energy and money collecting and reporting news from around the world meant that, on both sides of the Atlantic, the live sounds and reports of the war were only as far

away as the radio speaker. The temporal lag that had structured mass percep-
tion of First World War had collapsed during Second World War, and radio
afforded listeners around the world a new mediated means of gaining live
access to the scene of distant catastrophe. Indeed, a significant legacy of news
broadcasting during the Second World War was that it initiated a process
continuing down to the present day in which journalists and news organizations have utilized increasing technical capabilities to bring reports of dangerous and violent events from far-off places directly into the home in real time,
and often at great risk and expense.

Ultimately, the increasing prominence and abundance of broadcast news
starting in the 1920s did not spell ruin or even decline for newspapers. In fact,
sales of printed newspapers in both countries actually rose dramatically in
radio's first two decades. In Britain, the circulation of national newspapers
nearly doubled from 5.4 million to 10.6 million between 1921 and 1939. (The
circulation of local daily newspapers stayed constant.) In the United States,
total daily circulation rose from 27.8 million to 41.1 million between 1920 and
1940.[53] In practice, rather than posing a devastating competitive threat to the
newspaper business, radio instead contributed to an expanding multimedia
marketplace for news, and most listeners remained active purchasers and
readers of newspapers.

This continued growth of newspaper circulation was in many ways a
reflection of the fact that radio simply never came to substitute for the
newspaper as a news source. For the consumer, this in some ways had to do
with the ways that the newspaper offered the reader a greater degree of control
over what news he or she consumed than did radio. As the American
journalist Marlen Pew noted, radio had "physical difficulties which, in general
terms, makes it a poor competitor for the established newspaper. These
difficulties include the impossibility of exercise of the selective processes of
the reader—he sits at his radio and takes what is being sent, whether he likes it
or not, and he takes the full dose. With a newspaper the eye skips around on
printed pages, selecting that which it desires as food. Who will be willing to sit
through a radio reading of crop reports to get a craved baseball tidbit? Will
men retire when women's features are being read, and will women turn to the
phonograph for relief when tomorrow's racing entries are flowing from the
loud speaker?"[54] In addition to giving the reader more freedom of selection in
news consumption, newspapers also offered a vastly greater amount of news
content than did radio. According to one estimate in 1935, it would take,
depending upon how fast a radio announcer could read, somewhere between
fifty and eighty hours of continuous reading to get through a Sunday edition of
the *New York Times*, and that was not even factoring in the advertisements.
Though radio retained a tremendous appeal as a source of breaking news and
aural accounts of live events, newspapers always offered readers more control
over how to select from a greater quantity and range of reports. This kept

people in Britain and the United States buying newspapers in ever increasing numbers, even as radio grew in importance as a news source.[55]

By the Second World War, publishers and broadcasters had accommodated themselves to the distinct characteristics of their respective media, and most were clearly aware that the public wanted news from both radio and newspapers and that news organizations could grow and prosper providing that news in both media. As the BBC Director General W. J. Haley put it in November 1944, "The Press is one of our most enduring and vital heritages. Broadcasting has come to stay. In our different ways we must both help each other to serve the public well."[56] Though policy choices had created important structural differences between the broadcasting systems of Great Britain and the United States, those working within them had developed successful news broadcasting practices and operations, and many looked to the postwar period optimistic that the productive wartime partnership between broadcasting and the press in news reporting would continue.

NOTES

1. Susan Douglas, *Inventing American Broadcasting, 1899–1922* (Baltimore: Johns Hopkins University Press, 1987), 53–8; "The Mid-Ocean Daily," *Editor & Publisher*, 2/29 (January 10, 1903), 1; "Published at Sea," *Editor & Publisher*, 2/36 (February 28, 1903), 1.

2. "First True Mid-Sea Daily," *Editor & Publisher*, 3/52 (June 18, 1904), 1; Editorial, "A New Field," *Editor & Publisher*, 3/52 (June 18, 1904), 4.

3. Michele Hilmes, *Network Nations: A Transnational History of British and American Broadcasting* (New York: Routledge, 2012).

4. Asa Briggs, *The History of Broadcasting in the United Kingdom*, vol. 1: *The Birth of Broadcasting* (London: Oxford University Press, 1961), 45–9, 58.

5. Briggs, *Birth of Broadcasting*, 75, 82–5, 95–7; Hilmes, *Network Nations*, 37–9; Herbert Ridout, "Radio Boom Spreads to Britain But Will Be Restricted," *Editor & Publisher*, 55/3 (June 17, 1922), 32; Herbert Ridout, "Radio Is Making Slow Progress in Great Britain," *Editor & Publisher*, 55/10 (August 5, 1922), 6.

6. Adrian Johns, *Death of a Pirate: British Radio and the Making of the Information Age* (New York: Norton, 2011), 17; Ronald Coase, *British Broadcasting: A Study in Monopoly* (London: Longmans, Green and Co., 1950), 12–16; Briggs, *Birth of Broadcasting*, 115–16, 126; C. A. Lewis, *Broadcasting From Within* (London: George Newnes, 1924), 13–15.

7. Coase, *British Broadcasting*, 15–17; Johns, *Death of a Pirate*, 20.

8. Colin Seymour-Ure, "Northcliffe's Legacy," in Peter Catterall, Colin Seymour-Ure, and Adrian Smith (eds), *Northcliffe's Legacy: Aspects of the British Popular Press, 1896–1996* (London: Macmillan, 2000), 9; "Gives Northcliffe Chief Rank as Real Ruler of England," *Editor & Publisher* 51/30 (January 4, 1919), 9; Ridout, "Radio Boom Spreads to Britain But Will Be Restricted," 32; Briggs, *Birth of Broadcasting*, 130–2.

9. Briggs, *Birth of Broadcasting*, 130–3; Donald Read, *The Power of News: The History of Reuters, 1849–1989* (New York: Oxford University Press, 1992), 202; Herbert Ridout, "Radio Programs Must Pay Ad Rates, British Publishers Declare," *Editor & Publisher*, 55/40 (March 3, 1923), 6.
10. Lewis, *Broadcasting From Within*, 20–2, 29; Johns, *Death of a Pirate*, 21–5.
11. The Broadcasting Committee, *Report*, Cmd. 1951 (London: His Majesty's Stationery Office, 1923), 6; Briggs, *Birth of Broadcasting*, 172–3; Herbert Ridout, "British Press Fears Radio Monopoly is Danger to Nation," *Editor & Publisher*, 56/10 (August 4, 1923), 12.
12. The Broadcasting Committee, *Report*, 31, 36; Hilmes, *Network Nations*, 42–6; John Reith, *Broadcast over Britain* (London: Hodder and Stoughton, 1924), 15–19, 139–41, 147, 217.
13. Briggs, *Birth of Broadcasting*, 263–4; Paddy Scannell and David Cardiff, *A Social History of British Broadcasting*, vol. 1: *1922–1939: Serving the Nation* (Oxford: Basil Blackwell, 1991), 25–6, 281.
14. *Report of The Broadcasting Committee, 1925*, Cmd. 2599 (London: His Majesty's Stationery Office, 1926), 4, 22; Briggs, *Birth of Broadcasting*, 265.
15. "The Broadcasting Inquiry," *The Times* (December 18, 1925), 16; Briggs, *Birth of Broadcasting*, 340–1; David Lindsay, Earl of Crawford, *The Crawford Papers*, ed. John Vincent (Manchester: Manchester University Press, 1984), 505–6; *Report of the Broadcasting Committee, 1925*, 5–6, 10–11.
16. Briggs, *Birth of Broadcasting*, 340, 360–8; "B.B.C. and the Strike," *The Times* (May 19, 1926), 28; Harold McKenna, Letter to the Editor, *The Times* (May 14, 1926), 3; Percival Wolton, Letter to the Editor, *The Times* (May 21, 1926), 8.
17. Coase, *British Broadcasting*, 61; Jonathan Silberstein-Loeb, *The International Distribution of News: The Associated Press, Press Association, and Reuters, 1848–1947* (New York: Cambridge University Press, 2014), 157; Terence O'Brien, *British Experiments in Public Ownership and Control: A Study of the Central Electricity Board, British Broadcasting Corporation, and London Passenger Transit Board* (London: George, Allen & Unwin, 1937), 17; Johns, *Death of a Pirate*, 30–1.
18. *The B.B.C. Year-Book, 1930* (London: British Broadcasting Corporation, 1930), 183; "In Interview Hearst Speaks Plainly of Policies of his Organization," *Editor & Publisher*, 57/3 (June 14, 1924), 4; Michael Stamm, *Sound Business: Newspapers, Radio, and the Politics of New Media* (Philadelphia: University of Pennsylvania Press, 2011), 45–58.
19. Ellis Hawley, "Herbert Hoover and Economic Stabilization, 1921–22," in *Herbert Hoover as Secretary of Commerce: Studies in New Era Thought and Practice*, ed. Ellis Hawley (Iowa City: University of Iowa Press, 1981), 47; Radio Talk by Secretary Hoover, Washington, DC, March 26, 1924, 9–10, Commerce Period, Box 489, Folder Radio Correspondence, Press Releases, Misc. 1924 Jan.–March, Herbert Hoover Papers, Herbert Hoover Presidential Library, West Branch, Iowa; Statement by the Secretary of Commerce at the Opening of the Radio Conference on February 27, 1922, 1, Commerce Period Papers, Box 489, Folder Radio Correspondence, Press Releases, Misc. 1922 Jan.–March, ibid.
20. Hilmes, *Network Nations*, 49–50; Hudson Maxim, "Radio—The Fulcrum," *The Nation*, 119 (July 23, 1924), 91.

21. David Moss and Michael Fein, "Radio Regulation Revisited: Coase, the FCC, and the Public Interest," *Journal of Policy History*, 15/4 (2003): 389–416; *Tribune Company v. Oak Leaves Broadcasting Station*, reprinted in *Congressional Record*, 69th Cong., 2nd sess., 1926, 68, pt. 1: 216–17.

22. Louis Caldwell, "The Standard of Public Interest, Convenience or Necessity as Used in the Radio Act of 1927," *Air Law Review*, 1/3 (July 1930), 296; Stamm, *Sound Business*, 45–54, 195.

23. Warren Basset, "Radio Now Paid Advertising Medium Also Special Spot News Carrier," *Editor & Publisher*, 57/11 (August 9, 1924), 3–4.

24. Stamm, *Sound Business*, 32–3; G. C. Arnoux, "Radio Broadcasting—Is It Worth While?" *Editor & Publisher*, 55/39 (February 24, 1923), 27; Eugene Leuchtman, "Small City Newspaper Need Not Risk Fortune For Radio Success," *Editor & Publisher*, 55/42 (March 17, 1923), 12.

25. For a full discussion of the case, see Heidi Tworek's chapter in this volume.

26. "News Broadcasting Before A.P. Board," *Editor & Publisher*, 55/47 (April 21, 1923), 6; Jonathan Silberstein-Loeb, "Exclusivity and Cooperation in the Supply of News: The Example of the Associated Press, 1893-1945," *Journal of Policy History*, 24/3 (2012): 466–98.

27. "Year Report Shows Associated Press Spent Nearly $4,000,000 Covering World News," *Editor & Publisher*, 51/45 (April 17, 1919), 11; Louise Benjamin, *Freedom of the Air and the Public Interest: First Amendment Rights in Broadcasting to 1935* (Carbondale: Southern Illinois Press, 2001), 174–8.

28. Gwenyth Jackaway, *Media at War: Radio's Challenge to the Newspapers, 1924–1939* (Westport: Praeger, 1995), 15–19; "Chicago Tribune Defies Associated Press Rule to Radio Election Returns," *Editor & Publisher*, 57/22 (October 25, 1924), 3.

29. Philip Schuyler, "Press Radiocasting of Election Returns Gives Journalism New Ally," *Editor & Publisher*, 57/24 (November 8, 1924), 3; "A.P. Plans to Detect and Punish Possible Radio Rule Violators," *Editor & Publisher*, 57/25 (November 15, 1924), 8; "A.P. To Defer Action On Radio Cases," *Editor & Publisher*, 57/36 (January 31, 1925), 3; "A.P. Lawyers Consider Possible Broadcasting Test Case," *Editor & Publisher*, 57/27 (November 29, 1924), 6.

30. Douglas Craig, *Fireside Politics: Radio and Political Culture in the United States, 1920–1940* (Baltimore: Johns Hopkins University Press, 2000), 146–9; "Radio and Press Unite at A.P. Luncheon," *Editor & Publisher*, 60/49 (April 28, 1928), 13; "Press to Spread Election News Over Radio," *Editor & Publisher*, 61/24 (November 3, 1928), 9.

31. Warren Basset, "Radio Will Flash Big Fall News Events," *Editor & Publisher*, 57/19 (October 4, 1924), 5; Susan Douglas, *Listening In: Radio and the American Imagination* (Minneapolis: University of Minnesota Press, 2004), ch. 8; "Radio Accelerating Newspaper Circulations, Sarnoff Declares," *Editor & Publisher* 57/34 (January 17, 1925), 18.

32. Advertisement, *Editor & Publisher*, 60/17 (September 17, 1927), 17; "Fight Broadcasting Helped Sell Papers," *Editor & Publisher*, 60/19 (October 1, 1927), 5.

33. Stamm, *Sound Business*, ch. 2.

34. Jackaway, *Media at War*, 86–7.

35. Isabelle Keating, "Pirates of the Air," *Harper's Monthly Magazine*, 169 (August 1934), 463.

36. Stamm, *Sound Business*, 64.

37. "Press Radio Pact Has Failed, Says Dill," *Editor & Publisher*, 67/19 (September 22, 1934), 5–6.

38. Herbert Moore, "The News War in the Air," *Journalism Quarterly*, 12/1 (March 1935), 47, 49–50; "Network is Building its News Service," *Editor & Publisher*, 67/4 (June 9, 1934), 9; Bice Clemow, "I.N.S. Sells Full News Service For Sponsored Radio Broadcast," *Editor & Publisher*, 67/52 (May 11, 1935), 22; Jackaway, *Media at War*, 32–3; Isabelle Keating, "Radio Invades Journalism," *The Nation*, 140 (June 12, 1935), 677; Bice Clemow, "Saturation Point of Air News Near," *Editor & Publisher*, 68/31 (December 14, 1935), 11.

39. Asa Briggs, *The History of Broadcasting in the United Kingdom*, vol. 2: *The Golden Age of Wireless* (London: Oxford University Press, 1965), 6, 35; Scannell and Cardiff, *Social History of British Broadcasting*, 34, 41; Read, *The Power of News*, 203.

40. *B.B.C. Year-Book, 1930*, 183; Scannell and Cardiff, *Social History of British Broadcasting*, 48–9.

41. Matthew Arnold, "Up to Easter," *The Nineteenth Century*, 21/123 (May 1887), 638, emphasis in original; Martin Conboy, *Journalism: A Critical History* (Thousand Oaks: Sage Publications, 2004), 169–73, 189–91.

42. Quoted in Joel Wiener, "How New Was the New Journalism?," in *Papers for the Millions: The New Journalism in Britain, 1850s to 1914*, ed. Joel Wiener (Westport: Greenwood, 1988), 54.

43. *The B.B.C. Year-Book, 1933* (London: British Broadcasting Corporation, 1933), 177–8; Scannell and Cardiff, *Social History of British Broadcasting*, 118; James Curran and Jean Seaton, *Power without Responsibility: Press, Broadcasting and the Internet in Britain*, 7th edn (London: Routledge, 2010), 43.

44. Siân Nicholas, "All the News that's Fit to Broadcast: The Popular Press *versus* the BCC, 1922–45," in *Northcliffe's Legacy*, ed. Catterall, Seymour-Ure, and Smith, 142; *Report of The Broadcasting Committee, 1935*, Cmd. 5091 (London: His Majesty's Stationery Office, 1936), 27, 50.

45. Scannell and Cardiff, *Social History of British Broadcasting*, 118–23.

46. Douglas, *Listening In*, 162, emphasis in original; *BBC Year-Book, 1944* (London: British Broadcasting Corporation, 1944), 18, 29; Ernest Schier, "Radio Now Vital Arm in U.S. War Effort," *Washington Post* (December 27, 1942), L3.

47. Stamm, *Sound Business*, 101–3; James Rorty, "Radio Comes Through," *The Nation*, 147/16 (October 15, 1938), 372, 374; Douglas, *Listening In*, 189.

48. Siân Nicholas, "Keeping the News British: The BBC, British United Press and Reuters in the 1930s," in *Anglo-American Media Interactions, 1850–2000*, eds. Joel Wiener and Mark Hampton (New York: Palgrave Macmillan, 2007), 196, 200–1, 208–10.

49. Scannell and Cardiff, *Social History of British Broadcasting*, 121.

50. Asa Briggs, *The History of Broadcasting in the United Kingdom*, vol. 3: *The War of Words* (London: Oxford University Press, 1970), 47–8; Hilda Jennings and Winifred Gill, *Broadcasting in Everyday Life: A Survey of the Social Effects of the*

Coming of Broadcasting (London: British Broadcasting Corporation, 1939), 14, emphasis in original.

51. Jonathan Dimbleby, *Richard Dimbleby: A Biography* (London: Coronet, 1977), 68–71, 159.

52. Bob Edwards, *Edward R. Murrow and the Birth of Broadcast Journalism* (Hoboken: John Wiley & Sons, 2004), 72, 77.

53. Curran and Seaton, *Power Without Responsibility*, 38–9; Raymond Nixon, "Trends in Daily Newspaper Ownership Since 1945," *Journalism Quarterly*, 31/1 (Winter 1954), 7.

54. Marlen Pew, "Radio Discussed as Press Threat or Promise," *Editor & Publisher*, 56/37 (February 9, 1924), 7.

55. Clemow, "Saturation Point of Air News Near," 11.

56. "Broadcasting to Be Expanded," *London Times* (November 29, 1944), 2.

7

The Decline of Journalism since 1945

James L. Baughman

At the end of the Second World War, the United States and Britain had very different journalistic cultures.[1] America had roughly three times the population of Britain, and many more daily newspapers. In 1946, the United States had 1,763 compared to 116 in Britain.[2] Yet the British were far more likely than Americans to read a paper every day. Indeed, Britain had the most concentrated newspaper circulation in the world, according to a 1953 UNESCO report: 611 copies per 1,000 inhabitants in Britain compared to 353 per 1,000 in the United States, which was tied for tenth.[3] Demand in Britain rose even when government-imposed paper rationing reduced the size of papers. London newspapers, with the exception of the *Manchester Guardian*, dominated the national market; London dailies consumed 60.5 percent of all newsprint during and after the war.[4] The American system was far more decentralized. Less charitably, a British publisher in 1961 dismissed American newspapers as "a lot of little parish magazines scattered over the country."[5] Readers in the Middle West, South, and West had limited access to the nation's best daily, the *New York Times*. Because most American newspapers tended to favor local news, opinion leaders (or those who fancied themselves opinion leaders), seeking more national and international news, had to settle for a weekly newsmagazine, usually *Time*.[6]

How free were journalists in the world's two leading democracies to do their work? The threat of libel action could inhibit reporting in both countries, though this prospect lessened over the next seventy years. In the United States, a 1964 Supreme Court ruling limited the right of public officials to sue for libel.[7] Britain was much slower to follow. Two British legal scholars dubbed London "the libel capital of the world," while American journalists were known to call London "a town named Sue." A 1998 court decision, as well as one by the House of Lords in 2006, nudged Britain toward the protections American journalists enjoyed from libel proceedings.[8] Even so, in late 2012, the *Economist* concluded that "England's libel laws are exceptionally lousy—a lawyers' racket that grossly favours the rich and powerful."[9]

Reporters in the United States generally had greater access to government records, beginning in 1948, with a concerted campaign by the American Society of Newspaper Editors for stronger "open records" laws. These culminated in the Freedom of Information Act (1966), which required federal agencies to publish or make more information available to the public. "The act codified the ideal," wrote one journalism historian, "that federal agency and executive records should by definition be open to public inspection, unless officials could give specific reason for their closure."[10] A lack of formal access to local government proceedings and records in Britain "where governments cover up except on rare occasions" greatly diminished (but did not entirely account for) the quality of reporting, concluded a study conducted in 1976. But greater access did not make every American journalist a watchdog. Indeed, many watchdogs, their masters tied to local political and economic elites, were kept on short leashes or encouraged to nap.[11]

Outside courtrooms, a larger question needs to be addressed. Who made communication policy in Britain and the United States? In Britain, the government occasionally concerned itself with some aspect of communication oversight. But there was resistance, as one communication scholar found, "toward a single media ministry."[12] In the United States, Congress and, in the case of broadcasting, a weak regulatory agency set communication policy. The US Justice Department sometimes got involved.

Despite having so many cooks making policy after 1945, one common objective emerged in both countries. The market rather than the state became the preferred overseer. Competition among media systems was to be encouraged. The premise was simple enough. It was better to have two newspapers serving a community rather than one, or two television channels rather than one. With less enthusiasm, both countries over time relaxed restrictions on journalists in reporting state secrets. As a result, in the United States and Britain, a case could be made that by the mid-1970s the fourth estate had become the fourth estate, that is, relatively independent of government and party. An exception came in the late 1980s and early 1990s, when political pressures compelled the British Broadcasting Corporation (BBC) to restrain some of its reporting. Some of the advances by individual news organizations owed much to contingency, such as the character of ownership and changing composition of the audience. The *Los Angeles Times* became a great American daily after 1960 largely because its publisher, Otis Chandler, aspired to make it so.[13] Then the policy of media diversity arguably went too far. Both Britain and the United States fostered new technologies, in addition to other policies, that began to undermine the practice of serious journalism.

THE POSTWAR YEARS

In the late 1940s, critics of the press and broadcast news could be found on both sides of the Atlantic. In Britain, some noted the declining number of daily newspapers and the growing number of papers owned by single individuals or corporations.[14] The trend could be seen in America, where intra-city competition had disappeared in most smaller cities and towns. More and more papers—just over 40 percent—were held by "chains."[15] Many American newspapers had unabashedly opposed Franklin D. Roosevelt and the New Deal.[16] Members of Britain's Labour Party resented the support many papers had awarded the Conservatives in the 1945 elections.[17] Then, again, regardless of their publisher's party leanings, reporters in both countries could at times be too deferential to those in power. But the tendency was more pronounced in Britain. When Winston Churchill, prime minister again in 1953, suffered a stroke, three leading publishers cooperated in gagging the story; it only became public knowledge a year later when Churchill mentioned how ill he had been.[18]

The first dramatic change in communication policy in either country came with the passage of the Television Bill in Britain in 1954. The bill ended the BBC's monopoly in television broadcasting (it retained one in radio for another seventeen years). One long-time producer believed some within the Conservative Party, which returned to power in 1951, had blamed the BBC in part for their party's defeats in the 1945 and 1950 general elections.[19] At the same time, many, though not all, Tories had concluded that the country would be better served by giving the BBC a *commercial* rival. Competition would increase interest in television (some at the BBC had limited enthusiasm for the newest medium). Then, too, TV advertising, which the BBC did not run, might foster consumer demand and thus help the economy.[20] Proponents were sure Britain could adopt a commercial system without the excesses of America's. "There is also no reason why the standards of advertising in American television should be allowed in this country," Lord Bessborough, an advocate of a commercial system, wrote the *Times* in 1952. A commercial *British* channel could never resemble an American network, the Home Secretary commented, because "we are a much more mature and sophisticated people."[21] The Television Bill created an Independent Television Authority (ITA), which would air advertising. But even the more market-driven Tories only went so far. Although the BBC's commercial rival might not be a government entity, it was subject to various state-imposed rules and objectives. ITA initially awarded seven-year franchises to competing applicants to operate in different geographical regions and nationally at specified times. It was to ensure that entertainment programs would not be offensive, and that news shows were impartial and unsponsored. The government appointed the ITA board.[22]

In May 1955, an alliance of companies producing entertainment programming for ITA joined to launch Independent Television News (ITN). ITN deliberately set its own path. Its first editor, Aidan Crawley, encouraged human-interest stories. At the same time, Crawley grasped, better than his counterparts at BBC TV, that television news required *good visuals*. ITN offered the only film of the fighting during the Suez invasion of 1956. Crawley, a former MP, urged his interviewers to be less deferential. The *Daily Express* judged Robin Day's 1958 ITN interview of Prime Minister Harold Macmillan, "the most vigorous cross-examination a prime minister has been subject to in public." Crawley's formula won the first round. In the early 1960s, the *Economist* noted, ITN's public affairs programs had larger audiences than the BBC's.[23] The *New Yorker*'s London correspondent deemed some ITN current-affairs documentaries "excellent."[24]

The BBC had to play catch-up. The Corporation had not even offered TV news programming between 1946 and 1954, except for a brief late-night rebroadcast of a radio newscast.[25] By comparison, one American network, CBS, had been busily experimenting with televising the news during the Second World War, when few American homes (less than 8,000 in 1945) had TV receivers.[26] For the BBC, ITN's launch forced a change of heart. Audiences could not be taken for granted. "Presentation had to be brighter," one producer recalled.[27] News programs became more probing, less deferential. On the BBC's *Tonight*, a nightly news program launched in February 1957, the "approach to political interviewing was journalistic rather than reverential," one producer recalled.[28] "Above all," wrote one historian, "the programme consciously placed itself on the side of the citizen and the consumer rather than the minister or the official."[29] Over the next twenty-five years, the BBC came to identify with the needs of its audience rather than the government. It became, recalled one veteran manager, "an independent institution."[30]

Competing with ITA, the BBC secured an influential champion in 1962. A royal commission on broadcasting ignored ITA's effects on news programming by emphasizing its shortcomings elsewhere on the schedule. Chaired by Sir Harry Pilkington, the head of England's largest glassmaking concern, the commission determined that ITA scheduled too many quiz shows and violent programs.[31] The commission believed audiences would be drawn to more culturally ambitious programming *if given the choice*. And the government accepted the report's recommendation that a third television channel be awarded to the BBC, and not ITA.[32] The report had the effect of rededicating ITA to news programming.[33] *World in Action*, an award-winning news documentary series, ran from 1963 to 1998. One report, on seven-year-old British children, conveyed the country's class system; it became, at one producer's suggestion, the basis of subsequent *Seven Up!* documentaries. *World in Action*, the director Michael Apted recalled, "was always on the cutting edge and never frightened to speak its mind."[34]

In America in the 1950s, few political leaders involved themselves with communication policy. A prominent Republican senator, John W. Bricker of Ohio, criticized CBS for its coverage of his Constitutional amendment intended to curb the president's treaty-making authority. Though many Republicans eventually took up Bricker's cause, and became active critics of the national broadcast networks, he had few followers in the mid-1950s.[35] Democrats decried "the one-party press" that covered Republican candidates so generously, but sought no legislative relief.[36]

The one-party press critique lost some of its force over the course of the 1950s. More newspapers labored to present the news more objectively, eschewing the willful distortions that had often afflicted political reporting in the 1930s and 1940s. Not every newspaper, to be sure, offered balanced presentation. But Richard Nixon, among others, witnessed the change—with dismay. Nixon had run successfully for the United States Senate in California in 1950, enjoying the one-sided support of Los Angeles's dominant *Times*. Seeking the governorship twelve years later, Nixon realized that the *Los Angeles Times* had undergone a transformation. The *Times* labored to give each major candidate equal coverage. Reporters of his campaign were no longer publicists, but reporters, asking critical questions.[37]

Yet objective journalism could become stenography. A young Russell Baker, reporting from London for the *Baltimore Sun* in 1953, recalled writing a story on a speech in the House of Commons by Foreign Minister Anthony Eden. As Baker prepared his respectful account of Eden's address, a colleague from the *Guardian*, Harry Boardman, shared a copy of his story. "When he rose in the House," Boardman began, "Mister Eden had nothing to say but made the mistake of saying it at great length, omitting hardly a single flatulent Foreign Office cliché." "It was a revelation," Baker wrote. "Until that night I had held religiously to the American faith in 'objective journalism,' which forbade a reporter to go beyond what the great man said."[38]

If Harry Boardman had identified a great flaw in American reporting, A. J. Liebling found one in British journalism several years later. Liebling was America's leading press critic, and no fan of the stenography that Boardman had derided. But when Liebling was in London when Britain and France attacked Egypt, he was amazed by the one-sided reporting he found in Britain's dailies. The invasion bitterly divided Britain, a division reflected too well in the papers. "For those in London who read more than one paper," Liebling wrote, "it was hard to tell, on Wednesday morning after Sir Anthony Eden's cease-fire announcement, whether the end of the shooting in Egypt represented an acknowledgment of political bankruptcy or the magnanimous conclusion of an episode of triumph unparalleled in British history."[39]

BECOMING THE FOURTH ESTATE

Liebling's observation gave one indication of British newspapers' relations to the government. In 1956, they often reflected the political coloration of the individual paper. And that bias was already beginning to break down. When a major spy scandal beset the Macmillan government seven years later, there was no partisan, interpretive divide. Condemnations were widespread.[40]

In America the leading newspapers did not suffer so much from excessive partisanship as an excessive sense of "responsibility." That is, the nation's most prominent dailies regarded themselves as partners in governing the nation. The Defense Department correspondent for the *Washington Post* in 1965 was also a captain in the Navy reserve. Reporters and editors for such dailies might criticize individual actions but not challenge fundamental policies.[41]

What were the "leading" newspapers in the United States? It was, in fact, a very short list. In a 1942 University of Wisconsin survey of 500 American newspaper editors and publishers, 80 percent judged the *New York Times* the country's greatest newspaper.[42] The *Times* self-consciously retained its position in the postwar years, giving it the largest circulation among the opinion leadership.[43] With the greatest reporting resources of any American news organization, the *Times* was one of the few news organizations in 1963 to have a bureau in Saigon, South Vietnam. Its correspondent there, David Halberstam, was critical of the course of the Vietnam War. Tellingly, President John F. Kennedy tried unsuccessfully to have the reporter reassigned. The *Times* was the first major news organization to send a reporter to North Vietnam.[44] The sociologist Herbert J. Gans, in his 1979 study of TV network news, as well as the news magazines *Time* and *Newsweek*, was struck by the influence of the *Times* on whether or how certain stories were carried. "The *Times* is treated as *the* professional setter of standards," Gans concluded, "just as Harvard University is perceived as the standard setter of university performance."[45] Somewhat behind the *Times* in influence, Gans determined, was the *Washington Post*, which in the early 1970s began to compete for the opinion leadership.[46] A former *Post* reporter exaggerated only slightly when he wrote that the paper's publisher and her editor "dragged *The Post* out of the sea of the ordinary and made it great, made it a rival of *The New York Times*."[47]

Both newspapers changed in ways that deeply affected the relationship of the fourth estate to the government. In 1971 the *Times*, then the *Post*, published the "Pentagon Papers," a secret history of the Vietnam War, despite protests from the Nixon administration that doing so posed a risk to national security. Spurning the request was no small matter. The publishers were in effect substituting their judgment, and those of their reporters and editors, for that of the government. The legal counsel of both newspapers had advised against publication.[48]

Publisher Arthur O. Sulzberger of the *Times,* thinking he might face imprisonment, became so distracted one night that he burned the meal he was preparing on the grill for his family. "We dined that evening on salami sandwiches," his daughter remembered.[49] Still, both the *Times* and *Post* prevailed. In a 6–3 vote, the United States Supreme Court ruled against the government and allowed the newspapers to continue publication of the history. "Mr. Nixon," the *Economist* observed without enthusiasm, "suffered an unqualified defeat."[50]

Publishing the Pentagon history signaled the extent to which by 1971 the goodwill the federal government had enjoyed with much of the fourth estate in matters of national security had been largely spent. A credibility gap had grown between the federal government and much of the fourth estate. And the Vietnam War had become enormously unpopular. "The first step toward overcoming the national agony that Vietnam has caused us is to face the truth," declared the *Denver Post* in defense of the Pentagon Papers' publication.[51] These factors made it far more likely that a publisher would, as happened, turn down a personal request from the Attorney General.

A year after the Pentagon Papers decision, two *Washington Post* reporters, Bob Woodward and Carl Bernstein, began investigating the illegal activities of President Richard Nixon's reelection campaign. Their stories greatly boosted the *Post*'s standing as a serious rival to the *Times,* while perpetuating a professional mythology about the importance of investigative journalists. Many in the journalistic community drew a direct line between the *Post*'s reporting and Nixon's resignation from office in August 1974.[52]

In retrospect, it was not the Watergate reporting that marked a new independence by major dailies so much as the Pentagon Papers case. The United States Supreme Court all but sanctioned a more ambitious, even "adversarial" press while acknowledging the press's role in American democracy. The *Times* of London correspondent in Washington deemed the decision "a momentous reaffirmation of the extraordinary protection given to a free press in the American Constitution."[53] In a November 1974 Yale Law School lecture, Associate Justice Potter Stewart, who had voted with the majority in the Pentagon Papers case, agreed. Yet Stewart did not speak of a "reaffirmation." Rather, the justice regarded the aggressive behavior of the *New York Times* and the *Post* of recent origin. "The established American press in the past ten years, and *particularly in the past two years*," he remarked, "has performed precisely the function it was intended to perform by those who wrote the First Amendment to the Constitution."[54]

For many if not most press critics, the investigative reporting of some American dailies was unimaginable in Britain. Particularly for those on the Left, British newspapers were too beholden to those in power. "Why bother to muzzle sheep?" Foreign Minister Ernest Bevin once asked.[55] The Watergate investigation, wrote one prominent historian of the English press, was "regretfully cited as an impossibility under the British system."[56]

Yet some British journalists reported on national security issues, over the objections of the government. There could be penalties. In March 1963, two journalists who had written on a British spy ring were imprisoned for six months each for refusing to reveal their sources.[57] Some reporters remained unintimidated, notably Chapman Pincher, defense correspondent for the *Daily Express* from 1945 to 1979. One historian of the press wrote of Pincher's "truly jaw-dropping ability to get a scoop" on national security issues, often over lunch and a bottle of wine with a security official at the reporter's favorite French restaurant in Jermyn Street.[58] He had no American counterpart working for a major daily.[59] In 1959, an exasperated Prime Minister Harold Macmillan asked, "Can nothing be done to suppress or get rid of Mr. Chapman Pincher?"[60]

Britain even had its version of the Pentagon Papers case. In January 1975, the *Sunday Times* began publishing excerpts from the diaries of Richard Crossman, who had served in the Labour cabinet from 1964 to 1970. Crossman, who had died in April 1974, had hoped his candid observations on cabinet and civil service would paint a more realistic portrait of government, especially of deliberations in the cabinet. The diaries' reconstruction of exchanges between ministers and civil service were *too* realistic for some in the government, including John Hunt, the Cabinet Secretary. Hunt was empowered to approve prior to publication the memoirs of prime ministers and cabinet members; otherwise such publications were not to appear for thirty years, which was his original recommendation for the Crossman diaries. Hunt persuaded Harold Evans, the editor of the *Sunday Times* who had sought to run parts of the diaries, to delete some passages. But when the government moved to block the publication of Crossman's diaries in book form, Evans ran an excerpt from the book without Hunt's review. In the ensuing trial, the *Sunday Times* prevailed when Lord Widgery, the Lord Chief Justice, ruled in favor of the diaries' publication. Lord Widgery, the *Economist* exulted, "has joined the rest of us in disagreeing with the presumption that secrecy is good for the body politic and bureaucratic."[61]

THE POLITICAL AND APOLITICAL ECONOMY
OF NEWSPAPERS

There was a certain irony in the *Sunday Times'* position. Several generations of press critics had decried "media barons" like the owner of the *Sunday Times*, Lord Thomson. One historian dubbed him "a new and somewhat implausible

type of press magnate, who disclaimed the slightest interest in editorial policy
and described balance sheets as his 'favourite reading.'"[62] Yet Harold Evans
regarded Thomson as a model publisher, who stood by his decision to run
Crossman's diaries, despite the possible legal difficulties. "We had the steadfast
support of Thomson," Evans wrote: "He made good journalism possible."[63]

Five years after Thomson's death in 1976, his family elected to sell the *Times*
and *Sunday Times*—and the critics had a new villain. Rupert Murdoch, an
Australian publisher who already owned the *Sun* and *News of the World*,
sought to purchase the two papers. A decidedly controversial figure, Murdoch,
one journalism historian concluded, "has evoked more vituperation than any
press owner of the last 40 years."[64] He made no effort to disguise his contempt
for the "prestige press." His London and American tabloids practiced a
sensationalism that might have impressed, perhaps unnerved, past practitioners of the style like William Randolph Hearst and Lord Northcliffe. By
1978, the journalist Nick Davies later observed, Murdoch had transformed the
moribund *Sun* into England's most popular daily, relying on a formula of
"brash headlines, sensational stories and all the nudes that were fit to print."
"Mr. Murdoch has not invented sex," the *Times* of London cracked, "but
he does show a remarkable enthusiasm for its benefits to circulation."[65]
Murdoch's reputation among the chattering classes was not aided by his
papers' pronounced conservative politics, reflecting the proprietor's deeply
held worldview.[66] That bias did him no harm in seeking to purchase the *Times*
in 1981. Prime Minister Margaret Thatcher, who had enjoyed the ardent
support of Murdoch's papers in the 1979 general election, could have, under
the Monopolies and Mergers Act of 1965 and the Fair Trading Act of 1973,
ordered a formal inquiry and delayed the transaction. Both papers, however,
were losing money, a condition that ostensibly led the government to take no
action.[67] After much wooing (Murdoch could be exceedingly persuasive), most
in the news room, led by Evans, as well as the papers' unionized employees
supported Murdoch's bid. Then, too, Murdoch made a series of concessions that
he would maintain the quality of the *Times* and *Sunday Times*. His bid was
approved and he named Evans editor of the daily *Times*. The marriage proved
short-lived. Murdoch sacked him a year later. Although Murdoch did not
transform the *Times* into a tabloid, it did not practice the aggressive, investigative journalism Evans had championed at the *Sunday Times* in the 1970s.
Murdoch, commented another former *Times* editor, "is not in newspapers to
make the world a better place."[68] Murdoch was hardly finished. Indeed, he came
to loom over Anglo-American journalism more than any other publisher in the
late twentieth century, assembling a vast empire of newspapers, magazines,
television properties, and satellite relay systems.

Like any clever captain of commerce, Murdoch did not allow political
sentiments, even his national identity, to limit his freedom of action. When
his Australian citizenship prevented him from securing American television

licenses, he became an American citizen.[69] Despite his conservative politics, Murdoch was not mindlessly partisan. Self-interest could on occasion trump ideology. Although his papers had strongly supported the Conservatives in the late 1970s and 1980s, they reversed course and backed the Labour Party in the 1997 general election. (The switch came in part because the Labour leader, Tony Blair, had indicated that a Labour government would treat Murdoch's growing British media holdings gently.)[70] Labour won handily.

Murdoch's closeness to Thatcher proved decisive as he engineered a dramatic change in his London papers' production and union relations in 1986. Newspaper trade unions had been among the most militant and best compensated of any in Britain. And publishers in the past had been loath to risk a work stoppage because of the revenues lost from advertising. Concessions were routinely made, not only regarding compensation but also work rules and staffing levels. One scholar estimated that the London papers had three times as many workers as necessary.[71] Murdoch resolved to end such practices. Of his properties, the *Sun* was performing especially well, but he wanted to make more to help finance his American broadcast acquisitions.[72] New offset composition and printing technologies could greatly reduce labor costs. The printers' unions, however, would not accept their implementation because they would reduce the size of the workforce and worker autonomy. The impasse ended in January 1986 when 5,500 union members voted to strike in protest of Murdoch's plans to publish his papers at a new facility, using modestly new technologies, in Wapping. The job action had the opposite effect. Murdoch was able to publish all four papers at the new plant without the strikers. Ten years earlier, the unions would in all likelihood have forced Murdoch's hand. But the Thatcher government had sponsored legislation beginning in 1980 that had greatly curbed the power of organized labor. Secondary strikes were outlawed, the number of pickets at plant entrances limited. Observed a *Guardian* writer, Murdoch "does not just have the best cards, he's got the entire pack."[73] And the government provided Murdoch with a generous police presence—averaging 300 officers a day—around Wapping. At one point in 1986, a scholarly account of the controversy concluded, Wapping "was the most densely policed area in all of the United Kingdom."[74]

Murdoch had prevailed, and changed the rules of metropolitan newspaper publishing. The strikers relented, accepting a buyout in early 1987. Murdoch could then publish his papers with one tenth of the workforce and increase his papers' profitability threefold.[75] Other London papers followed suit. The upmarket broadsheets in particular benefited, by being able to offer larger editions with more sections appealing to more and younger upscale readers.[76]

By the time Murdoch moved his operations to Wapping, American newspapers had fixed their labor and technology costs, including adopting automated typesetting. The victorious proprietors, however, did not need government legislation to tip the scale in their favor, just perseverance. As in

Britain, publishers had to reckon with the opposition of their unionized typesetters, who rightly regarded the new technology as a threat to their status as skilled craftsmen. Photo composition hardware was simpler to operate than the Linotype, which newspapers had used to set pages since the late nineteenth century. A Linotype might require four years to master. Much negotiation followed, and the number of unionized typesetters began to shrink. Some accepted generous buyouts, others were simply let go. The profits of newspapers grew significantly. Among the first was the Missoula (Montana) *Missoulian*, whose profits increased from $259,749 in 1968 to $843,223 in 1975.[77]

Publishing a newspaper in America had become a very lucrative endeavor. Despite the quick spread of television, a daily paper remained for local retailers the best buy. For them, the publisher John S. Knight remarked in 1963, "The newspaper continues to be the basic advertising medium."[78] Classified advertising took on added importance, accounting for 41 percent of newspaper ad revenues in 1988. In the 1980s, the industry analyst Leo Bogart noted, newspapers claimed pre-tax profits in the range of 20 percent, well above the pre-tax profit average (13.6 percent) of Standard and Poor's 400 leading industry companies in 1986.[79] In real terms, newspapers had two-and-a-half times more advertising income in 2,000 than in 1950.[80]

At about the same time, however, newspapers drew the attention of the US Internal Revenue Service (IRS), which found itself making communication policy. The IRS began to challenge the valuations newspaper owners ascribed to their properties for gift and estate tax purposes. In essence, the IRS insisted that newspapers were worth more than their owners claimed, and raised the estate tax accordingly to around 70 percent. This in turn had the effect, along with another IRS rule, of encouraging family-owned newspapers to sell to chains. "A publisher can't leave enough negotiable securities to meet the death tax," a dour John Knight commented in 1977 a few years before his death. "His family must sell to big chains in order to pay off the government."[81]

Some newspaper publishers also had to worry about the Justice Department, which challenged joint-operating agreements (JOAs) between papers competing in the same communities. Beginning in the 1930s, some competing daily papers agreed to share advertising revenues, printing facilities, and distribution costs while maintaining separate editorial operations.[82] JOA newspapers insisted that without the efficiencies achieved by the agreements, one of the competing papers would cease operations. Justice Department investigators, however, deemed JOAs a violation of the Sherman Anti-Trust Act.

Congress stepped in, passing the Newspaper Preservation Act of 1970. Introduced by Democratic Senator Daniel K. Inouye of Hawaii, the law sanctioned joint operating agreements in twenty-two cities. Heavily lobbied by their hometown publishers, members of Congress and President Nixon accepted the industry argument that without JOAs, competing papers would close. Declared Inouye, "We have saved one paper in each of 22 cities from going out of business," including in Inouye's hometown of Honolulu.[83] Although the prominent press critic Ben H. Bagdikian cast the Newspaper Preservation Act in the worst possible light (it did benefit some major newspaper chains), the law did help to prop up many dailies for a generation. There is little doubt that communities *were* better served having two newspapers even when, as one study found in the wake of the closing of the *Cincinnati Post* in 2007, the second daily had a modest circulation and reporting resources.[84]

Newspaper regulation in Britain came to resemble that in the United States. Many especially in the Labour Party had long worried about the possibility of an individual proprietor controlling too many papers with too much circulation. That publisher might insist that his papers advance a specific, often Tory, political agenda. In 1965, under the Labour government of Harold Wilson, Parliament passed the Monopolies and Mergers Act, which made any newspaper purchase subject to governmental review. In theory, the government was to consider whether the proposed acquisition granted the buyer too large a share of national circulation. In practice, governments—Labour and Conservative—gave greater weight to the financial woes of the property. If, as happened in 1981, the *Times* was losing money, then the government refused to hold up a sale by conducting a formal inquiry.[85]

ON THE AIR

For more than half a century, the American government encouraged broadcast journalism. It did so without ever seriously considering the formation of a federal network along the lines of the BBC. The prevailing assumption among policymakers in the 1920s and 1930s was that commercial entities would operate most radio stations and do so in "the public interest." Because the radio spectrum is limited, Congress empowered the Federal Radio Commission (FRC), then the Federal Communication Commission (FCC), to award radio, then television, licenses. In the process, federal overseers listed various *types* of programs, including news, which license holders were to offer. To obtain a renewal of their license, after three years, broadcasters had to demonstrate they had in fact upheld the public interest by airing these program "types." The expectation was vague. Neither the FRC nor FCC stipulated that a specific percentage of the schedule had to be dedicated to such programs.[86] Yet station managers understood they could not run their operations like a movie house, which might show a newsreel, or might not. Although the broadcast networks were not subject to direct federal oversight, they owned profitable radio licenses. They assiduously sought the goodwill of regulators and influential members of Congress. As a result, the two dominant networks, CBS and NBC, spent considerable resources on news, but much of this investment only came on the eve of the Second World War, when public interest in—and advertiser demand for—news broadcasts grew enormously.[87]

With the advent of television in the late 1940s, the networks labored to please the FCC and Congress, without losing their shirts. Various ratings services indicated that most viewers preferred entertainment to informational programming.[88] Nonetheless, the networks made small concessions to the guardian class, notably in telecasting an especially newsworthy Congressional hearing and the national party conventions. But such public-spirited gestures became less common as the total audience for television grew, along with advertiser interest in sponsoring entertainment programming. A case in point came in early 1954 regarding the airing of a Senate hearing investigating charges by Senator Joseph R. McCarthy, Jr. that the Army had lax internal security procedures. The allegations, by the nation's foremost and notorious anti-Communist crusader, caused a sensation. Yet CBS declined to televise any of the hearings, and NBC dropped its telecasts after several days. Too much money could be made airing regularly scheduled daytime entertainment programs. ABC did air the hearings, but many of its affiliates declined to carry some or all of the telecasts. Four years later, CBS canceled the critically praised documentary program, *See It Now*, hosted by Edward R. Murrow. Although many decried the network's decision, *See It Now* had been expensive to produce and had been unable (and, in truth, unwilling) to compete for viewer favor.[89] CBS and NBC shifted to a more calculated strategy about news programming. Each would concede some hours to news, but closely monitored costs and, in most instances, secured sponsors.[90]

In the early 1960s, CBS and NBC, which remained the dominant TV networks, poured more resources into their early evening newscasts. They were attracting advertisers and viewers. The problem was their length. Since the late 1940s each newscast ran fifteen minutes. More commercials could be sold and money made if each program could run a half-hour. Here the federal government quietly intervened. The FCC under Newton N. Minow, a John F. Kennedy appointee, had made clear its enthusiasm for news programming. This was a calculated bias. Minow had dismissed television as "a vast waste-land" in a May 1961 speech. But later in the year, his praise of specific entertainment programs provoked a furor. Even some allies in the press questioned the propriety of an FCC chairman volunteering a positive judgment on individual programs. Minow retreated; instead of suggesting entertainment productions he found worthy, he stressed the need for more educational programming for children and, even more, the virtues of informational programming. This made political sense. Many in broadcasting and Congress might defend the cultural value of the Western *Bonanza*. Yet at the time most opinion leaders, especially within the Kennedy administration, welcomed the airing of more news programs, which tended then to flatter those in power. And this preference was subtly conveyed to network affiliates, who had been unwilling to surrender an extra fifteen minutes to the networks, or, in many cases, increase their own newscasts.[91] CBS and NBC expanded their evening newscasts to a half-hour in September 1963. ABC, which had far less money—and enthusiasm for news—followed four years later.

Into the early 1980s the networks' early evening newscasts enjoyed a comfortable position. The structure of American broadcasting created what might be called a "benevolent oligopoly." The newscasts' producers had a largely captive audience. In most markets, set owners were only served by network-affiliated stations, which tended to schedule their newscasts at the same time. A viewer in such communities who turned on her set in 1970 at 6:30 (ET) could only select from one of the three newscasts. That circumstance fueled advertiser demand, making the newscasts highly profitable. Despite pressure to lead in the ratings, the three network newscasts were in fact only competing *with each other*. That is, they did not have to contend with channels or stations that did not offer news. So the evening newscasts could and did take an essentially serious approach to information, with the occasional feature story aired near the end of the program.[92] For viewers, civics class was required.[93]

A different journalistic culture developed among local American TV stations. After 1963, stations increased their early evening and morning news programs not because of any hints from the FCC but because they could earn much more money. Stations owned their news shows; they did not have to pay a hefty rights fee to rerun a popular network series. And local newscasts attracted advertisers, who in turn pressed stations to boost their ratings. Station news producers could have followed the lead of their network colleagues and adhered to a more sober agenda, one that, for example, prioritized news about government and politics. Most took the money and ran. Certain types of stories—with good visuals and emotional appeal to a lower middle- and lower-class audience—trumped others.[94]

Even network news executives, who regarded their local station counterparts with growing disdain, became more calculating about what they aired in the evening. Hour-long documentaries, which had been a mainstay on the schedule, might impress critics, but they were usually too unpopular to justify continued production. In their place came news "magazines," notably *60 Minutes*, which covered multiple stories in engaging, sometimes melodramatic, ways. (It bore some resemblance to the BBC's *Panorama*.) Again, federal encouragement was no longer a factor. The popularity of *60 Minutes* determined its place on the schedule. It had become a very profitable franchise, earning as much as $2 billion for CBS between its launch in 1968 and 2004. Murrow's partner, Fred Friendly, was not impressed. Except for one story, he remarked in 1983, "It is hard for me to remember a single broadcast of *60 Minutes* that played an important part in making the American people think hard about a complex issue. It is a very successful program. I watch and enjoy it, but it isn't what Murrow did. It prides itself first on the audience and the revenues and then on the program."[95]

Americans had alternatives to this increasingly commercial journalistic culture. In 1967, Congress passed the Public Broadcasting Act, which combined a string of educational television stations into a public broadcasting network (PBS). National Public Radio soon followed. Both PBS and NPR produced news programming but neither enjoyed recourse to a license fee like the BBC.[96] Different commissions funded by the Carnegie Corporation emphasized public broadcasting's financial woes. The 1979 commission spoke of "the system's chronic poverty." The 2008 panel concluded that "funding remains its greatest problem."[97]

By comparison, the British government remained more committed to broadcast journalism. In 1982, the government awarded a fourth channel, to the Independent Broadcasting Authority (IBA), the successor to ITV. Again, there were strings. Channel Four was expected to produce public service programming, which occupied about half of evening prime time. These included the well-regarded *Channel Four News* and the *Friday Alternative*.[98]

At the same time, the government's attitude toward the BBC underwent a sea change. Many Tories, among them Prime Minister Thatcher, deeply mistrusted the BBC. In 1982, during the Falklands War, the BBC's reporting appeared too objective for some Conservatives. They were more exasperated by what they construed to be the BBC's apparent sympathy for the Irish Republican Army.[99] The Thatcher government commenced a not too subtle attempt to restrain the BBC's journalism. The prime minister appointed individuals who shared her misgivings about the Corporation to its Board of Governors (such appointments had previously been non-partisan); she also installed a like-minded board chairman. By 1987, Thatcherites constituted a majority of the board. The director-general was removed and replaced by Michael Checkland, an accountant. He and his deputy, John Birt, worked to rein in producers. Birt disdained documentaries that he regarded as too "bitty." Programs or newscast features that might upset the Conservatives (who remained in power until 1997) were pulled.[100]

Thatcher's policies diminished the editorial independence of the news productions of both the BBC and IBA. Her government's communication policy fostered more competition through the introduction of cable television and satellite dish systems, and an additional broadcast channel.[101] The 1990 Broadcasting Act weakened the IBA's public-interest orientation. The Act had the effect of changing broadcast journalism at ITN, which, for the first time, would have to seek advertising. And ITN began imitating its American counterparts. News from overseas was reduced.[102] "Its approach to news," wrote one British media scholar, "became more popular, more concerned with 'human interest' stories."[103] ITN moved its 10 p.m. newscast later to allow for more popular entertainment programming and eventually dropped *World in*

Action. The program's disappearance, wrote the former editor of the *Sunday Times* (and heretofore a champion of broadcast competition), denoted the extent to which television news in Britain pursued "a tabloid agenda with an emphasis on consumer concerns and stunts."[104]

ITN also had to reckon with the growth of cable and satellite systems that afforded many more channels. The Thatcher government sanctioned Murdoch's Sky satellite system. Murdoch promised British viewers a new world of choices—and relief not only from BBC but from IBA as well. "Broadcasting in this country," he remarked in 1988, "has for too long been the preserve of the old Establishment that has been elitist in its thinking and in its approach to programming." Sky would give consumers choices they did not have with the on-air system.[105] Subscribers could view the Movie Channel, the Family Channel, the Children's Channel, the American Cable News Network, as well as Murdoch's Sky News, and several devoted to sports. This much longer menu attracted more and more Britons. By 2002, just under 40 percent of all British homes had cable or satellite links.[106]

America similarly came to accept the potential of cable. At first, the FCC fretted that cable might adversely affect, even wipe out, smaller stations. Commission regulations had the effect of inhibiting cable's growth. (Local governments, in their licensing of cable operations, often slowed cable's expansion as well.) Eventually Congress intervened, passing the Cable Communications Act of 1984, which essentially freed the industry from much FCC and local oversight.[107] The percentage of homes with cable increased from 19.8 percent in 1980 to 51.1 percent eight years later.[108]

Cable's spread in America provided alternatives to network news. Viewers no longer *had* to watch a network newscast at 6:30 (or nothing at all). Between 1981 and 2001, the total audience of the three early evening newscasts fell by 40 percent.[109] The explosion of choice had notable effects on younger viewers. Most never took up their parents' habit of watching local and network newscasts, favoring more entertaining alternatives on cable. This had arguably negative consequences for the political culture.[110] Some evidence suggested that younger consumers, both in the United States and Britain, had developed a more cynical attitude toward citizenship.[111] This sensibility in turn caused many to regard the task of staying informed less seriously, if they regarded it at all. Some spurned the consumption of news (both broadcast and print) altogether or limited their informational diet to satirical news presentations on cable comedy channels. The broadcast networks responded by deemphasizing news from abroad and Washington. The new agenda dismayed traditional champions of TV news. "The networks have cheapened the news," Newton Minow noted in 1997.[112] But nothing could reverse the downward trend.

British broadcast journalism was traveling a similar path. In the early 2000s, homes with cable or satellite access were much less likely to watch the BBC's current event programs, *Correspondent, Newsnight,* and *Horizon.* In this more competitive world, the marketing of news programs suddenly became important, even at the BBC. "We are over-serving white, middle-class 55-year-olds," one BBC executive confessed in 2007.[113] ITN news producers were lectured on the importance of the younger viewer, the 16–34-year-old demographic, while being warned, in one instance, not to include three-syllable words in the script. Another, pitching a documentary on the Falklands War, was asked, "What's in this for the woman under thirty-five?"[114] Mourning the passing of his old producer, Denis Forman of Granada Television, the director Michael Apted remembered "lively times and I doubt we'll see their like again as the business has become more fragmented and its values compromised."[115]

The market as regulator displaced an older standard regarding broadcast news. That standard had never been fixed, hardly perfect, and certainly not democratic. Simply put, news judgment—that is, what stories should be covered, in what order or proportion—was to be based on more than audience demand. *Producers* were expected to weigh the relative importance of news as opposed to what might most engage viewers. But viewer interest increasingly affected news judgment. In that sense, the market assumed control of the news agenda. In July 2013, both of the channels of America's leading cable news network, CNN, offered continuous coverage of the trial of George Zimmerman, a neighborhood watch volunteer accused of killing an unarmed youth. Slighted were reports on the deaths of nineteen firefighters in Arizona and a coup in Egypt. CNN was gambling that the Zimmerman trial would be another "blockbuster" story that would draw more viewers to their channels.[116]

In some cases, the *relaxation* of government oversight had consequences for broadcast journalism. In 1987 the FCC rescinded the Fairness Doctrine, which had required broadcast licensees to give balanced treatment of controversial issues. If a radio talk show host proved decidedly one-sided on an important matter, the Commission could force the station to offer those with opposing viewpoints a reasonable opportunity to present their opinion.[117] For decades, the doctrine had the effect of inhibiting speech, especially that exercised by those on the extremes of the political spectrum.[118] The end of the Fairness Doctrine brought forth a thousand radio talk show hosts—or so it seemed, overwhelmingly conservative.[119] Roger Ailes drew on the right-wing opinionated-news model when he started the Fox News Network in 1996. It proved a great financial success, and prompted MSNBC, another news channel, to adopt a liberal slant. "By some measures," wrote one reporter in 2012, "the partisan bitterness on cable news has never been as stark—and in some ways, as silly or small."[120]

Conservative talk radio challenged the credibility of American journalism. Denigrating the messenger was not peculiar to the United States. The Murdoch newspapers had relentlessly criticized the BBC in the 1980s.[121] Beginning in the early 2000s, American talk radio hosts regularly and stridently assailed the mainstream news media, including local newspapers, accusing them of liberal bias.[122] There was some irony here. Many if not most talk show hosts had no journalistic credentials. The most notorious, Rush Limbaugh, had been a radio disc jockey. Yet many listeners cared little about the host's background. They were drawn to his expression of a deeply felt, probably long-held, resentment toward the fourth estate. Talk radio was their safe harbor. As Thomas Frank observed in his study of many Kansans' turn to the hard right, "They can turn to nearly any station on the AM dial to hear their views confirmed."[123]

THE NEXT NEW THING

The rise of opinionated talk in America marked only the first round of a frontal assault on traditional journalism. A far greater challenge in both America and Britain came with the Internet, which offered immediate access to a host of commercial and informational sites. Access depended on having a computer or mobile device. And until the last decades of the twentieth century, computers were very large, data-processing machines operated by government agencies and businesses. They might occupy an entire room or more. But American computer scientists, many of them young entrepreneurs, created the personal computer (PC), a much smaller machine that could be installed in a person's workstation or home—and could be something more than a powerful calculator.[124]

Such an advance would not likely have occurred, or have occurred when it did, without federal patronage. The American government played a major role in funding computer technologies. Between 1949 and 1959, one study concluded, the American government accounted for 59 percent of all domestic investment in computer research and development. Much of this largesse, it should be realized, resulted from the Cold War rivalry with the Soviet Union, which also generously supported computer R&D. New computer technologies were expected to serve military ends.[125] Among those ends was the Internet. For various reasons, among them a search for a decentralized communication system in the event of a nuclear attack, in the 1960s and 1970s the American Defense Department provided funds for university scientists to work on a computer-based information network.[126] The commercial possibilities were not evident, even after a successful demonstration of the Internet in 1972; AT&T declined an offer to take over the project.[127] In 1983, the Defense Department surrendered partial control over Internet research by allowing the formation of a separate unit that would focus on the civilian uses of the technology. This division hurried the technology's development, as did the steady spread of personal computers in the 1980s. Research universities were among the first to acquire Internet access. Many businesses followed. Not content to let the private sector resolve matters, Congress appropriated $2 billion in 1991 in part to advance a high-speed network.[128] Although Britain had led the world in 1939 in what became computer technology, it was unable to sustain a domestic computer industry and had to settle for promoting the diffusion of personal computers in education and the workplace in the 1980s and 1990s.[129] What was initially envisioned as a new means of interpersonal communication became something else. In the early 1990s, a British computer scientist, Tim Berners-Lee, developed what became the World Wide Web. At relatively low cost, individuals and corporations could launch websites to sell their goods or ideas. "The Web," Janet Abbate wrote, "completed the Internet's transformation from a research tool to a popular medium."[130]

As a popular medium, the Internet posed enormous challenges to the established mass media, notably daily newspapers. Although American newspaper publishers were not indifferent to the new technology, few realized *how* disruptive the Web would be to their operations. Websites matched the printed media's textual representation, and could be updated quickly, without regard to fixed production and delivery deadlines. Moreover, the Web's capacity for instantaneous delivery possessed more mass appeal than many in the news media initially grasped. "Most consumers really do not have a pressing need for instant information," a prominent industry analyst wrote in 1993.[131] In fact, many younger consumers would no longer wait for the arrival of a morning paper, if mobile devices afforded them immediate access to news or a soccer score. An "on-demand" news culture grew enormously.[132]

Nor did most editors and publishers initially recognize that certain websites would weaken their control over the news agenda. An early harbinger of the new media landscape came in 1998. A special prosecutor was considering charging President Bill Clinton with perjury concerning his sexual liaisons. A *Newsweek* reporter learned that a key witness, a former White House intern, had a sexual relationship with the president. His editors chose not to run the story. Five hours later that decision appeared on a website, the *Drudge Report*, a one-man operation based in Los Angeles, and was soon picked up by news outlets everywhere.[133] Clinton subsequently faced impeachment and removal from office.[134]

The Web had effects on the demand side of journalism. Using the Web, consumers could tailor their acquiring of information according to personal interest. In a 1993 talk, the popular writer Michael Crichton looked forward to being able to assemble his own news agenda. "I will have artificial intelligence agents roaming the databases, downloading stuff I am interested in, and assembling for me a front page, or a nightly news show, that addresses *my* interests. I'll have the top stories that I want."[135] Crichton, who fancied himself a futurist, did not anticipate that the Web would contribute to a more partisan journalism. In his address, Crichton decried "the impulse to polarize every issue."[136] Yet some websites, like talk radio programs, only encouraged this tendency. Some had clear political leanings and, for an increasing number of Americans, became informational enclaves. A reporter covering the 2012 South Carolina Republican presidential primary observed, "More and more citizens" no longer read their morning papers, instead "tucking themselves inside information silos where they see mainly what they already agree with. The result, according to voters, campaign strategists and a raft of studies that track users' news choices, is an electorate in which conservatives and liberals often have not only their own opinions but also their own set of facts, making it harder than ever to approach common ground."[137]

In the end, government policy mattered to American and British journalism, though not in the ways some planners imagined. The law of unintended consequences was at work. Consider two of the most significant actions by the American government. Many conservative advocates of deregulation, including President Ronald Reagan, ardently supported the end of the Fairness Doctrine. Yet some on the right feared the doctrine's demise would unleash the "liberal" media.[138] The opposite occurred. The World Wide Web allowed for the creation of a myriad of individual sites, some of which could and did challenge the financial health and reportorial authority of the established news media.

The Web's effects on newspapers deserve special mention. Many, if not most, younger Britons and Americans have no special attachment to the newspaper. It seems something a grandparent read most avidly. Its importance to a democratic society hardly appears obvious. Yet even in the new, wired century, newspapers produced perhaps 85 percent of all of the news, in other words, information that had not been known. (Much of the news upon which website contributors and radio talk show hosts commented had, in fact, been revealed by a newspaper.)[139] But the Web left the traditional daily imperiled. The Web all but wiped out newspaper classified advertising, which had been a major revenue stream.[140] With advertising and subscriber revenues falling, metro dailies had to cut costs. In Britain, newspaper advertising spending shrank by 10.2 percent in 2012; forecasts indicated advertising on newspaper websites would make up only about 25 percent of the 400 million pounds expected to be lost by the end of 2014.[141] In both countries, reporting staffs were slashed. In America, the total number of newspaper editorial employees fell from about 60,000 in 1992 to 38,000 in 2012. The circulation of the *Los Angeles Times* fell by nearly 50 percent between 2000 and 2010, as did the size of its newsroom. "We need a paper that's more, and this is less," one longtime reader complained in 2011. "It used to be a world-class paper."[142]

In Britain, falling circulations and a loss of advertising revenue wiped out the gains of the Wapping Revolution. Except for the *Daily Telegraph*, all of the quality dailies, including Murdoch's *Times* and *Sunday Times*, were losing money. The list included the *Guardian*. It had moved its editorial operations to London in the 1960s and had many admirers. But it struggled to find enough of them, or hold them. Its average circulation fell from 403,297 in October 2005 to 217,190 in March 2012. Of the country's eleven national dailies, the *Guardian* ranked tenth in circulation. The finances were equally depressing. £40 million in classified advertising had been lost. The newspaper division of the Guardian Media Group, which included the *Observer*, lost £37 million in the 2009–10 financial year. Operations of the *Guardian* alone absorbed losses of £33 million in 2011, roughly £100,000 a day, and despite several rounds of layoffs. "The feeling persists," wrote one journalist, "that the *Guardian* may be heading full steam towards an iceberg."[143]

Perhaps. Even in the worst of times, the *Guardian* could produce great journalism. Beginning with a major 2003 investigation on the illegal activities of an arms manufacturer, the *Guardian* began running stories that had extraordinary consequences at home and abroad. It revealed that reporters and editors working for Rupert Murdoch had illegally "hacked" or gained access to the voicemails of various celebrities, including the Prince of Wales and, most disturbingly, a July 2011 story revealed, those of a murdered teenage girl. Some 3,000 voicemails may have been hacked. This reporting excess had persisted in part because Murdoch's minions had cultivated, via cash and other inducements, the goodwill of Scotland Yard. The reporting brought great dishonor to a media baron who had, in fact, little if any honor to spare. Murdoch closed the *News* and withdrew his bid to assume full control of Britain's largest satellite broadcaster. "A once feared colossus," the *Economist* remarked, "has become a pantomime villain, hissed from the stage."[144] Two years later, the *Guardian* reported on a vast surveillance program by the US National Security Agency, raising the paper's profile, the *Washington Post* observed, "to an Everest-like peak."[145]

Possibly the *Guardian* and other traditional news outlets can find a way to survive. Optimists noted the popularity of the *Guardian*'s website, which in 2012, ranked among the five most viewed newspaper sites in the world. Americans made up a third of its traffic. (In the 1980s, it is worth noting, Americans would have had to find a very good newsstand or university library to secure a hard copy of the *Guardian*, published some days earlier.) Nevertheless, the *Guardian* has yet to find a way to make the website support its journalism, and it may die a slow death.[146] What will take its place? Who will monitor the misdeeds of government and buccaneers like Murdoch? Perhaps journalism will reinvent itself, and the huge role some news organizations have played in gathering and presenting information can be replicated online. Some hope that nonprofit organizations will make up the difference, or, more generally, that a generation of "citizen journalists" will effectively replace newspaper reporters.[147] The last prospect may be very wishful thinking, as one wag cracked, akin to taking one's spouse to a fine restaurant only to discover that the meal will not be prepared by a trained chef, but a couple at another table. They *might* be very good cooks, or they might not.

NOTES

1. The author thanks Mitchell Bard, Harvey Black, Martin Conboy, Anuj C. Desai, Robert Drechsel, and Lucas Graves for their counsel, and Samuel Gale and Caitlin Cieslik-Miskimen for their research assistance.
2. Great Britain, Royal Commission on the Press, *Memoranda of Evidence Submitted to the Royal Commission on the Press* (London: HM Stationery Office, 1947), 2; Christopher H. Sterling and Timothy R. Haight, *The Mass Media: Aspen Institute Guide to Communication Industry Trends* (New York: Praeger, 1978), 20.
3. UNESCO, *The Daily Press: A Survey of the World Situation in 1952* (Paris: Clearing House, Department of Mass Communication, 1953), 19.
4. J. Edward Gerald, *The British Press under Government Economic Controls* (Minneapolis: University of Minnesota Press, 1956), 69, 87, 191; Graham Murdock and Peter Golding, "The Structure, Ownership and Control of the Press, 1914–76," in *Newspaper History: From the 17th Century to the Present Day*, ed. George Boyce, James Curran, and Pauline Wingate (London: Constable, 1978), 132–3.
5. Pat Munroe, "British Tycoon [Cecil King] Lords It Over Our Press," *Editor & Publisher* (May 20, 1961), 18.
6. James L. Baughman, *Henry R. Luce and the Rise of the American News Media* (Baltimore: Johns Hopkins University Press, 2001), 51–3, 170.
7. *New York Times v. Sullivan*, 376 US 254 (1964). The decision did not prove as liberating as hoped. See Kermit L. Hall and Melvin I. Urofsky, *New York Times v. Sullivan: Civil Rights, Libel Law, and the Free Press* (Lawrence: University Press of Kansas, 2011), 182, 190–8; Anthony Lewis, *Make No Law: The Sullivan Case and the First Amendment* (New York: Random House, 1991), ch. 18, 244–5; Ronald Dworkin, "The Coming Battles over Free Speech," *New York Review of Books* (June 11, 1992), 55, 63–4.
8. Geoffrey Robertson and Andrew Nicol, *Media Law*, 5th edn (London: Sweet & Maxwell, 2007), xiii–xiv, 93–5, 97–101. See also Lord Thomson of Fleet, "On Reform of the Libel Laws," May 25, 1966, reprinted in *The British Press since the War*, ed. Anthony Smith (Newton Abbot: David & Charles, 1974), 225–6.
9. "Hacked to Pieces," *The Economist*, December 2, 2012, 12.
10. James L. Aucoin, "The Re-emergence of American Investigative Journalism," *Journalism History*, 21 (Spring 1995), 10. Aucoin notes that many states followed suit. See also "Freedom of Information Bill Enacted," *1966 Congressional Quarterly Almanac*, 556–9.
11. David Murphy, *The Silent Watchdog: The Press in Local Politics* (London: Constable, 1976), 11, 168. See also David L. Paletz, Peggy Reichert, and Barbara McIntyre, "How the Media Support Local Governmental Authority," *Public Opinion Quarterly*, 35 (Spring 1971): 80–92 and Henry Fairlie, "Bound to Sell," *Harper's*, 258 (June 1979), 80.
12. Jeremy Tunstall, *The Media in Britain* (New York: Columbia University Press, 1983), ch. 16.
13. Jack R. Hart, *The Information Empire: The Rise of the Los Angeles Times and the Times Mirror Corporation* (Washington, DC: University Press of America, 1981), ch. 9; Otis Chandler obituary, *New York Times*, February 28, 2006.

14. Statement of the National Union of Journalists, June 3, 1947, *Memoranda of Evidence*, 2, 5.
15. Communities with competing dailies had declined from 502 in 1923 to 137 in 1943. See James L. Baughman, "Wounded But Not Slain: The Orderly Retreat of the American Newspaper," in *The History of the Book in America*, vol. 5: *The Enduring Book: Print Culture in Postwar America*, ed. David Paul Nord, Joan Shelley Rubin, and Michael Schudson (Chapel Hill: University of North Carolina Press, 2009), 122-3.
16. See, e.g., George Wolfskill and John A. Hudson, *All But the People: Franklin D. Roosevelt and his Critics, 1933-1939* (New York: Macmillan, 1969), ch. 7. The charge has been qualified by some scholars, including Graham J. White, *FDR and the Press* (Chicago: University of Chicago Press, 1979), chs 4-6.
17. Even though, as the Northcliffe Newspaper Group, among others, reminded the Royal Commission, the Tories were badly beaten. See *Memoranda of Evidence*, 66, 141. Stephen E. Koss believes the 1945 campaign marked the beginning of the end of the old party press model in England, though the political class was slow to realize the transformation taking place. See *The Rise and Fall of the Political Press in Britain*, 2 vols (London: Hamish Hamilton, 1981-4), vol. 2, 623-32, 658-9. Partisanship returned in the mid-1970s, James Curran and Jean Seaton forcefully argue. See *Power without Responsibility: Press, Broadcasting and the Internet in Britain*, 7th edn (London: Routledge, 2010), 68-73.
18. Jeremy Tunstall, *Newspaper Power: The New National Press in Britain* (Oxford: Clarendon Press, 1996), 243-4; John Colville, *The Fringes of Power: 10 Downing Street Diaries 1939-1955* (New York: W. W. Norton, 1985), 668-9.
19. Grace Wyndham Goldie, *Facing the Nation: Television and Politics 1936-1976* (London: The Bodley Head, 1977), 105-6.
20. Asa Briggs, *The BBC: The First Fifty Years* (New York: Oxford University Press, 1985), 270, 278.
21. Tom O'Malley, "'Typically Anti-American'? The Labour Movement, America and Broadcasting in Britain from Beveridge to Pilkington, 1949-62," in *Anglo-American Media Interactions, 1850-2000*, ed. Joel H. Wiener and Mark Hampton (New York: Palgrave Macmillan, 2007), 242. On divisions within the Conservative Party over commercial television, see "TV Rift Prompts Churchill Parley," *New York Times*, June 18, 1953.
22. Briggs, *The BBC: The First Fifty Years*, 257-71, 278-87.
23. "TV with Auntie," *The Economist*, June 30, 1962, 1288; Warren Hoge, "Robin Day, 76, BBC Grand Inquisitor, Dies," *New York Times*, August 9, 2000; Andrew Crisell, *An Introductory History of British Broadcasting* (London: Routledge, 1997), 91-3.
24. Mollie Panter-Downes, "Letter from London," *New Yorker*, July 14, 1962, 69.
25. Crisell, *British Broadcasting*, 92.
26. Mike Conway, *The Origins of Television News America: The Visualizers of CBS in the 1940s* (New York: Peter Lang, 2009). The BBC, in contrast, had suspended television production during the war. See Robert Foot, "Looking Forward," *BBC Yearbook 1944* (London: British Broadcasting Corporation, 1944), 38.
27. Goldie, *Facing the Nation*, 110-12.

28. Goldie, *Facing the Nation*, 215. See also Briggs, *BBC: The First Fifty Years*, 288, 304–5; Colin Seymour-Ure, *The British Press and Broadcasting since 1945*, 2nd edn (Oxford: Blackwell, 1996), 187; Alasdair Milne, *DG: The Memoirs of a British Broadcaster* (London: Hodder & Stoughton, 1988), ch. 2.

29. David Kynaston, *Modernity Britain: Opening the Box, 1957–59* (London: Bloomsbury, 2013), 17.

30. Milne, *Memoirs of a British Broadcaster*, 212–13.

31. Briggs, *BBC: The First Fifty Years*, 327. See also Richard Atcheson, "St. Pilkington vs. the Dragon," *Show* (September 1962), 100; *Report of the Committee on Broadcasting, 1960* (London: HM Stationery Office, 1962).

32. *Report of the Committee on Broadcasting*, 17–18, 286; Briggs, *BBC: The First Fifty Years*, 328–30.

33. Crisell, *British Broadcasting*, 112–13.

34. Michael Apted, "How Granada TV Chairman Sir Denis Forman Changed my Life," *The Guardian*, March 4, 2013, <http://www.theguardian.com/media/2013/mar/04/michael-apted-granada-denis-foreman>; Stephen Moss, "Denis Forman Democratised Television," *The Guardian*, February 25, 2013, <http://www.theguardian.com/media/2013/feb/25/denis-forman-television>; Paul Vitello, "Denis Forman, British TV Innovator, Is Dead at 95," *New York Times*, February 27, 2013.

35. James L. Baughman, *Same Time, Same Station: Creating American Television, 1948–1961* (Baltimore: Johns Hopkins University Press, 2007), 239.

36. Adlai E. Stevenson, "The One-Party Press," in *Major Campaign Speeches of Adlai E. Stevenson, 1952* (New York: Random House, 1953), 78–82; Nathan B. Blumberg, *One-Party Press? Coverage of the 1952 Presidential Campaign in 35 Daily Newspapers* (Lincoln: University of Nebraska Press, 1954).

37. Stephen E. Ambrose, *Nixon: The Education of a Politician, 1913–1962* (New York: Simon and Schuster, 1987), 651–2, 664; Roger Morris, *Richard Milhous Nixon: The Rise of an American Politician* (New York: Henry Holt & Co., 1990), 589, 606, 615.

38. Russell Baker, *The Good Times* (New York: William Morrow, 1989), 237–8.

39. A. J. Liebling, *The Press* (New York: Ballantine Books, 1961), 258–66.

40. Alistair Horne, *Harold Macmillan*, 2 vols (New York: Viking, 1989), vol. 2, 479–80. See also Tunstall, *Newspaper Power*, 303–4.

41. Robert G. Kaiser, "Ben Bradlee, Legendary Washington Post Editor, Dies at 93," *Washington Post*, October 21, 2014. See also Chalmers Roberts, *In the Shadow of Power: The Story of the Washington Post*, rev. edn (Cabin John, Md.: Seven Locks Press, 1989), 271.

42. "Editors Vote 'Times' World's Greatest Paper," *New York Times*, May 5, 1942.

43. Baughman, *Luce*, 170.

44. Daniel C. Hallin, *The "Uncensored War": The Media and Vietnam* (New York: Oxford University Press, 1986), 34, 147.

45. Herbert J. Gans, *Deciding What's News: A Study of "CBS Evening News," "NBC Nightly News," "Newsweek," and "Time"* (New York: Pantheon, 1979), 126, 180–1.

46. Ibid., 180.

47. David Remnick, "Citizen Kay," *New Yorker*, January 20, 1997, 62. See also David Wigg, "Katherine Graham: The Woman who Opened Watergate," *The Times* (London), June 4, 1973.

48. Harrison Salisbury, *Without Fear or Favor: An Uncompromising Look at "The New York Times"* (New York: Times Books, 1980), 249, 251; Remnick, "Citizen Kay," 70.
49. Clyde Haberman, "The Times Pays Tribute to a Publisher Called 'Punch,'" *New York Times*, October 6, 2012. See also James C. Goodale, *Fighting for the Press: The Inside Story of the Pentagon Papers and Other Battles* (New York: CUNY Journalism Press, 2013), 45–165.
50. "Clashes of Principle," *The Economist*, July 3, 1971, 47–8; *New York Times Co. v. United States*, 403 U.S. (1971). See also David Rudenstine, *The Day the Presses Stopped: A History of the Pentagon Papers Case* (Berkeley: University of California Press, 1996); Sanford J. Ungar, *The Papers and the Papers: An Account of the Legal and Political Battle over the Pentagon Papers* (New York: Columbia University Press, 1989).
51. *Denver Post*, June 16, 1972.
52. Michael Schudson, *Watergate in American Memory: How We Remember, Forget, and Reconstruct the Past* (New York: Basic Books, 1992), 103–7, 123–6; Louis Heren, "Backroom Boys of Watergate," *The Times* (London), July 17, 1974.
53. Fred Emery, "Victory for US Press in Supreme Court," *The Times* (London), July 1, 1971.
54. Potter Stewart, "Or of the Press," *Hastings Law Journal*, 26 (1974–5), 631.
55. Christopher Moran, *Classified: Secrecy and the State in Modern Britain* (New York: Cambridge University Press, 2013), 96–7.
56. Koss, *Rise and Fall of the Political Press in Britain*, vol. 2, 678.
57. Horne, *Harold Macmillan*, vol. 2, 461–4.
58. Moran, *Classified*, 100–9, 113, 129–30, 136–48; Douglas Martin, "Chapman Pincher, Fleet St. Scoop Specialist, Dies at 100," *New York Times*, August 10, 2014; Richard Norton-Taylor, "Spycatcher Defense Correspondent Chapman Pincher Has Died, Aged 100," *The Guardian*, August 6, 2014; "Chapman Pincher: Farewell to Fleet Street's Greatest Spycatcher," *Daily Express*, August 7, 2014.
59. The closest comparable was likely David Wise, reporting for the *New York Herald Tribune* in the late 1950s and early 1960s. Alas, the *Trib* ceased publication in 1966. See Richard Kluger, *The Paper: The Life and Death of The New York Herald Tribune* (New York: Knopf, 1986), 588.
60. Fortunately, Norman Brook, the Cabinet Secretary, better served Macmillan than those around Henry II. The prime minister was persuaded to let Pincher alone. He was a "respectable chap," Brook remarked, and no "danger to the nation." Moran, *Classified*, 129–30.
61. "Stand down, the Palace Guard," *The Economist*, October 4, 1975, 15; "No Conviction," ibid., July 19, 1975, 16–17; "Ten-Year Rule?" ibid., February 8, 1975, 23–4; Philip Howard, "Cabinet Did Not Pass Crossman Diaries," *The Times* (London), January 27, 1975; Jack Hayward, "The Crossman Diaries," *Index on Censorship*, 4 (1975), 26–30; Eric J. Evans, *Thatcher and Thatcherism*, 3rd edn (London: Routledge, 2013), 17–26; Moran, *Classified*, 241–50.
62. Koss, *Rise and Fall of the Political Press in Britain*, vol. 2, 661.
63. Evans, *Thatcher and Thatcherism*, 6–8, 13.
64. John J. Pauly, "Rupert Murdoch and the Demonology of Professional Journalism," in *Media, Myths, and Narratives: Television and the Press*, ed. James W. Carey

(Newbury Park, Calif.: Sage Publications, 1989), 246, 257. See also Charles B. Seib, "Murdoch's Warning: Enliven News or Wither," *Washington Post*, May 13, 1977; "Comment," *Columbia Journalism Review*, 18 (January/February 1980), 23; Patrick Brogan, "Citizen Murdoch," *New Republic*, 187 (October 11, 1982): 19–22.

65. Nick Davies, *Hack Attack: The Inside Story of How the Truth Caught Up with Rupert Murdoch* (New York: Faber & Faber, 2014), 211.

66. David McKnight persuasively argues that Murdoch privileged advancing his political agenda over commercial considerations. See "Rupert Murdoch's News Corporation: A Media Institution with A Mission," *Historical Journal of Film, Radio and Television*, 30 (2010): 303–16.

67. Michael Palmer and Jeremy Tunstall, *Liberating Communications: Policy-Making in France and Britain* (Oxford: NCC Blackwell, 1990), 238, 295; Evans, *Thatcher and Thatcherism*, 142. See also Tunstall, *Newspaper Power*, 380–6.

68. William H. Meyers, "Murdoch's Global Power Play," *New York Times Magazine*, June 12, 1988, 41. See also William Shawcross, *Murdoch* (New York: Simon & Schuster, 1992), 161–74, 180–9, 197, 227.

69. Daniel Rosenheim and Charles Storch, "Murdoch Group to Buy Metromedia," *Chicago Tribune*, May 7, 1985.

70. Tunstall, *Newspaper Power*, 251–3; McKnight, "Rupert Murdoch's News Corporation," 305; "Why the British Press Holds Such Sway over Politicians," *The Economist*, April 28, 2012, 66; Nick Davies, *Hack Attack*, 212–14. See also Koss, *Rise and Fall of the Political Press in Britain*, vol. 2, 667.

71. Suellen M. Littleton, *The Wapping Dispute: An Examination of the Conflict and its Impact on the National Newspaper Industry* (Aldershot: Avebury, 1992), 4–5, 9, 17.

72. Ibid., 44; Shawcross, *Murdoch*, 256.

73. Littleton, *Wapping Dispute*, 28, 29, 52. See also Tunstall, *Newspaper Power*, ch. 2.

74. Littleton, *Wapping Dispute*, 92, 96, 102, 119–20, 132, 135.

75. Ibid., 134, 135.

76. Tunstall, *Newspaper Power*, 164–5.

77. Elizabeth MacIver Neiva, "Chain Building: The Consolidation of the American Newspaper Industry, 1953–1980," *Business History Review*, 70 (Spring 1996), 3–24.

78. Knight, "A Few Newspapers Die but Many Still Thrive," *Akron Beacon Journal*, November 3, 1963, clipping in Knight Papers, University of Akron, Series F. See also "Why Newspapers Are Making Money Again," *Business Week*, August 29, 1970, 35, 37.

79. Leo Bogart, *Press and Public: Who Reads What, When, Where, and Why in American Newspapers*, 2nd edn (Hillsdale, NJ: Lawrence Erlbaum Associates, 1989), 45–8. Between 1987 and 1997, profits for the Thomson chain of newspapers ranged from 33.9 to 17.6 percent. See William Prochnau, "In Lord Thomson's Realm," in *Leaving Readers Behind: The Age of Corporate Newspapering*, ed. Gene Roberts (Fayetteville: University of Arkansas Press, 2001), 291.

80. Robert G. Picard, "U.S. Newspaper Ad Revenue Shows Consistent Growth," *Newspaper Research Journal*, 23 (Fall 2002): 21–33.

81. Charles Whited, *Knight: A Publisher in the Tumultuous Century* (New York: E. P. Dutton, 1988), 331–2. See also Neiva, "Chain Building," 26–7, 34–5.

82. Ed Adams, "Combating Economic Decline during the Great Depression: News-paper Chain Scripps-Howard's Steps to Economic Recovery," paper presented at the Business History Conference, Columbus, Ohio, March 22, 2013.

83. "Congress Enacts Bill to Preserve Ailing Newspapers," *1970 Congressional Quarterly Almanac* (Washington, DC: Congressional Quarterly, Inc., 1971), 238–43.

84. Ben Bagdikian, *The Media Monopoly*, 6th edn (Boston: Beacon Press, 2000), ch. 5; Steven H. Chaffee and Donna G. Wilson, "Media Rich, Media Poor: Two Studies of Diversity in Agenda-Holding," *Journalism Quarterly*, 54 (Autumn 1977): 466–76; Sam Schulhofer-Wohl and Miguel Garrido, "Do Newspapers Matter? Short-Run and Long-Run Evidence from the Closure of *The Cincinnati Post*," Federal Reserve Bank of Minneapolis, Research Department, Working Paper 686, April 2011. See also Paul Farhi, "The Death of the JOA," *American Journalism Review* (September 1999): 49–52; Robert G. Picard, "Natural Death, Euthanasia, and Suicide: The Demise of Joint Operating Agreements," *Journal of Business Studies*, 4 (2007): 41–64.

85. Tunstall, *Newspaper Power*, 380–90.

86. See "In the Matter of the Application of Great Lakes Broadcasting Company," in US Federal Radio Commission, *Annual Report* (1929), 32–5.

87. See, e.g., Gerd Horten, *Radio Goes to War: The Cultural Politics of Propaganda during World War II* (Berkeley: University of California Press, 2002), 22–32; Michael J. Socolow, "'We Should Make Money on Our News': The Problem of Profitability in Network Broadcast History," *Journalism*, 11 (December 2011), 682–3.

88. Baughman, *Same Time*, 219.

89. Ibid., 220–48.

90. Michael Curtin, *Redeeming the Wasteland: Television Documentary and Cold War Politics* (New Brunswick: Rutgers University Press, 1995), 125, 127; Socolow, "'We Should Make Money on Our News,'" 686.

91. James L. Baughman, *Television's Guardians: The FCC and the Politics of Programming, 1958–1967* (Knoxville: University of Tennessee Press, 1985), ch. 4, 78–86; Newton N. Minow, "More Regulation or More Competition," *AAUP Journal of Academic Freedom*, 55 (March 1962), 156–8; Robert E. Kintner, "Television and the World of Politics," *Harper's* (May 1965), 132.

92. Sheldon Zalaznick, "The Rich, Risky Business of TV News," *Fortune*, 79 (May 1969), 92–7; John E. Cooney, "Air War: News Departments of the TV Networks Join Ratings Battle," *Wall Street Journal*, January 2, 1980; Gans, *Deciding What's News*, 180, 230, 248.

93. Not all attended, it should be noted. One study suggested more than half did not watch *any* of the network newscasts over a two-week period in 1969. See John P. Robinson, "The Audience for National TV News Programs," *Public Opinion Quarterly*, 35 (Autumn 1971): 403–5.

94. Phyllis Kaniss, *Making Local News* (Chicago: University Of Chicago Press, 1991), 107–13; Kaniss, "Too Few Reporters," *American Journalism Review*, 15 (September 1993): 20, 21; Harry F. Waters, "Sex and the Anchor Person," *Newsweek*, December 15, 1980, 65–6; Tony Schwartz, "What's Wrong with Local TV News?" *New York Times*, February 21, 1982; Max Frankel, "The Murder Broadcasting System,"

New York Times Magazine, December 17, 1995, 46–7; Craig M. Allen, *News is People: The Rise of Local TV News and the Fall of News from New York* (Ames, Ia: Iowa State University Press, 2001), ch. 12; Allen, "Discovering 'Joe Six Pack' Content in Television News: The Hidden History of Audience Research, News Consultants, and the Warner Class Model," *Journal of Broadcasting & Electronic Media*, 49 (December 2005): 363–82. A 2013 survey of local TV news in America suggested an average of 40 percent of airtime went to sports, weather, and traffic. Between 2005 and 2012 stories involving politics and government fell by 50 percent. See Mark Jurkowitz et al., "The Changing TV Landscape," <www.stateofthemedia.org/2013>.

95. *The Edward R. Murrow Heritage: Challenge for the Future*, ed. Betty Houchin Winfield and Lois B. DeFleur (Ames, Ia: Iowa State University Press, 1986), 15; David Blum, *Tick ... Tick ... Tick ...: The Long Life & Turbulent Times of "60 Minutes"* (New York: Harper Collins, 2004), 1 and *passim*. See also Richard Campbell, *"60 Minutes" and the News: A Mythology for Middle America* (Urbana: University of Illinois Press, 1991).

96. While working on the public broadcasting bill, some aides to President Johnson recommended that a special tax on the sale of new televisions and radios be used to endow public broadcasting, but a key House committee chairman blocked this and other funding proposals. See Robert J. Blakely, *To Serve the Public Interest: Educational Broadcasting in the United States* (Syracuse: Syracuse University Press, 1979), ch. 8; Memoranda, James Gaither to Joe Califano, January 3, 1968, Joe Califano to the President, November 7, 1967, James Gaither Files, box 190, Lyndon B. Johnson Library, Austin, Texas.

97. *A Public Trust: The Report of the Carnegie Commission on the Future of Public Broadcasting* (New York: Bantam Books, 1979), 94; *The Meeting of Two Cultures: Public Broadcasting on the Threshold of the Digital Age: A Report of the Carnegie Corporation of New York* (New York: Carnegie Corporation, 2008), 22.

98. Jeremy Isaacs, *Look Me in the Eye: A Life in Television* (London: Little, Brown, 2006), ch. 16.

99. Curran and Seaton, *Power without Responsibility*, 200–1, 203; Tunstall, *Newspaper Power*, 413–15; Milne, *Memoirs of a British Broadcaster*, 88–93, ch. 12; Tom O'Malley, *Closedown? The BBC and Government Broadcasting Policy 1979–92* (London: Pluto Press, 1994), 7, 54–8, 68–9.

100. Georgina Born, *Uncertain Vision: Birt, Dyke and the Reinvention of the BBC* (London: Secker & Warburg, 2004), 57–8, 386–7, 400; O'Malley, *Closedown?* 7, 9, 11, 137–40; Curran and Seaton, *Power without Responsibility*, 206–10; David Childs, *Britain since 1945: A Political History*, 7th edn (London: Routledge, 2012), 250–1; Seymour-Ure, *British Press and Broadcasting since 1945*, 69. Despite efforts to inhibit BBC journalists, they still managed to upset future governments. See, e.g., Sarah Lyall, "The BBC Loses a Bit of its Luster," *New York Times*, September 25, 2003.

101. O'Malley, *Closedown?* 10 and *passim*.

102. Curran and Seaton, *Power without Responsibility*, 247–8. On the more domestic-focused agenda of American network news, see Andrew Tyndall, "Climbing Down from Olympus," *Media Studies Journal*, 12 (Fall 1998), 140.

103. Crisell, *British Broadcasting*, 228–9.
104. Andrew Neil quoted in George Brock, *Out of Print* (London: Kogan Page, 2013), 72.
105. Shawcross, *Murdoch*, 341–4, 349–51, 379–82, 389; Palmer and Tunstall, *Liberating Communications*, 288–90.
106. Curran and Seaton, *Power without Responsibility*, 224. In 2002, American cable penetration was just over 80 percent. See Geraldine Fabrikant, "In Fight between Cable and Satellite, Customers Gain an Edge," *New York Times*, December 1, 2003. Cable was the preferred carrier in America. In early 2002, 73 million homes had cable compared to 17 million with satellite. See Laura M. Holson and Seth Schiesel, "Diverse Group Opposes EchoStar-DirecTV Deal," *New York Times*, January 30, 2002.
107. "Cable Deregulation Passed," *1984 Congressional Quarterly Almanac* (Washington, DC: CQ Press, 1985), 286–8; Thomas R. Eisenmann, "The U.S. Cable Television Industry, 1948–1995: Managerial Capitalism in Eclipse," *Business History Review*, 74 (Spring 2000), 6–19. See also Don L. Le Duc, *Cable Television and the FCC: A Crisis in Media Control* (Philadelphia: Temple University Press, 1973); William E. Lee, "A Regulatory Lock Box on Cable TV," *Wall Street Journal*, October 15, 1984.
108. *Statistical Abstract of the United States 1989* (Washington, DC: US Government Printing Office, 1989), 544.
109. Leonard Downie, Jr. and Robert G. Kaiser, *The News About the News: American Journalism in Peril* (New York: Knopf, 2002), 112.
110. Markus Prior, "News vs. Entertainment: How Increasing Media Choice Widens Gaps in Political Knowledge and Turnout," *American Journal of Political Science*, 49 (July 2005): 577–92.
111. See Joseph S. Nye, Jr., "Introduction: The Decline of Confidence in Government," in *Why People Don't Trust Government*, ed. Joseph S. Nye, Philip D. Zelikow, and David C. King (Cambridge, Mass.: Harvard University Press, 1997), 1–2, and Gary Orren, "Fall from Grace: The Public's Loss of Faith in Government," in ibid., 77–107; Born, *Uncertain Vision*, 375.
112. Quoted in James McCartney, "News Lite," *American Journalism Review* (June 1997), 19. See also Walter Goodman, "Some Hard Charges over Soft TV News," *New York Times*, March 18, 1997; Howard Kurtz, "Lite 'n' Lively 'Nightly,'" *Washington Post*, February 17, 1997; Bernard Gwertzman, "Memo to the *Times* Foreign Staff," *Media Studies Journal*, 7 (Fall 1993), 37.
113. "The Future of the BBC," *The Economist*, January 6, 2007, 47–8; Born, *Uncertain Vision*, 255–6, 281–2. See also Stephen Cushion, "Rolling Service, Market Logic: The Race to Be 'Britain's Most Watched News Channel,'" in *The Rise of 24-Hour News Television*, ed. Stephen Cushion and Justin Lewis (New York: Peter Lang, 2010), 127.
114. Isaacs, *Look Me in the Eye*, quoting several producers, 421–2.
115. Apted, "How Granada TV Chairman Sir Denis Forman Changed my Life."
116. Jack Mirkinson, "George Zimmerman Trial Completely Dominates Cable News," *TheHuffingtonPost.com*, July 2, 2013, <http://www.huffingtonpost.com/2013/07/02/george-zimmerman-cable-news_n_3532682.html>. See also Bill Kovach and Tom Rosenstiel, *Warp Speed: America in the Age of Mixed Media* (New York:

Century Foundation Press, 1999), 7–8, 75–6. On the decline of the public service ideal, see Curran and Seaton, *Power without Responsibility*, 341ff.

117. The FCC for political and legal reasons had asked Congress to agree with the doctrine's repeal. Majorities in both houses rejected the recommendation and passed a bill reaffirming the doctrine. President Reagan vetoed the measure; his veto was not overridden. See his letter to the Senate, press release, June 20, 1987, Office of the Press Secretary, copy in Alan C. Raul Files, OA 19141, and memo, David Gergen to the President, May 10, 1982, Gergen Files OA 9022, Ronald Reagan Library, Simi Valley, California. See also Robert Britt Horwitz, *The Irony of Regulatory Reform: The Deregulation of American Telecommunications* (New York: Oxford University Press, 1989), 159, 260 and *passim*.

118. See, e.g., Heather Hendershot, *What's Fair on the Air: Cold War Right-Wing Broadcasting and the Public Interest* (Chicago: University of Chicago Press, 2011), ch. 4.

119. John Leland, "Why the Right Rules the Radio Waves," *New York Times*, December 8, 2002. A liberal alternative talk radio network, Air America, proved short-lived. See James Rainey, "Clearing the Air on Talk Radio," *Los Angeles Times*, January 27, 2010.

120. Jeremy W. Peters, "Dueling Bitterness on Cable News," *New York Times*, November 6, 2012; Project for Excellence in Journalism, Pew Research Center, "Winning the Media Campaign 2012: Coverage of the Candidates by Media Sector and Cable Outlet," November 2, 2012, <www.journalism.org>. On Ailes, see Gabriel Sherman, *The Loudest Voice in the Room: How the Brilliant, Bombastic Roger Ailes Built Fox News—And Divided a Country* (New York: Random House, 2014). In the early 2000s, the British government's impartiality guidelines discouraged British news networks, even one owned by Murdoch, from adopting the Fox model. See Stephen Cushion and Justin Lewis, "Towards a 'Foxification' of 24-Hour News Channels in Britain?" *Journalism*, 10 (2009): 131–53.

121. O'Malley, *Closedown?* 36–44.

122. See, e.g., Nicholas Lemann, "Right Hook," *New Yorker*, August 29, 2005, 34–9.

123. Thomas Frank, *What's the Matter with Kansas? How Conservatives Won the Heart of America* (New York: Henry Holt and Co., 2004), 142.

124. Martin Campbell-Kelly, et al., *Computer: A History of the Information Machine*, 3rd edn (Boulder, Col.: Westview, 2014), 229–51.

125. James W. Cortada, *The Digital Flood: The Diffusion of Information Technology across the U.S., Europe, and Asia* (New York: Oxford University Press, 2012), 48–50. Government subsidies, Kenneth Flamm suggested, advanced the development of computer technologies several decades: Flamm, *Creating the Computer: Government, Industry, and High Technology* (Washington, DC: The Brookings Institution, 1988), 252–5. See also Mariana Mazzucato, *The Entrepreneurial State: Debunking Public vs. Private Sector Myths* (London: Anthem Press, 2013), 76–9.

126. Thomas P. Hughes, *Rescuing Prometheus* (New York: Pantheon Books, 1998), 255–6, 269, 272–3. Roy Rosenzweig insists that the Defense Department's patronage of research on the Internet has been obscured by some early histories. See "Wizards, Bureaucrats, Warriors, and Hackers: Writing the History of the Internet," *American Historical Review*, 103 (December 1998), 1534–7.

127. Janet Abbate, *Inventing the Internet* (Cambridge, Mass.: MIT Press, 1999), 195.

128. Ibid., 185–6, 195, 199, 202; "Bill Enacted To Advance High-Speed Computing," *Congressional Quarterly Almanac 1991* (Washington: CQ Press, 1992), 244–5. Another governmental patron was the National Science Foundation, which had been supporting computer science research at many research universities since the 1960s and fostered the wiring or connection of computer networks. Abbate, *Inventing the Internet*, 191–4.

129. Cortada, *Digital Flood*, 95–106.

130. Abbate, *Inventing the Internet*, 214–17. See also Campbell-Kelly, *Computer*, 287.

131. John Morton, "Papers Will Survive Newest Technology," *American Journalism Review*, 15 (June 1993): 48.

132. "Overview," "The State of the News Media 2009," <www.stateofthemedia.org/2009>.

133. Kovach and Rosenstiel, *Warp Speed*, 11–12 and *passim*.

134. Blaming Matt Drudge for the ensuing controversy, Richard A. Posner argued, is foolish. The story would have broken out eventually. Moreover, Posner wrote, the fault ultimately rested with the panel of judges who had authorized the Independent Counsel to look into the sexual affair. See Richard A. Posner, *An Affair of State: The Investigation, Impeachment, and Trial of President Clinton* (Cambridge, Mass.: Harvard University Press, 1999), 246–8.

135. Emphasis added. Crichton, "The Mediasaurus," *Wired* (October 1993), 57–8.

136. Ibid., 59.

137. Marc Fisher, "Polarized News Market Has Altered the Political Process in South Carolina Primary," *Washington Post*, January 20, 2012.

138. Memorandum, Henry M. Gandy to William L. Ball III, April 15, 1987, David Backorney Files OA 17459, Reagan Library; Frankie Clogston, "The Repeal of the Fairness Doctrine: Ideational Conflict, Institutional Complexity and Unintended Consequences," paper presented at the Policy History Conference, June 2010, Columbus, Ohio.

139. See, e.g., Alex S. Jones, *Losing the News: The Future of the News that Feeds Democracy* (New York: Oxford University Press, 2009), 3–4.

140. David Barboza, "Classified Ads Are Rapidly Finding a New Home on the Internet," *New York Times*, May 13, 1995; Brock, *Out of Print*, 139–40.

141. Mark Sweney, "UK Newspapers' Print Ad Revenue to Shrink by 400 M by the End of 2014," *The Guardian*, June 19, 2013 <http://www.theguardian.com/media/2013/jun/19/uk-newspapers-print-ad>.

142. Jeremy W. Peters, "Despite Distinctions, Los Angeles Times Loses Standing at Home," *New York Times*, January 24, 2011; Rick Edmonds, "ASNE Census Finds 2,600 Newsroom Jobs were Lost in 2013," *Poynter.org*, June 26, 2013, <http://www.poynter.org/news/mediawire/216617/asne-census-finds-2600-newsroom-jobs-were-lost-in-2012/>; Leonard Downie, Jr. and Michael Schudson, *The Reconstruction of American Journalism* (New York: Columbia Journalism School, 2009), 17.

143. Tim de Lisle, "Can The Guardian Survive?" *Intelligent Life Magazine*, July/August 2012, <http://moreintelligentlife.co.uk/content/ideas/tim-de-lisle/can-guardian-survive?page=full>.

144. "How to Lose Friends and Alienate People," *The Economist*, July 16, 2011, 25. The best account to date on the scandal is Nick Davies'. See also "No End in Sight," *The Economist*, July 16, 2011, 27–8; Felix Gillette, "Rupert Murdoch, News Corp. Dodge Phone-Hacking Ruin," *Bloomberg Business*, April 18, 2013; Anthony Lane, "Hack Work," *New Yorker*, August 1, 2011, 24–6. Very much the Houdini of Anglo-American journalism, Murdoch, three years after the scandal broke, appeared to be surviving nicely. See Ravi Somaiya, "News Corp. Slowly Putting Phone-Hacking Scandal Behind It," *New York Times*, June 30, 2014.

145. Paul Farhi, "The Guardian: Small British Paper Makes Big Impact with NSA Stories," *Washington Post*, July 1, 2013; "How Whistleblower Exposed Secrets of a Surveillance State," *The Guardian*, August 22, 2013. See also Christine Haughney and Noam Cohen, "Guardian Makes Waves, and Is Ready for More," *New York Times*, June 11, 2013.

146. Ken Auletta, "Freedom of Information," *New Yorker*, October 7, 2013, 48, 56.

147. Downie and Schudson, *Reconstruction of American Journalism*, 34–73; Dan Gillmor, *We the Media: Grassroots Journalism by the People, for the People* (Sebastopol, Calif.: O'Reilly, 2006); C. W. Anderson, Emily Bell and Clay Shirky, *Post-Industrial Journalism: Adapting to the Present* (New York: Tow Center for Digital Journalism, 2012).

8

Protecting News before the Internet

Heidi J. S. Tworek

Newspapers in the nineteenth century commonly copied from each other without legal sanction. American newspapers, for instance, extracted around 30 percent of their stories from other papers, generally receiving them through the system of newspaper exchange organized by the post.[1] Horace Greeley, founder and editor of the hugely influential *New York Tribune*, told a British parliamentary commission in 1851 that "all the evening journals copy from us and we rather like it."[2] In 1873, Frederic Hudson, managing editor of the *New York Herald*, argued that the increased speed of newspaper production provided sufficient protection of news value from would-be copiers. According to Hudson, the ability of the *New York Herald* to print one hundred thousand copies in one hour meant "newspapers must continue to find their copyright in their superior enterprise, their superior machinery, their superior circulation, and in their superior means of delivering their papers to the public."[3] For Hudson, exclusive access to news until the time of publication was all the legal protection that publishers required. Now that publishers could print with greater rapidity and in large quantities, it was simply a question of who had the news first and could scoop everyone else.

Although newspapers and news agencies partially heeded Hudson's advice, they also began to seek other means of protecting their products. Such a narrow temporal window of exclusivity proved inadequate as new means of distribution enabled publishers to increase their circulation. Telegraphy also allowed enterprising newsgatherers to transmit news at a faster pace than newspapers could travel. To increase the shelf life of exclusives, publishers sought out public protection for news value through law. This chapter traces how, when, and why particular news providers sought protection, while exploring why these efforts so often failed to provide the relief that providers had anticipated.

In recent years, legal strategies to protect the value in news reports have become an integral element of attempts to "save" the news business. Publishers and news organizations in countries ranging from Germany to the United States have become convinced that the law has a significant role to play in protecting news. Since at least the early nineteenth century, publishers have turned to the law for succor from the winds of competition, but courts and legislatures have been reluctant to grant them safe harbor. Simultaneously, news providers have devised private solutions to protect or prolong the exclusive value of news through contracts and business organization. These private mechanisms have proven far more effective.

The pursuit of public protection required the imprimatur of the state; private means to protect exclusivity relied on cooperation among news providers. The public and private pursuit of mechanisms to protect news value overlapped. The efficacy of private strategies like contracts and market mechanisms affected the degree to which publishers felt a need to turn to the state for protection. Conversely, de facto property rights generated through private ordering were subject to state regulation and sanction. More broadly, the domestic search for private and public means of protecting news value intertwined with the operation of national news agencies and associations abroad as well as attempts to devise international treaties for the protection of intellectual property. Making news was a transatlantic and, indeed, a global enterprise. So was protecting it.

The ability to use and reproduce news reports rested on the types of rights accorded to those reports and the parties involved. Attempts to protect news value mainly revolved around the legal concepts of property rights and licenses. Legally speaking, a property right is defined as a right over things; this right is enforceable against other persons. It is a right against the world. Licenses, on the other hand, are contracts. Licenses grant permission for use and are good only against the signatories to the license. Contracts between news providers often effectively allowed one provider a license to use news reports from another.

If news reports were accorded the status of property, however, news providers could exclude rivals or free-riders from using them. In Great Britain, the contention that news was property relied on extending John Locke's labor theory to the collection of news. For Locke, "Man has a *Property* in his own *Person*"; therefore, the fruit of a man's labor was "the unquestionable Property of the Laborer."[4] Locke's labor theory or interpretations of it became a foundational element of arguments about property rights from the mid-eighteenth century.[5] From the 1880s onwards, British and imperial news procurers attempted to combine Locke's labor theory with the cost of collecting news, hoping to create an indivisible association between protecting labor and protecting financial outlay.

American news providers also pursued the idea that news reports constituted a form of property. In the United States, however, contractual rights between competitors within the news business ultimately proved more important than property rights. Attempts by certain news providers to establish control over news reports through contracts that excluded other providers shaped the business of news and competition. For British and American news providers, protecting expenses incurred in gathering news provided the key rationale for legal action. Economic motivations justified legal methods.

Different strategies for protecting news value in Britain and the United States reflected the market structures prevalent in each country. In the United States in the 1840s, the New York Associated Press (NYAP) started as a partnership of New York papers that shared the costs of news transmission by telegraphy and post. In the 1850s, the NYAP expanded and granted franchises to newspaper publishers that joined the organization as members. Franchises entitled members to exclusive use of the association's news reports within a specific geographic area. In return, members were obliged to pay assessments and to supply the association with the breaking news of their vicinity. This approach entailed a careful calibration of the size of the association. On the one hand, a larger membership reduced the costs of news-gathering incurred by each member and expanded the coverage of the association's news reports. On the other hand, restricting the size of membership increased the value of member franchises. These restrictions encouraged the establishment of competing newsgatherers to serve the portion of the newspaper market excluded from membership. Successors to the NYAP, including the Associated Press (AP), incorporated in Illinois in 1892, were organized along similar lines. This method of organization relied fundamentally on members sharing their news with the association before publication. Sharing news before publication, as opposed to after, enabled the association to share it with members exclusively. More than a clearinghouse for news, the AP became a mechanism for propagating exclusive control over news reports. For this reason, the AP was particularly concerned to protect the news of its members prior to publication. Concerns about competition checked the AP's pursuit of private and public protection for its news reports. If private, contractual mechanisms of generating exclusivity proved too effective, the AP might fall prey either to competition or regulation. If a public property right proved forthcoming, the AP might be reconceived of, and regulated as, a public utility.

Limited oligopolistic competition engendered by private contracting and public regulation of monopoly characterized the American newsgathering market. In Britain, by contrast, exclusive joint-operating agreements among firms perpetuated comparatively small enterprises and limited competition. Reuters, established in 1851, served as the principal supplier of overseas news to Great Britain. From 1851 to 1930, it functioned more like "a trading company operating in news."[6] The Press Association (PA), a cooperative organization established in 1868 and comprising the principal provincial newspapers, was the primary provider of domestic news and the exclusive licensee for the distribution of

Reuters' news reports outside London. The London newspapers largely fended for themselves, but occasionally negotiated through trade associations to further their mutual interests. As a consequence, Reuters' business lay principally overseas, chiefly in the British Empire, and particularly India.

Just as the AP and Reuters created contractual relationships with domestic news organizations to increase news value and to share the costs of gathering news, they signed exclusive contractual relationships with foreign news agencies for similar purposes. The "Big Three" news agencies (Reuters, Agence Havas, and Wolff's Telegraphisches Bureau) participated in a cartel agreement by which they divided the world into exclusive markets for the collection and sale of their news. These agreements lasted from the mid-nineteenth century until the outbreak of the Second World War. From 1893 to 1934, the AP was a signatory to these cartel contracts. After the Second World War, Reuters and the AP became the two major western news agencies alongside Agence France Presse (AFP) and United Press International (UPI), while TASS (Telegraph Agency of the Soviet Union) and Xinhua were the two major Communist agencies. News agencies' needs often differed fundamentally from newspapers. Newspapers had national or regional audiences. Correspondingly, they focused on domestic litigation to protect their interests. News agencies collected and disseminated news internationally. Reuters, in particular, supplied imperial as well as national customers. These agencies sought protection for their products outside the countries in which they were headquartered. News agencies pursued their agendas in international conferences and in national courts and legislatures. Ultimately, however, private strategies continued to order the collection and distribution of news more effectively than the public mechanisms that news providers constantly craved.

NEWS AND COPYRIGHT

Although the problem of copying news had irked newspaper publishers and editors long before news agencies emerged, the business structure and global nature of news agencies made these companies the primary drivers of efforts to protect news from the 1880s onwards. News piracy was a concern as early as the eighteenth century, but at that time verbatim copying was a rampant practice and newspapers often did not cite their sources. The standardization of copyright law and the abolition of stamp duties on paper and advertisements in Britain by the mid-nineteenth century reignited debates about property in news reports. Over a century after the Statute of Anne in 1710, the 1842 Copyright Act standardized and consolidated British copyright law. The Copyright Act even included a clause that protected "any Encyclopedia, Review, Magazine, Periodical Work, or Work published in a series of Books or

Parts." Section 7 of Britain's International Copyright Act of 1852 then added the idea of citing sources by allowing newspapers to reprint foreign articles on politics if the source was stated.

Just three years after the International Copyright Act, the abolition of the stamp tax unleashed a campaign for the protection of news by newspapers such as the *Times*, which had an extensive and expensive apparatus of news collection and dissemination. These newspapers feared that smaller and provincial papers would now telegraph news from London and reprint it. This would preempt the arrival of the *Times* in those provincial areas and reduce its sales. The Chancellor of the Exchequer proposed a clause to protect news for twenty-four hours from publication into the bill to repeal the stamp duty. The attempt failed probably because of resistance from provincial papers which argued that news was not property and that any copyright on news would hinder the free flow of information.[7]

In fact, even the definition of a newspaper or periodical work was unclear until the Newspaper Libel and Registration Act (1881). This Act classified newspapers as "any paper containing public news, intelligence or occurrences, or any remarks or observations thereon printed for sale" and published in England or Ireland every 26 days or less.[8] That same year, a court case clarified that newspapers only needed to register once to qualify for protection under English copyright law.[9] This relatively well-defined copyright regime contrasted markedly with other countries' more permissive approaches, as international conferences in the 1880s made clear.

The Berne Convention on copyright was signed in 1886 after several negotiating conferences and is still in force today. The Convention built on various bilateral agreements and aimed to prevent international piracy of nationally copyrighted works. It explicitly covered creative works and forms of expression. Article 7 of the Convention was devoted specifically to periodical literature. Article 7 articulated a division between categories of newspaper articles that began to exclude certain types of news from copyright. On the one hand, Article 7 allowed reproduction of newspaper and magazine articles if the authors or publishers had not specifically prohibited it. This amounted in effect to a blanket license provision for newspapers to reprint articles. On the other hand, Article 7 stated that prohibition of reprinting articles "cannot in any case apply to articles of political discussion, to the news of the day, or to current topics." As these types of news were considered information and not creative works, they remained unprotected.

These debates aroused opposition from the British Foreign Office delegation of Francis Ottiwell Adams, a lawyer and diplomat, and Sir John Henry Gibbs Bergne, a frequent British delegate to international conventions on copyright and industrial property in the 1880s and 1890s. The delegation requested the removal of Article 7, as British law already required newspapers to indicate their sources when reprinting foreign articles. Other delegations explained that Article 7 was not intended to change British domestic law and the British motion was defeated by ten votes to two. However, the British delegation won the small victory that countries party to the Berne Convention could always require their newspapers to adhere to stricter domestic legislation on naming sources for articles.[10] While British law remained stricter than the Berne Convention on copyright in the 1880s, later copyright legislation in Britain followed the Berne Convention's provisions on news more closely.

After multiple failed attempts in the late 1890s to ratify copyright bills that included news, the British government seized the chance to promulgate a new Copyright Act in 1911 to conform to the Berlin revisions of the Berne Convention that had occurred in 1908.[11] The 1911 Copyright Act classified articles in newspapers and magazines as akin to the contents of a book. The Act did not protect factual content, however, and it excluded news articles using the Berne Convention's definition of news. British domestic legislation had become entangled with international conventions and had partially acquired their approaches to news too.

The international participants in the Berlin revision found protecting any potential creativity in news less important than the possible political, economic, and social benefits of informing the public about current events.[12] News articles were viewed as cosmopolitan because the participants thought that the news belonged not to a particular producer, but to everyone in the world.[13] The Convention's creators and revisers privileged the global dissemination of news over journalists' revenue. In 1908, Article 9 of the Berlin revision altered what had formerly been Article 7 to affirm that the Convention "does not apply to news of the day or to miscellaneous news having the character merely of press information."[14] Original articles discussing political topics could be protected, but daily news was not. To put it another way, the Berne Convention distinguished between facts and accounts. These developments sharpened the divide between accounts produced by newspaper journalists and factual items supplied by news agencies that often presented news of the day. After the First World War, Article 306 of the Versailles Treaty stated that pre-war trade, artistic, and literary property rights should be restored. A final change in 1967 to the Convention confirmed the exclusion of news reports.[15] By 1908, news reports had no place in international copyright conventions that were designed explicitly to protect authorial creativity.

Matters were rather more complicated back in Britain. By the 1890s, British courts had actually strengthened common-law copyright in news reports. *Walter v. Steinkopff* (1892) surpassed the Berne Convention's division between fact and account to argue that the form of expression should be protected regardless of an article's content. The London *Times* had sought redress from newspapers copying literary articles by Rudyard Kipling and three "copyrighted" news articles on current events. For Justice North, there was "little doubt but that there is copyright in the literary form given to news – not in the substance of the news itself, but in the form in which it is conveyed, and this even where it consists of a mere statement or summary, and the information with respect to the current events of the day."[16] This did not mean that all news was automatically protected. North distinguished between Kipling and news articles, drawing a line between literary expressions and reporting. Indeed, North's judgment was one of the first to draw the distinction between fact and expression.

As the number of cases grew in the 1890s, courts did not just rely on definitions of creativity. They also took account of the expense incurred in creation. In *Pall Mall Gazette v. Evening News and others* (1895), the court granted an injunction to prevent the *Evening News* from reprinting the results of Australian cricket matches, which the *Pall Mall Gazette* had procured by telegraph.[17] The cost of overseas telegrams thus helped to settle a national case and to make financial outlay a legitimate factor in court cases on news.

Given that most newspapers relied heavily on news agencies for news, these cases were particularly relevant for Reuters. Reuters had campaigned in vain since the 1870s for protection of its news reports to the colonies and dominions. The legal status of news reports varied greatly throughout the Empire, particularly after the spread of telegraphy. Several Australian states (starting with Victoria) created laws to protect foreign telegrams in the early 1870s after the arrival of submarine cable connections.[18] These laws provided precedents for other colonies, such as Ceylon in 1898, rather than Britain. Other colonies rejected the insertion of protection for news reports into legislation. Most prominently, Indian vernacular newspapers strongly opposed the proposed introduction of a bill assigning thirty hours of exclusivity to news reports in 1899. Despite support from some Anglo-Indian papers, vernacular newspapers and the Indian National Congress believed that the law might restrict free speech in India. Vernacular newspapers were often too poor to afford a subscription to Reuters. They copied Reuters' news from English-language newspapers and would have found themselves in an impossibly precarious situation without that free news. Lord Curzon, newly appointed Viceroy of India, dropped the bill in 1900, as he did not wish to inflame Indian nationalist passions.[19] The politics of the British Empire had temporarily ended the possibility of streamlining legislation to protect news reports.

As late as 1936, however, Sir Roderick Jones, Reuters' managing director from 1916 to 1941, deplored the difference between Britain and the myriad rules governing news in the colonies and dominions. In a rousing speech to the Empire Press Union, Jones claimed that British newspapers and news agencies had reached a "happy understanding which amounts, in practice, to recognition and acceptance of the news property principle, liberally interpreted." He worried, by contrast, that news organizations in Australia might "flout contracts and convention" to garner news "in defiance of all accepted journalistic concern," while India seemed filled with "parasitical prints" of news telegraphed by "pirates" in London.[20] In the interwar period, the AP of

India (owned by Reuters since 1919) complained that Indian news-papers copied Reuters' telegrams and even claimed that not a single paper subscribed to Reuters.[21] Yet, the grievances aired by Jones and the AP of India belied the fact that imperial business was booming for Reuters. In 1939, Reuters' income from India outstripped its income from the United Kingdom. Similarly, Reuters' revenue from South Africa almost equaled that from Britain.

Disputes over the provision of information to the Empire lay at the heart of Reuters' concerns over public provisions to protect news. These issues accelerated after the creation of the BBC in 1922. Reuters negotiated on behalf of a consortium of news agencies from 1922 until the end of the Second World War to supply news to the BBC. From the mid-1930s, however, Reuters' insistence on legal protection for its news increasingly convinced the BBC that Reuters' financial concerns were diametrically opposed to the BBC's mission to serve the public interest. Reuters wished to preface the BBC news bulletins with "copyright reserved" to prevent newspapers from copying news from the radio and printing it as their own. There was no legal basis for enforcing this reservation, but Reuters and the BBC negotiated continuously for the next few years over Reuters' purported rights to the news that it supplied the BBC.

Arguments between the BBC and Reuters became particularly heated over the global and imperial distribution of news. As the 1930s progressed, the two organizations repeatedly came to blows over the global dissemination of news and its purpose in fighting fascism. Reuters feared that wireless enabled hostile countries like Italy to broadcast in multiple languages around the world and undermine the business of newspapers and news agencies. While Reuters wished to restrict access to the news through copyright, the BBC hoped to distribute its news as widely as possible to counteract fascist propaganda. Simultaneously, Reuters wanted to use copyright to secure its income from supplying news to the Empire after the BBC launched a news bulletin for the Empire in 1932. Until the Second World War, Reuters pushed heavily for a copyright notice for its news in the BBC's Empire news bulletins to try to prevent Indian newspapers from copying the broadcast matter.[22] The disagreement over copyright even spurred the BBC to start to develop its own news collection services in the 1930s. As so often, Reuters claimed that the lack of legal protection had harmed its revenue. But this rhetoric disguised the reality of Reuters' financial and operational stability, even without more stringent legal protection of its news reports.

Over and above common law and statutory measures, Reuters tried to find everyday practices to protect its news. The company sought legal advice continuously from the mid-1880s onwards, but lawyers' responses barely agreed on any aspect of protection. One lawyer claimed in 1895 that Reuters' news from abroad was fully protected under the Copyright Act of 1842 if

Reuters put that news into printed form and registered its periodical under copyright.[23] Reuters had published selected telegrams in its own version of a newspaper, *Reuter's Journal*, from February 1890. It offered the *Journal* for sale from its headquarters in Old Jewry to secure statutory copyright for telegrams that Reuters had received from abroad. Still, Article 7 of the Berne Convention could not prevent a foreign paper's correspondent from copying Reuters' news in England and sending it to a newspaper abroad. Reuters also printed a *Reuter's Indian Journal* from 1895 and simultaneously asked all its agents and correspondents throughout the world to sign over their rights to their telegrams and news to Reuters.[24]

Given the cost of printing the *Journal*, Reuters continued to look for cheaper methods to protect its telegrams. In 1911, it hoped to remove the "considerable expense" of printing the journal by following the Exchange Telegraph Company's approach.[25] The Exchange Telegraph Company typed up its telegraphic news on a sheet, offering it for sale. It registered each day's cables at Stationers Hall as a periodical entitled *The Exchange Telegraph Company's Stock Exchange News*. This approach succeeded in 1895, when the Exchange Telegraph Company secured an injunction against another company's use of its stock market ticker. The court held that the Exchange Telegraph Company had a common-law right of property in the information contained in its news reports before publication. The court granted the company injunctive relief from companies such as Gregory, which had surreptitiously acquired the Exchange Telegraph Company's stock and price information before it was published.[26] Lawyers advised Reuters that any common-law rights it possessed in unpublished news would disappear after publication. Reuters published its *Journal* until 1979.[27] Legal protection influenced Reuters' publication practices for nearly a century, but did not satisfy Reuters' concerns about protecting its news abroad.

In the United States too, news providers remained discontented with domestic arrangements. The legal protection of news became an important topic in the United States in the 1880s, just like in Britain. Although British law on the subject was still in a state of flux, by the 1880s, it was clear that American copyright law did not cover news reports. The AP would thereafter pursue a property right in its news reports through litigation rather than legislation.

Prior to the 1880s, American debates respecting property in news reports primarily addressed two issues: the creativity and the originality of news. Article 1, Section 8, Clause 8 of the United States Constitution stated that copyright was essential "to promote the Progress of Science and useful Arts, by securing for limited Times to Authors and Inventors the exclusive Right to their respective Writings and Discoveries." The first attempt to protect news revolved around defining the word "science." In 1829, the Court for the Southern District of New York held that "the term science cannot, with any propriety, be applied to a work of so fluctuating and fugitive form as that of a newspaper or pricecurrent, the subject-matter of which is daily changing, and is of more temporary use."[28] Although newspaper editors extensively discussed the issue of crediting sources and copying, the next major court case occurred over fifty years later. Building on the judgment of 1829, the United States Supreme Court ruled in 1880 that newspapers' ever-changing subject matter excluded them from the category of "science" that deserved protection.[29]

Starting in the 1880s, American news agencies campaigned for the protection of news through statutory and common law. Whereas in Britain, Reuters pursued legislative protection of the news reports it sent to the colonies, the NYAP and Western AP pushed for domestic legislation. In 1884, they sent a representative, Henry Watterson, to Washington DC to campaign for an act of Congress that would grant copyright to news for eight hours after publication.[30] Watterson argued before the House Committee on the Judiciary that English common law already recognized copyright in news reports and the United States should follow suit.[31] Yet, Watterson later described the mission as "a fool's errand."[32] The initiative aroused great opposition from smaller newspapers that relied on copying from other newspapers and a rival news agency, the United Press. Unlike the British inclusion of newspapers in statutory copyright in the 1880s, the American bill died in the Committee of the Library before it reached Congress. That exclusion also had broad consequences for the history of copyright. Up to that point, copyright had included items that were not original, but had involved significant intellectual labor, such as directories or maps. By rejecting the idea that labor was a sufficient justification for protection, the debate over copyright in news reports transformed copyright into a law designed to protect originality and creativity, rather than products of intellectual labor like daily news.[33]

Internationally, the Committee of the Library's attitude to copyright in news mirrored the United States' broader stance on participating in international copyright legislation. The United States remained outside the Berne Convention until 1988, despite observer Boyd Winchester's support for American membership in the mid-1880s and W. E. Simonds' pleas in his report on international copyright in 1890. Simonds employed Lockean labor theory to argue that an author owned the rights to a literary creation and called an author's property right a "self-evident natural right," like life, liberty, and the pursuit of happiness. Simonds compared authors' intangible property rights to railroad, telephone, and telegraph franchises. As the state or a municipality explicitly granted franchises, Simonds implicitly argued that copyright should be considered as a bundle of contractual rights exercised against specific individuals, rather than property conferring rights against the world. Notwithstanding an appendix with a long list of newspapers and associations in favor of American adoption of international copyright, however, the report failed to convince Congress to accede to Berne.[34]

Contemporaries also emphasized the enormous benefits for publishers of reprinting foreign works without paying copyright dues. The exclusion of news items from copyright law meant that American news providers would have to pursue other routes, if they wished to protect their products through public mechanisms.

Despite its aloof stance to the Berne Convention, the United States was a signatory to the more regional Pan-American Copyright Convention. Like Berne, the Pan-American Convention excluded news from protection as a creative product. In 1909, the United States revised its copyright law to mirror these provisions. It provided legal protection for newspaper and magazine articles that were deemed original creations, but again not for news of the day.[35] The United States Copyright Act of 1976 allowed newspapers to display a blanket copyright on their front pages, which covered copyright for all the sections in the newspaper. However, this blanket copyright provision remained valid only for those parts of a newspaper that could be copyrighted in the first place. News reports, then, remained excluded from that provision.

Although the avenue of statutory copyright law to protect news closed in the 1880s, the AP readily and swiftly adapted its rhetoric and strategy to changing legal circumstances. The AP turned to common law and the doctrine of unfair competition to protect news value. In 1918, these efforts culminated in the decision of the United States Supreme Court in *INS v. AP*. To rely on unfair competition to obtain the protection it sought, the AP had to argue that news was not original enough to be covered by copyright. It thus cemented a key difference from British law, where major court cases of the 1890s had refined the place of news reports in copyright, but not excluded them completely.

NEWS AND PROPERTY

Although the Berne Convention and subsequent revisions excluded news of the day, news agencies continued to seek alternative public means to protect their newsgathering enterprises internationally and to complement the private contractual arrangements of the news agency cartel. The AP and Reuters pursued two rather different paths to insert news into international conventions. While the AP tried to regulate news as intellectual property through the League of Nations, Reuters sought to categorize news as industrial property through the Convention on Industrial Property. These alternative approaches by AP and Reuters did not arise from fundamentally different conceptions of news, but from the two agencies' pragmatic attempts to seize upon international mechanisms to protect their news reports.

By the early 1900s, the AP had developed an extensive private system of contractual obligations concerning news sharing and member duties.[36] Still, these private mechanisms had limitations, particularly vis-à-vis competitors in the news agency business. To solve those issues, the AP turned to public property rights to attempt to secure greater protection for its news. In 1879, AP general agent, James W. Simonton, believed that the AP possessed "a property in news, and that property is created by the fact of our collecting it and concentrating it."[37] While Simonton did not specify when that property right expired, the AP remained committed to creating some form of property rights in news to protect its control over members' news.

Melville Stone, general manager of the AP from 1893 to 1918, claimed to have campaigned tirelessly for protection from the later nineteenth century onwards. His passion purportedly began soon after he had founded the penny newspaper, *Chicago Daily News*, in 1876. Stone's paper shared an office with the *Post and Mail*, owned by the McMullen brothers. Stone realized that the McMullens were waiting for other papers to appear at 3 a.m. and then reprinting that news in their paper, which was published a few hours later. Stone played a trick to catch the McMullens. On 2 December 1876, his *Chicago Daily News* published an article on the distress in Serbia that included the following quotation from a local mayor: "*Er us siht la Etsll iws nel lum cmeht.*" The afternoon edition of the *Post and Mail* contained the same item verbatim; it took a friend to point out to the McMullens that read backwards the quotation spelled out: "the McMullens will steal this sure." After the McMullens were "literally laughed to death," Stone bought the paper and its AP franchise at a greatly reduced price less than two years later.[38]

Stone's vocabulary indicated that he saw the matter rather differently than courts at the time. Stone conceived of news as a form of property: he called the *Post and Mail* "a news thief."[39] Stone believed fervently that news items were property that deserved some sort of protection. He suspected that the new technology of telegraphy had helped to generate the problem of theft: while books and paintings could be registered before publication to ensure copyright, there was no time for this with news reports. Stone was nothing if not persistent in his quest, campaigning for over thirty years to create legal protections for news that would account for the increased speed of news dissemination.

Stone doggedly pursued and followed court cases on protecting news reports after the failed attempt to procure copyright for news through an act of Congress in 1884. This defeat led Stone to believe by the early 1900s that the only solution was to look for protection from common law on property, rather than copyright.[40] This involved redefining the meanings of both "property" and "publication." First, property had to be redefined to cover more than "movables" and "immovables." It had to include everything with an "exchangeable value." Second, Stone intended to reconceive the concept of publication. He aimed to limit other publishers' ability to reproduce telegraphed news after its initial publication and to establish norms to protect news prior to its publication. This would increase the exclusive shelf life of news reports and enhance the AP's position over its competitors. Stone's search for property rights drove him to seek public mechanisms that would bolster the AP's position vis-à-vis competitors and complement its private law system amongst AP members.

The AP pursued many lawsuits in various states, but none gave rise to a common-law property right in news reports. For instance, a case in 1900 concluded that publishers could not copyright entire editions of a newspaper, because newspapers contained public facts that could not be protected under copyright law.[41] The case confirmed the custom that there was no private property right in published news items. Another case provided the AP with a different avenue for protection through the contractual mechanisms of unfair competition and by extending the definition of property. In *National Telegraph News Co. v. Western Union Telegraph Co.* (1902), the Illinois Supreme Court held that courts of equity should extend protection to intangible elements related to property like news items.[42] The court restrained the defendants from copying Western Union's ticker tape service for sixty minutes after it had been printed.

The judgment involved two departures from established precedent. First, the court held that copying a company's information on prices violated a form of intangible property. In a somewhat convoluted statement, the court explained its logic as follows: "though the immediate thing [ticker news reports] to be acted upon by the injunction is not itself, alone considered, property, it is enough that the act complained of will result, even though somewhat remotely, in injury to property."[43] The printed ticker tape temporarily acquired limited attributes of property, but only for a short time period before competitors could use the news printed on the tape.

Second, the court based its understanding of the legal limits of property on recent developments in the law of unfair competition with respect to unregistered trademarks. The court reasoned that gathering and transmitting news constituted a form of business and that Western Union's ticker tape stock quotations, sporting results, and other reports were inherently commercial products. The court confirmed the exclusion of such news reports from copyright law. However, the court found that Western Union's news reports deserved legal protection under common law because Western Union had expended labor and money to gather the news. Furthermore, Western Union had generated value through the "precommunicatedness of the information," i.e. by distributing its news earlier than anyone else.[44] This quality of speed created the commercial value of the printed ticker tape and made the tape a commercial product that could receive protection through the laws of unfair competition.

The court held further that Western Union needed protection not just for its own sake, but also for the sake of the public. If a competitor continued to reproduce Western Union's financial news, the business would cease to be profitable and Western Union might stop providing news entirely. As the court evocatively concluded, "the parasite that killed, would itself be killed, and the public would be left without a service at any price."[45] According to the court, protecting the public interest required applying the law of unfair competition to prevent freeriding by competitors. To achieve this result, the court was obliged to consider news reports as a form of intangible property for a limited time.

In 1905, the United States Supreme Court confirmed that companies could rely on the law of unfair competition to bar unlicensed use of price quotations.[46] The "precommunicatedness" of news formed an important argument in understanding competition among news providers. Thus, the Supreme Court's ruling recognized that news providers garnered value from news by sending it to their customers first and before their competitors. This opened the door for the AP to seek similar protection from its rivals.

Rivalry with fellow news agencies over reporting during the First World War finally provided the AP with the opportunity to pursue the matter further. Once the United States declared war on Germany in 1917, the demand for swift and accurate reports on news from Europe increased. William Randolph Hearst (1863–1951) had founded a news agency, International News Service (INS), in 1909. After INS reported rather hostilely on British losses during the first years of the First World War, Allied authorities in Europe banned INS from using telegraph lines to collect news. Rather than admit defeat to the AP, INS purportedly gained access to AP stories by bribing AP employees as well as copying from early editions of newspapers and news bulletin boards. Hearst's newspapers on the West Coast were published three hours after those on the East Coast. INS agents on the East Coast telegraphed published AP news reports to the West Coast in time for publication there. Stone had found the opportunity he had anticipated for decades.[47] In 1917, the AP brought a suit against INS for illegally obtaining AP news prior to publication through bribery and for copying AP news from bulletin boards and early editions of AP newspapers to resell to INS customers. Judge Augustus Hand, sitting in the Second District Court of New York, had little trouble characterizing the acts of bribery as a tortious interference with contracts. When he turned his attention to the copying of information from publicly available bulletin boards and early editions of AP member newspapers, however, Hand had greater difficulty. Hand sought to reconcile the established view that news became public property upon publication with a contrary desire to protect the value the AP had created in its news through its investments of labor and expense. Hand concluded there was an implied contract between the parties that precluded competitors from copying news while it remained valuable. Hand did not assign a property right to news reports.[48] The Circuit Court of Appeals granted the AP a preliminary injunction "against any bodily taking of the words or substance of [AP] news."[49]

In 1918, the case came before the United States Supreme Court. The Supreme Court's contested majority decision focused on the question of rights between competitors. In the Supreme Court's opinion of December 23, 1918, Justice Pitney, speaking for the majority, held that news could not in law be copyrighted, as news items were not creative, but rather constituted "a report of matters that ordinarily are *publici juris*; it is the history of the day."[50] Pitney built on previous cases to argue news reports deserved protection for commercial reasons. The collection of global news cost a great deal and the AP needed some profit "as an incentive to effective action in the commercial world," wrote Pitney. This made news collection "a legitimate business."[51] Like the Illinois Supreme Court's decision in *Inter-Ocean Publishing Co v. AP* (1900), Pitney's opinion seemed to have a strange duality. It argued that news agencies were private businesses whose products could be subject to regulation through laws of unfair competition. Simultaneously, however, Pitney asserted that news reports were *publici juris*, implying that news agencies were businesses trading in reports that belonged to the public.[52]

In line with Pitney's separation between the private business of news providers and the public-interest value of news, the United States Supreme Court focused on the private aspects of news agencies' business dealings. Pitney concluded that the case revolved around whether INS's behavior constituted unfair competition in the news business because INS had resold the AP's news before its commercial value had disappeared. Each business possessed its own character, argued Pitney. While news items could not be owned "in the absolute sense," they were "stock in trade," because the AP and INS expended "enterprise, organization, skill, labor, and money" to gather and distribute news. This made news similar to other merchandise. In the news business, however, Pitney distinguished between the rights of competitors vis-à-vis each other as opposed to their rights vis-à-vis the public. Pitney also distinguished between the rights news providers held over news reports before and after publication. Pitney concluded that the AP and INS had no property interest in news reports after publication vis-à-vis the public, but they retained property interests against each other, as they were competitors within the same business.

Pitney thus regarded news in this context as simply "the material out of which both parties are seeking to make profits at the same time and in the same field." With these caveats and noting that these rights only existed between competitors, Pitney concluded that news was "quasi property, irrespective of the rights of either [party] as against the public."[53] A quasi-property right meant that the AP had a property right against INS, its competitor within the news business, to prevent the misappropriation of the AP's news.[54] The case went some way to achieving Stone's goals of establishing a property right in news, but it did so only against competitors, not against the world.

In one of two written dissents from the majority opinion, Justice Louis Brandeis expressed concerns about both the legal implications of the case and the majority opinion's interpretation of the concept of publication. Brandeis wrote that the Supreme Court had used nonproprietary terms to justify a doctrine of quasi-property. Furthermore, wrote Brandeis, quasi-property was a new concept and such innovation was a matter for the legislature. Brandeis opined that common-law protection already existed for unpublished works, even if they were just facts reported through telegraphy. In this case, however, Brandeis saw the bulletin boards as a form of publication and reasoned that INS therefore had a right to use those news reports, because the AP had made them public.[55] Brandeis disagreed with both the legal grounds for the judgment and the majority's definition of publication.

Despite Brandeis' dissent, the Supreme Court upheld the Circuit Court of Appeals' injunction against appropriating the plaintiff's news *"until its commercial value as news to the complainant and all its members has passed away."*[56] Pitney had focused on the abstract principles of competition and creating the new concept of a quasi-property right that was only good against competitors. Ironically, even the notion of competitors was highly ambiguous below the surface of the case. Several Hearst newspapers actually held AP franchises. The outcome sharpened the exclusivity of their franchise, even as it seemed to restrict INS's freedom of maneuver to gather news. The news agency and newspaper markets overlapped substantially, further complicating the creation of a quasi-property right.

Subsequent interpretations have often claimed that Pitney introduced a new common-law rule whereby those who freeload on the labor and financial investment of a competing firm can be prosecuted for misappropriation. This has since become known as the doctrine of "hot news." Scholars have since critiqued Pitney's majority opinion as illogical, while others have argued that Pitney recognized neither the AP's anti-competitive tendencies nor its use of the case to protect its newspaper franchise members from competitors such as the United Press.[57] The AP sought to employ public mechanisms to protect its private business model of supplying its franchise members with each other's news.

After the case was decided, the AP changed its requirements for how newspapers should designate AP reports. Now, newspapers had to label these items with either "Associated Press" or "AP," along with printing a note in every issue stating that the AP was "entitled exclusively to the use for republication of all news dispatches credited to it or not otherwise credited in this newspaper and all the local news published herein."[58] While these changes theoretically allowed the AP to claim ownership over news, they also changed the AP's place in the market of international news. The AP felt bound to follow the decision in *INS v. AP* internationally and it refrained from copying from foreign newspapers, which it had frequently done in the past.[59] Yet, the AP found itself embattled at home because its rival, the United Press, continued to copy from foreign papers. To rectify the situation, Kent Cooper, AP general manager from 1925 to 1943, turned to the League of Nations to advocate for international quasi-property rights in news that would buttress the AP's position at home.

The United States was not a member of the League of Nations. Ironically, however, the AP saw the Conference of Press Experts at the League of Nations in 1927 as the ideal opportunity to internationalize the idea of quasi-property.[60] The conference's preparatory committee drafted a resolution that divided news into three categories: unpublished, published, and official. The League proposed that official news could be freely reproduced. The League aimed to protect published and unpublished news through property rights for a limited period of time. Within a number of hours after receipt, a news item would then become public property. Cooper introduced the resolution at the conference, seeing this as a key means to internationalize *INS v. AP*.

The British government and Reuters rejected the idea of international legislation. They believed that domestic cases such as *INS v. AP* or ordinances on protecting news telegrams in various British colonies and dominions had shown that protection was a widely accepted principle. Most English lawyers, Reuters believed, thought that if a test case were brought to the House of Lords, the House's judgment would mirror that of the United States Supreme Court in *INS v. AP*.[61] At the conference, Reuters mainly intervened to protest that British newspapers "by their very practice recognize the principle of property rights in news."[62] Reuters saw no reason to rock the legislative boat.

Due to opposition from various quarters, particularly the German delegation, Cooper's resolution was defeated at the conference.[63] Delegates agreed to divide news into official, pre-, and post-publication, to forbid any protection of official news, and to agree on the importance of protecting news prior to publication. They rejected, however, any attempt to create international regulation on news reports after publication, arguing that each nation's different legal traditions made agreement impossible. Although further conferences of press experts convened in Copenhagen in 1932 and Madrid in 1933, the participants never discussed the issue of news protection further.[64]

Still, the League's resolution mattered because it upheld a commercial justification for the protection of news reports. The conference's final resolution declared that: "newspapers, news agencies, and other news organisations are entitled to the fruits of their labour, enterprise and financial expenditure upon the production of news reports."[65] The resolution and conference participants also adopted the American rhetoric of unfair competition and recognized the principle of assessing the labor and time involved in the collection and dissemination of news. In his closing speech, Lord Burnham, the conference president, declared that "the Conference does not wish to establish any monopoly in news or prejudicial control of the sources of public information, but it does wish to protect against unfair competition those great journalistic enterprises which, by their initiative and their organization, bring the world's news at great cost of time and skilled labour to the use of the reading public."[66] An important AP member, the *New York Times*, declared triumphantly that the conference's resolution had established "a universal concept" that news was property and deserved protection.[67] Creativity was no longer the central notion underlying attempts to protect news internationally. Rather, labor, enterprise, and financial expenditure had become the three interrelated concepts that buttressed legal arguments for granting protection to news reports.

Although Reuters' managing director, Roderick Jones, had dismissed the AP's attempts to internationalize *INS v. AP*, Reuters remained highly interested in international legislation on news reports. In the mid-1920s, the AP sought to solve domestic problems through an international conference at the League of Nations. In the mid-1930s, Jones tried to use international legislation to streamline imperial legislation. He argued for the inclusion of news in the International Convention for the Protection of Industrial Property, which dealt principally with patents and trademarks. When ratified, the Convention applied throughout the Empire. Jones perceived that if news reports were included in the Convention, it would act, like the Berne Convention, to harmonize legislation on protection for news reports throughout the British Empire.

Jones intended to use the international consensus reached at the League of Nations as a springboard to simplify the protection of news within the British Empire through international legislation. He drew on American developments to justify his approach, even using religious language to glorify *INS v. AP*. Jones proclaimed that the judgment had "ultimately imposed upon U.S. journalists, for their eternal salvation, the doctrine that news after publication as well as before is as much an article of property as coal, or cabbages, or diamonds."[68] Jones repeatedly adopted the vocabulary of *INS v. AP*, declaring in 1923 that he too preferred the term "property rights in news" over the "rather misleading term" of copyright. Jones believed that the language of property rights was better suited to underscore news agencies' investment in procuring news items.[69]

Despite this affinity with American approaches, Jones argued that news did not constitute quasi-property, but was in fact industrial property deserving of protection under the International Convention for the Protection of Industrial Property. As early as 1924, Reuters had enlisted its partners in the Agences Alliées, the interwar European trade association of national news agencies, to explore the alternative of classifying news as industrial property as early as 1924. Trademarks protect forms of expression such as logos, titles, and service marks; they often protect titles of serial publications, such as the *Encyclopedia Britannica*. The news agencies hoped that their news reports might qualify as serial publications. At the first general conference of the Agences Alliées in 1924, the agencies decided unanimously to address the Bureau of Industrial

Property in Berne as well as the relevant national authorities. The agencies hoped to revise Article 10*bis* on unfair competition to punish unauthorized reproduction of articles.[70] In 1934, after discussions on news at several international conferences on industrial property, Reuters acted as the official representative of the European news agencies at the conference convened in London to revise the Industrial Property Convention. Reuters proposed that "all news obtained by a newspaper or news agency, whatever its form or content and whatever the method by which it has been transmitted, shall be regarded as the property of such newspaper or agency for as long as it retains its commercial value."[71] In a vote on a proposition to protect news for twenty-four hours after publication, thirteen countries voted in favor, five against (including the United States), and twelve, including Britain, abstained. Despite further reports and discussions, by the 1938 conference it had become clear that delegates could agree neither on what constituted illicit means of news procurement nor on the wording of the potential addition to Article 10*bis*. The outbreak of the Second World War ended any concerted joint action by the European news agencies.

THE POSTWAR BUSINESS OF NEWS

After heightened international efforts to protect news reports in the interwar period, postwar disputes mainly occurred within national borders. Reuters became a nonprofit trust in 1941. Although the BBC continued to worry about Reuters' commercial ambitions, a 1944 agreement allowed the BBC further control over its news from Reuters. The board of Reuters appointed a journalist knowledgeable about the BBC to supervise the composition of the news reports Reuters sent to the BBC.[72] After the war, the BBC continued to expand its own newsgathering services, but it remained Reuters' largest single customer in 1960.[73] The BBC External Services' subscription also effectively provided hidden subsidies to Reuters' overseas services throughout the 1960s and 1970s before the BBC ended its External Services contract in 1980. After Reuters was floated on the London Stock Exchange and the NASDAQ in 1984, Reuters' close government connections and indirect government subsidies finally ended in 1986, when the relationship became openly commercial.[74]

The AP discovered that public mechanisms could cut both ways. The United States government brought an anti-trust case against the AP that challenged its exclusionary bylaws.[75] During the case, the AP tried to head off accusations that it had restrained trade by arguing that the company was not subject to the rules of commerce and that it was under no obligation to share its news with everyone who could pay. The AP presented news prior to publication as a noncommercial good. The Supreme Court and Judge Learned Hand of the Second Circuit, on the other hand, found it more important to allow competition amongst newspapers within franchise districts than to maintain competition between the AP and its newsgathering rivals.[76] In *INS v. AP*, the courts had focused on competition between news providers, specifically between news agencies. In the anti-trust case, the courts shifted to focusing on the consumers of news and their rights to choose between competing newspapers. In June 1945, the courts found that the AP had violated the Sherman Act and the AP was forced to open its membership. This allowed more newspapers to join the AP, reconfiguring the private law and franchise systems of the association. Concerns about restraint of trade had plagued the AP since at least 1900, when the AP moved its corporate offices from Chicago to New York following an injunction to prevent the AP from expelling a member for violating its bylaws.[77]

After the mid-1950s, the AP rarely relied on the logic of *INS v. AP* to protect its news reports. Prior to 1945, AP members had disagreed in their attitudes toward radio. While Reuters sought to control what news the BBC could broadcast and when it could broadcast it, the AP pursued legal sanctions against radio stations that broadcast the association's news in competition with AP members.[78] Television news followed similar patterns to print. Network television news relied heavily on print media for stories, particularly news agency wires from the AP and United Press International (UPI) as well as the *New York Times*. In December 1968, NBC sourced 70 percent of its domestic stories from AP and UPI wire services.[79] As late as 1979, television news editors still used AP and UPI wires constantly to check reporters' work for errors. Twenty-five years later, little had changed in television news despite broader shifts in the overall news environment and significant declines in viewer figures.[80] Although networks selected which stories to cover, they followed a news agenda set by news agencies and print newspapers of record. The protection of news too has continued to revolve around news agencies, particularly the AP.[81] Similarly, other groundbreaking cases on fair use, such as *Harper & Row v. Nation Enterprises* (1985), have relied on the ruling in *INS v. AP*.[82]

In the postwar international world, Reuters and the AP retained their positions as the major western news agencies (with AFP close behind). After the Second World War, the AP embarked on an extensive program of overseas expansion and Reuters strengthened its position in post-colonial Africa. Meanwhile, UNESCO and the United Nations focused on reorganizing the global flows of news. Reports by UN bodies on communications, such as the MacBride Report (1980), did not mention legal protection. The MacBride Report focused on how to reconfigure the status quo in favor of a "new information order" that might remove the privileged position of western news agencies in global reporting.[83] These aspirational discussions dismissed property and legislative protection for news. Participants sought to establish a nonprofit model for news provision to counter western political influence. The authors of the MacBride Report viewed ideas about free trade in news as synonymous with western domination of news provision. The interests of Reuters and the AP in the business of news contrasted sharply with UNES-CO's political project for news. Agencies like Reuters or the AP did not participate in UNESCO's commissions, and felt unfairly attacked by them.[84] These competing conceptions about news provision have kept the protection of news out of the international legislative agenda until debates since 2012 over a "Google tax."

CONCLUSION

The availability of news on the Internet has accelerated the decline in news-paper subscriptions that dated back to the 1980s. In response, newspapers and news agencies have turned once again to the law to protect their organizations from new competitors. In so doing, they have revived a raft of older arguments about the legal status of news. In these earlier debates, as well as in their more recent variants, news providers floated a variety of arguments, depending on their audience and objectives. In a statement before a 1923 government commission in which he argued for exclusivity, for example, Reuters managing director Roderick Jones defined news somewhat vaguely as "an impalpable thing" and "whatever is interesting to the man in the street."[85] When Jones tried to persuade his journalistic colleagues to lobby for the creation of a property right in news, in contrast, he focused more narrowly on the "labour, cost and enterprise" that was necessary to creating a news report.[86] Jones was but one of the many news agency publicists who tried to transform news into property. Here, as in so many other realms, rhetoric did not translate into law. When confronted with specifics, both jurists and lawmakers challenged self-serving definitions of news in order to strike a balance between the competing claims of public access and private control.

Nationally-based legal conventions have unquestionably shaped how news providers have behaved. Yet the political economy rather than law has done the most to sustain the business strategies of producing and distributing news. In Britain, Reuters' agreement with the PA led the British press to lobby lawmakers to protect the PA's revenue base. In the United States, the AP's national franchise system led AP lobbyists to try to convince jurists to invest news with property rights. While these approaches were nation-specific, appeals to the law played a key role on both sides of the Atlantic. Here, as in many similar instances, news providers used the law not to change the status quo, but to perpetuate it.

Technological change and market competition have often spurred news providers to seek legal protection for news. In the past, as today, these factors frequently crossed national boundaries. It is for this reason that, despite major differences in legal norms and business models, news agencies in Britain and America have tried to obtain similar kinds of legal protection. Newspapers in both countries have also tried at various times to protect the news, yet they have rarely equaled the dedication of news agencies. In the late nineteenth century, British and American news agencies first invested their hopes in national legislation before shifting to common law. In each country, news agencies devised a business strategy that effectively managed the tricky balance between the exclusion of rivals and the creation of access to news. In the interwar period, news agencies in both countries tried, mostly unsuccessfully, to insert news into international conventions. In this debate, news agencies tried to protect the rights, prerogatives, and customary arrangements of news providers; the consumers of news or the public were of far less concern. Following the Second World War, these issues largely lay dormant in each country until the Internet threatened well-established business models. The global transformation of the news business since the 1990s helps to explain why so many news providers in so many different countries are simultaneously trying once again to protect the news. Yet if history is any guide, public rights-based jurisprudence will prove to be less effective in protecting the interests of news providers than the negotiation of private contract-based agreements. While lawsuits will doubtless retain their allure, strategic investments in shaping the political economy of news will probably pay off better in the long run.

NOTES

1. Richard Kielbowicz, *News in the Mail: The Press, Post Office, and Public Information, 1700–1860s* (New York: Greenwood Press, 1989), 155.
2. Quoted in Victor Rosewater, *History of Coöperative News-Gathering in the United States* (New York: D. Appleton and Company, 1930), 279.
3. Frederic Hudson, *Journalism in the United States, from 1690–1872* (New York: Harper & Brothers, 1873), 727.
4. John Locke, *Two Treatises of Government* (London: Printed for Awnsham Churchill, 1690), part 2, ch. 5, "Of Property," section 27.
5. Lionel Bently and Brad Sherman, *The Making of Modern Intellectual Property Law: The British Experience, 1760–1911* (Cambridge: Cambridge University Press, 1999), 23. On justifications for intellectual property protection, see Steven Wilf, "Intellectual Property," in *A Companion to American Legal History*, ed. Sally E. Hadden and Alfred L. Brophy (Hoboken: Wiley-Blackwell, 2013), 441–59.
6. Jonathan Silberstein-Loeb, *The International Distribution of News: The Associated Press, Press Association, and Reuters, 1848–1947* (Cambridge: Cambridge University

Press, 2014), 165. For more on Reuters and AP, see James Brennan's chapter in this volume.

7. Lionel Bently, "The Electric Telegraph and the Struggle over Copyright in News in Australia, Great Britain and India" in *Copyright and the Challenge of the New*, ed. Brad Sherman and Leanne Wiseman (The Netherlands: Kluwer Law International, 2012), 55–69; Will Slauter, "How News Becomes Property," paper presented at the Annual Workshop of the International Society for the History and Theory of Intellectual Property, American University School of Law, September 24, 2010.
8. Newspaper Libel and Registration Act (1881), s. 1.
9. *Walter v. Howe* 17 Ch. D 708 (1881).
10. *Actes de la 2me conférence internationale pour la protection des oeuvres littéraires et artistiques* (Berne: K. J. Wyss, 1885), 32, 46. See Lionel Bently and Brad Sherman, "Great Britain and the Signing of the Berne Convention in 1886," *Journal of the Copyright Society of the U.S.A.*, 48 (2001): 311–40.
11. See Isabella Alexander, *Copyright Law and the Public Interest in the Nineteenth Century* (Oxford: Hart Publishing, 2010), ch. 7; Catherine Seville, *The Internationalisation of Copyright Law: Books, Buccaneers and the Black Flag in the Nineteenth Century* (Cambridge: Cambridge University Press, 2006), 281–95.
12. In 1897, the International Congress of the Press (ICP) advocated property rights in news and prosecution under the law of unfair competition, not copyright. The ICP played no role at conferences to revise Berne. Ulf Jonas Bjork, "The First International Journalism Organization Debates News Copyright, 1894–1898," *Journalism History*, 22/2 (1996): 56–63.
13. William Briggs, *The Law of International Copyright, with Special Sections on the Colonies and the United States of America* (London: Stevens & Haynes, 1906), 336.
14. *Actes de la conférence réunie à Berlin du 14 octobre au 14 novembre 1908* (Berne: Bureau de l'Union internationale littéraire et artistique, 1909), 45, 203–7.
15. Article 2 (8). See Sam Ricketson, *The Berne Convention for the Protection of Literary and Artistic Works: 1886–1986* (London: Centre for Commercial Law Studies, Queen Mary College, 1987), 302–6.
16. *Walter v. Steinkopff* 3 Ch. 489 (1892), 495. A similar case in the United States, *Chicago Record-Herald Co. v. Tribune Ass'n.* 275 F. 797 (7th Circ. 1921), decided that newspapers could copyright stories that were literary productions. *Baker v. Selden* 101 U.S. 99 (1880) also distinguished between fact and expression.
17. Discussed in Briggs, *The Law of International Copyright*, 541.
18. Lionel Bently, "Copyright and the Victorian Internet: Telegraphic Property Laws in Colonial Australia," *Loyola of Los Angeles Law Review*, 38/1 (2004): 71–176.
19. Lionel Bently, "Copyright, Translations, and Relations between Britain and India in the Nineteenth and Early Twentieth Centuries," *Chicago-Kent Law Review*, 82 (2007): 71–5.
20. Roderick Jones, *Property in News* (London: Waterlow, 1936), 5–7.
21. Letter from AP of India to Moloney, July 16, 1924, Reuters Archive, London (henceforth RA) RA 1/9011508, LN520.
22. Interview at 9 Carmelite Street between William Turner, Reuters' Overseas General Manager, and Jardine Brown, May 25, 1930, BBC Written Archives Centre, Caversham (henceforth WAC) WAC R28/162/1.

23. RA 1/867515, LN30, opinion by T. E. Scrutton, December 27, 1895.
24. Amelia Bonea, "All the News that's Fit to Print? Reuter's Telegraphic News Service in Colonial India," in *Global Communication Electric: News, Business, and Politics in the World of Telegraphy*, ed. M. Michaela Hampf and Simone Müller-Pohl (Frankfurt am Main: Campus, 2013), 223–45.
25. RA 1/867515, LN30, opinion by F. D. McKinnon, April 10, 1911.
26. *Exchange Telegraph Co. v. Gregory and Co.* 1 Q.B. 147 (1895).
27. Donald Read, *The Power of News: The History of Reuters*, 2nd edn (Oxford: Oxford University Press, 1999), 52.
28. *Clayton v. Stone* 5 F. Cas. 999 (C.C.S.D.N.Y. 1829), 1003.
29. *Baker v. Selden* 101 U.S. 99 (1880).
30. See Barbara Cloud, "News: Public Service or Profitable Property," *American Journalism*, 13 (1996): 140–56.
31. He referenced *Cox v. Land and Water Journal Company* LR 9 Eq 324 (1869), which had found grounds for copyright infringement against a periodical copying another periodical's directory of hunts.
32. Henry Watterson, *"Marse Henry": An Autobiography*, vol. 2 (New York: G. H. Doran, 1919), 104.
33. See Robert Brauneis, "The Transformation of Originality in the Progressive-Era Debate over Copyright in News," *Cardozo Arts & Entertainment Law Journal*, 27 (2009): 9–11.
34. International Copyright Report by W. E. Simonds, June 10, 1890 reprinted in *The Question of Copyright: A Summary of the Copyright Laws at Present in Force in the Chief Countries of the World*, ed. George Haven Putnam (New York: G. P. Putnam's Sons, 1891), 115–68. See also Meredith McGill, "Copyright," in *A History of the Book in America*, vol. 3: *The Industrial Book, 1840–1880*, ed. Scott Casper et al. (Chapel Hill: University of North Carolina Press, 2007), 158–77.
35. Section 5b of the Copyright Act of 1909 allowed registration of "periodicals, including newspapers."
36. *Charter and By-Laws of the Associated Press, Incorporated in New York* (1901).
37. Cited in Daniel J. Czitrom, *Media and the American Mind: From Morse to McLuhan* (Chapel Hill: University of North Carolina Press, 1982), 26.
38. Melville Elijah Stone, *Fifty Years a Journalist* (Garden City, NY: Doubleday, Page and Co., 1921), 63–4. It was common practice to disseminate incorrect news to catch copying.
39. Stone, *Fifty Years a Journalist*, 355.
40. "Will End Piracy, Stone Says," *New York Times*, March 30, 1917, 9.
41. *Tribune Co. of Chicago v. Associated Press* 116 F. 126 (D.C. Ill. 1900). For the simultaneous debate in the courts about whether the AP should be regulated as a public utility, see Silberstein-Loeb, *International Distribution of News*, 54–6. Note that the Supreme Court of Missouri ruled in 1901 that the AP was not a monopoly in part because it did not believe there could exist a property right in news any more than in "information" or "knowledge." *Star Publishing Co. v. Associated Press* 159 Mo. 410, 60 S. W. 91 (1901).
42. The presiding judge, Peter Grosscup, was Melville Stone's neighbor; the two had frequently discussed the merits of investing news reports with property rights in the years preceding this case.

43. *National Telegraph News Co. v. Western Union Telegraph Co.* 119 F. 300 (7th Circuit 1902). For a similar judgment, see *Dodge Co. v. Construction Information Co.* 183 Mass. 62 (1903).

44. *National Telegraph News Co. v. Western Union Telegraph Co.* 119 F. 298 (7th Circuit 1902).

45. *National Telegraph News Co. v. Western Union Telegraph Co.* 119 F. 296 (7th Circuit 1902).

46. *Board of Trade v. Christie Grain and Stock Co.* 198 U.S. 236 (1905). On prices as a form of property, see Stuart Banner, *American Property: A History of How, Why, and What We Own* (Cambridge, Mass: Harvard University Press, 2011), 79–84.

47. One scholar labeled it a "concocted controversy." Douglas G. Baird, "The Story of INS v. AP: Property, Natural Monopoly, and the Uneasy Legacy of a Concocted Controversy (Unfair Competition)," in *Intellectual Property Stories*, ed. Jane C. Ginsburg and Rochelle Cooper Dreyfus (New York: Foundation Press, 2006), 11–18.

48. *INS v. AP* 240 F. 983 (S.D.N.Y. 1917).

49. *INS v. AP* 245 F. 253 (2nd Circuit 1917).

50. *INS v. AP* 248 U.S. 234 (1918).

51. *INS v. AP* 248 U.S. 235 (1918).

52. The Illinois Supreme Court's classification of the AP as a public utility in 1900 pushed the AP to move to New York and incorporate under New York state law. *Inter-Ocean Publishing Co. v. AP* 184 Ill. 438 (1900). See Silberstein-Loeb, *International Distribution of News*, 53–7.

53. *INS v. AP* 248 U.S. 236 (1918).

54. See Victoria Smith Ekstrand, *News Piracy and the Hot News Doctrine: Origins in Law and Implications for the Digital Age* (New York: LFB Scholarly Publishing, 2005); Richard A. Epstein, "International News Service v. Associated Press: Custom and Law as Sources of Property Rights in News," *Virginia Law Review*, 78/1 (1992): 85–128. The contention of AP lobbyists that *INS v. AP* created a property right in news has been challenged by legal scholars. See Shyamkrishna Balganesh, "'Hot News': The Enduring Myth of Property in News," *Columbia Law Review*, 111/3 (2011): 419–97.

55. See Steven Wilf, "Making Intellectual Property Law in the Shadow of Law: International News Service v. Associated Press," *WIPO Journal*, 5/1 (2013), 88–95.

56. *INS v. AP* 248 U.S. 222 (1918). Emphasis in original. The Court did not specify how long news retained commercial value.

57. Jonathan Silberstein-Loeb, "Exclusivity and Cooperation in the Supply of News: The Example of the Associated Press, 1893–1945," *Journal of Policy History*, 24/3 (2012): 466. See also Leo J. Raskind, "The Misappropriation Doctrine as a Competitive Norm of Intellectual Property Law," *Minnesota Law Review*, 75 (1991): 865–905; Douglas G. Baird, "Property, Natural Monopoly, and the Uneasy Legacy of INS v. AP," John M. Olin Program in Law and Economics Working Paper no. 246 (2005), 1–43.

58. Cited in Baird, "Property," 30.

59. The *Chicago Tribune* even took the AP to court during the Boer War for buying the London *Times*, copying its war news, and cabling it to the United States, even though the *Tribune* had paid the *Times* for the exclusive right to carry its news in the

United States. Stone and the AP won the case with the argument that this form of copying did not constitute theft. *Tribune Co. v. AP* 116 F. 126 (C.C.N.D. Ill. 1900).

60. On Cooper's plans, which included creating an "international league of news associations" akin to the League of Nations, see Silberstein-Loeb, *International Distribution of News*, ch. 7.

61. League of Nations Archive (henceforth LNA) R1343 Document 53289, Letter from Reuters to Sir Eric Drummond, July 25, 1925.

62. LNA Conf. E.P. P.V.4, Fourth Plenary Session of the Conference of Press Experts, August 25, 1927, 47.

63. See Heidi J. S. Tworek, "Journalistic Statesmanship: Protecting the Press in Weimar Germany and Abroad," *German History*, 32/4 (2014): 559–78.

64. See Heidi J. S. Tworek, "Peace through Truth? The Press and Moral Disarmament through the League of Nations," *Medien & Zeit*, 25/ 4 (2010): 16–28.

65. "Declaration and Resolutions Adopted by the Conference of Press Experts," *League of Nations Official Journal (46th Session of the Council)*, 10 (Geneva: League of Nations, 1927), 1155.

66. LNA Conf. E.P.13. (General.1927.15), Conference of Press Experts, Final Report, Geneva, October 25 1927, Lord Burnham's closing speech of the Conference, August 29, 1927, 9.

67. "Ownership Doctrine Prevails," AP dispatch, *New York Times*, August 27, 1927, 13.

68. Jones, *Property in News*, 5.

69. Sykes Broadcasting Commission, June 5, 1923, Royal Mail Archive (henceforth RM), London, POST 89/20, 1998, 2115.

70. First Resolution, General Conference of Agences Alliées, Berne, June 6–11, 1924, Archives Nationales, Paris (henceforth AN) 5AR/469. On Agences Alliées, see Heidi J. S. Tworek, "The Creation of European News: News Agency Cooperation in Interwar Europe," *Journalism Studies*, 14/5 (2013): 730–42.

71. Sent to Agences Alliées on May 4, 1932, AN 5AR/484.

72. Agreement between Reuters and BBC, July 27, 1944, BBC WAC, R152/3.

73. Read, *The Power of News*, 335.

74. Read, *The Power of News*, 397–8.

75. *AP v. US* 326 U.S. 1 (1945).

76. Silberstein-Loeb, "Exclusivity and Cooperation in the Supply of News," 486.

77. *Inter-Ocean Publishing Co. v. AP* 184 Ill. 438 (1900).

78. See Michael Stamm's chapter in this volume. Important cases include *AP v. KVOS, Inc.* 80 F. 2d 575 (9th Circ. 1935), *Veatch v. Wagner* 109 F. Supp. 537 (D.C. Alaska 1953) and 116 F. Supp 904 (D.C. Alaska 1953).

79. Edward Jay Epstein, *News from Nowhere: Television and the News* (Chicago: I. R. Dee, 2000), 142.

80. Herbert J. Gans, *Deciding What's News: A Study of CBS Evening News, NBC Nightly News, Newsweek, and Time* (Evanston: Northwestern University Press, 2004), xvi–xvii, 86.

81. E.g. *Kregos v. AP* 937 F. 2d 700 (2nd Circuit 1991) and *AP v. All Headline News Corp.* 608 F. Supp. 2d 454 (S.D.N.Y. 2009).

82. *Harper & Row, Publishers, Inc. v. Nation Enterprises* 471 U.S. 539 (1985).

83. *Many Voices, One World. Toward a New, More Just and More Efficient World Information and Communication Order* (London and New York: UNESCO, 1980).
84. For Reuters, see Read, *The Power of News*, 393–4. In protest at what they saw as UNESCO's increasing politicization, Britain and the United States withdrew from UNESCO, respectively, in 1984 and 1985, but rejoined in 1997 and 2003.
85. Sykes Broadcasting Commission, June 5, 1923, RM POST 89/20, p. 2030.
86. Jones, *Property in News*, 3.

9

Protecting News Today

Robert G. Picard

Since the millennium, the changing digital environment has altered the businesses of traditional news providers in Britain and the United States. These changes have compounded difficulties for companies already wrestling with mature media markets and a general decline in the public's consumption of traditional news media. Combined with the recession of 2007–9, a decline in advertising revenue and readership created precarious financial conditions for traditional news providers. These challenges reduced revenue and profits, forced layoffs and company restructurings, and stripped wealth from the news industry.[1] Simultaneously, digital media has become central to news provision and consumption.[2]

In light of these difficulties, traditional news providers have struggled to protect their traditional business models and secure the value of their news reports. This chapter focuses on news providers' attempts to protect the value of their news reports. To secure exclusive control over their news reports, news providers have, broadly speaking, sought either to obtain various forms of legal protection for their businesses or attempted to devise new methods of business organization that contend with the novel technological problems the Internet has generated. News providers have relied on copyright law, the doctrines of unfair competition and misappropriation, and they have attempted to secure new legislation that would protect their business models. None of these efforts, however, has proven successful in insulating them against the technological changes and shifts in patterns of consumption that are now occurring.

Despite enormous opportunities created by the digital environment, legacy news providers remain the primary sources of news[3] and new private licensing regimes are yet to emerge online that displace news organizations, such as the AP, which evolved to control the exclusive value of news reports in an age of telegraphy and broadcasting. Alternative forms of organization are emerging and evolving, but even after a number of years of operation they remain incipient and small.

Although forecasting is always difficult, the news business in the Internet age is likely to involve a wider variety of news providers that will derive revenue from a greater range of sources than in the twentieth century. These actors will have different approaches to the economic value of news, but commercial providers will continue to put great emphasis on protecting their content and its market value. Circulation, listeners, viewers, and unique visitors are still critical to success, but the instantaneous distribution of news via the Internet and social media makes it difficult to retain control of one's news product and audiences. Retaining control of news once gathered and published will therefore continue to be a priority for news providers. As in the past, a property rights approach is unlikely to be fully successful in the Internet age, despite strong continuing support for it among news enterprises. A contract-based approach, predicated on exclusive licensing agreements, may be helpful, but history suggests that such efforts are likely to produce a race for new forms of technology and business organization that better secure exclusive access to news content or establish new methods of funding news provision in which such protection is less central. The social costs of such a race are unknown. When deliberating how to regulate the supply of news in the age of the Internet, social media, and mobile digital distribution, media firms, policymakers, legislators, and judges must weigh the advantages and disadvantages of greater legal protection against those of private initiatives intended to compensate for the absence of an effective property rights regime in news.

WHY THE INTERNET AND MOBILE DISTRIBUTION POSE SUCH A THREAT TO TRADITIONAL NEWS MEDIA

News providers were initially enthusiastic about the potential for digital distribution. In the 1970s and 1980s, publishers on both sides of the Atlantic experimented with and offered videotext and teletext services that piggybacked on cable and broadcast systems. In 1973, the BBC made the first use of teletext services to display text information on television screens.[4] During the age of mainframe computers, publishers offered dial-up services. Publishers hoped that these new technologies might enable them to move away from printing newspapers, which accounted for 60 to 75 percent of their total costs.[5] From 1983 to 1986, Knight Ridder Newspapers managed to attract 20,000 paying subscribers for its Viewtron service, but the project was short-lived and was shut down at considerable loss.[6] In the late 1990s, after the arrival of the Internet, some publishers tried to introduce paid-for news sites and they created a national digital advertising network in the United States, but they failed to attract sufficient consumers to maintain the efforts. By the early 2000s, most news sites provided content free of charge, but the continuing loss of classified advertising in—and readers for—paid print editions led to apprehension, a concern compounded by the inability to produce significant advertising revenues online.

The discomfort of newspaper publishers was in part a reaction to their commercial success in the twentieth century. American newspapers derived about half their income from advertising and half from circulation in the 1880s, but by 1950 70 percent of their income came from advertising. At the start of the new millennium, American newspapers received 82 percent of their income from advertising. The growth in advertising during the second half of the twentieth century increased newspaper advertising 2.6 times in real terms.[7] Newspaper enterprises grew wealthy and accustomed to 20 percent or higher annual returns on sales,[8] but as advertising revenue dropped, so did projected earnings and the value of the newspapers. In 1997, the *Minneapolis Star-Tribune*—circulation 387,000—sold to McClatchy Newspapers for $1.4 billion, but by 2012, the eight newspapers of the Tribune Co., including the *Chicago Tribune, Los Angeles Times*, and *Baltimore Sun*, were valued at less than $623 million.

The impact of the Internet has differed from that of previous communications technologies. Unlike broadcasting or television, the Internet is a substitute for the printed word. It does not directly compete for the same advertising resources, but it has destroyed the market for paid classified advertising—taking about one third of the advertising revenue from print. This is different from technologies appearing in the nineteenth and twentieth centuries. The telegraph was not a viable substitute for newspapers because it was not available to general consumers, although tickertape did partly supplant the supply of share prices by newspaper to financial institutions. Radio became an imperfect substitute for the printed word. Radio broadcasts generally carried less news than newspapers, and radio was ill suited for display and classified advertising. Although television was a better substitute for some types of display advertising, it was not a replacement for the printed word. After television emerged, however, it slowly became the news medium of choice for most of the public, but the increase in the popularity of television neither significantly reduced newspaper readership nor advertising in newspapers. Despite the growing use of radio and television, including 24-hour cable news channels, American newspaper circulation increased until 1985, and newspaper advertising revenue continued to grow until it peaked in 2005. Newspapers continued to serve as the primary local medium for reading and advertising and newspaper valuations remained robust.

In attempting to understand these new technologies and their political economies, analogies are useful in helping to establish systems of classification that inform regulation.[9] In the nineteenth century, policymakers in the United Kingdom drew an analogy between the Post Office, a state-owned monopoly, and telegraphy; telegraphy was said to be post by another means. In the United States, policymakers drew an analogy between railroads, a private business, and telegraphy.[10] The influence of these two differing analogies helps to explain why the telegraph was nationalized in the United Kingdom but not in the United States. In the United Kingdom, the analogy between the post and telegraphy was later extended to wireless telegraphy, which helps account for the Post Office's control over radio as well.[11] In the United States, where different analogies informed policy, the regulation of radio followed a different trajectory based on private commercial ownership and operation of broadcast stations.

The Internet shares features with both print and broadcast technologies. Unlike newspapers, telegraphy, broadcasting, and television, the Internet provides a way in which to "broadcast" the written word, as well as audio, video, and graphics. The Internet is also similar to broadcasting in eliminating the interval in time between when news is produced in a comprehensible form and when it is received for consumption. Unlike newspapers that must first be printed and then distributed—which introduces a delay between the time news content is produced and consumed—there is no such delay with broadcasting or the Internet.[12]

In the nineteenth century, telegraphy enabled news providers to take advantage of the interval in time between when the news was gathered and when it could be published. The success of the business model of the AP, for example, depended on the ability to exchange news exclusively after it had been collected and before it was published. Whether communications traveled from east to west, or west to east, the difference in time between one side of the United States and the other or between Britain and the United States determined the advantage in time that the AP had over its rivals. Whether the time difference increased or decreased the shelf life of the AP's news reports correspondingly determined the advantages that accrued to the AP's method of organization.[13] Once the news was published, it became possible for competing organizations to copy and redistribute to newspapers published later. The dispute in *INS v. AP* arose out of this problem and the AP's desire to maintain the exclusive value of its news reports even after its member newspapers had published the news that the association relied on to compile its reports.[14] Radio, television, and the Internet have all eliminated the interval between the time of reporting and distribution and the interval between the time of publication and worldwide consumption. By eliminating these two intervals in the traditional print publication process, the Internet has undermined the methods newsgatherers developed to protect the value of their news reports in the ages of telegraphy and telephony. News providers are now struggling to devise new methods and adapt existing ones to preserve the value of their news products in the Internet age.

LEGAL ATTEMPTS TO PROTECT NEWS AND
BUSINESS MODELS

As shown in earlier chapters, the pursuit of legal protection for news reports has been largely unsuccessful in the past. The decision of the United States Supreme Court in *INS v. AP* is the exception that proves the rule.[15] Despite the heavily publicized efforts of news organizations to obtain greater legal protection for their newspapers, the democratic qualities attributed to news in Britain and the United States, and the corresponding desire that news should be widely disseminated, have made legislators and judges wary of extending broad copyright protection to news reports.[16] In the past forty years, a growing quantity of national and international legislation devoted to protecting copyrights has increasingly shielded all kinds of content. However, legislation such as the American Copyright Act, the Digital Millennium Copyright Act, the EU Copyright Directive, and the WTO TRIPS agreements offer no apparent new protection for news.[17] Efforts to secure even a limited-duration copyright, such as twenty-four hours, on news or information have also proved fruitless.[18]

The protracted and self-damaging attempt by Belgian newspapers to prevent Google from indexing their articles for use in Google News is illustrative of the difficulties copyright claims encounter.[19] The doctrine of "fair use" (or "fair dealing" as it is known in England) has been of little assistance in preventing copying, linking, or sharing on the Internet, despite some court rulings backing news producers.[20] Copyright trolls, entities that acquire a tailored interest in a copyrighted work with the objective of enforcing claims relating to it, have engendered considerable public backlash and are no longer seen as an effective means in protecting the fleeting value of news reports online because of their lack of sociopolitical legitimacy.[21] Given that news providers are struggling to establish what rights, if any, they have in their content, and how to protect these rights, even the creation of platforms for trading digital licenses for news content is unlikely to be highly successful except among the largest entities that share similar interests in such a system.

Whatever protection *INS* may have afforded news providers in the past, it is no longer applicable law because the United States Supreme Court decided *INS* before the abolition of so-called "federal common law." After the decision of the Supreme Court in *Erie Railroad v. Tompkins*, the federal common-law origins of *INS* are no longer binding in federal courts, but the cause of action is still recognized under the laws of various states, including New York.[22] Attempts to unify and harmonize American law relating to intellectual property led to the enactment of the Copyright Act in 1976[23] and Congress recognized that some forms of misappropriation survived the passage of the Act. Misappropriation of "hot news," however, is a branch of the doctrine of unfair competition, a narrow version of which survives pre-emption.[24] Its application in different states remains disparate.[25] As a consequence, broader readings of *INS* in broadcasting cases from the 1940s and 1950s—in which newspapers and news agencies attempted to restrict use of their news by radio and television broadcasters—are also no longer helpful in seeking protection for digital news.[26] Insofar as such protection continues to exist at the state level, claims arising out of the misappropriation doctrine in *INS* have been significantly circumscribed.

The United States Court of Appeals Second Circuit has led the way in developing the modern and narrower doctrine. In *NBA v. Motorola*, a case concerning the provision of scores and other statistics from ongoing basketball games, the court held the Copyright Act pre-empted the NBA's misappropriation claims. "Hot news" *INS*-like claims were said to be limited to cases where a plaintiff generates or gathers information at cost, the information is time-sensitive, a defendant's use of the information constitutes freeriding on the plaintiff's efforts, the defendant is in direct competition with a product or service offered by the plaintiff, and the ability of other parties to free-ride on the efforts of the plaintiff or others "would so reduce the incentive to produce the product or service that its existence or quality would be substantially threatened."[27] This last requirement, which is likely to be difficult to prove in many cases, makes a finding of misappropriation remote, especially where others generate information for different purposes.

The decision of the Second Circuit in the more recent case of *Barclays Capital v. Theflyonthewall.com* confirms that the scope of the doctrine developed by the majority in *INS* has been narrowed and circumscribed. The case concerned the investment reports and recommendations of several leading banks and financial institutions. Each morning, the several banks and financial institutions circulated these reports to potential investors to generate investments placed through their services. Theflyonthewall.com, a financial news website, obtained access to the information contained in these reports, which it then published on the Internet. The plaintiffs alleged "hot news" misappropriation and copyright infringement as to their securities recommendations. The United States District Court for the Southern District of New York held in favor of the plaintiffs, but the Second Circuit reversed and remanded. It concluded that the plaintiff's claim did not meet the exceptions for a "hot news" misappropriation as recognized by the court in *NBA*, therefore it was pre-empted by the Copyright Act. Having held that the claim was pre-empted, the court found no need to apply the test in *NBA*.[28] Neither *NBA* nor *Theflyonthewall* preclude the possibility of a successful *INS*-related claim, at least not in New York, but the hurdle over which plaintiffs must climb will be substantial. Even so, the survival of the *INS* doctrine, albeit in a limited form, may be a sufficient threat to curtail some clearly obvious and repeated misappropriation of news and information on the Internet.

In an attempt to preserve their business models before bringing their claims, the plaintiffs in *Theflyonthewall* took measures to prevent or curtail pre-market public dissemination of their recommendations. The firms informed their employees that the unauthorized dissemination of their equity research or its contents was a breach of loyalty to their employers that could result in disciplining and firing; they included provisions prohibiting the redistribution of their content in their licensing agreements with third-party distributors and in their reports; and the plaintiffs used Internet technologies to seek to find the source of leaks and to plug them.[29] The efforts the plaintiffs employed to shore up leaks of their content to unintended recipients are reminiscent of those that the AP and other organizations employed to protect the exclusive value of their news reports before *INS*.[30] That the methods used by the institutions producing financial recommendations were unsuccessful is indicative of the difficulties associated with securing information on the Internet. The use of these methods, and the fact that they have for so long been common practice among information providers in the absence of established property rights, also suggests that news providers will continue to struggle to secure control over their content in the future.

The inability of American news providers to depend on broad protection from the *INS* doctrine, and the absence of a similar doctrine in Britain, accounts partly for the bevy of alternative unfair competition claims that traditional news providers have launched against their rivals. There is nothing particularly new about these efforts, which have existed as long as there have been threats to the newspaper business. In recent years the *bêtes noires* of traditional news providers have been search engines and other news aggregators. News organizations and publishers associations have heavily criticized Google, Yahoo!, MSN, and others, arguing that use of newspaper and news agency material amounts to theft, takes customers away from print, and makes it impossible to get readers to pay for news online.[31] In Britain, the BBC is another whipping post of the traditional media. Ever since its formation in 1923, commercial news providers have claimed that the BBC's license fee creates unfair competition, but such arguments have come to naught,[32] and the European Commission specifically accepts public service broadcasting license fees in competition policy. The success of traditional news providers in limiting the remit of public broadcasters in other European countries has been similarly lackluster, although significant limits have been put in place in Germany with regards to online news activities of public service broadcasters.[33]

Campaigns against unfair competition have produced proposals for legislation intended to insulate traditional news providers from competitors and rivals. In Germany, France, and the United States, legislators have considered laws to require search engines such as Google to pay for linking to news stories.[34] American and British regulators have acknowledged the difficulties confronting the traditional news business, and the interests of democracy and social policy at stake in maintaining a robust press, but few practical solutions have emerged. After hearings by the United States Federal Trade Commission in 2009, the Commission staff suggested wide-ranging policy measures, including extending copyright to news, a statutory "hot news" doctrine, subsidies, and antitrust exemptions for news organizations.[35] The proposals were criticized for being protectionist and backward-looking, and have produced no further action.[36] Ofcom, the British communications regulator, has acknowledged that local news is important to social and political participation, but has provided few practical solutions likely to receive widespread support or parliamentary approval.[37] Similarly, a United States Federal Communications Commission report concluded that significant impediments exist for news provision at the local level despite digitalization, a proliferation of news media, and an expanded number of content distribution systems.[38]

Other legislative proposals to protect traditional news providers have included tax breaks for the press. In the United States, there have been proposals that newspapers should be accorded not-for-profit status, but still be permitted to engage in commercial and political activities, such as political endorsements that are prohibited under rules for charitable organizations.[39] Other suggestions include providing tax-exempt status for not-for-profit digital news start-ups. Tax authorities have been reluctant to support such measures. Similar concerns have also prevented granting newspapers new tax advantages in Britain.[40] A proposal from German publishers that the government require search engines to pay each time they linked to a newspaper article led Google to launch an online campaign, backed by print media advertising, to develop opposition by Internet users,[41] and has led others to question its efficacy given the performance of protective measures in media history.[42] In France, newspaper interests promoted a proposal to tax Internet searches. The money from the tax was intended to help create a fund to compensate publishers.[43] Although Google threatened to remove all French publications from its index if the law passed,[44] eventually the press and the search engine agreed to establish a €60 million ($82 million) fund to help publishers improve digital operations and online business models.[45]

Scholars supporting intervention to address challenges to news provision in the digital age have argued that governments ought to take an active interest in protecting the news industry in the name of democracy and social welfare. They have argued that government, foundations, and the public should support newsgathering and distribution that serves public interests.[46] Proposals for achieving these aims include protectionist changes to the tax code, increased philanthropic support, refocusing public broadcasting toward local needs, involving educational institutions in local news provision, and introducing a federal levy on broadcasters and Internet service providers to generate funding for local news coverage. These suggestions for increased public support mirror similar practices established in Western Europe in the 1960s and 1970s to slow newspaper mortality.[47]

Conversely, other academics have criticized using the state to shore up legacy news providers for interfering with a technological transformation that might produce new forms of newsgathering and distribution better suited to the digital age.[48] These anti-protectionists argue that news organizations "need to get better at partnering with individuals, organizations, even loose networks, both to expand their purview and reduce their costs."[49] Partnering and cooperation are old tactics that news providers have used extensively since the mid-nineteenth century. A difficulty confronting the establishment of partnerships and cooperation is finding the incentives necessary to encourage coordination. Finding the incentive necessary to encourage news providers with disparate needs and in different locations to share resources has always been problematic. In the past, the promise of exclusivity encouraged news providers to cooperate and this enticement was critical to the formation of the AP and similar organizations.[50]

Today, there exist a greater number of different types of news providers, from bloggers to newspapers to aggregators and broadcasters. This variety makes coordination more complicated. Indeed, the wide variety of news providers with differing motives and varying revenue models has undermined the possibility of using exclusive access to the news as a compelling incentive to encourage cooperation. An alternative to outright protection might be for governments to provide incentives for news organizations to cooperate by granting privileges that would encourage disparate news providers to join.

NOVEL APPROACHES TO DIGITAL NEWS PROVISION

Absent the creation of large-scale partnerships and cooperative arrangements to supply news, social activists and civil society organizations are attempting to use the Internet to meet the demands of niche markets for various types of news reports and to fill the gap in news provision left by struggling traditional media organizations. Some of these efforts have focused on establishing new digital ventures, others on finding alternative funding for news organizations. Local and specialized start-up news organizations, often funded by foundations, wealthy patrons, civil society organizations, and readers, provide ways to fill some of the gaps that exist in news provision.[51] A variety of start-up journalistic enterprises have emerged, many staffed by journalists who formerly worked for legacy news organizations. Most of these news start-ups, however, remain small, local, or specialized[52] and research indicates they are not challenging legacy media, but supplementing it by serving niche audiences or supplying large media outlets.[53] Major news providers have had some success establishing online news portals, such as cnn.com. Other successful ventures have emerged from legacy firms, such as Politico and Slate, and still others have formed as independent start-ups, such as the Huffington Post. The *New York Times* now gains nearly a quarter of its revenue from digital activities and the *Guardian* has more digital readers outside Britain than print readers in that country, but most traditional news organizations have lowered their commercial expectations and reorganized to adapt to the digital environment.[54]

CONCLUSION

New technology often creates instability and disrupts incumbent businesses, hastening innovation, adaptation, and the creation of new institutional arrangements.[55] In the face of creative destruction, established firms that fail to innovate or adapt typically seek state protection. The news business has been confronted by challenges posed by new technology for hundreds of years. Although the telegraph, radio, and television did not disrupt traditional news providers as much as the Internet, on each occasion government protection ultimately proved unavailing. Instead, news providers relied on private con- tractual methods to protect their assets, whether through licensing agreements or novel forms of business organization.

Today, given the huge number and variety of news providers, their collect- ive inability to control news reporting, and the ease with which it is possible to copy and share the news, it is hard to imagine circumstances in which effective contract-based cooperative news reporting regimes may once again emerge. Even so, the establishment of private cooperative regimes would seem to be a better option for news providers than the pursuit of property rights protection for news content. In addition to the traditional unwillingness of British and American lawmakers to grant news reports property rights protection, nation- based property rights regimes are ill matched to the global reach of the Internet. Private cooperative regimes, when effectively structured and oper- ated, have in the past helped news providers protect their investments in newsgathering and news outlets obtain access to news reports at a reasonable price. In addition, these cooperative regimes have often obtained legal protec- tion in different jurisdictions over long periods of time. Governments may find it worthwhile to encourage such institutional arrangements in the future, as they have in the past.

The challenge of protecting news is influenced by the myriad ways in which news production and distribution are financed and the extent to which news providers remain dependent on different institutional arrangements for sup- port. As the number of news providers has proliferated, news providers have come to rely on several different business models. Some news providers sell access to news directly to users and protect their content by limiting access to it through conditional-access technologies such as paywalls. Others rely more heavily on advertising, license fees, or foundation funding. News providers who provide news for free—by relying on advertising, license fees, or foundation funding—tend to be less concerned about limiting access to their content than news providers who rely on paywalls. The growing divergence of interests between different news providers reduces the effectiveness of traditional legal approaches, since it complicates the task of predicting the likely consequences of a particular legal ruling on the production and distribution of news.

The legal and economic environment in which news is currently produced and distributed makes it hard for news providers that rely for protection on copyright and competition law to thrive, even if lawmakers champion their claims. Licensing agreements and technical fixes will almost certainly be more effective at providing news providers with protection, yet even these institutional arrangements are likely to be of limited utility in protecting the news providers' traditional monopoly over breaking news, since this monopoly no longer exists as a result of technological innovations and the growing importance of social media. To protect tomorrow's news, alternative institutional arrangements must be devised.

NOTES

1. Between 2000 and 2012, advertising revenues for the American newspaper industry dropped from $49 billion to $22 billion, a 55 percent decline. That figure was $20 billion in 2014 for a comparable advertising income stream. In 2000, American newspapers employed 56,000 people in their newsrooms; by 2011, the number had dropped to 40,000. The value of news companies has melted away. At the beginning of 2000, shares in the New York Times Company traded at $49; by January 2014 shares sold for $15. See Lucy Küng, Ruth Towse, and Robert G. Picard (eds), *The Internet and the Mass Media* (London: Sage Publications, 2008); Andrew Currah, *What's Happening to Our News* (Oxford: Reuters Institute for the Study of Journalism, University of Oxford, 2009); David Levy and Rasmus Nielsen, *The Changing Business of Journalism and its Implications for Democracy* (Oxford: Reuters Institute for the Study of Journalism, 2010); Robert G. Picard, "The Future of the News Industry," in *Media and Society*, ed. James Curran (London: Bloomsbury Academic, 2010), 366–79.

2. By 2013, the Internet was the primary source of news for 50 percent of the population between the ages of 18 and 44, and 25 percent of the population 45 years of age and above. One third of digital users received news on at least two digital devices and 12 percent of Americans with digital access paid for their news. Reuters Institute, *Digital News Report 2013* (Oxford: Reuters Institute for the Study of Journalism, 2013).

3. Reuters Institute, *Digital News Report 2014* (Oxford: Reuters Institute for the Study of Journalism, 2014).

4. Leonard Graziplene, *Teletext: Its Promise and Demise* (Bethlehem, Penn.: Lehigh University Press, 2000).
5. Robert G. Picard, *The Economics and Financing of Media Companies*, 2nd edn (New York: Fordham University Press, 2011).
6. "Knight Ridder is Closing its Videotext Service," *Los Angeles Times*, March 18, 1985, <http://articles.latimes.com/1986-03-18/business/fi-27148_1_videotext>; Howard Finberg, "Before the Internet there was Viewtron," Poynter.org, October 27, 2003, <http://www.poynter.org/uncategorized/17738/before-the-web-there-was-viewtron/>.
7. Robert G. Picard, "U.S. Newspaper Ad Revenue Shows Consistent Growth," *Newspaper Research Journal*, 23/4 (2002), 21–33.
8. Robert G. Picard, "Shifts in Newspaper Advertising Expenditures and their Implications for the Future of Newspapers," *Journalism Studies*, 9/5 (2008), 704–16.
9. Ithiel de Sola Pool, *Technologies of Freedom* (Cambridge, Mass.: Belknap Press of Harvard University Press, 1984).
10. Richard John, *Network Nation: Inventing American Telecommunications* (Cambridge, Mass: Belknap Press of Harvard University Press, 2010); William S. Jevons, "On the Analogy between the Post Office, Telegraphs and Other Means of Conveyance of the United Kingdom as Regards Government Control," *Transactions of the Manchester Statistical Society* (1867): 89–104.
11. Jonathan Silberstein-Loeb, *The International Distribution of News: The Associated Press, Press Association, and Reuters, 1848–1947* (Cambridge: Cambridge University Press, 2014), chs 3–4.
12. Alan B. Albarran and Angel Arrese (eds), *Time and Media Markets* (Mahwah, NJ: Lawrence Erlbaum Associates, 2003).
13. Silberstein-Loeb, *The International Distribution of News*, ch. 7.
14. Silberstein-Loeb, "Exclusivity and Cooperation in the Supply of News: The Example of the Associated Press, 1893–1945," *Journal of Policy History*, 24/3 (2012), 466–98.
15. 248 U.S. 215 (1918).
16. Richard Pérez-Peña, "A.P. Seeks to Rein in Sites Using its Content," *New York Times*, April 6, 2009, <http://www.nytimes.com/2009/04/07/business/media/07paper.html?hp&_r=0>; Bruce Sanford, Bruce Brown, and Laurie Babinski, "Saving Journalism with Copyright Reform and the Doctrine of Hot News," *Communications Lawyer*, 26 (2008–9): 8; Doug Kramer, "Idea for Protecting Newspapers Draws National Spotlight, Bloggers' Ire," *Cleveland Plain Dealer*, July 22, 2009; Brian Westley, "How a Narrow Application of Hot News Misappropriation Can Help Save Journalism," *American University Law Review*, 60 (2010–11): 691.
17. United States, Digital Millennium Copyright Act, Pub. L. No. 105-304, 112 Stat. 2860 (October 28, 1998); European Commission, "The Copyright Directive," Directive 2001/29/EC of the European Parliament and of the Council of 22 May 2001; World Trade Organization, "Agreement on Trade-Related Aspects of Intellectual Property Rights," <http://www.wto.org/english/tratop_e/trips_e/t_agm0_e.htm>.
18. France, "Presidential Commission on the Press" (Paris: Etats Généraux de la Press Ecrite, 2008); The Netherlands, "Dutch Government Innovation Press Committee," 2009; US Federal Trade Commission Workshop, "From Town Crier to

Bloggers: How Will Journalism Survive in the Internet Age?" December 1–2, 2009; US Senate Committee on Commerce, Science, and Transportation, Hearing, "The Future of Newspapers: The Impact on the Economy and Democracy," May 6, 2009; US House of Representatives Joint Economic Committee, Hearing, "The Future of Newspapers: The Impact on the Economy and Democracy," September 24, 2009.

19. Aoife White, Associated Press, "Belgian Newspapers Want $77M from Google," *USA Today*, May 27, 2008, <http://usatoday30.usatoday.com/tech/world/2008-05-27-belgium-google_N.htm>; Stephanie Bodoni, "Google Belgian Copyright Case Could Set European Policy," Bloomberg.com, February 24, 2011, <http://www.bloomberg.com/news/2011-02-23/google-belgian-copyright-appeal-could-deter mine-european-policy.html>; Matthew Lasar, "Google v. Belgium 'Link War' Ends after Years of Conflict," *Ars Technica*, July 19, 2011, <http://arstechnica.com/tech-policy/2011/07/google-versus-belgium-who-is-winning-nobody/>; Google, "Belgian Papers Reach Accord on Copyright," December 13, 2013, <http://news.yahoo.com/google-belgian-papers-reach-accord-copyright-100505932–finance.html>.

20. Scott Parrott, "News Producers Often Prevail Against 'Fair Use' Claims," *Newspaper Research Journal*, 33/3 (2012): 6–20.

21. Shyamkrishna Balganesh, "The Uneasy Case Against Copyright Trolls," *Southern California Law Review*, 86 (2013): 723–81. See also Nate Anderson, "Rightshaven, Still Angering Judges, Finally Pays Cash for its Mistakes," *Ars Technica*, August 3, 2011, <http://arstechnica.com/tech-policy/2011/08/righthaven-still-angering-judges-finally-pays-for-its-mistakes/>; David Krevets, "Newspaper Chain Drops Right-haven: It Was a Dumb Idea," *Wired*, August 9, 2011, <http://www.wired.com/threatlevel/2011/09/medianews-righthaven-dumb-idea/>; Parrott, "News Producers Often Prevail."

22. 304 U.S. 64 (1938); *Associated Press v. All Headline News Corp.*, 608 F.Supp.2d 454 (S.D.N.Y. 2009), 459; Douglas G. Baird, "Common Law Intellectual Property and the Legacy of International News Service v. Associated Press," *Chicago Law Review*, 50 (1983): 411.

23. 17 U.S.C.A. (West 2010).

24. *Financial Information Inc. v. Moody's Investors Service, Inc.* 808 F.2d 204 (2nd Cir. 1986), 209.

25. See *Associated Press v. All Headline News Corp.*, 608 F.Supp.2d 454 (S.D.N.Y. 2009), 459–60.

26. *National Basketball Ass'n. v. Motorola, Inc.*, 105 F.3d 841 (2nd Cir. 1997), 852.

27. *National Basketball Ass'n* at 845.

28. *Barclays Capital Inc. v. Theflyonthewall.com, Inc.*, 650 F.3d 876 (2nd Cir. 2011).

29. *Barclays Capital Inc.* at 880.

30. Silberstein-Loeb, *International Distribution of News*, ch. 2.

31. John Sturm, "Statement of John Sturm before the United States Congress Joint Economic Committee Hearing on 'The Future of Newspapers: The Impact on the Economy and Democracy,'" September 24, 2009.

32. Silberstein-Loeb, *International Distribution of News*, ch. 4.

33. Germany, 13 Rundfunkänderungsstaatsvertrag [13th Interstate Treaty on Broadcast and Telemedia], 2010. An English language version is available at <http://www.docstoc.com/docs/150063484/Interstate-Treaty-on-Broadcasting-and-Telemedia-KJM>; J. Johannes Weberling, *Mapping Digital Media: German*

Public Service Broadcasting and Online Activity (London: Open Society Media Program, Open Society Foundations, 2011); Josef Trappel, "Online Media within the Public Service Realm? Reasons to Include Online into the Public Service Mission," *Media, Culture & Society*, 34 (2012): 181–94.

34. Loek Essers, "German Cabinet Backs Law that Could Allow News Publishers to Sue Google," *PC World*, August 29, 2012, <http://www.pcworld.com/article/261585/german_cabinet_backs_law_that_could_allow_news_publishers_to_sue_google.html>; Eric Pfanner, "Germany Trying to Cut Publishers in on Web Profits," *New York Times*, March 11, 2012, <http://www.nytimes.com/2012/03/12/business/global/germany-trying-to-cut-publishers-in-on-web-profits.html?pagewanted=all&_r=0>; Robert G. Picard and Kit Kowel, "Content Taxes in the Digital Age: Issues in Supporting Content Production with Levies on ISPs, Telecoms, Search and Aggregator Firms, and Digital Products," Policy Brief, Reuters Institute, University of Oxford, February 2014.

35. Federal Trade Commission, Staff Discussion Draft, "Potential Policy Recommendations to Support the Reinvention of Journalism," 2010.

36. Robert G. Picard, "Getting It Wrong: The FTC and Policies for the Future of Journalism," *The Media Business*, June 12, 2010, <http://themediabusiness.blogspot.com/2010/06/getting-it-wrong-ftc-and-policies-for.html>.

37. Ofcom, Local and Regional Media in the UK, "Discussion Document," September 22, 2009; Ofcom, Local and Regional Media in the UK: Nations and Regions Studies, "Discussion Document Annex," September 22, 2009.

38. Steven Waldman, *The Information Needs of Communities: The Changing Media Landscape in a Broadband Age* (Washington, DC: Federal Communications Commission, 2011), available at <http://www.fcc.gov/document/information-needs-communities>.

39. Statement of Paul Starr, Joint Economic Committee Hearing on "The Future of Newspapers: The Impact on the Economy and Democracy," September 24, 2009.

40. David Levy and Robert G. Picard, *Is There a Better Structure for News Providers? The Potential in Charitable and Trust Ownership* (Oxford: Reuters Institute for the Study of Journalism, 2011).

41. AP, "Google Launches Campaign in Germany against Proposed Law that Could Establish Fees for Content," 2012, <http://news.yahoo.com/google-launches-campaign-against-possible-fees-104100488–finance.html>.

42. Heidi J. Tworek and Christopher Buschow, "Lessons: Why Germany's 'Google Tax' Won't Work," *Nieman Reports*, October 23, 2014, <http://niemanreports.org/articles/history-lessons-why-germanys-google-tax-wont-work/>.

43. "France to Act to Force Google to Pay for News," *Chicago Tribune*, October 29, 2012, <http://www.chicagotribune.com/business/breaking/chi-france-to-act-to-force-google-to-pay-for-news-links-20121029,0,1550062.story>.

44. "Google Threatens French Media Ban over Proposed Law," BBC News, October 18, 2012, <http://www.bbc.com/news/technology-19996351>.

45. "Agence France-Presse, Google Reaches Deal with French News Websites," February 2, 2013, <http://www.ndtv.com/world-news/google-reaches-deal-with-french-news-websites-512130>.

46. Leonard Downie, Jr. and Michael Schudson, "The Reconstruction of American Journalism," *Columbia Journalism Review*, October 19, 2009.

47. Anthony Smith, *Subsidies and the Press in Europe*, Political and Economic Planning, 43/569 (London: PEP in association with the International Press Institute, 1977); Robert G. Picard, *The Press and the Decline of Democracy: The Democratic Socialist Response in Public Policy* (Westport, Conn.: Greenwood Press, 1985); Robert G. Picard, "Patterns of State Intervention in Western Press Economics," *Journalism Quarterly*, 62 (Spring 1987): 3–9; Robert G. Picard, "Regression Analysis of State Role in Press Economics," *Journalism Quarterly*, 64 (Winter 1987): 846–50; Robert G. Picard, "Subsidies for the Media," in *The International Encyclopedia of Communication*, vol. 11, ed. Wolfgang Donsbach (Oxford: Wiley-Blackwell, 2008), 4891–5.

48. Chris Anderson, Emily Bell, and Clay Shirky, *Post-Industrial Journalism: Adapting to the Present* (New York: Tow Center for Digital Journalism, 2012).

49. Anderson, Bell, and Shirky, *Post-Industrial Journalism*, 92.

50. Silberstein-Loeb, *International Distribution of News*, chs 1–3.

51. David Westphal, "The State of Independent Local Online News: Start-Ups Look for Foundation Support," *Online Journalism Review*, November 3, 2008, <http://newmediaskool.org/index.php?option=com_content&view=article&id=1833:the-state-of-independent-local-online-news-start-ups-look-for-foundation-support&catid=1:latest-news&Itemid=50>; Jan Schaffer, *New Voices: What Works* (J-Lab: Institute for Interactive Journalism, 2010), <http://www.kcnn.org/WhatWorks/introduction/>.

52. Nicola Bruno and Rasmus Nielsen, *Survival is Success: Journalistic Online Start-Ups in Western Europe* (Oxford: Reuters Institute for the Study of Journalism, 2012); Knight Foundation, *Finding a Foothold: How Nonprofit News Ventures Seek Sustainability* (Miami: Knight Foundation, 2013).

53. Esa Sirkkunen and Clare Cook (eds), *Chasing Sustainability on the Net* (Tampere, Finland: Tampere Research Centre for Journalism, Media and Communication, 2012), 117.

54. "The New York Times Company Reports 2014 Third-Quarter Results," October 30, 2014, <http://investors.nytco.com/investors/investor-news/investor-news-details/2014/The-New-York-Times-Company-Reports-2014-Third-Quarter-Results/default.aspx>; Guardian US Press Office, "The Guardian Is Now the World's Third Most Read Newspaper Website," July 26, 2012, <http://www.theguardian.com/gnm-press-office/8>.

55. Howard Aldrich and C. Marlene Fiol, "Fools Rush In? The Institutional Context of Industry Creation," *Academy of Management Review*, 19/4 (1994): 645–70; Debora Spar, *Ruling the Waves: From the Compass to the Internet: A History of Business and Politics along the Technological Frontier* (New York: Mariner Books, 2003).

Epilogue

Tomorrow's News

Richard R. John and Jonathan Silberstein-Loeb

Newsgathering has always been a tricky business. High-quality news reporting is costly and even the best journalism is highly perishable. Once a news report becomes publicly available, it is almost impossible to prevent it from becoming copied. Unlike a fine meal or a pair of dress shoes, news becomes more valuable when it is shared. And no matter how valuable it may become, once news becomes public it has left the control of the news provider that created it. It is for these reasons that news fits the classic definition of a public good: the revenue it can generate cannot match the cost of its production. News is a public good for an additional reason: the information that it conveys is essential to civic life.

The fact that news is a public good has long challenged news providers. No business can long thrive that cannot match costs with revenue, and in Britain and America news has been a business since the seventeenth century. To subsidize its production, lawmakers and news providers have devised a raft of institutional arrangements. Prominent among them have been monopoly grants, government subventions, the bundling of news with advertising, and the establishment of exclusionary mechanisms to limit supply.

The bundling of news with advertising has long been a recipe for success. From the 1770s until the first decades of the twenty-first century, the print-and-paper newspaper remained a much-sought-after platform not only for news, but also for display and classified advertising. By leasing advertising space—a private good—newspaper publishers helped fund news reporting—a public good. Even after the commercialization of radio and television, the newspaper retained its strong position as an advertising platform. Here, as so often in the history of journalism, technological innovations had less draconian consequences for legacy media than one might have predicted. For many late twentieth-century newspaper publishers, news became the journalistic equivalent of a loss leader in the retail food business. Just as supermarkets sometimes offer certain highly sought-after items at unusually low prices as an enticement to shoppers, so newspaper publishers spent large sums on news-gathering in the expectation that advertising revenue would cover their costs. Only with the rise of online advertising would newspapers lose their monopoly on the attention span of a large and coveted audience. It is primarily for this reason that sponsored content has posed such a challenge. If high-quality journalism is to be sustained, the bright line between advertising and news must be carefully maintained to discourage news providers from conflating news with advertising or skimping on news altogether to maximize revenue from the leasing of advertising space.

The earliest newspapers did not recycle gossip. Rather, they offered their mostly elite readership a paper window on the world. Almost all of the news that found its way into print was international and national; the first news-papers to specialize in local news would not emerge until the nineteenth century. The paucity of local news in early newspapers is easily explained. Certain kinds of local news might ruffle feathers, making it problematic for the editor, while the routine coverage of local political events was little sought-after, since readers could be expected to have already learned by word-of-mouth about events that occurred in their immediate vicinity.

Prior to the codification of legal safeguards for journalists, the establishment of reliable postal systems, and the opening of legislatures to the public, news-gathering was costly, haphazard, and rare. During the eighteenth century, printers unabashedly and frequently republished news reports that originated in other publications, a practice that in certain respects anticipated the pro-miscuous information sharing that has become such a ubiquitous feature of the digital age. No one was paid for this content. Some London newspapers received brief news reports from unpaid correspondents abroad. A few fea-tured paragraphs and brief essays culled by a salaried editor, a vocational identity that in Britain originated in the 1760s. Most simply copied foreign news, without remuneration, from the Dutch and French press. Provincial English newspapers, in turn, freely lifted news reports from the London press. Colonial American printers were equally cosmopolitan, at least until the 1760s, when, spurred by political exigency, they increased their coverage of North American affairs.

Once news providers discovered that newsgathering could give them a comparative advantage, they began to invest in news reporting, a journalistic genre that emerged in Britain and America more or less simultaneously around 1800. The emergence of news reporting was slow and halting. Well into the nineteenth century, news providers typically spent more money on paper and printing and, in Britain, on stamp and advertising duties. The absence of copyright protection for news, a constant in the history of British and American journalism, significantly lowered the expense of obtaining "copy."

The unremunerated reprinting of news reports would long remain a staple feature of British and American journalism. The ubiquity of this practice was highlighted in 1851 in a parliamentary hearing at which the prominent New York City newspaper editor Horace Greeley was asked by a British lawmaker if he had any qualms about news "piracy" in the United States. Was Greeley troubled, the lawmaker asked, if a rival editor who had "not himself been at the expense of obtaining news" copied a news report "immediately" from Greeley's *New York Tribune*? Greeley was not: "It is talked of for effect's sake; yet, on the whole, I would rather that those who do not take it should copy than not ... the evening journals all copy from us, and we rather like it."[1]

To reduce the cost of news reporting, publishers banded together to form cooperative associations known as news agencies. In the United States, the New York Associated Press (NYAP) and its successor, the Associated Press (AP), limited their newsfeeds to member newspapers, which profited from their exclusivity through higher advertising rates and increased sales. In Britain, Reuters and the Press Association subsidized the British provincial press at the expense of the London press, the colonial press, and several colonial governments.

The existence of cooperative associations helps to explain the equanimity with which Greeley contemplated the sharing of original content. For Greeley was in 1851 a member of the NYAP, a news agency that permitted member newspapers, such as Greeley's *New York Tribune*, to obtain exclusive access to high-quality news reports. Enterprising publishers had always recognized the value of "exclusives"; the novelty of these institutional arrangements lay rather in the ingenuity with which news agencies like the NYAP used the telegraph to provide member newspapers with exclusive access to breaking news.[2] Cooperative newsgathering preceded the telegraph; yet it would not be until the completion in the late nineteenth century of a globe-girdling cable network that the exclusive coverage of late-breaking international news stories would become a journalistic staple.[3]

The legality of these exclusionary practices was affirmed in a landmark 1918 Supreme Court case, *INS v. AP*. The catalyst for this lawsuit was the circumvention by newspaper magnate William Randolph Hearst of the AP's exclusionary policy. By taking advantage of the time differential between New York City and San Francisco, Hearst was able to telegraph AP news reports from New York City to San Francisco *after* they had appeared in print in New York City, but *before* they were published in San Francisco. In its ruling, the Supreme Court rejected the AP's expansive claim that a news agency could copyright facts. Yet it affirmed the AP's narrower contention that a rival news provider could not "misappropriate" a news agency's news reports even after they had been published.

News providers in the digital age confront enormous challenges in retaining exclusive access to their news reports, since the time interval between the collection of news and its circulation has largely vanished. News providers like Bloomberg that specialize in real-time financial information remain committed to technical fixes, such as the Bloomberg terminal, that enable them to sell exclusivity. In the future, exclusivity is likely to remain an arrow in the news providers' quiver. Yet as the economic value of this kind of inside information becomes increasingly confined to the financial sector, this practice raises in a new form venerable questions about the relationship between the private interest and the public good.

Champions of high-quality journalism often invoke the metaphor of the "marketplace of ideas." In theory, this metaphor encourages the laudatory presumption that everyone can have a voice in public affairs; in practice, however, market-channeling institutional arrangements have often done more to facilitate high-quality journalism. A case in point was the London *Times* in the Age of Revolution. Protected from rivals by government subventions and high taxes that only wealthy newspapers could afford, the *Times* capitalized on its commercial success to transform itself into a politically independent "Fourth Estate." In the United States, in contrast, the unprecedented proliferation of newspapers hastened by the market-friendly Post Office Act of 1792 paradoxically obliged many journalists to curry government favor in order to generate the necessary revenue to balance their books.

"Free trade" was in Victorian Britain a shibboleth for a generation of political radicals who took it for granted that the unimpeded circulation of information would uplift the people and promote the public good. Communications policy in the nineteenth-century United States had a different, and even more expansive, civic mandate.[4] In addition to eliminating constraints upon the circulation of information—the primary goal of the British radicals—the federal government massively subsidized the circulation of information on market trends and public affairs in order to create and sustain an educated citizenry.[5]

In the digital age, it has become increasingly plain to thoughtful observers that the news business no longer resembles a marketplace of ideas. Merely to eliminate restrictions on the flow of information, the goal of the nineteenth-century British radicals, is a less realistic policy option than the subsidization of certain valued categories of information, long the norm in the United States.[6] Tomorrow's news, like yesterday's news, will best thrive in a political economy in which the market is channeled in a socially productive direction, rather than one in which its supposedly emancipatory potential in unleashed.

Among the most restrictive of the institutional arrangements that have shaped the news business have been government-sanctioned monopolies. In the United States, government-sanctioned news monopolies have been rare. In Britain, in contrast, monopoly has long been the law of the land. In the seventeenth century, the London-based Stationers' Company retained tight control over the press; following Parliament's buyout of the telegraph in 1868, the British Post Office granted the Press Association a monopoly over the distribution of provincial news inside Britain. The commercialization of radio followed an analogous trajectory. Having gained control of the electromagnetic spectrum, the British Post Office encouraged radio manufacturers to band together to establish the country's broadcasting infrastructure. To realize this goal, Parliament granted radio manufacturers a monopoly over the sale of radio sets. This monopoly eventually transmogrified into the BBC, which to this day collects from users an annual license fee on every radio and television in the United Kingdom.[7] Whether similar institutional arrangements will emerge in the future is unknown. Yet it is worth observing that the BBC, long an exemplar of high-quality journalism, emerged in a political economy in which competition was anathema and monopoly the rule.

Nowhere in recent years has the marketplace-of-ideas metaphor been more pervasive than in the public debate over network neutrality. Network neutrality, posited legal scholar Tim Wu in a seminal 2003 law review article that is widely credited with popularizing the "network neutrality" meme, is a principle that gives network users the right to use network applications and innovators the freedom to supply them.[8] By fostering competition, it is intended to establish a digital-age equivalent of the marketplace of ideas. The Victorian lineage of the marketplace metaphor is often obscured by hyperbolic techno-jargon. The powers-that-be at Google intend "to keep the Internet awesome for everybody," blogged one Google enthusiast in 2010. "Awesome" for the blogger meant network providers should be prohibited from "discriminating against certain services, applications, or viewpoints on the Web," and required to "be transparent about how they manage their networks."[9] Awesome networks are neutral networks. The Google blogger fixed his gaze on the future. Yet sometimes the Victorian lineage of the marketplace-of-ideas metaphor can still be discerned. The principle shaping the "promotion" of the marketplace-of-ideas concept, Wu elaborated, in invoking a controversial contention that had been originally popularized by the nineteenth-century British sociologist Herbert Spencer, was the promotion of "Darwinian competition among every conceivable use of the Internet" so that "only the best survive."[10]

Network neutrality is the social Darwinism of the digerati. While compelling as a catchphrase, it is a poor substitute for a sober-minded analysis of the limitations and possibilities of news reporting in the digital age. The political economy of journalism was never neutral in the past and it is disingenuous to assert that it can ever be neutral in the future. Every communications network encourages certain media and discourages others. Rather than pursue the utopian project of network neutrality, lawmakers would be well advised to be mindful of institutional arrangements that have been established to foster high-quality journalism.

In the digital age, the often tenuous link between the cost of making news and the revenue that news reporting can generate is badly frayed. There are simply too many news providers and too few barriers to entry. To complicate matters even further, online advertisers can now obtain fine-grained data on the preferences of the audiences that news providers aspire to reach. The Victorian marketplace-of-ideas metaphor no longer reigns supreme in theory, yet in practice, competition for audience-share, or "eyeballs," has never been more intense. Until the invention of market studies in the 1930s, audience preferences were largely a black box that was almost never opened. No longer. Should the monitoring of online audiences be perfected, as it is widely assumed it will be, even the most iconoclastic of journalists may well be encouraged, and even pressured, to tailor their news reports to their advertisers' expectations.

The political economy of journalism in the digital age presents new challenges and opportunities and it is high time rhetoric caught up with reality. News providers should recognize the de facto locality-based monopolies that once protected the distribution of news have vanished, almost certainly for good, and that contractually based cooperative arrangements to improve news reporting—e.g. Reuters, the AP—may well prove to be more effective in safeguarding the collective interests of news providers than quixotic legal campaigns to create property rights where none existed. Lawmakers should recognize that high-quality journalism has always been subsidized, reject the marketplace-of-ideas metaphor, and stop defending network providers that oppose the creation of the kind of market-channeling institutional arrangements that have protected high-quality journalism in the past. Tomorrow's high-quality news providers are likely to bundle news with advertising or some related non-news-specific revenue source even as they perpetuate the high ethical standards and sound journalistic skills long associated with the newspaper newsroom. In addition, they can be expected to invent a new array of institutional arrangements in the perennial quest to protect not only the channels that connect the news and its audience, but also, and even more fundamentally, the organizational capabilities that up until now have proved necessary to the making of high-quality news.

NOTES

1. "Report from the Select Committee on Newspaper Stamps" (1851), *Parliamentary Papers*, 558, 393.
2. Richard R. John, *Network Nation: Inventing American Telecommunications* (Cambridge, Mass.: Belknap Press of Harvard University Press, 2010), ch. 4.

3. Jonathan Silberstein-Loeb, "The Political Economy of Media," in *The Routledge Companion to British Media History*, ed. Martin Conboy and John Steel (London: Routledge, 2014), 80.
4. Richard R. John, "The Political Economy of Postal Reform in the Victorian Age," *Smithsonian Contributions to History and Technology*, 55 (2010): 3–12.
5. Richard R. John, "From Franklin to Facebook: The Civic Mandate for Communications," in *To Promote the General Welfare: The Case for Big Government*, ed. Steven Conn (New York: Oxford University Press, 2012), 156–72.
6. Richard R. John, *Spreading the News: The American Postal System from Franklin to Morse* (Cambridge, Mass.: Harvard University Press, 1995), chs 1–2.
7. Jonathan Silberstein-Loeb, *The International Distribution of News: The Associated Press, Press Association, and Reuters, 1848–1947* (Cambridge: Cambridge University Press, 2014), chs 4–5.
8. Tim Wu, "Network Neutrality, Broadband Discrimination," *Journal on Telecommunications and High Technology Law*, 2 (2003): 142.
9. Rick Whitt, "Hey FCC, Keep the Internet Open—and Awesome!" Google Public Policy Blog, January 14, 2010, <http://googlepublicpolicy.blogspot.com>, last accessed on October 4, 2014.
10. Wu, "Network Neutrality, Broadband Discrimination," 142.

Select Bibliography

Albarran, Alan B. and Angel Arrese (eds). *Time and Media Markets*. Mahwah, NJ: Lawrence Erlbaum, 2003.

Amory, Hugh and David D. Hall (eds). *A History of the Book in America*, vol. 1: *The Colonial Book in the Atlantic World*. Cambridge: Cambridge University Press, 2000.

Anderson, Chris, Emily Bell, and Clay Shirky. *Post-Industrial Journalism: Adapting to the Present*. New York: Tow Center for Digital Journalism, 2012.

Ayerst, David. *The Manchester Guardian: Biography of a Newspaper*. Ithaca, NY: Cornell University Press, 1971.

Baird, Douglas G. "Common Law Intellectual Property and the Legacy of International News Service v. Associated Press," *Chicago Law Review*, 50 (1983): 411–29.

Baird, Douglas G. "The Story of INS v. AP: Property, Natural Monopoly, and the Uneasy Legacy of a Concocted Controversy (Unfair Competition)," in Jane C. Ginsburg and Rochelle Cooper Dreyfuss (eds), *Intellectual Property Stories*, 11–18. New York: Foundation Press, 2006.

Balganesh, Shyamkrishna. "'Hot News': The Enduring Myth of Property in News," *Columbia Law Review*, 111/3 (2011): 419–97.

Barker, Hannah. *Newspapers, Politics, and Public Opinion in Late Eighteenth-Century England*. New York: Oxford University Press, 1998.

Barnard, John et al. (eds). *The Cambridge History of the Book in Britain*, 7 vols. Cambridge: Cambridge University Press, 1999–2014.

Baughman, James L. *Republic of Mass Culture: Journalism, Filmmaking, and Broadcasting in America since 1941*, 3rd edn. Baltimore: Johns Hopkins University Press, 2006.

Benjamin, Louise. *Freedom of the Air and the Public Interest: First Amendment Rights in Broadcasting to 1935*. Carbondale, Ill.: Southern Illinois Press, 2001.

Bently, Lionel. "Copyright and the Victorian Internet: Telegraphic Property Laws in Colonial Australia," *Loyola of Los Angeles Law Review*, 38/1 (2004): 71–176.

Bently, Lionel. "The Electric Telegraph and the Struggle over Copyright in News in Australia, Great Britain and India," in Brad Sherman and Leanne Wiseman (eds), *Copyright and the Challenge of the New*, 55–69. Netherlands: Kluwer Law International, 2012.

Bjork, Ulf Jonas. "The First International Journalism Organization Debates News Copyright, 1894–1898," *Journalism History*, 22/2 (1996): 56–63.

Black, Jeremy. *The English Press in the Eighteenth Century*. London: Croom Helm, 1987.

Blondheim, Menahem. *News over the Wires: The Telegraph and the Flow of Public Information in America, 1844–1897*. Cambridge, Mass.: Harvard University Press, 1994.

Botein, Stephen. "'Meer Mechanics' and an Open Press: The Business and Political Strategies of Colonial American Printers," *Perspectives in American History*, 9 (1975): 127–225.

Botein, Stephen. "Printers and the American Revolution," in Bernard Bailyn and John B. Hench (eds), *The Press and the American Revolution*, 11–57. Worcester, Mass.: American Antiquarian Society, 1980.

Boyd-Barrett, Oliver. *The International News Agencies*. London: Constable, 1980.

Brauneis, Robert. "The Transformation of Originality in the Progressive-Era Debate over Copyright in News," *Cardozo Arts & Entertainment Law Journal*, 27 (2009): 321–74.

Briggs, Asa. *The History of Broadcasting in the United Kingdom*, vol. 1: *The Birth of Broadcasting*. London: Oxford University Press, 1961.

Briggs, Asa. *Victorian Cities*. New York: Harper & Row, 1963.

Briggs, Asa. *The History of Broadcasting in the United Kingdom*, vol. 2: *The Golden Age of Wireless*. London: Oxford University Press, 1965.

Briggs, Asa. *The History of Broadcasting in the United Kingdom*, vol. 3: *The War of Words*. London: Oxford University Press, 1970.

Briggs, Asa. *BBC: The First Fifty Years*. New York: Oxford University Press, 1985.

Brown, Lucy. *Victorian News and Newspapers*. Oxford: Clarendon Press, 1985.

Campbell-Kelly, Martin, et al. *Computer: A History of the Information Machine*, 3rd edn. Boulder, Colo.: Westview, 2014.

Catterall, Peter, Collin Seymour-Ure, and Adrian Smith (eds). *Northcliffe's Legacy: Aspects of the British Popular Press, 1896–1996*. London: Macmillan, 2000.

Clark, Charles. *The Public Prints: The Newspaper in Anglo-American Culture, 1665–1740*. New York: Oxford University Press, 1994.

Cloud, Barbara. "News: Public Service or Profitable Property," *American Journalism*, 13 (1996): 140–56.

Coase, Ronald. *British Broadcasting: A Study in Monopoly*. London: Longmans, Green & Co., 1950.

Conboy, Martin. *Journalism: A Critical History*. Thousand Oaks: Sage Publications, 2004.

Copeland, David. *Colonial American Newspapers: Character and Content*. Newark: University of Delaware Press, 1997.

Craig, Douglas. *Fireside Politics: Radio and Political Culture in the United States, 1920–1940*. Baltimore: Johns Hopkins University Press, 2000.

Cronon, William. *Nature's Metropolis: Chicago and the Great West*. New York: W. W. Norton, 1991.

Currah, Andrew. *What's Happening to our News*. Oxford: Reuters Institute for the Study of Journalism, 2009.

Curran, James and Jean Seaton. *Power without Responsibility: Press, Broadcasting and the Internet in Britain*, 7th edn. London: Routledge, 2010.

Daly, Christopher B. *Covering America: A Narrative History of a Nation's Journalism*. Amherst: University of Massachusetts Press, 2013.

Dimbleby, Jonathan. *Richard Dimbleby: A Biography*. London: Coronet, 1977.

Douglas, Susan. *Inventing American Broadcasting, 1899–1922*. Baltimore: Johns Hopkins University Press, 1987.

Douglas, Susan. *Listening In: Radio and the American Imagination*. Minneapolis: University of Minnesota Press, 2004.

Downie, Jr., Leonard and Robert G. Kaiser. *The News about the News: American Journalism in Peril*. New York: Knopf, 2002.

Downie, Jr., Leonard and Michael Schudson. "The Reconstruction of American Journalism," *Columbia Journalism Review*, October 19, 2009.

Edwards, Bob. *Edward R. Murrow and the Birth of Broadcast Journalism*. Hoboken: John Wiley & Sons, 2004.

Einhorn, Robin L. *Property Rules: Political Economy in Chicago 1833–1872*. Chicago: University of Chicago Press, 1991.

Ekstrand, Victoria Smith. *News Piracy and the Hot News Doctrine: Origins in Law and Implications for the Digital Age*. New York: LFB Scholarly Publishing, 2005.

Epstein, Richard A. "'International News Service v. Associated Press': Custom and Law as Sources of Property Rights in News," *Virginia Law Review*, 78/1 (1992): 85–128.

Ferdinand, C. Y. *Benjamin Collins and the Provincial Newspaper Trade in the Eighteenth Century*. Oxford: Clarendon Press, 1997.

Graziplene, Leonard. *Teletext: Its Promise and Demise*. Bethlehem, Pa.: Lehigh University Press, 2000.

Gross, Robert A. and Mary Kelley (eds). *A History of the Book in America*, vol. 2: *An Extended Republic: Print, Culture, and Society in the New Nation, 1790–1840*. Chapel Hill: University of North Carolina Press, 2010.

Hall, David, et al. (eds). *A History of the Book in America*, 5 vols. Chapel Hill: University of North Carolina Press, 2007–10.

Hamilton, John M. *Journalism's Roving Eye: A History of American Foreign Reporting*. Baton Rouge: Louisiana State University Press, 2009.

Hampton, Mark. *Visions of the Press in Britain, 1850–1950*. Urbana, Ill.: University of Illinois Press, 2004.

Harris, Bob. *Politics and the Rise of the Press: Britain and France, 1620–1800*. London and New York: Routledge, 1996.

Harris, Michael. *London Newspapers in the Age of Walpole: A Study of the Origins of the Modern English Press*. Cranbury, NJ: Associated University Presses, 1987.

Hawley, Ellis (ed). *Herbert Hoover as Secretary of Commerce: Studies in New Era Thought and Practice*. Iowa City: University of Iowa Press, 1981.

Hilmes, Michele. *Network Nations: A Transnational History of British and American Broadcasting*. New York: Routledge, 2012.

Jackaway, Gwenyth. *Media at War: Radio's Challenge to the Newspapers, 1924–1939*. Westport: Praeger, 1995.

Jevons, William S. "On the Analogy between the Post Office, Telegraphs and Other Means of Conveyance of the United Kingdom as Regards Government Control," *Transactions of the Manchester Statistical Society* (1867): 89–104.

John, Richard R. *Spreading the News: The American Postal System from Franklin to Morse*. Cambridge, Mass.: Harvard University Press, 1995.

John, Richard R. *Network Nation: Inventing American Telecommunications*. Cambridge, Mass.: Belknap Press of Harvard University Press, 2010.

Johns, Adrian. *Death of a Pirate: British Radio and the Making of the Information Age*. New York: Norton, 2011.

Junger, Richard. *Becoming the Second City: Chicago's Mass News Media, 1833–1898*. Urbana, Ill.: University of Illinois Press, 2010.

Kemp, Geoff and Jason McElligott (eds). *Censorship and the Press, 1580–1720*, 4 vols. London: Pickering & Chatto, 2009.

Klatt, Wayne. *Chicago Journalism: A History.* Jefferson, NC: McFarland, 2009.

Knight Foundation. *Finding a Foothold: How Nonprofit News Ventures Seek Sustainability.* Miami: Knight Foundation, 2013.

Knightley, Phillip. *The First Casualty: The War Correspondent as Hero and Myth-Maker from the Crimea to Iraq.* Baltimore: Johns Hopkins University Press, 2004.

Küng, Lucy, Ruth Towse, and Robert G. Picard (eds). *The Internet and the Mass Media.* London: Sage Publications, 2008.

Levy, David and Rasmus Nielsen. *The Changing Business of Journalism and its Implications for Democracy.* Oxford: Reuters Institute for the Study of Journalism, 2010.

Levy, David and Robert G. Picard. *Is There a Better Structure for News Providers? The Potential in Charitable and Trust Ownership.* Oxford: Reuters Institute for the Study of Journalism, 2011.

Moore, James R. *The Transformation of Urban Liberalism: Party Politics and Urban Governance in Late Nineteenth-Century England.* Aldershot, UK: Ashgate, 2006.

Moran, Christopher. *Classified: Secrecy and the State in Modern Britain.* New York: Cambridge University Press, 2013.

Morris, James McGrath. *Pulitzer: A Life in Politics, Print, and Power.* New York: Harper, 2010.

Moss, David and Michael Fein. "Radio Regulation Revisited: Coase, the FCC, and the Public Interest," *Journal of Policy History,* 15/4 (2003): 389–416.

Nixon, Raymond. "Trends in Daily Newspaper Ownership since 1945," *Journalism Quarterly,* 31/1 (Winter 1954): 3–14.

Nord, David Paul. *Communities of Journalism: A History of American Newspapers and their Readers.* Urbana: University of Illinois Press, 2001.

O'Brien, Terence. *British Experiments in Public Ownership and Control: A Study of the Central Electricity Board, British Broadcasting Corporation, and London Passenger Transit Board.* London: George, Allen & Unwin, 1937.

O'Malley, Tom. *Closedown? The BBC and Government Broadcasting Policy, 1979–92.* London: Pluto Press, 1994.

Parrott, Scott. "News Producers Often Prevail Against 'Fair Use' Claims," *Newspaper Research Journal,* 33/3 (2012): 6–20.

Pasley, Jeffrey L. *"The Tyranny of Printers": Newspaper Politics in the Early American Republic.* Charlottesville: University of Virginia Press, 2001.

Pettegree, Andrew. *The Invention of News: How the World Came to Know about Itself.* New Haven: Yale University Press, 2014.

Picard, Robert G. *The Press and the Decline of Democracy: The Democratic Socialist Response in Public Policy.* Westport, Conn.: Greenwood Press, 1985.

Picard, Robert G. "Patterns of State Intervention in Western Press Economics," *Journalism Quarterly,* 62 (Spring 1987): 3–9.

Picard, Robert G. "Regression Analysis of State Role in Press Economics," *Journalism Quarterly,* 64 (Winter 1987): 846–50.

Picard, Robert G. "U.S. Newspaper Ad Revenue Shows Consistent Growth," *Newspaper Research Journal,* 23/4 (2002): 21–33.

Picard, Robert G. "Shifts in Newspaper Advertising Expenditures and their Implications for the Future of Newspapers," *Journalism Studies,* 9/5 (2008): 704–16.

Picard, Robert G. "Subsidies for the Media," in Wolfgang Donsbach (ed.), *The International Encyclopedia of Communication*, vol. 11, 4891–5. Oxford: Wiley-Blackwell, 2008.

Picard, Robert G. "The Future of the News Industry," in James Curran (ed.), *Media and Society*, 366–79. London: Bloomsbury Academic, 2010.

Picard, Robert G. *The Economics and Financing of Media Companies*, 2nd edn. New York: Fordham University Press, 2011.

Platt, Harold L. *Shock Cities: The Environmental Transformation and Reform of Manchester and Chicago*. Chicago: University of Chicago Press, 2005.

Pool, Ithiel de Sola. *Technologies of Freedom*. Cambridge, Mass.: Belknap Press of Harvard University Press, 1984.

Potter, Simon J. *News and the British World: The Emergence of an Imperial Press System, 1876–1922*. Oxford: Clarendon Press, 2003.

Raymond, Joad. *The Invention of the Newspaper: English Newsbooks 1641–1649*. Oxford: Clarendon Press, 1996.

Raymond, Joad (ed.). *The Oxford History of Popular Print Culture*, vol. 1: *Cheap Print in Britain and Ireland to 1660*. Oxford: Oxford University Press, 2011.

Read, Donald. *The Power of News: The History of Reuters, 1849–1989*. New York: Oxford University Press, 1992.

Reuters Institute for the Study of Journalism. *Reuters Institute Digital News Report 2014*. Oxford: Reuters Institute for the Study of Journalism, 2014.

Roberts, Matthew. *Political Movements in Urban England, 1832–1914*. New York: Palgrave Macmillan, 2009.

Robertson, Geoffrey and Andrew Nicol. *Media Law*, 5th edn. London: Sweet & Maxwell, 2007.

Rodgers, Daniel T. *Atlantic Crossings: Social Politics in a Progressive Age*. Cambridge, Mass.: Belknap Press of Harvard University Press, 1998.

Scannell, Paddy and David Cardiff. *A Social History of British Broadcasting*, vol. 1: *1922–1939: Serving the Nation*. Oxford: Basil Blackwell, 1991.

Schaffer, Jan. *New Voices: What Works*. Washington, DC: J-Lab: Institute for Interactive Journalism, 2010.

Schwarzlose, R. A. *The Nation's Newsbrokers*, 2 vols. Evanston, Ill.: Northwestern University Press, 1988–90.

Seymour-Ure, Colin. *The British Press and Broadcasting since 1945*, 2nd edn. Oxford: Blackwell, 1996.

Shawcross, William. *Murdoch*. New York: Simon & Schuster, 1992.

Silberstein-Loeb, Jonathan. "Exclusivity and Cooperation in the Supply of News: The Example of the Associated Press, 1893–1945," *Journal of Policy History*, 24/3 (2012): 466–98.

Silberstein-Loeb, Jonathan. *The International Distribution of News: The Associated Press, Press Association, and Reuters, 1848–1947*. New York: Cambridge University Press, 2014.

Sirkkunen, Esa and Clare Cook (eds). *Chasing Sustainability on the Net*. Tampere, Finland: Tampere Research Centre for Journalism, Media and Communication, University of Tampere, 2012.

Slauter, Will. "The Paragraph as Information Technology: How News Traveled in the Eighteenth-Century Atlantic World," *Annales: H.S.S.* [English version], 67/2 (April–June 2012): 253–78.

Slauter, Will. "Upright Piracy: Understanding the Lack of Copyright for Journalism in Eighteenth-Century Britain," *Book History*, 16 (2013): 34–61.

Smith, Anthony. "Subsidies and the Press in Europe," *Political and Economic Planning*, 43/569 (1977): 1–113.

Smythe, Ted C. *The Gilded Age Press, 1865–1900.* Westport, Conn.: Praeger, 2003.

Sommerville, C. John. *The News Revolution in England: Cultural Dynamics of Daily Information.* New York: Oxford University Press, 1996.

Stamm, Michael. *Sound Business: Newspapers, Radio, and the Politics of New Media.* Philadelphia: University of Pennsylvania Press, 2011.

Starr, Paul. *The Creation of the Media: Political Origins of Modern Communications.* New York: Basic Books, 2004.

Steele, Ian K. *The English Atlantic, 1675–1740: An Exploration of Communication and Community.* New York: Oxford University Press, 1986.

Trappel, Josef. "Online Media within the Public Service Realm? Reasons to Include Online into the Public Service Mission," *Media, Culture & Society*, 34 (2012): 181–94.

Tunstall, Jeremy. *Newspaper Power: The New National Press in Britain.* Oxford: Clarendon Press, 1996.

Tworek, Heidi J. S. "Journalistic Statesmanship: Protecting the Press in Weimar Germany and Abroad," *German History*, 32/4 (Winter 2014): 559–78.

Warner, William. "Communicating Liberty: The Newspapers of the British Empire as a Matrix for the American Revolution," *ELH*, 72/2 (Summer 2005): 339–61.

Wendt, Lloyd. *Chicago Tribune: The Rise of a Great American Newspaper.* Chicago: Rand McNally, 1979.

Westley, Brian. "How a Narrow Application of Hot News Misappropriation Can Help Save Journalism," *American University Law Review*, 60 (2010–11): 691–729.

Whyman, Susan E. *The Pen and the People: English Letter Writers 1660–1800.* Oxford: Oxford University Press, 2009.

Wiener, Joel and Mark Hampton (eds). *Anglo-American Media Interactions, 1850–2000.* New York: Palgrave Macmillan, 2007.

Wiener, Joel H. (ed.). *Papers for the Millions: The New Journalism in Britain, 1850s to 1914.* Westport, Conn.: Greenwood Press, 1988.

Wiener, Joel H. *The Americanization of the British Press, 1830s–1914: Speed in the Age of Transatlantic Journalism.* New York: Palgrave Macmillan, 2011.

Wilf, Steven. "Making Intellectual Property Law in the Shadow of Law: International News Service v. Associated Press," *WIPO Journal*, 5/1 (2013): 88–95.

Williams, Kevin. *Read All About It: A History of the British Newspaper.* London: Routledge, 2010.

Wilson, Kathleen. *Sense of the People: Politics, Culture, and Imperialism in England 1715–1785.* Cambridge: Cambridge University Press, 1995.

Winseck, Dwayne R. and Robert M. Pike. *Communication and Empire: Media, Markets and Globalization, 1860–1930.* Durham: Duke University Press, 2007.

Zarkin, Kimberly A. and Michael J. Zarkin. *The Federal Communications Commission: Front Line in the Culture and Regulation Wars.* Westport, Conn.: Greenwood, 2006.

Index

Printed and bound by CPI Group (UK) Ltd, Croydon, CR0 4YY